MERGERS AND ACQUISITIONS

Also edited by Greg N. Gregoriou

ADVANCES IN RISK MANAGEMENT
ASSET ALLOCATION AND INTERNATIONAL INVESTMENTS
DIVERSIFICATION AND PORTFOLIO MANAGEMENT OF MUTUAL FUNDS
PERFORMANCE OF MUTUAL FUNDS

Mergers and Acquisitions
Current Issues

Edited by

GREG N. GREGORIOU

and

KARYN L. NEUHAUSER

Selection and editorial matter © Greg N. Gregoriou and Karyn L. Neuhauser 2007
Individual chapters © contributors 2007

All rights reserved. No reproduction, copy or transmission of this
publication may be made without written permission.

No paragraph of this publication may be reproduced, copied or transmitted
save with written permission or in accordance with the provisions of the
Copyright, Designs and Patents Act 1988, or under the terms of any licence
permitting limited copying issued by the Copyright Licensing Agency,
90 Tottenham Court Road, London W1T 4LP.

Any person who does any unauthorized act in relation to this publication may be liable
to criminal prosecution and civil claims for damages.

The authors have asserted their rights to be identified as the authors of this work in
accordance with the Copyright, Designs and Patents Act 1988.

First published 2007 by
PALGRAVE MACMILLAN
Houndmills, Basingstoke, Hampshire RG21 6XS and
175 Fifth Avenue, New York, N.Y. 10010
Companies and representatives throughout the world

PALGRAVE MACMILLAN is the global academic imprint of the Palgrave
Macmillan division of St. Martin's Press, LLC and of Palgrave Macmillan Ltd.
Macmillan® is a registered trademark in the United States, United Kingdom
and other countries. Palgrave is a registered trademark in the European
Union and other countries.

ISBN-13: 978-0230-55379-8
ISBN-10: 0-230-55379-6

This book is printed on paper suitable for recycling and made from fully
managed and sustained forest sources. Logging, pulping and manufacturing
processes are expected to conform to the environmental regulations of the
country of origin.

A catalogue record for this book is available from the British Library.

Library of Congress Cataloging-in-Publication Data
Mergers and acquisitions: current issues / edited by
   Greg N. Gregoriou and Karyn L. Neuhauser.
      p. cm.
   Includes index.
   ISBN 0-230-55379-6 (alk. paper)
   1. Consolidation and merger of corporations. I. Gregoriou, Greg N.,
      1956– II. Neuhauser, Karyn L.
   HD2746.5.M4365 2007
   338.8'3—dc22   2007021799

10 9   8   7   6   5   4   3   2   1
16 15 14 13 12 11 10 09 08 07

Printed and bound in Great Britain by
Antony Rowe Ltd, Chippenham and Eastbourne

To my mother Evangelia and in loving memory of
my father Nicholas (GNG)

To my mother, Helen Lieck, and in remembrance of my father,
Arthur Louis Lieck, who together taught me
what was important in life (KLN)

Contents

Acknowledgments		xi
Notes on the Contributors		xiii
Introduction		xxi

1 Mergers and Acquisitions: A Global View — 1
 Karyn L. Neuhauser

2 What Drives Acquisitions? A Market-Manager Rationality Framework — 5
 Antonios Antoniou and Huainan Zhao

   2.1 Introduction — 5
   2.2 Hypothesis development — 7
   2.3 Data and descriptive statistics — 8
   2.4 Methodology — 10
   2.5 Empirical results — 11
   2.6 Conclusion — 24

3 Misadventure and the Form of Payment in Corporate Acquisitions — 27
 Tyrone M. Carlin, Guy Ford and Nigel Finch

   3.1 Introduction — 27
   3.2 Factors influencing the form of consideration in acquisitions — 31
   3.3 A price too far? The acquisition of Howard Smith Ltd by Wesfarmers Ltd — 33
   3.4 Financial analysis — 35

3.5	Assessment of the transaction	38
3.6	Conclusion	40

4 An Essay on the History of a Merger: The Case of the National Bank of Canada — 42
Raymond Théoret and François-Éric Racicot

4.1	Introduction	42
4.2	The structures of the two merged banks	43
4.3	The new merged bank	50
4.4	A low P/E ratio for the stock of national bank	53
4.5	Conclusion	54

5 Corporate Diversification: The Costs and Benefits of Synergy — 56
Felipe Balmaceda

5.1	Introduction	56
5.2	Related literature	58
5.3	The model	60
5.4	The analysis	64
5.5	Robustness	67
5.6	Conclusion	73

6 The Influence of M&As on Firm Value: The Turkish Experience — 83
M. Nihat Solakoğlu and Mehmet Orhan

6.1	Introduction	83
6.2	Data and methodology	85
6.3	Discussion of results	87
6.4	Conclusion	93

7 Price Volatility in Stocks Subject to Tender Offers — 96
Elaine Hutson

7.1	Introduction	96
7.2	Previous research and theoretical background	97
7.3	The econometric analysis: market effect and volatility	101
7.4	Data and preliminary results	102
7.5	Econometric results	106
7.6	Trading volumes	110
7.7	Conclusion	114

8 Merger Arbitrage: An Introduction — 118
Greg N. Gregoriou and François-Serge Lhabitant

8.1	Introduction	118
8.2	Merger arbitrage: the strategy	119
8.3	Key sources of merger arbitrage risk	128
8.4	Historical performance	132
8.5	Conclusion	136

9 The Impact of Cross-Border Mergers and Acquisitions on Financial Analysts' Forecasts: Evidence from the Canadian Stock Market — 139
Alain Coën, Aurélie Desfleurs and Claude Francoeur

9.1	Introduction	139
9.2	Conceptual framework	141
9.3	Measures of financial analysts' forecast errors and data	142
9.4	Empirical results and analysis	145
9.5	Conclusion	151

10 The Economic Analysis of US Antitrust Merger Law — 155
Germán Coloma

10.1	Introduction	155
10.2	Theoretical literature	156
10.3	Statute and case law	160
10.4	Empirical studies	163
10.5	Conclusion	165

11 Ethical Issues in Mergers and Acquisitions — 168
Robert W. McGee

11.1	Introduction	168
11.2	Ethical approaches	168
11.3	Review of the literature	173
11.4	Conclusion	175

12 The Use of Equity Swaps in Mergers — 178
Paul U. Ali

12.1	Introduction	178
12.2	Equity swaps	179
12.3	Hedging of swap exposure	180
12.4	"Fear and loathing" in takeover battles	180
12.5	Conclusion	185

13 Banking Performance in Domestic and Cross-Border Acquisitions — 188
Sergio Sanfilippo Azofra, Belén Díaz Díaz, Myriam García Olalla and Carlos López Gutiérrez

13.1	Introduction	188
13.2	Cross-border M&As: a literature review	190
13.3	Empirical analysis: definition of sample, variables and methodology	192
13.4	Results from empirical analysis	199
13.5	Conclusions	208

14 Mergers between European Energy Firms: National Champions and Markets — 213
Francesc Trillas

14.1	Introduction	213
14.2	The issues at stake	214
14.3	The behavior of target firms	217
14.4	Expanding firms	221
14.5	Competition policy and national champions	228
14.6	Conclusion	231

15 A Deal Too Far: The Case of the Killer Acquisition — 234
Tyrone M. Carlin, Nigel Finch and Guy Ford

15.1	Introduction	234
15.2	Overview of the focal company	236
15.3	A string of acquisitions	239
15.4	Exploring a killer deal	241
15.5	Conclusion	244

16 Trends in Chinese M&A: A Look at Lenovo's Acquisition of IBM PC — 249
Margaret Wang

16.1	Introduction	249
16.2	History of Lenovo	249
16.3	Lenovo's acquisition of IBM PC	250
16.4	After the merger	253
16.5	Conclusion	255

Index — 259

Acknowledgments

We would like to thank Stephen Rutt, Alexandra Dawe and Lisa von Fircks at Palgrave Macmillan for guiding us through the process. We also thank Keith Povey Editorial Services and his staff for the excellent work in editing this manuscript, and thanks also to a handful of anonymous referees who assisted in the selection of articles for this book.

GNG
KLN

Notes on the Contributors

The Editors

Greg N. Gregoriou is Professor of Finance in the School of Business and Economics at State University of New York (Plattsburgh), USA. He obtained his joint PhD in Finance from the University of Quebec at Montreal, which pools the resources, with Montreal's three major universities (McGill University, Concordia University and Hautes-Etudes (Commerciales). He is co-editor of the *Journal of Derivatives and Hedge Funds* and an editorial board member of the *Journal of Wealth Management* and the *Journal of Risk, Management in Financial Institutions*. He has written over fifty articles on hedge funds and managed futures in various peer-reviewed publications, including the *Journal of Portfolio Management, European Journal of Operational Research, Annals of Operations Research, Journal of Banking and Finance, Journal of Futures Markets, Journal of Derivatives Accounting, European Journal of Finance* and *Journal of Asset Management*. He has authored one book with Professor Joe Zhu and edited nineteen books with Elsevier-Butterworth-Heinemann, John Wiley & Sons, Palgrave Macmillan and Risk Books.

Karyn L. Neuhauser is an Assistant Professor of Finance at the State University of New York (Plattsburgh), USA. She earned her doctorate in Finance from Louisiana State University and has published articles in the *Journal of Real Estate Finance and Economics* and the *Journal of Financial Research*. She recently edited a special issue of the *International Journal of Managerial Finance*. She is actively involved in the Financial Management Association, the Eastern Finance Association and the Southwestern Finance Association, and has served as an ad hoc reviewer for the *Quarterly Review of Economics and Finance* and the *Institute for Global Management Research* at George Washington University. Her research focuses on mergers and acquisitions, corporate control and governance, securities issuance, and dividend policy. Her work has been presented at numerous national and regional conferences.

The Contributors

Paul U. Ali is Associate Professor in the Faculty of Law at the University of Melbourne, Australia. He was previously a finance lawyer in Sydney. Paul has published several books on finance and investment law including, most recently, *Innovations in Securitization*. His articles have appeared in *Derivatives Use, Trading and Regulation*, *Journal of Alternative Investments*, *Journal of Banking Regulation* and *Journal of International Banking Law and Regulation*.

Antonios Antoniou is currently the Dean of the Durham Business School, Durham University, UK. His areas of research include risk management, derivatives markets and their impact on the underlying markets, tests of asset pricing models and market anomalies, market integration, mergers and acquisitions, and capital structure decisions. He has published widely in a variety of academic journals, including *Journal of Financial and Quantitative Analysis*, *Journal of Banking and Finance*, *The Economic Journal*, *European Financial Management Journal*, *Journal of Empirical Finance*, *Journal of International Money and Finance*, and *Journal of Business Finance and Accounting*. He has also published a book with J. Appiah-Kusi on African stock markets. He studied at the London School of Economics and York University, and previously held an academic position at Brunel University, all in the UK.

Felipe Balmaceda is Assistant Professor at the Industrial Engineering Department at the University of Chile. He was Visiting Assistant Professor at Dartmouth College, Assistant Professor of the Ilades–Georgetown Ms program in economics. He has been a consultant for the IADB and World Bank. He specializes in contract theory, industrial organization and game theory. His articles have appeared in the *Journal of Labor Economics* and the *Journal of Industrial Organization* and he has written several book chapters related to the industrial organization of energy markets.

Tyrone M. Carlin is a Professor of Management and Director of Academic programs at the Macquarie Graduate School of Management (MGSM) in Sydney, Australia. His current research interests lie in interdisciplinary work on corporate governance and corporate financial reporting. He teaches in the areas of commercial law, mergers and acquisitions, and insolvency and restructuring. He has published articles in a range of international journals, including *Management Accounting Research*, *Financial Accountability & Management*, *Public Management Review*, *Australian Accounting Review*, *Sydney*

Law Review, University of New South Wales Law Review and *Australian Business Law Review*. He co-edits *Journal of Law and Financial Management* and *Journal of Applied Research in Accounting and Finance*.

Alain Coën is an Associate Professor of Finance at the University of Quebec in Montreal (UQAM), Canada. He obtained his PhD in Finance from the University of Grenoble and holds a Master's degree in Economics with a major in Macroeconomics from Laval University. He teaches, does research and consults in the areas of investment and corporate finance. His research interests focus on asset pricing, earnings forecasting and financial econometrics. He has published in several international journals and written a book on financial management.

Germán Coloma obtained his Bachelor's degree in Public Accounting at the National University of La Plata, Argentina. He also holds an MPP degree from the Torcuato Di Tella Institute in Buenos Aires, and a PhD in economics from the University of California, Los Angeles. He is a full-time Professor of Economics at CEMA University in Buenos Aires, where he teaches courses on microeconomic theory, industrial organization and the economic analysis of law. He is also the Director of the graduate program in project evaluation at the university, co-editor of *Journal of Applied Economics*, and a Visiting Professor of the graduate program in Law and Economics at the University of Buenos Aires School of Law. Since 1999, he has been affiliated with LECG and LLC, and in that role has acted as a consultant on many cases concerning antitrust issues and public utility regulation. His professional experience also includes an appointment as Chief Economist of the Argentine Competition Commission (CNDC) in 1997 and 1998. He has published several papers on microeconomic theory, industrial organization, competition policy, public utility economics, and economic analysis of law. These have appeared in journals such as *Empirical Economics, International Review of Law and Economics, Review of Industrial Organization* and *Journal of Economic Dynamics and Control*. He has also published three books.

Aurélie Desfleurs is an Assistant Professor of Finance in the Accounting School at Laval University, Quebec, Canada. She received her MBA and PhD in finance from Laval University. She teaches investment and corporate finance. Her research interests include mergers and acquisitions, and earnings forecasting. She has published several papers in the fields of multinational finance and financial analysts' forecasts.

Belén Díaz Díaz is an Associate Professor of Finance at the University of Cantabria, Santander, Spain. She also teaches postgraduate courses in banking and financial markets. After receiving her Bachelor's degree in Business, she completed her PhD in Finance at the University of Cantabria. She has been a visiting researcher at the University of California – Berkeley, the London School of Economics, and the University of Technology in Sydney. Professor Díaz is the author of several papers on banking and corporate finance, published in various academic journals. She has presented her research at international conferences.

Nigel Finch is a lecturer in management at the Macquarie Graduate School of Management (MGSM) in Sydney, Australia. He specializes in the fields of managerial accounting and financial management. His research interests lie in the areas of accounting and managerial decision-making, finance and investment management, and corporate governance and reporting. Prior to joining MGSM, he worked as a financial controller for both public and private companies, operating in the manufacturing, entertainment, media and financial services industries. Subsequently, he worked as an investment manager specializing in Australian growth stocks for institutional investment funds. He is the founding editor of *Journal of Applied Research in Accounting and Finance*.

Guy Ford is an Associate Professor of Management at the Macquarie Graduate School of Management (MGSM) in Sydney, Australia. He teaches in the areas of financial management, corporate acquisitions, insolvency and restructuring, and financial institutions management. Formerly serving with the Treasury Risk Management division of the Commonwealth Bank of Australia, he has published papers in a wide range of scholarly refereed journals and presented his work at a wide variety of international research gatherings. He is a founding co-editor of *Journal of Law & Financial Management*, and the author of two books: *Financial Markets and Institutions in Australia* and *Readings in Financial Institutions Management*.

Claude Francoeur is an Assistant Professor of Finance and Accounting in the Accounting Department at HEC Montreal, Canada. He holds a CGA, an MBA and a PhD in Finance from the University of Quebec in Montreal, Canada. He teaches accounting for financial instruments and corporate governance and is also a consultant in financial accounting and financial management for various institutions. He has published in several international journals. His research interests focus on mergers and acquisitions, and corporate governance.

Myriam García Olalla is a full Professor of Financial Economy at the University of Cantabria, Santander, Spain. She received her PhD in Economics and Business Sciences from the University of Oviedo. Her research focuses on banking, financial markets and corporate finance. She has directed several PhD students in these subjects and is the author of numerous publications in national and international journals, and several textbooks. She is currently the Director of a Master's program in Banking and Financial Markets at the University of Cantabria. This program was developed in collaboration with one of the principal banks in the world, the Santander Group.

Elaine Hutson holds a PhD in Finance from the University of Technology, Sydney, Australia where she worked as a Lecturer in Finance for nine years. In 1999, she moved to Dublin, Ireland, where she is now a Lecturer in the School of Business at University College Dublin. She has published widely in a variety of finance journals including *Journal of Empirical Finance*, *Journal of International Financial Markets, Institutions and Money*, *International Review of Financial Analysis*, *Journal of the Asia Pacific Economy* and *Venture Capital*. Her research interests are broad, and include small business finance, mergers and acquisitions, the performance, regulation and history of managed funds (including hedge funds), and international risk management.

François-Serge Lhabitant is the Chief Investment Officer at Kedge Capital. He was formerly a Member of Senior Management at Union Bancaire Privée, where he was in charge of quantitative risk management and subsequently, of the quantitative research for alternative portfolios. Prior to this, he was a Director at UBS/Global Asset Management, in charge of building quantitative models for portfolio management and hedge funds. On the academic side, he is currently a Professor of Finance at the University of Lausanne, Switzerland and at the EDHEC Business School, France. He was formerly a visiting professor at the Hong Kong University of Science and Technology, held the Deloitte & Touche Chair on Risk Management at the University of Antwerp, Belgium, and was an associate professor of finance at Thunderbird, the American Graduate School of International Management. His specialist skills are in the areas of quantitative portfolio management, alternative investments (hedge funds), and emerging markets. He is the author of several books on these subjects and has published numerous research and scientific popularization articles. He is also a member of the Scientific Council of the Autorité des Marches Financiers, the French regulatory body.

Carlos López Gutiérrez is Assistant Professor of Finance at the University of Cantabria, Santander, Spain. He holds a PhD in Finance and a Bachelor's degree and Diploma in Business with highest honors. He is the author of several papers on corporate finance, corporate financial distress, and efficiency of bankruptcy law. He has taken part in several prestigious national and international professional meetings presenting his work.

Robert W. McGee is a Professor at the Andreas School of Business, Barry University in Miami, Florida, USA. He has published more than 370 articles and more than 40 books in the areas of accounting, taxation, economics, law and philosophy. He is a lawyer, certified public accountant, and economist.

Mehmet Orhan is an Assistant Professor in the Economics Department of Fatih University, Istanbul, Turkey. He is also the Director of the Social Sciences Institute, responsible for the coordination of several graduate programs. He earned his PhD from Bilkent University, Ankara, Turkey, and graduated from the Industrial Engineering Department of the same university. He had a full scholarship until he got his PhD degree. His main interest is econometrics, both theoretical and applied. He has published articles in *Economics Letters*, *International Journal of Business* and *Journal of Economic and Social Research*. His theoretical research interests include HCCME estimation, robust estimation techniques and Bayesian inference. He is currently working on studies of initial public offering performance in Turkey, hedge fund returns, tax revenue estimation, and international economic cooperation.

François-Éric Racicot is Associate Professor of Finance in the Department of Administrative Sciences of the University of Quebec in Outaouais (UQO), Hull, Quebec, Canada. He holds a Master's degree in Economics with a major in financial econometrics from the University of Montreal and received his PhD in Finance from the University of Quebec, Montreal (UQAM). He is also a permanent member of the Laboratory for Research in Statistics and Probability (LRSP) of Carlton University and University of Ottawa. His research interests focus on developing econometric methods applied to financial problems. He has also written several books on quantitative finance and financial econometrics, and is a consultant in quantitative finance for various banks and investment firms.

Sergio Sanfilippo Azofra is an Assistant Professor of Finance at the University of Cantabria Santander, Spain. He also teaches postgraduate courses in banking and financial markets. After completing his Bachelor's degree in Economics, he gained his PhD in Finance at the University of Cantabria. He has been a visiting researcher at Cass Business School (City University of London). He has research interests in banking and corporate finance, has published several papers in academic journals, and presented papers at national and international conferences.

M. Nihat Solakoğlu is Assistant Professor in the Department of Banking and Finance at Bilkent University, Ankara, Turkey. Previously he was Assistant Professor in the Department of Management at Fatih University, Istanbul, Turkey. Before joining Fatih University, he worked for American Express in the USA in international risk management, international information management and information and analysis. He received his PhD in Economics and Master's degree in Statistics from North Carolina State University, USA. His main interests are applied finance and international finance. His papers have been published in *Applied Economics*, *Journal of International Financial Markets, Institutions & Money* and *Journal of Economic and Social Research*.

Raymond Théoret, PhD, is Professor of Finance at École des sciences de la gestion, University of Quebec, Montreal, Canada. He has to his credit many books and articles on banking, portfolio management, and the technical aspects of financial engineering. He was previously senior economist in a major Canadian financial institution and a Professor at HEC Montreal.

Francesc Trillas is a Lecturer in Economics at the Universitat Autònoma de Barcelona, Spain. He has published articles on regulated industries and corporate control in international journals such as *Oxford Economic Papers*, *Review of Network Economics*, *Telecommunications Policy* and *Utilities Policy*. He holds a PhD in Economics from the European University Institute in Florence, Italy, where he wrote a dissertation on privatized utilities, regulatory reform and corporate control. He is a former research fellow for the regulation initiative at the London Business School.

Margaret Wang is a Lecturer in the School of Law, and an associate of the Centre for International Corporate Governance Research, Faculty of Business and Law at Victoria University, Melbourne, Australia. Before taking up her position with Victoria University she worked in law firms in Taiwan and Hong Kong, where she specialized in corporate advisory matters and capital market transactions. She is also licensed to practice in Australia. She has published a number of articles on various aspects of corporate law in Asia, including one in the *European Business Law Review*. Her latest project involves examining the mergers and acquisitions practices of Chinese companies.

Huainan Zhao is currently a Lecturer in Finance at Cass Business School, London. He received his Bachelor's degree in Information Management from Fudan University, Shanghai, China. His Master's degree in Finance and Investment from the University of York, UK, and his PhD in Finance from Durham University, UK. Prior to joining Cass, he was a Lecturer in Finance at Durham University Business School. His research interests include mergers and acquisitions, corporate finance and risk management.

Introduction

In Chapter 1, the history of waves of mergers and acquisition in the USA is sketched, and well-documented empirical regularities summarized. The analysis is then extended to encompass contemporary trends and the landscape of current mergers and acquisitions, particularly the effects of economic globalization and private equity funding.

In Chapter 2 the authors answer the question of what driving force of acquisitions is of crucial importance for us to understand merger activities. Following the emergence of the market timing theory of mergers, recent studies that focus on overvalued bidders have found evidence in support of the theory. Equally important, however, undervalued targets form the other part of misvaluation theory, which has unfortunately been relatively neglected. This paper therefore examines the undervaluation part of the story and provides supportive evidence that stock market misvaluation and the market timing ability of managers are the likely driving forces behind merger activities.

Chapter 3 examines an often overlooked feature of control premiums in the context of fixed exchange ratio scrip mergers – the impact of a rise in the acquiring firm's share price over the duration of the offer period. While this has traditionally been seen as an affirmation of deal value by capital markets, in this chapter it is argued that a better analysis may be that such transactions destroy value for acquiring shareholders.

Chapter 4 deals with the difficult beginnings of the National Bank of Canada, the product of a merger between the Canadian National Bank and the Provincial Bank. It presents a model of the net income ratio of the National Bank compared with other big Canadian banks. It shows that the net income ratio of the National Bank reverts to a long-term level that is quite low compared with those of other banks, and more generally with the banking standards.

In Chapter 5, the author provides an explanation, based on agency conflicts, for why some firms pursue value-decreasing diversification, while others pursue value-increasing diversification. There is a vast empirical literature suggesting that diversification is value-maximizing for some firms and value-destroying for others.

In Chapter 6, the increasing role of mergers and acquisitions (M&As) in the Turkish economy is examined. The authors investigate the short-term impact of M&As on firm value. Consistent with earlier work, we find that target firms realize most of the gains in the short run. In addition, the increasing trend observed in the cumulative average abnormal return may indicate the existence of information spillovers before the announcement date. We also show that the probability of observing a positive abnormal return is positively related to the existence of international transactions and family ownership at the firm level.

Chapter 7 shows that there is a large body of evidence demonstrating that target company shareholders earn substantial excess returns around takeover announcements. There has been less academic interest in the second moment of target returns. Are high bid period returns for target firms associated with higher price volatility? We show that conditional volatility in fact falls during the bid period, and with some important exceptions, volume tends to follow. The decline in volatility is larger for targets of cash bids relative to non-cash bids, for targets of successful bids versus failed bids, and for friendly versus hostile bids. This is consistent with our suggestion that the reduction in volatility is a result of convergence of trader opinion regarding the value of the target stock, because the greater the certainty about the takeover's outcome, the greater the drop-off in volatility. While trading volume falls in the successful, friendly and cash sub-samples, it remains unchanged or increases for targets of failed, hostile and non-cash bids.

Chapter 8 examines merger arbitrage strategy, elucidating how merger arbitrageurs function when a merger or takeover is revealed, along with the positions they assume as well as hedging is performed by concurrently short selling the acquiring firm's stock. The chapter also addresses the various risks encountered by merger arbitrageurs, and summarizes returns since the early 1990s.

Chapter 9 investigates financial analysts' performance before and after cross-border mergers and acquisitions transactions on the Canadian stock markets over the period 1990–2004. The chapter focuses on the consequences of M&A on the accuracy and quality of earnings forecasts, using financial analysts' forecast consensus provided by the IBES database. The results highlight an increase of financial analysts' forecast errors after the mergers, and the pre-merger level of accuracy is restored only two years after the event. Light is also shed on the over-optimism shown by financial analysts in their forecasts for US targets.

Chapter 10 is about the economic literature that analyzes mergers and merger law from an antitrust perspective. Its focus is on US antitrust law, although some of the reviewed literature can also be applied to other countries. The chapter has three main sections. In the first the most important theoretical papers are reviewed, with an emphasis on the basic trade-off between cost reduction and market power that many mergers generate. The second section analyzes the development of US antitrust merger law and its increasing link with economic theory, which becomes especially clear in the passing of the Hart–Scott–Rodino Act (1976) and the publication of the DOJ–FTC Merger Guidelines (1992). Third, a section is included about the basic empirical methods used in economics to analyze the antitrust effects of mergers, and several important case studies that have used those methods are reviewed. Basic conclusions are summarized in the last section.

Chapter 11 analyzes the topic of acquisitions and mergers from the perspectives of utilitarian ethics and rights theory, and discusses the ethical issues involving hostile takeovers and attempts that have been made to prevent them. Most mergers meet the utilitarian ethics test. Preventing or increasing the cost of mergers violates property and contract rights. These issues have not been discussed much in the literature; this chapter attempts partially to fill that gap.

Chapter 12 discusses the equity swaps that are used routinely by professional investors to synthesize equity investments and create equity-linked exposure for their portfolios. Now a new use for these investment instruments has emerged: the accumulation of pre-bid stakes in target companies. This chapter examines the application of equity swaps to takeover contests.

Chapter 13 analyzes the profitability obtained by the acquirer in domestic and cross-border acquisitions. The analysis is carried out on a sample of European banks during the period 1992–2000. The results show that domestic acquisitions improve acquirers' performance, especially in the long term, while cross-border operations do not have a significant effect on acquirers' performance.

Chapter 14 examines European Union electricity and gas directives, aimed at the creation of an internal energy market, that triggered a wave of mergers and acquisitions. National and European authorities took a somewhat incoherent stance *vis-à-vis* such processes, at times promoting such transactions and on other occasions opposing them. This chapter reviews a number of recent takeover bids (both successful and unsuccessful), and examines the winners and the losers in this process through an analysis of stock market (event study) and other data. The interaction between competition policy and ownership constraints is revealed as a key determinant of public policy.

Chapter 15 examines the substantial literature on the subject of mergers and acquisitions, suggesting that many changes in control transactions result in value destruction. While undesirable, in most cases this loss of value is not sufficiently profound to threaten the ongoing existence of the enlarged firm. However, some transactions – which are dubbed "killer acquisitions" do have this effect. This chapter is devoted to a discussion of this relatively under-investigated topic.

Chapter 16 examines the Chinese company Lenovo's acquisition of the personal computer (PC) division of the world's third most valuable brand, IBM, which shocked the world when the proposed deal was first announced in late 2004. This acquisition has been described as 'a snake swallowing an elephant'. This chapter explains the key elements of the transaction and its economic rationale, as well as considering whether this transaction may be an indicator for future M&A transactions involving Chinese companies as acquirers.

CHAPTER 1

Mergers and Acquisitions: A Global View

Karyn L. Neuhauser

Many theories have been offered to explain why mergers and acquisitions (M&As) occur. Efficiency theories suggest that mergers occur to exploit economies of scale or synergies. Market power theories argue that consolidation creates oligopoly benefits. Agency theories suggest that mergers and acquisitions may solve agency problems by acting as a mechanism to remove ineffective managers or, alternatively, that mergers and acquisitions may be a manifestation of agency problems with managers making unwise acquisitions as a result of hubris or empire-building motives. Benefits from diversification or tax considerations have also been suggested as a motive for M&A activity. Although no single cohesive theory of mergers and acquisition has been developed, most of these theories have received at least some empirical support.

The short-run valuation effects of M&A transactions have been documented in numerous event studies. These studies consistently find positive cumulative abnormal returns to target shareholders on the order of 15 percent to 40 percent, depending on the time period and types of transaction studied. While the abnormal returns for bidders appear to be close to zero, or perhaps even slightly negative, the combined bidder-target returns are universally positive, suggesting that M&A activity creates value overall. Other well-known regularities are that the target stock price reactions are on average significantly higher for cash offers compared with stock offers; tender offers compared with mergers; hostile offers compared with friendly offers; and multiple-bidder rather than single-bidder contests. These characteristics tend to have the opposite effect on bidder returns. Thus bidder returns tend to be lower for stock-financed offers; merger transactions; hostile offers; and multiple-bidder contests.

Another known regularity is that merger and acquisition activity occurs in waves. Mitchell and Mulherin (1996) and Harford (2005) find that industry-specific merger waves occur in response to economic, regulatory and technological shocks accompanied by sufficient capital liquidity. This suggests that M&A activity will be high when certain industries are experiencing changes that require large-scale redeployment of assets during a business expansion or bull market.

There have been six periods of intense merger and acquisition activity in the USA. Interestingly, each of these periods occurred during a strong economic expansion and robust stock market, and was followed by a large decline in stock prices. The first M&A wave occurred around the start of the twentieth century, when consolidation took place in the oil, steel, mining and tobacco industries. Much of this activity was aimed at creating monopoly power. The second wave occurred in the 1920s, when the booming stock market led to consolidation in the communications, utilities and automobile industries. Due to the enactment of antitrust legislation that made the creation of monopolies illegal, much of the activity in this period focused on vertical integration. Unlike the earlier waves, the third wave, which occurred in the 1960s, was characterized by a large number of unrelated acquisitions and is often referred to as the wave of conglomerate mergers.

The fourth M&A wave, which occurred in the 1980s, is often remembered for bust-up takeovers, leveraged buyouts (LBOs), and junk-bond financed deals. During this period, M&A transactions were undertaken to reverse the corporate diversification of previous decades, eliminate excess capacity, and discipline poor management. The rise in institutional ownership during this period facilitated these takeovers by creating a group of large shareholders that were willing to tender their shares to bidders who promised to increase share values (Holmstrom and Kaplan, 2001). The 1980s also saw the proliferation of takeover defense strategies such as poison pills and anti-takeover amendments. However, although many observers associate the 1980s with hostile takeovers, fewer than 15 percent of these deals were hostile.[1]

After a brief decline in the early 1990s, takeover activity again increased, reaching record levels in the late 1990s and ushering in the fifth M&A wave. Unlike the takeover wave of the 1980s, however, leverage and hostility were uncommon in the M&A wave of the 1990s. Instead, takeover activity was dominated by cross-border mergers, and mergers in the service sectors, most notably telecommunications, broadcasting, health care and banking. In fact, these three industries accounted for one-third of worldwide mergers by value in 1999. Andrade et al. (2001) refer to this wave as 'the decade of deregulation'. In contrast to the conglomerate mergers of the 1960s, much of the M&A activity in the 1990s was driven by consolidation within these industries, and by synergistic and strategic considerations.

In addition, much of the activity in the late 1990s was driven by economic globalization. In 1999, cross-border merger activity exceeded US$1 trillion for the first time, and accounted for about one-third of all M&A activity. Merger activity in Europe was encouraged by the introduction of a common currency, the euro. While cross-border transactions accounted for only about 10 percent of US mergers and acquisitions, over 30 percent of European M&A's involved cross-border deals. This trend of increased global M&A activity was also strengthened by the privatization of state-owned enterprises, deregulation, and the liberalization of trade and capital markets. Another striking characteristic of the 1990s merger wave is that over 70 percent of the transactions were financed with stock, because of the unusually high market values accorded to companies during this period.

The sixth merger wave began toward the end of 2003 and is still under way today. In fact, in 2006, the worldwide M&A deal total was US$4 trillion, beating the previous record of US$3.3 trillion set in 2000. US and European firms accounted for almost 80 percent of these deals. This increased M&A activity is attributable partly to high corporate cash balances and low interest rates. In contrast to the 1990s wave, almost 75 percent of recent deals have been paid for with cash. Many of the larger deals occurring during this period have involved companies in the same line of business seeking to cut redundant costs and thereby increase profitability via mergers.

Another major force in the current merger wave has been private equity investors, who typically buy companies by loading them up with debt and then attempting to make them more efficient so that they can service the debt and resell them at a profit within a few years, either to another firm or through an initial public offering (IPO). After playing a large role in the many leveraged buyout deals of the 1980s takeover wave, private equity virtually vanished in the 1990s. In recent years, however, private equity has made a comeback, playing a leading role in about 20 percent of worldwide deals.

Cross-border mergers have been the driving force behind the increase in foreign direct investment (FDI) since the mid-1990s. In this age of corporate globalization, cross-border mergers allow companies to obtain operations around the world quickly. Recently, cross-border mergers, particularly among European companies, have accounted for about 40 percent of total deal volume.

Past studies have generally concluded that the long-run performance of merged firms is typically less than that of a matching peer group, but interestingly, some studies are emerging that suggest the subsequent performance of M&As in the current wave will be better. This may in part be because of the lower premiums being offered. Historically, merger premiums have often reached levels of 40 percent to 60 percent but in the most recent wave they are averaging about 25 percent. All else being equal, this would imply that bidders are less likely to be overpaying for targets. In addition, the focus of the current wave on concrete benefits obtainable through the merger, such as the elimination of duplicate operations, may lead to better long-run performance.

NOTE

1. However, this is a higher level of hostility than in other M&A waves. See Andrade et al. (2001).

REFERENCES

Andrade, Gregor, Mitchell, Mark and Stafford, Erik (2001) "New Evidence and Perspectives on Mergers", *Journal of Economic Perspectives*, 15 103–20.

Harford, Jarrad (2005) "What Drives Merger Waves?", *Journal of Financial Economics*, 77, 529–60.

Holmstrom, Bengt and Kaplan, Steven N. (2001) "Corporate Governance and Merger Activity in the United States: Making Sense of the 1980s and 1990s", *Journal of Economic Perspectives*, 15, 121–44.

Mitchell, Mark L. and Mulherin, J. Harold (1996) "The Impact of Industry Shocks on Takeover and Restructuring Activity", *Journal of Financial Economics*, 41, 193–229.

CHAPTER 2

What Drives Acquisitions? A Market-Manager Rationality Framework

Antonios Antoniou and Huainan Zhao

2.1 INTRODUCTION

Recent studies on merger waves (for example, Maksimovic and Phillips (2001) and Javanovic and Rousseau (2001)) have established that high merger activity is correlated with high stock market valuations. This finding is particularly important, since it indicates that high stock market valuations, which *ex post* frequently turn out to have been misvaluations, may have an impact on merger activities in a systematic way. It is therefore of little surprise that recent studies on the wealth effects of mergers have documented a growing body of anomalies; for example, cash offers systematically outperform stock offers (Loughran and Vijh, 1997); value acquirers outperform glamour acquirers (Rau and Vermaelen, 1998); and small bidders outperform large bidders (Moeller, *et al*. 2004).

In order to explain and reconcile the growing body of evidence of significant stock-market merger anomalies, Shleifer and Vishny (2003) and Rhodes-Kropf and Viswanathan (2004) develop models whereby stock market misvaluations drive merger activities. The fundamental assumption in their models is that financial markets are inefficient/irrational, and therefore some firms are valued/priced incorrectly, while bidder managers are completely rational, understand market misvaluation and therefore time the market to take advantage of it. This market timing theory is supported directly by recent empirical studies such as Rhodes-Kropf *et al.* (2005), Ang and Chen (2006) and Dong *et al.* (2006).

The market timing theory is, however, a direct contradiction to Roll's (1986) hubris hypothesis based on the opposite assumption: namely, that financial markets are strong-form efficient, while bidder managers are infected by hubris in making their merger decisions. Roll's theory has been well supported by empirical evidence, and gained great popularity in the later 1980s and early 1990s. This hypothesis has, however, become harder to reconcile with the growing evidence of the stock-market merger anomalies discussed above. An important outcome of this debate is the light it throws on the plausibility of the assumptions embedded in each theory. As Roll (1986) puts it "perhaps one of the long-term benefits of studying takeovers is to clarify the notion of market efficiency". Therefore, a thorough investigation of the competing models not only facilitates a greater understanding of merger activities but also provides an opportunity to evaluate alternative behavioral assumptions concerning the rationality of corporate managers and financial markets.

We know from many past event study results that merger announcements signal important new information to the capital markets. Under the hubris hypothesis, the announcement of either a cash or a stock offer is indicative of overconfidence by the bidder management and therefore on average such offers must deliver negative news to the markets.[1] The empirical implications of the market timing theory is, however, not that unambiguous. For a pure stock offer, it is likely that either the bidder is overvalued or the target is undervalued (that is, relative to the bidder). However, for a pure cash offer, the only reason for making an acquisition is, as Shleifer and Vishny (2003) put it, "the undervaluation of the target" (that is, relative to target fundamental values). Dong *et al.* (2006) argue that, under the market timing theory, bidders profit by buying undervalued targets for cash at a price below its fundamental value. But if managers are acting in the shareholders' interests, it is also possible that the bidders may choose to pay cash when they know that their shares are undervalued (Myers and Majluf, 1984). Even in this case, given the large merger premiums typically paid to the targets,[2] target firms must be even more undervalued relative to the bidders. In a nutshell, cash-financed mergers signal unambiguous information to the market: either management overconfidence under the hubris hypothesis, or target undervaluation under the market timing theory.

Rhodes-Kropf *et al.* (2005), Ang and Chen (2006) and Dong *et al.* (2006), find direct evidence supporting the market timing theory. In general, they find that overvaluation increases the probability of a firm becoming a bidder, the use of stock as a method of payment, and that bidding firms perform poorly both on announcement of the merger and in subsequent periods. The above studies, however, have focused mainly on one side of the story: bidder overvaluation. We argue that target undervaluation constitutes the other side of the market timing theory and is therefore an issue that deserves to be examined closely. Given the clarity of the signalling effect of cash announcements mentioned above, we therefore focus in this chapter exclusively on the target undervaluation story by examining cash-financed mergers.

We are aware that, though merger activities are a universal phenomenon, most if not all of the evidence relating to this debate has been based on US data. In this chapter, we present UK evidence on this issue. We chose the UK as a representative sample of European evidence, since the UK accounts for the majority of European deals in terms of both numbers and value (for example, in Faccio and Masulis (2005), 65.3 percent of their thirteen European country mergers are UK bidders). Moreover, since our study involves cash-financed deals only, we are particularly interested in the fact that most UK bids are financed entirely by cash (for example, Faccio and Masulis (2005) report that 80.2 percent of the UK transactions in their sample were cash offers). This is in sharp contrast with the US data. Andrade et al. (2001) report that 70 percent of US deals involve stock payments, and that 58 percent are exclusively stock offers. Thus the UK sample is particularly interesting given the focus of our research.

Based on our analysis of a sample of UK public cash mergers between 1985 and 2004, we find that the stock-market reaction to merger announcements in both the short and long run are consistent with the prediction of the market timing theory, and that the pre-announcement performance of both targets and bidders are also in line with the theory. Our results therefore lend support to the proposition that stock market misvaluation and the market timing ability of managers are more likely to be the driving forces behind merger activities.

The rest of the chapter is organized as follows: section 2.2 develops the testable hypotheses; section 2.3 describes the data; section 2.4 introduces the methodology used in our empirical study; section 2.5 reports and discusses the empirical findings; and section 2.6 concludes.

2.2 HYPOTHESIS DEVELOPMENT

Although a target stock already has an observable market price, bidders clearly conduct their own valuations of the potential targets. Normally, the bid is abandoned (offered) if the valuation is below (above) the target's current market price.[3] If an offer is made, the difference between the offer price and the pre-announcement market price of the target is called the "merger premium".

As discussed in the Introduction, given a cash-financed merger: (i) under the hubris hypothesis, high merger premiums represent systematic mistakes/misvaluations by bidders driven by their excellent pre-bid performance, which endows bidder management with both excessive overconfidence (hubris) and free cash flows; and (ii) under the market timing theory, high merger premiums represent high deal synergy, since bidder management understands the potential incremental value associated with buying undervalued targets (for example, Dong et al. (2006) find that targets with lower valuations on average receive higher merger premiums). Based on this, we develop two hypotheses, as shown below.

Hypothesis 1 – Hubris: irrational managers, rational markets

The higher the merger premium paid for the target, the more severe will be the bidder management's overconfidence/overpayment, and therefore the worse the market's reaction to the merger announcement will be.

Hypothesis 2 – Market timing: rational managers, irrational markets

The higher the merger premium paid for the target, the larger the target's undervaluation or the greater are the synergies of the deal, and therefore the better will be the market's reaction to the merger announcement.

2.3 DATA AND DESCRIPTIVE STATISTICS

We examine a UK sample of successful public cash-financed mergers occurring between 1985 and 2004. The sample is drawn from the Securities Data Corporation (SDC) merger and acquisition database based on the following criteria: (i) all bidders are UK public firms, and target firms are UK or international public firms; (ii) the deal value is at least 10 million US dollars;[4] (iii) financial and utilities firms are excluded; (iv) bidders acquire at least 50 percent of the target's common stock; (v) for the purpose of this study, we require that the one-month merger premium data[5] is either available directly from the SDC or can be calculated from the information provided by the SDC; and (vi) we require that all transactions are paid entirely by cash and all firms that meet the above criteria must have stock prices, size (market value) and book-to-market ratios available from Thomson Financial Datastream. Some 191 bidders met all of the above mentioned criteria for the period 1985–2004.

Table 2.1 presents descriptive statistics for the sample. Column 2 reports the number of mergers that occurred in each calendar year. It is evident that the UK acquisition market experienced a boom in the late 1980s, slowed down between 1990 and 1996 and experienced another boom between 1997 and 2001. Our sample is thus representative of the transactions that occurred during the UK merger waves of the late 1980s and 1990s. Column 3 provides the mean and median one-month merger premiums paid for

Table 2.1 Descriptive statistics for mergers announced and completed, 1985–2004

Year	Firms	Premium (%)	Deal value (£m)	Bidder Size (£m)	Bidder B/M ratio	Diversifying (%)	Domestic (%)
1985	2	110(110)	337(337)	1742(1742)	0.29(0.29)	100	100
1987	13	49(46)	157(139)	1486(937)	0.27(0.30)	62	31
1988	26	56(52)	289(61)	872(471)	0.57(0.52)	73	54
1989	16	38(39)	110(41)	397(269)	0.16(0.51)	63	56
1990	9	42(56)	50(14)	215(156)	0.57(0.52)	78	78
1991	5	54(69)	100(95)	2125(1124)	0.48(0.45)	40	60
1993	3	63(43)	86(21)	1318(128)	0.25(0.27)	33	33
1994	5	35(38)	166(121)	1152(732)	0.36(0.29)	80	40
1995	6	33(37)	115(116)	1816(1136)	0.45(0.48)	67	67
1996	3	35(29)	108(125)	2022(2670)	0.40(0.40)	100	33
1997	12	49(52)	159(83)	1213(843)	0.63(0.63)	42	67
1998	20	43(37)	222(76)	1522(445)	0.48(0.32)	55	75
1999	26	52(40)	365(76)	2547(764)	0.49(0.42)	54	73
2000	15	48(50)	280(209)	3243(850)	0.66(0.50)	47	60
2001	16	38(36)	190(143)	3510(3009)	0.39(0.29)	31	44
2002	6	41(26)	64(14)	634(238)	0.67(0.61)	17	100
2003	6	37(41)	105(119)	3788(1671)	0.36(0.38)	33	17
2004	2	66(66)	61(61)	184(184)	0.61(0.61)	100	0
Total	191	47(41)	206(84)	1749(575)	0.47(0.41)	56	59

Notes: The sample consists of 191 UK public bidders that have acquired one or more public target firms with a deal value above 10 million US dollars between 1985 and 2004. The merger premium is defined as the four-week pre-announcement premium. It equals the difference between the initial bid price and the target market price four weeks prior to the initial merger announcement divided by the same target price four weeks prior to the announcement. The deal value (£million) is the total value of the consideration paid by the acquirer, excluding fees and expenses. Bidder size is the market capitalization of acquirers at the time of the merger announcement. Bidder book-to-market ratio is the book value of equity divided by the market capitalization at the time of merger announcement. Diversifying is the percentage of diversifying merger deals. A deal is classified as diversifying when the acquirer takes over a target with a different two-digit SIC industry code. Domestic is the percentage of domestic merger deals. The median values are shown in parentheses.

sample targets. Average premiums each year range from 33 percent to 110 percent for the whole sample period. Column 4 shows the mean and median deal values. Average deal value range from £50 million to £365 million each year. The bidders' mean and median market values each year are reported in Column 5. As can be seen, bidders are much larger than the targets they buy, on average about nine times larger. Column 6 shows mean and median book-to-market ratios of bidders average ranging from 0.16 to 0.67. Finally, Columns 7 and 8 show that on average 56 percent of deals are diversifying mergers[6] and 59 percent are domestic mergers.

2.4 METHODOLOGY

2.4.1 Short-run method

We follow Fuller *et al.* (2002) and Dong *et al.*'s (2006) standard event study methodology to calculate the cumulative abnormal returns (CARs) for the three-day (-1 to $+1$) and the five-day (-2 to $+2$) event windows surrounding merger announcements. We calculate abnormal return based on daily market-adjusted returns:

$$AR_i = R_i - R_m \tag{2.1}$$

where R_i is the daily return for event firm i, and R_m is the corresponding value-weighted market index return.

2.4.2 Long-run method

We calculate both the buy-and-hold abnormal return (BHAR) and the calendar time abnormal return (CTAR) for our long-run (3-year) post-merger studies. We also calculate the cumulative abnormal return (CAR) for the long-run (1-year) pre-merger investigation. In all cases, we use the return on a single control firm matched for industry, size and book-to-market ratio as the expected/normal return for our sample firms. The matching method is in the spirit of Barber and Lyon (1997), Lyon *et al.* (1999) and Megginson *et al.* (2004). We match for industry in addition to size and book-to-market ratio since Andrade and Stafford (1999) show that mergers tend to cluster in calendar time by industry. Mitchell and Mulherin (1996) find that industry shocks lead to increased same-industry takeover activity. Kahle and Walkling (1996) and Walker (2000) show that industry-matching of benchmark firms surpasses pure size-matched benchmarks in performance analysis. Thus industry is an important factor to be adjusted for in mergers.

We note that matching for size and book-to-market ratio during the event month and employing the same control firm for several years can bias the expected return benchmark, since, for frequent acquirers, size and book-to-market ratios can fluctuate considerably over time. This creates serious biases in using a single control firm matched at the merger event throughout the long-run event window. However, nearly all previous studies employing the control firms/portfolios approach fail to consider this long-run mismatching problem. Further, for event and control firms alike, size and book-to-market ratios may drift in a systematic fashion as a result of major corporate events such as mergers. Thus a systematic event-induced drift could cause event firms and control firms to be mismatched in long-run event studies (Cowan and Sergeant, 2001).

To overcome the above-mentioned mismatching problems, we match event and control firms dynamically. We follow Brav and Gompers (1997) and Cowan and Sergeant (2001), who allow the size and book-to-market control portfolio to change quarterly. This quarterly rematching approach allows us to overcome both the long-run mismatch problem and the event-induced risk drifting problem.

Briefly, the control firm is selected as follows: (i) for each year at the merger completion month (for the post-merger study) or 12 months prior to the merger announcement month (for the pre-merger study), we identify all firms listed on the London Stock Exchange that have the same two-digit standard industrial classification (SIC) code as the sample firm;[7] (ii) we then identify all firms with a market capitalization (size) of between 70 percent and 130 percent of the sample firm market capitalization; and (iii) we then select the firm with the closest book-to-market ratio to the event firm. The control firm matched as described above is employed as the expected return for each sample firm over a 3-month horizon. We repeat the above-mentioned matching process every three months, which ensures that a new control firm is obtained quarterly should the acquiring firm's characteristics change significantly over this period; otherwise, the original control firm is utilized. If an event firm is delisted during the 36-month post-merger event window, we calculate and report only the abnormal returns for either 12-months and/or 24-months.

2.5 EMPIRICAL RESULTS

We will now test our hypotheses developed in section 2.2 in three different event windows: namely, the announcement, post-merger, and pre-merger periods. The hubris hypothesis or the market timing theory, whichever is the main driving force for merger activities, should produce consistent evidence in all three periods under investigation. We first report our empirical results for the announcement period.

2.5.1 Acquirer announcement period stock performance

Under Shleifer and Vishny's framework, some firms may be valued incorrectly, possibly because of a lack of information or ineffective arbitrage. Since merger announcement reveals new information to the market about the target, and the bidder's value and the synergy of the deal, the market's immediate reaction to the announcement is thus an important testimony to our hypotheses. If some firms are misvalued temporarily before the announcement, the market, during the announcement period, will reassess and react on the basis of whether it perceives the deal as value-destroying (that is, the bidder overpaying because of hubris) or value-creating (the buying of undervalued targets by rational managers).

Table 2.2 presents the short-run (3- and 5-day) CARs of the full sample and three sub-samples sorted by the merger premiums. For the full sample, we find that bidders experience small and insignificant 3- and 5-day CARs that are consistent with the majority of the existing evidence, which documents that bidders normally break even during the announcement period. According to our hypotheses, the rational market/irrational bidder hubris hypothesis predicts that high-premium-paying acquirers should experience worse returns than low-premium acquirers, while the market timing hypothesis predicts that high-premium acquirers would have better performance than low-premium ones. Table 2.2 shows that the 3- and 5-day CARs of low-premium acquirers are negative (−1.60 percent and −1.65 percent respectively) and statistically significant at the 1 percent signifi-

Table 2.2 Announcement period CARs of bidders

Days	All	Low (30%)	Medium (40%)	High(30%)	High–Low
(−1, +1)	−0.0035	−0.0160[a]	0.0012	0.0028	0.0188[c]
	[−0.86]	[−2.50]	[0.19]	[0.34]	[1.80]
(−2, +2)	−0.0034	−0.0165[a]	0.0008	0.0042	0.0207[c]
	[−0.74]	[−2.55]	[0.10]	[0.46]	[1.86]

Notes:
The sample consists of 191 UK public bidders that have acquired one or more public target firms with a deal value above US$10 million between 1985 and 2004. The merger premium is defined as the four-week pre-announcement premium. It equals the difference between the initial bid price and the target market price four weeks prior to the initial merger announcement divided by the same target price four weeks prior to the announcement. Acquiring firms are ranked by merger premiums and partitioned into three portfolios according to their rankings. Low-premium portfolio comprises the lowest 30 percent premium paying firms. Medium-premium portfolio comprises the middle 40 percent firms. High-premium portfolio comprises the highest 30 percent firms. We calculate abnormal return based on the market-adjusted returns: $AR_i = R_i - R_m$, where R_i is the return on event firm i and R_m is the value-weighted market index return. T-statistics are reported in square brackets.
[a] Denotes significance at the 1 percent level.
[b] Denotes significance at the 5 percent level.
[c] Denotes significance at the 10 percent level.

cance level. For the high acquirer sub-portfolio, both the 3- and 5-day CARs are positive (0.28 percent and 0.42 percent, respectively) though statistically insignificant. The high-low return differentials are 1.9 percent and 2.1 percent for 3- and 5-day event windows, respectively; and both are significant at the 10 percent significance level. This evidence is consistent with the prediction of Hypothesis 2 (market timing) in that high-premium-paying bidders outperform their low-premium counterparts, given that high-premium may represent a large undervaluation of the target and therefore have high deal synergy.

2.5.2 Robustness checks

In order to conduct some robustness checks, we now control for a variety of known firm and deal characteristics–namely, size, relative size, book-to-market ratio, diversification, and target origin, to ascertain the persistence and robustness of our preliminary results reported in Table 2.2. Because of the limitations of our small sample size (191 firms), we are unable to use multidimensional sorting methods to control merger premiums and all the other characteristics simultaneously. However, we are at least able to use two-dimensional sorting methods to correct for some misclassification problems that are inherent in a one-variable approach. We thus proceed to sort sample firms according to both merger premium and one other distinct firm or deal characteristic and then reexamine whether the short-run CARs obtained under the new sorting method are consistent with those reported in Table 2.2.

Acquirer size and merger premiums

The size effect has been documented widely in the finance literature. Banz (1981) and Reinganum (1981) find that small-cap stocks earn higher abnormal returns. In mergers, Moeller *et al.* (2004) show that small firms earn higher announcement period abnormal returns than do large firms. However, if our general result (Table 2.2) is valid, it should not be significantly affected by the size of the bidders.

Panel A of Table 2.3 reports the results for bidder size and merger premium. For large-size bidders, the 3- and 5-day CARs for the large+low sub-samples are negative (-1.70 percent and -2.60 percent respectively) and statistically significant at 10 percent and 1 percent level, respectively. However, the CARs for the large+high sub-samples are small and insignificant. The respective high–low return differentials are positive but statistically insignificant. For small-size bidders, the CARs for the small+low sub-samples are negative, while being positive for small+high. The 3-day high–low return differential is 2.28 percent and significant at the 10 percent level. Thus Panel A shows similar patterns to those observed in Table 2.2 after controlling for bidder size differences.

Table 2.3 CARs of bidders sorted by merger premium and other characteristics

Characters	Low (30%)	Medium (40%)	High (30%)	High–Low
Panel A: bidder size				
Day (−1, +1)				
Large	−0.0170c	0.0111	−0.0022	0.0149
	[−1.82]	[1.17]	[−0.15]	[0.88]
Small	−0.0150c	−0.0090	0.0079	0.0228c
	[−1.68]	[−1.11]	[0.95]	[1.87]
Day (−2, +2)				
Large	−0.0259a	0.0124	−0.0040	0.0219
	[−2.60]	[1.05]	[−0.28]	[1.27]
Small	−0.0068	−0.0111	0.0126	0.0194
	[−0.85]	[−1.10]	[1.14]	[1.42]
Panel B: Relative size between target and bidder				
Day (−1, +1)				
Large	−0.0174b	−0.0042	0.0016	0.0190
	[−2.39]	[−0.44]	[0.14]	[1.36]
Small	−0.0146	0.0067	0.0039	0.0186
	[−1.36]	[0.82]	[0.34]	[1.17]
Day (−2, +2)				
Large	−0.0122	−0.0060	0.0027	0.0149
	[−1.63]	[−0.54]	[0.22]	[1.04]
Small	−0.0210c	0.0078	0.0057	0.0267c
	[−1.95]	[0.71]	[0.42]	[1.75]
Panel C: Book-to-market ratio				
Day (−1, +1)				
Value	−0.0086	−0.0021	−0.0046	0.0040
	[−0.89]	[−0.23]	[−0.48]	[0.30]
Glamour	−0.0220b	0.0045	−0.0003	0.0217
	[−2.28]	[0.43]	[−0.02]	[1.25]
Day (−2, +2)				
Value	−0.0073	−0.0050	−0.0088	−0.0015
	[−0.80]	[−0.48]	[−0.73]	[−0.10]
Glamour	−0.0232b	0.0060	0.0094	0.0326c
	[−2.31]	[0.45]	[0.62]	[1.79]

(Continued)

Table 2.3 Continued

Characters	Low (30%)	Medium (40%)	High (30%)	High–Low
Panel D: Focused or diversified deal				
Day (−1, +1)				
Focused	−0.0116	−0.0051	0.0052	0.0169
	[−1.35]	[−0.46]	[0.36]	[0.99]
Diversified	−0.0154	0.0031	0.0008	0.0163
	[−1.54]	[0.44]	[0.09]	[1.19]
Day (−2, +2)				
Focused	−0.0154	−0.0068	−0.0041	0.0113
	[−1.45]	[−0.50]	[−0.26]	[0.59]
Diversified	−0.0141	0.0042	0.0106	0.0246[c]
	[−1.61]	[0.48]	[1.05]	[1.85]
Panel E: Domestic or foreign				
Day (−1, +1)				
Domestic	−0.0160[c]	0.0003	−0.0005	0.0154
	[−1.75]	[0.04]	[−0.05]	[1.03]
Foreign	−0.0184	0.0027	0.0093	0.0277[c]
	[−1.65]	[0.25]	[0.90]	[1.83]
Day (−2, +2)				
Domestic	−0.0154	0.0013	0.0065	0.0219
	[−1.64]	[0.16]	[0.50]	[1.36]
Foreign	−0.0258[b]	0.0056	0.0014	0.0271[c]
	[−2.24]	[0.38]	[0.12]	[1.68]

Notes:

The sample consists of 191 UK public bidders that have acquired one or more public target firms with a deal value above US$ 10 million between 1985 and 2004. The merger premium is defined as the four-week pre-announcement premium. It equals the difference between the initial bid price and the target market price four weeks prior to the initial merger announcement divided by the same target price four weeks prior to the announcement. Acquiring firms in each panel are ranked by merger premiums and partitioned into three portfolios according to their rankings. Low-premium portfolio comprises the lowest 30 percent premium paying firms. Medium-premium portfolio comprises the middle 40 percent firms. High-premium portfolio comprises the highest 30 percent firms. We calculate abnormal return based on the market-adjusted returns: $AR_i = R_i - R_m$, where R_i is the return on event firm i, and R_m is the value-weighted market index return. T-statistics are reported in brackets.

[a] Denotes significance at the 1 percent level.
[b] Denotes significance at the 5 percent level.
[c] Denotes significance at the 10 percent level.

Relative size and merger premiums

Many studies have also examined the impact of the relative size of target to bidder on acquiring firms' stock performance. Asquith *et al.* (1983) find that acquirers' abnormal returns depend on their relative size. Ang and Kohers

(2001) report that relative size significantly affects bidder's post-merger stock performance. Fuller *et al.* (2002) show that the larger the relative size (in the acquisition of public targets), the lower the acquirers' abnormal returns. Given the above evidence, we control for both relative size and merger premium in our study.

Panel B of Table 2.3 reports results for sub-samples sorted by both relative size and merger premiums. We can see that all low-premium sub-samples earn negative CARs regardless of the relative size, and among them half are statistically significant. On the other hand, all high-premium sub-sample CARs, no matter what their relative size, are positive, though statistically insignificant. All high–low return differentials are positive, the 5-day high–low return differentials for relatively small-size bidders are 2.67 percent and significant at the 10 percent level. Thus our general results (see Table 2.2) are, by and large, not affected by the relative size and there is no sign of any evidence supporting the hubris hypothesis.

Book-to-market ratio (value/glamour acquirer) and merger premium

The performance extrapolation hypothesis (Rau and Vermaelen, 1998) states that investors over-extrapolate the past positive performance of glamour acquirers (characterized as having a low book-to-market ratio), while penalizing value acquirers (characterized as having a high book-to-market ratio) based on the idea that poor recent performance will persist. Thus, bidder status (value or glamour) affects their stock performance. However, if market timing is the main reason for merger activities, then our general results reported in Table 2.2 should generally not be affected by the book-to-market ratio of the bidders.

Panel C of Table 2.3 reports the results for sub-samples sorted by both book-to-market ratio and merger premium. Again, we find all low premium sub-samples, regardless of their value/glamour status, earn negative 3- and 5-day CARs. For example for glamour+low acquirers, the 3- and 5-day CARs are −2.20 percent and −2.32 percent, respectively, and both are significant at the 5 percent level. For high premium sub-samples, the CARs are again small and statistically insignificant. The 5-day high-low return differential for glamour acquirers is 3.26 percent and significant at the 10 percent significance level. Thus Panel C, after controlling for the bidder status is, by and large, consistent with the market timing theory.

Diversification and merger premium

Morck *et al.* (1990) and Maquiera *et al.* (1998) find that capital markets react negatively to diversifying mergers. Megginson *et al.* (2004) find a significant positive relationship between corporate focus and long-term merger performance. In contrast, however, Agrawal *et al.* (1992) find that diversifying deals earn higher post-merger stock returns. Thus diversification is an important factor that should be controlled when measuring merger performance.

Panel D of Table 2.3 presents results sorted by both diversification and merger premium. We again observe negative CARs for all low-premium sub-samples, and positive CAR for most high premium sub-samples regardless whether the deal is a diversifying or a focused one. All high–low return differentials are positive. The 5-day high–low return differential of diversifying deals is 2.46 percent and significant at the 10 percent level. Thus Panel D again presents evidence that supports the market timing theory after controlling for the diversification effect.

Target origin and merger premium

In our sample, though all bidders are UK public firms, the targets are either UK or international public firms. Thus some transactions are domestic, while others involve foreign acquisitions. In general, the literature suggests different market reactions to domestic versus foreign acquisitions.[8] We thus control for both target origin and merger premium in our test.

Panel E of Table 2.3 reports results sorted by both domestic/foreign deal and merger premiums. As can be seen, Panel E clearly repeats the results of the previous panels. All low-premium sub-sample CARs are negative, and among them half are statistically significant, while the CARs are small and insignificant for the high-premium sub-samples, regardless of whether the deal is domestic or cross-border. All the high–low return differentials are positive, and half of them are statistically significant. Once again, after controlling for target origin, we find similar evidence to that reported in Table 2.2, which lends supports to the market timing theory of mergers.

Taken together, we find in Table 2.3 consistent evidence supporting the prediction of the market timing theory. We note, however, that the CARs of high-premium-paying acquirers are small and insignificant, which may be because rational targets, knowing that their firms are severely undervalued and thus requiring a much higher premium, exhausts the potential abnormal gains of the bidders.

2.5.3 Announcement period abnormal returns of combined firms

We have so far reported short-run evidence only for acquiring firms. However, our hypotheses also make clear predictions for combined CARs (target and bidder). Since the market timing theory predicts value creation through buying undervalued targets, according to our Hypothesis 2, we should observe that the higher the premiums offered, the larger the combined CARs of targets and bidders. However, Hypothesis 1 predicts no combined gains (zero-sum), since, under hubris, target gains are bidder losses.

Table 2.4 Announcement period combined CARs of target and bidder

Day	All	Low (30%)	Medium (40%)	High (30%)	High–Low
(−1, +1)	0.0322[a]	0.0101	0.0323[a]	0.0543[a]	0.0443[a]
	[5.84]	[1.22]	[4.66]	[4.20]	[2.89]
(−2, +2)	0.0364[a]	0.0097	0.0365[a]	0.0630[a]	0.0533[a]
	[5.90]	[1.04]	[4.37]	[4.64]	[3.24]

Notes:
[a] Denotes significance at the 1 percent level.
[b] Denotes significance at the 5 percent level.
[c] Denotes significance at the 10 percent level.

The sample consists of 191 UK public bidders that have acquired one or more public target firms with a deal value above US$ 10 million between 1985 and 2004. The merger premium is defined as the four-week pre-announcement premium. It equals the difference between the initial bid price and the target market price four weeks prior to the initial merger announcement divided by the same target price four weeks prior to the announcement. Acquiring and target firms are ranked by merger premiums and partitioned into three portfolios according to their rankings. Low-premium portfolio comprises the lowest 30 percent premium paying firms. Medium-premium portfolio comprises the middle 40 percent firms. High-premium portfolio comprises the highest 30 percent firms. We calculate abnormal return for target and bidder based on the market-adjusted returns: $AR_i = R_i - R_{mv}$ where R_i is the return on event firm i and R_m is the value-weighted market index return. We then calculate the value-weighted CAR for the combined firm (target and bidder). T-statistics of the combined CARs are reported in square brackets.

Table 2.4 presents the short-run value-weighted CARs for the combined firms (target and acquirer). For the full sample, both the 3- and 5-day weighted CARs are positive (3.22 percent and 3.64 percent, respectively) and statistically significant at the 1 percent level. This result indicates that shareholders at the combined level gain from the announcement of cash mergers. The combined CARs for low-premium deals are small and insignificant, while CARs become larger and more significant with the increase of merger premium. For example, the high-premium 3- and 5-day combined CARs are 5.43 percent and 6.30 percent, respectively, and both are significant at the 1 percent level. Further, the high–low return differentials are positive (4.43 percent for 3-day, and 5.33 percent for 5-day) and highly significant at the 1 percent level. Thus, the combined results are also consistent with the predictions of the market timing theory.

2.5.4 Acquirer long-run post–merger stock performance

Our short-run analysis suggests that merger premiums may be a better proxy for the amount of deal synergy. This is in line with the market timing theory, but stands in sharp contrast with the hubris hypothesis. For further evidence, we now turn to the long-run study. In Shleifer and Vishny's framework, although the market is initially mispriced will correct itself in the long run. If this is the case, we should not expect to observe any significant

Table 2.5 Bidders' long-run post-merger BHARs and CTARs

Year	All	Low (30%)	Medium (40%)	High (30%)	High–Low
Panel A: BHAR					
1	−0.0602[c]	−0.0293	−0.0580	−0.0941	−0.0648
	[−1.72]	[−0.47]	[−1.02]	[−1.49]	[−0.73]
2	−0.1710	−0.0800	−0.2780	−0.1176	−0.0370
	[−1.58]	[−0.70]	[−1.14]	[−1.24]	[−0.25]
3	−0.0667	−0.0140	−0.0640	−0.1220	−0.1080
	[−1.07]	[−0.13]	[−0.59]	[−1.18]	[−0.71]
Panel B: CTAR					
1	−0.0076[c]	−0.0073	−0.0025	−0.0108[c]	−0.0035
	[−1.68]	[−0.84]	[−0.41]	[−1.90]	[−0.34]
2	−0.0053[b]	0.0003	−0.0070	−0.0083	−0.0083
	[−2.06]	[0.01]	[−1.36]	[−1.59]	[−1.11]
3	−0.0053[a]	−0.0045	−0.0032	−0.0104[c]	−0.0059
	[−2.55]	[−1.11]	[−0.75]	[−1.98]	[−0.89]

Notes:
[a] Denotes significance at the 1 percent level.
[b] Denotes significance at the 5 percent level.
[c] Denotes significance at the 10 percent level.
The sample consists of 191 UK public bidders that have acquired one or more public target firms with a deal value above US$ 10 million between 1985 and 2004. The merger premium is defined as the four-week pre-announcement premium. It equals the difference between the initial bid price and the target market price four weeks prior to the initial merger announcement divided by the same target price four weeks prior to the announcement. Acquiring and target firms are ranked by merger premiums and partitioned into three portfolios according to their rankings. Low-premium portfolio comprises the lowest 30 percent premium paying firms. Medium-premium portfolio comprises the middle 40 percent firms. High-premium portfolio comprises the highest 30 percent firms. Both buy-and-hold abnormal returns (BHAR) and Calendar-time abnormal returns (CTAR) are calculated for the full samples and sub-samples formed on the basis of merger premium. For CTAR, acquirers enter the portfolio on the effective month of the merger and remain for 12, 24, and 36 months respectively. Calendar portfolios are rebalanced each month to include firms that have just completed a merger and to disregard the ones that have just fulfilled 12, 24, or 36 months. T-statistics are reported in square brackets.

long-run performance differentials between high- and low-premium sub-samples. However, hubris hypothesis predicts that high-premium acquirers underperform low-premium ones, since high acquirers overpay severely and thus lead to long-run underperformance.

We calculate our long-run results by using both the buy-and-hold abnormal return (BHAR) and the calendar time abnormal return (CTAR) approaches. Under BHAR, Panel A of Table 2.5 shows no statistically significant evidence of long-run underperformance in the three years following merger for both the full sample and sub-samples sorted by merger premiums. Although the 1- to 3-year high–low return differentials are negative, they are statistically insignificantly different from zero. Under the CTAR, Panel B shows that while the long-run monthly average abnormal returns are statistically significant for the full sample, and for most of the high premium sub-samples, none of the high–low return differentials are statistically significant. Thus our long-run results taken as a whole show that there are no statistically significant return differentials between high and low premium acquirers in the 1 to 3 years following merger, which is in line with the market timing theory.

2.5.5 Target and acquirer pre-merger stock performance

Target firms

Under our Hypothesis 1, financial markets are efficient/rational and therefore all target firms are correctly priced by the market prior to the merger announcement. According to this, target firms should not experience any risk-adjusted abnormal returns prior to the announcement. On the other hand, our Hypothesis 2 assumes an inefficient market, and thus the only reason for a rational bidder to make cash-financed mergers is the undervaluation of the targets. According to this, high-merger premiums imply severe undervaluation of the targets. We would therefore expect to see, prior to the merger announcements, high-premium targets experience a period of poor performance comparing to the low premium ones.

Figure 2.1 depicts the 12-month pre-announcement CARs of UK target firms that are acquired by the low- and high-premium bidders.[9] For the low premium targets, we do not observe any significant pre-merger abnormal returns compared to their matching firms. However, high-premium targets

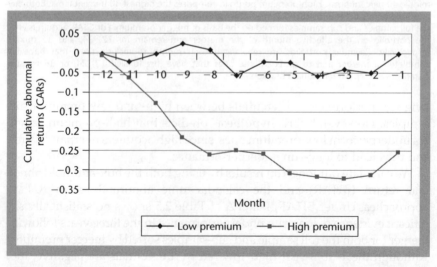

Figure 2.1 One-year pre-announcement CARs of UK low- and high-premium targets

severely underperform their matching firms throughout the 12-month pre-announcement period. The patterns depicted in Figure 2.1 are therefore consistent with the prediction of the market timing theory.

Table 2.6 calculates the 12-month pre-announcement CARs of all UK target firms and the respective low- and high-premium targets. For the full

Table 2.6 UK target firms' 12-month pre-merger CARs

Months	All	Low (30%)	High (30%)	High–Low
−12	−0.0057	−0.0014	−0.0074	−0.0060
	[−0.28]	[−0.03]	[−0.15]	[−0.10]
−11	−0.0131	−0.0226	−0.0639	−0.0414
	[−0.47]	[−0.42]	[−1.01]	[−0.50]
−10	−0.0429	−0.0027	−0.1287	−0.126
	[−1.21]	[−0.04]	[−1.64]	[−1.15]
−9	−0.0642	0.0229	−0.2169^b	−0.240^b
	[−1.61]	[0.27]	[−2.63]	[−2.04]
−8	−0.0961^c	0.009	−0.261^b	−0.270^c
	[−1.95]	[0.09]	[−2.57]	[−1.89]
−7	−0.1160^b	−0.058	−0.250^b	−0.192
	[−2.19]	[−0.53]	[−2.48]	[−1.29]
−6	−0.0955^c	−0.021	−0.258^b	−0.237
	[−1.85]	[−0.18]	[−2.29]	[−1.44]
−5	−0.0995^c	−0.024	−0.308^b	−0.284^c
	[−1.92]	[−0.23]	[−2.67]	[−1.85]
−4	−0.1118^c	−0.060	−0.317^b	−0.257
	[−1.74]	[−0.46]	[−2.10]	[−1.29]
−3	−0.1358^b	−0.042	−0.321^c	−0.279
	[−1.99]	[−0.33]	[−1.91]	[−1.31]
−2	−0.1374^c	−0.052	−0.314^c	−0.262
	[−1.88]	[−0.36]	[−1.96]	[−1.22]
−1	−0.0744	−0.003	−0.254	−0.250
	[−1.04]	[−0.02]	[−1.63]	[−1.18]

Notes:
The sample consists of 112 UK public targets that have been acquired by UK public bidders with a deal value above US$ 10 million between 1985 and 2004. The merger premium is defined as the four-week pre-announcement premium. It equals the difference between the initial bid price and the target market price four weeks prior to the initial merger announcement divided by the same target price four weeks prior to the announcement. Acquiring and target firms are ranked by merger premiums and partitioned into two portfolios according to their rankings. Low-premium portfolio comprises the lowest 30 percent premium paying firms. High-premium portfolio comprises the highest 30 percent firms. Cumulative abnormal returns (CAR) are calculated for the full samples and sub-samples formed on the basis of merger premium. T-statistics are reported in square brackets.
^{a} Denotes significance at the 1 percent level.
^{b} Denotes significance at the 5 percent level.
^{c} Denotes significance at the 10 percent level.

sample, seven out of twelve CARs (from month −8 to −2) are negative and statistically significant. However, when looking at the sub-sample results, we find that none of the CARs of low-premium targets are significant, while eight out of twelve CARs of high-premium targets are negative and significant. All high–low return differentials are negative, and three out of twelve are significant. Table 2.6 thus provides evidence that high-premium targets underperform their low-premium counterparts 12 months prior to the merger announcement, which is in line with the market timing theory.

Acquiring firms

Under our Hypothesis 1, bidder managers are irrational who overpay the acquisitions because they are infected by hubris, which may result from excellent pre-bid performance. Thus bidders paying high merger premiums must experience superior pre-bid performance relative to low-premium-paying acquirers. The market timing theory, however, predicts no difference on pre-merger performance for high- and low-premium acquirers, since the only reason for making cash-financed acquisitions is the undervaluation of the targets.

Figure 2.2 depicts the 12-month pre-announcement CARs of low- and high-premium-paying acquirers. It shows no obvious differences between CARs of the high and low premium sub-samples for the 12-month period prior to the announcement. The patterns shown in Figure 2.2 are therefore consistent with the prediction of market timing theory.

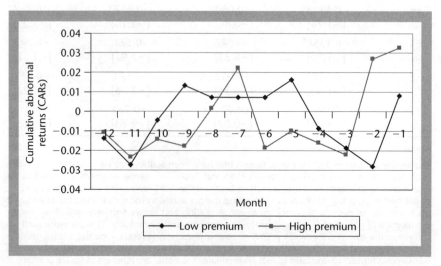

Figure 2.2 One-year pre-announcement CARs of UK low- and high-premium bidders

Table 2.7 calculates the 12-month pre-announcement CARs for all acquirers, and the high- and low-premium acquirers. As can been seen, none of the 12-month low-premium sub-sample CARs are statistically significant, and the same applies to high-premium-acquirer CARs. Further,

Table 2.7 Bidding Firms' 12-month pre-merger CARs

Months	All	Low (30%)	High (30%)	High-Low
−12	0.00399	−0.0139	−0.0107	0.0032
	[0.40]	[−0.67]	[−0.71]	[0.13]
−11	−0.0024	−0.0272	−0.0233	0.0039
	[−0.19]	[−1.15]	[−1.14]	[0.12]
−10	0.0200	−0.0043	−0.0140	−0.0097
	[1.33]	[−0.14]	[−0.64]	[−0.25]
−9	0.0268	0.0132	−0.0177	−0.0310
	[1.58]	[0.44]	[−0.63]	[−0.75]
−8	0.0319^c	0.0073	0.0016	−0.0058
	[1.83]	[0.22]	[0.06]	[−0.13]
−7	0.0514^a	0.0075	0.0223	0.0149
	[2.60]	[0.24]	[0.64]	[0.32]
−6	0.0341	0.0075	−0.0185	−0.0260
	[1.54]	[0.19]	[−0.53]	[−0.49]
−5	0.0467^b	0.0163	−0.0100	−0.0263
	[2.04]	[0.35]	[−0.28]	[−0.45]
−4	0.0291	−0.0087	−0.0161	−0.0074
	[1.20]	[−0.19]	[−0.42]	[−0.12]
−3	0.0195	−0.0185	−0.0219	−0.0035
	[0.73]	[−0.35]	[−0.55]	[−0.05]
−2	0.0324	−0.0278	0.0270	0.0548
	[1.18]	[−0.54]	[0.57]	[0.78]
−1	0.0425	0.0080	0.0325	0.0246
	[1.52]	[0.15]	[0.67]	[0.34]

Notes:
^{a} Denotes significance at the 1 percent level.
^{b} Denotes significance at the 5 percent level.
^{c} Denotes significance at the 10 percent level.

The sample consists of 191 UK public bidders that have acquired one or more public target firms with a deal value above US$ 10 million between 1985 and 2004. The merger premium is defined as the four-week pre-announcement premium. It equals the difference between the initial bid price and the target market price four weeks prior to the initial merger announcement divided by the same target price four weeks prior to the announcement. Acquiring and target firms are ranked by merger premiums and partitioned into two portfolios according to their rankings. Low premium portfolio comprises the lowest 30 percent premium paying firms. High premium portfolio comprises the highest 30 percent firms. Cumulative abnormal returns (CAR) are calculated for the full samples and sub-samples formed on the basis of merger premium. T-statistics are reported in square brackets.

none of the 12-month high–low return differentials are statistically significant. Thus we conclude that there are no significant performance variations between high- and low-premium-paying acquirers 12 months prior to the merger announcement. This is again in line with the prediction of the market timing theory.

2.6 CONCLUSION

Recent studies on testing the market timing theory of mergers (Shleifer and Vishny, 2003) have provided supportive evidence of the theory in the USA. These studies have also focused mainly on examining the overvaluation of acquirers. Equally important, target undervaluation constitutes the other side of the misvaluation theory, which surprisingly has been relatively ignored to date. In this chapter, we test the undervaluation side of the story under a new framework of market/manager rationality.

We find that stock market reactions to UK merger announcements in both the short and the long run are consistent with the prediction of the market timing theory of mergers. Further, the evidence for the pre-announcement period is also in line with the theory. Taken together, our results lend support to the proposition that stock market misvaluation and the market timing ability of managers are the main driving forces behind merger activities. Our results also provide evidence supportive of the growing field of behavioral corporate finance that views managerial decisions as primarily being driven by misvaluations by financial markets and managers' attempts to time the market.

NOTES

1. Under the hubris hypothesis, stock offer signals management overconfidence affected by excellent pre-bid performance and high valuation of bidder's stock; while cash offer signals management hubris affected by excess cash flows of the bidder.
2. The average merger premium in our sample for cash-financed deals is 47 percent.
3. Because the bidder understands that the target shareholders will not sell their shares for below the current market price, when the bidder's valuation turns out to be less than the target's market price clearly no offer will (should) be made.
4. Although we apply the 10 million dollars cut-off point, 72 percent of our sample firms have a deal value above 50 million dollars, and 55 percent above 100 million dollars.
5. Evidence has shown that the most significant market value changes for target firms occur on the merger announcement date or on the day before the announcement. Thus the use of one-month merger premiums should capture the difference between the offer price and the target's pre-merger price. See, for example, Dodd (1980), Asquith (1983), Dennis and McConnell (1986), Huang and Walkling (1987), and Bradley and Jarrell (1988). The one-month merger premium equals the difference between the initial bid price and the target market price four weeks prior to the initial merger announcement divided by the same target price four weeks prior to the announcement.

6. Diversifying deals are mergers where acquirers and target firms do not have the same two-digit SIC code.
7. The use of the two-digit SIC code is consistent with Daley *et al.* (1997), Desai and Jain (1999), and Megginson, *et al.* (2004).
8. See for example, Doukas and Travlos (1988); Kang (1993); Eun *et al.* (1996); Fatemi and Furtedo (1998); Goergen and Renneboog (2004); Conn *et al.* (2005); and Gregory and McCorriston (2005).
9. Because of the data limitation in finding the industry code, size and book-to-market ratio information for both international target firms and their respective control firms, we restrict our analysis in Figure 2.1 and Table 2.6 to UK public targets which possess the above required data and account for 59 percent of the total target firms.

REFERENCES

Agrawal, A., Jaffe, J. F. and Mandelker, G. N. (1992) "The post-merger performance of Acquiring Firms: A Re-examination of an Anomaly", *Journal of Finance*, 47: 1605–22.

Andrade, G. and Stafford, E. (1999) "Investigating the Economic Role of Mergers", Working paper, Harvard Business School.

Andrade, G., Mitchell, M. and Stafford, E. (2001) "New Evidence and Perspectives on Mergers", *Journal of Economic Perspectives*, 15: 103–20.

Ang, J. and Cheng, Y. (2006) "Direct Evidence on the Market-driven Acquisition Theory", *Journal of Financial Research*, 29: 199–216.

Ang, J. and Kohers, N. (2001) "The Takeover Market for Privately Held Companies: The US Experience", *Cambridge Journal of Economics*, 25: 723–48.

Asquith, P. (1983) "Merger Bids, Uncertainty, and Stockholder Returns", *Journal of Financial Economics*, 11: 51–83.

Asquith, P., Bruner, R. F. and Mullins, D. W. (1983) "The Gains to Bidding Firms from Merger", *Journal of Financial Economics*, 11: 121–39.

Banz, R. (1981) "The relationship between Return and Market Value of Common Stock," *Journal of Financial Economics*, 9: 3–18.

Barber, B. M. and Lyon, J. D. (1997) "Detecting Long-run Abnormal Stock Returns: The Fuller, K., Netter, J. M. and Stegemoller, M. (2003) "What Do Returns to Acquiring Firms Tell US? Evidence from Firms that Make Many Acquisitions", *Journal of Finance*, 57: 1763–94.

Goergen, M. and Renneboog, L. (2004) "Shareholder Wealth Effects of European Domestic and Cross-border Takeover Bids", *European Financial Management*, 10: 9–45.

Gregory, A. and McCorriston, S. (2005) "Foreign Acquisitions by UK Limited Companies: Short and Long Run Performance", *Journal of Empirical Finance*, 12: 99–125.

Huang, Y. S. and Walkling, R. A. (1987) "Target Abnormal Returns Associated with Acquisition Announcements, Payment, Acquisition Form, and Managerial Resistance", *Journal of Financial Economics*, 19: 329–49.

Javanovic, B. and Rousseau, P. (2001) "Mergers and Technological Change: 1885–2001", Working paper, New York University.

Kahle, K. and Walkling, R. (1996) "The Impact of Industry Classifications on Financial Research", *Journal of Financial and Quantitative Analysis*, 31: 309–35.

Kang, J. K. (1993) "The International Market for Corporate Control. Mergers and Acquisitions of US Firms by Japanese Firms", *Journal of Financial Economics*, 34: 345–71.

Loughran, T. and Vijh, A. M. (1997) "Do Long-term Shareholders Benefit from Corporate Acquisitions?", *Journal of Finance*, 52: 1765–90.

Lyon, J. D., Barber, B. M. and Tsai, C. (1999) "Improved Methods for Tests of Long-run Abnormal Stock Returns", *Journal of Finance*, 54: 165–201.

Maksimovic, V. and Phillips, G. (2001) "The Market for Corporate Assets: Who Engages in Mergers and Asset Sales and Are There Efficiency Gains?", *Journal of Finance*, 56: 2019–65.

Maquiera, C., Megginson, W. and Nail, L. (1998) "Wealth Creation versus Wealth Redistribution in Pure Stock-for-stock Mergers", *Journal of Financial Economics*, 48: 3–33.

Megginson, W. L., Morgan, A. and Nail, L. (2004) "The Determinants of Positive Long-term Performance in Strategic Mergers: Corporate Focus and Cash", *Journal of Banking and Finance*, 28: 523–52.

Mitchell, M. and Mulherin, H. J. (1996) "The Impact of Industry Shocks on Takeover and Restructuring Activity", *Journal of Financial Economics*, 41: 193–229.

Moeller, S. B., Schlingemann, F. P. and Stulz, R. M. (2004) "Firm Size and the Gains from Acquisitions", *Journal of Financial Economics*, 73: 201–28.

Morck, R., Shleifer, A. and Vishny, R. (1990) "Do Managerial Objectives Drive Bad Acquisitions?", *Journal of Finance*, 45: 31–48.

Myers, S. C. and Majluf, N. S. (1984) "Corporate Financing and Investment Decisions When Firms Have Information That Investors Do Not Have", *Journal of Financial Economics*, 13: 187–221.

Rau, P. R. and Vermaelen, T. (1998) "Glamour, value and the Post-acquisition Performance of Acquiring Firms", *Journal of Financial Economics*, 49: 223–53.

Reinganum, M. R. (1981) "Misspecification of Capital Asset Pricing: Empirical Anomalies Based on Earnings' Yields and Market Values", *Journal of Financial Economics*, 9: 19–46.

Rhodes-Kropf, M. and Viswanathan, S. (2004) "Market Valuation and Merger Waves", *Journal of Finance*, 59: 2685–717.

Rhodes-Kropf, M., Robinson, D. T. and Viswanathan, S. (2005) "Valuation Waves and Merger Activity: The Empirical Evidence", *Journal of Financial Economics*, 77: 561–603.

Roll, R. (1986) "The Hubris Hypothesis of Corporate Takeovers", *Journal of Business*, 59: 197–216.

Shleifer, A. and Vishny, R. W. (2003) "Stock Market Driven Acquisitions", *Journal of Financial Economics*, 70: 295–311.

Walker, M. (2000) "Corporate Takeovers, Strategic Objectives, and Acquiring Firm Shareholder Wealth", *Financial Management*, 29: 53–66.

CHAPTER 3

Misadventure and the Form of Payment in Corporate Acquisitions

Tyrone M. Carlin, Guy Ford and Nigel Finch

3.1 INTRODUCTION

If the share price of a firm rises on the announcement of its intention to acquire another firm, it is generally perceived to be a positive signal from the market of the logic of the proposed transaction, and the likelihood that the transaction will consummate. Notwithstanding that some portion of the rising price may be as a result of speculators hoping to realize a windfall gain over the offer period, the increase in price may also be interpreted as an initial reflection of the expected value to be created from the proposed combination of the two entities. In the light of a significant body of evidence suggesting that returns arising from acquisitions are negative – or, at best, neutral – to shareholders in bidding firms,[1] a rising share price for a bidding firm should be a cause for celebration.

Further, if shares in the bidding firm form part, or all, of the consideration for the target firm, the celebration associated with a rising share price should be intensified, given the existence of a separate body of evidence that finds share-exchange acquisitions earn negative excess returns relative to matching stock, while cash-based acquisitions earn positive excess returns relative to matching stock.[2] Given the large weight of evidence that stacks against the share price of an acquiring firm rising during the period from announcement to closure of the offer, a rising share price for a bidding firm is indeed a strong signal that the market expects the present value of synergies arising from the transaction to exceed any premium implicit in the offer.

This signal is intensified when a share-exchange features in the structure of the offer. An aspect of share-exchange acquisition overlooked surprisingly often is that a rising share price for the bidding firm also increases the premium paid for the target. This simple observation appears to be lost on some sharemarket investors, and even some investment bankers. In this sense, this chapter represents a cautionary tale.

While a rising share price for the bidding firm in a share-exchange acquisition may appear to manifest itself as a win–win situation for both bidding and target shareholders – bidders gaining from a positive market assessment of the transaction, and sellers gaining from an increase in the value of the offer for their stake – our years of working and teaching in finance have taught us to treat any claim of a "win–win" situation with care (and a dose of skepticism). Some commentators go so far as to claim that in a share-exchange acquisition, the payment of a premium to target shareholders cannot be justified on the grounds that shareholders of both constituent firms remain shareholders in the post-acquisition entity, and are thus able to participate pro rata in any gains arising from the combination.[3] The fact that premiums *are* observed in share-exchange acquisitions, and that these premiums are not materially different from premiums in cash-acquisitions, leads these commentators to seek alternative explanations for the payment of premiums in share-exchange acquisitions (other than as a medium for sharing some proportion of acquisition gains with target shareholders in order to gain control of the target firm).

Hamermesh (2003), for example, finds that the existence of acquiring firm shareholder voting rights – in terms of shareholder approval for the acquisition – reduces merger premiums in share-exchanges by 18.65 percent.[4] According to this view, in order to ensure the support of acquiring shareholders, management must offer lower premiums. This implies that, if no such approval is required, there is no constraint on the size of acquisition premiums.

While there is no doubt a range of factors behind the decision of management to use shares in the bidding firm as part or full consideration for an acquisition – some of which we shall review shortly – it is our position that premiums exist in share-exchange acquisitions for the same reason that they exist in cash-based acquisitions. Be it in the form of cash, shares or some other instrument, bidding firms must pay a premium to target shareholders in order to gain control of the target, and do so in the knowledge that some proportion of the expected gains from the transaction will be transferred to target shareholders.

In this context, it is erroneous to view a share-exchange acquisition as being materially different from a cash-based acquisition. In both mechanisms, there exist a buyer and a seller, and the value of the acquisition from the perspective of the buyer will depend on the extent to which there is a wealth transfer from buyer to seller that exceeds the value of the seller's assets in the hands of the buyer. Put simply, the value-creation principles that apply to a corporate acquisition should not differ from those that apply to the purchase of any asset.

This leads us to the main focus of this chapter. A key factor in the structure of a share-exchange acquisition is the predetermined exchange ratio, which represents the number of the acquirer's shares that are offered for each share of the target. The exchange ratio determines how the overall added value of an acquisition will be shared between shareholders of the acquiring company and the target company. If the exchange ratio is fixed, the value of a share-exchange offer will fluctuate with movements in the share price of the bidding firm. For example, if an exchange ratio in an offer is set and the acquirer's share price subsequently increases, then the net cost of the acquisition to acquiring company's shareholders also increases. This transfers a proportion of the gains from the acquisition from acquiring shareholders to shareholders in the target company. Conversely, a falling share price for the bidding firm will reduce the value of the consideration paid to shareholders of the target firm, and reduce the probability that the deal will be supported by target shareholders over the offer period.

In general, an increase in the acquirer's share price will occur on the announcement of a takeover bid, to the extent that the market believes synergies and other benefits arising from control will be realized in the acquisition. Specifically, for value to be created for the shareholders of the bidding firm, the present value of expected synergies and other control benefits, net of integration and transaction costs, must exceed the premium paid for control of the target firm. Price fluctuations will also be influenced by the view of the market as to the probability of the offer being accepted at the minimum threshold.

These complications need to be considered by the acquiring company when setting the exchange ratio for the offer. In this regard, the bidding firm needs to assess how its share price is likely to change during the period between the announcement of the offer and the anticipated closing date of the offer, which, with extensions, may be many weeks. Deal makers must assess not only market reactions to the proposed transaction – which may fluctuate contingent upon release of independent expert reports and other information over the period – but also factors unrelated to the deal that may influence the share price of the bidding firm. These could be firm-specific factors related to other aspects of the firm's operations, or general market-wide factors.

It is our observation that most of the literature related to risk in the form of payment in acquisitions tends to focus on the adverse consequences of the share price of the bidding firm falling, either over the offer period or post-acquisition. A price decline may result if the market doubts the realization of synergies, or if it interprets an equity exchange as a signal from management that the bidding firm is overvalued. If shareholders in the target firm fear that the share price of the bidding firm will fall over the offer period – and they believe they should share in any value that their stake creates for bidding shareholders – they may be less likely to accept the offer. Similarly, target shareholders may fear that management in the bidding firm have been overzealous in their estimation of the amount or timing of expected synergies, and that the share price of the bidding firm will fall post-acquisition as the market subsequently recasts its expectations on the value of the new entity.

In this chapter we focus on the risk that over the offer period the share price of the bidding firm overshoots the expectations of those structuring the deal. This may arise if the market overvalues the expected gains from the transaction. This phenomenon may have largely escaped the vision of commentators seduced by perceptions of the "win–win" situation under rising share prices for bidding firms. As argued earlier, we consider this win–win view to be misguided.

Although significantly more complex, an acquisition should not be viewed separately from any other asset purchase. What distinguishes a share-exchange offer from a cash offer is that, under the former, the net present value of the acquisition will be influenced by subsequent share price movements over the offer period. If the target receives a consideration in excess of the intrinsic value of the acquisition to the acquirer, then the acquirer has overpaid and the transaction is value-destroying from the perspective of the bidding firm.

An alternative way to view this is in terms of an opportunity loss to the bidding firm. If management in the bidding firm genuinely expected its market price to overshoot the value associated with expected synergies in the deal, it could have offered a cash price for the target and financed the transaction by issuing equity in the market at the overvalued price. The surplus cash raised could subsequently be used for other purposes within the entity. Alternatively, management could have set a lower share-exchange ratio in the structure of the offer.

The rest of this chapter is structured as follows. In section 2.3 we examine various factors that may influence the decision to use cash, shares or some combination of cash and shares as the form of consideration in acquisitions. We then demonstrate in section 3.3 how rising share prices over the offer period for an acquiring firm may lead to overpayment for the target entity, using the case of a recent transaction in Australia – the acquisition of Howard Smith Limited by Wesfarmers Limited.

This off-market transaction, which involved a combination of cash and equity as the form of consideration – was awarded the INSTO deal of the year in Australia in 2001. Our focus is on the steep rise in the share price of the bidding firm over the offer period – which went from a pre-bid price of US$21.86 to a closing bid price of US$29.80 – and the fixed share-exchange ratio in the transaction. This substantial increase in price was heralded by investment bankers and analysts as market support for the transaction, and evidence that the acquisition demonstrated the creation of significant shareholder value.[5] We offer a counter view.

Based on a discounted cash flow analysis of the transaction, using data published at the time on expected synergies and integration costs, we find that the rising share price of the bidding firm resulted in a significant transfer of value from shareholders in the acquiring firm to shareholders in the target firm, such that the deal was net present value negative to the shareholders of the acquiring firm. While our analysis has been conducted without specific inside information on the part of either the bidding or target firm, the analysis, at the very least, serves as a reminder that rising share prices on the part of the bidding firm represent a very real transaction risk in fixed share-exchange acquisitions.

3.2 FACTORS INFLUENCING THE FORM OF CONSIDERATION IN ACQUISITIONS

In keeping with Miller and Modigliani (1958), the form of consideration in a corporate acquisition should have no influence on the value of the transaction when capital markets are perfect. It thus should come as no surprise that the literature focusing on factors driving the form of consideration centres on market imperfections such as information asymmetries, taxation, managerial stakes in bidding and target firms, and the share price performance of the bidding firm over a specific period leading up to an offer announcement. In this section we review briefly some of the major findings of this literature.

Hansen (1987) argues that the risk of overpayment is higher in a cash bid than in a share exchange, because in a cash bid the bidding firm assumes the full risk that synergies turn out to be lower than expected. In a share exchange, this risk is shared with the shareholders of the target firm. For this reason, a cash bid may be seen by the market as a positive sign of the confidence of management of the bidding firm of the realization of synergies and other benefits. Travlos (1987) finds the share-exchanges as a means of payment typically result in significant losses to shareholders of bidding firms, based on the hypothesis that given the choice between a cash offer and a share offer, the latter delivers negative information regarding the value of the assets of bidding companies. This is the so-called signaling hypothesis associated with equity issues. In a similar vein, Fishman (1989) finds that cash offers convey positive information regarding the valuation of the assets of the bidder. Loughran and Vijh (1997) review 947 deals and compare post-acquisition returns of companies to the returns on matching stock chosen to control for size and market-to-book value effects. They find that share-exchange acquisitions earn negative excess returns relative to matching stock returns (−24 percent), while the returns on cash offer acquisitions outperform matching stock (19 percent).

The fact that most empirical studies find that share-exchange offers result in declining share prices in bidding firms provides one explanation as to why market commentators appear less focused on the potential negative impact that arises when share prices for the bidding firm rise over the offer period. If the overriding evidence is that share prices in bidding firms fall on announcement of share-exchange acquisitions, it is probable that this will feature heavily in their risk assessment of the transaction. It is easy to forget, however, that, while a falling share price may mean the transaction is less likely to be accepted by target shareholders when bidding firm shares feature in the consideration, conversely, the value of the potential acquisition will be rising to the acquiring shareholders.

Taxation issues related to the form of consideration tend to center on the potential liability for capital gains tax for shareholders in target firms who accept their consideration in cash. If capital gains tax rollover relief applies, shareholders in the target firm who accept their consideration in shares in the bidding firm are not required to pay tax on any capital gains they may realize in the transaction until disposal of the shares. Thus, all else being equal, a cash offer could bring about higher premiums relative to a share exchange if the bidding firm deems that the offer will not be accepted unless target shareholders are compensated for the more immediate tax burden arising in a cash offer.

Stulz (1988) finds that share exchanges are used less in transactions where the ownership stake of management in bidding firms is larger. Amihud *et al.* (1990) find that in cash financing deals the top five officers and directors hold around 11 percent of the company's shares, while for share financing the equivalent figure is around 7 percent. Ghosh and Ruland (1998) find a positive relationship between the use of cash financing in an acquisition and the degree of managerial ownership in the bidding firm, over a sample of 212 acquisitions. These findings suggest that management in bidding firms are reluctant to use shares as the main payment mechanism in order not to dilute their control in the merged entity.

Bishop *et al.* (2004) examine the cumulative abnormal price behavior of target and bidding companies in Australia around the time of takeover announcements, where abnormal returns are measured as actual returns less market-wide movements over the period. They identify positive abnormal returns for bidding firms in the 36-month period leading up to announcement of a proposed acquisition. Strong share price performance in the period leading up to an acquisition on the part of bidding firms may encourage the use of shares as the form of acquisition currency.

However, as already discussed, a critical factor in measuring the value of an acquisition to bidding-firm shareholders – when shares are used as the acquisition currency – is the subsequent movement of share prices over the offer period. If the market overvalues the expected synergies, the deal may destroy value for bidding-firm shareholders in the sense that the acquisition premium exceeds the present value of synergies and control benefits. In the following section we examine an actual transaction where we believe this is likely to have been the case.

3.3 A PRICE TOO FAR? THE ACQUISITION OF HOWARD SMITH LTD BY WESFARMERS LTD

Wesfarmers Limited is a diversified corporation with interests in a range of sectors including energy, hardware and forest products, fertilizers and chemicals, rural services, and insurance and service businesses in Australia. On 13 June 2001 it announced a takeover offer for Howard Smith Limited. At the time of the takeover announcement, Howard Smith was operating through two core businesses – Hardware Distribution and Industrial Distribution. Hardware Distribution operated under the BBC Hardware, Hardwarehouse and Benchmark Building Supplies names, while the industrial distribution group included Blackwoods, AE Baker, Alsafe and NZ Safety. The Hardware group serviced retail and trade customers through its network of warehouse and conventional hardware stores. The Industrial Distribution Group serviced customers in the manufacturing, resources and services sectors through the supply and distribution of tools, parts, safety equipment and consumables.

The acquisition of Howard Smith was considered complementary to the Wesfarmers Bunnings Warehouse operations. The CEO of Wesfarmers, Michael Chaney, claimed that Howard Smith's most significant business operation, BBC Hardware, was an attractive fit with Bunnings, a major business unit of Wesfarmers. The acquisition would give Wesfarmers sixty-one Hardwarehouse stores and forty-seven Bunnings Warehouse stores. Wesfarmers expected to close only nine stores as a result of the acquisition. The Hardwarehouse stores of Howard Smith were located predominantly in New South Wales (NSW) and Queensland, which was Bunnings' weakest market. All stores expected to operate under the Bunnings brand, with some exceptions in NSW and New Zealand.

Some key points related to the transactions are as follows:

- At the time of the offer, BBC Hardwarehouse achieved sales of US$17 million per warehouse store compared to Wesfarmers US$27 million per Bunnings store. Wesfarmers targeted sales to increase to US$22 million per BBC Hardwarehouse store within two years of the acquisition.

- In 2000, Howard Smith achieved an EBIT to sales ratio of 6.8 percent in its Hardware operations. Wesfarmers achieved 9.2 percent in its Bunnings group. Wesfarmers claimed significant scope for improvements in the Howard Smith operations.

- Wesfarmers estimated upgrades of US$500,000 per Hardwarehouse store – a total sum of approximately US$30 million. In a later interview, the CEO of Wesfarmers reported that the costs of rationalization, including store closures, would be between US$80 million and US$90 million.

- Wesfarmers targeted US$40 million in cost savings in the first year of operation. These savings expected to come from Howard Smith head office rationalization, and IT and logistics initiatives.

- In January 2002, the managing director of Bunnings Building Supplies claimed the business unit could extract annual savings of US$60 million from the integration of the businesses.[6] However, he warned that delays related to the integration would mean that full benefits would not be realized until the second year of operation of the combined entity.

The takeover was subject to Australian Competition and Consumer Commission (ACCC) approval, but it was anticipated that this would not be a contentious issue, given the fragmentation of the Australian hardware market, with three major players (BBC Hardware, Bunnings and Mitre 10) commanding only 25 percent of the market. Other players include Kmart and BIG W hardware departments and Danks (Thrifty-Link, and Home Timber and Hardware). The merged business was expected to have a 13 percent market share, and ACCC approval was subsequently granted. Further, the offer was subject to the Wesfarmers acquiring a relevant interest in at least 90 percent of all Howard Smith ordinary shares. The significance of this threshold in Australia is that a bidder who has received acceptance for 90 percent or more of the shares following a takeover bid may acquire the remaining shares compulsorily.

On a pre-goodwill basis, it was estimated that the earnings per share of Wesfarmers would increase from US$1.18 pre-deal to US$1.25 for the full-year 2002, based on a 1 July acquisition date. The structure of the offer was US$12.00 cash and two Wesfarmers shares for every five Howard Smith shares. At the time of the offer, Howard Smith shares were trading at US$9.75. Based on the Wesfarmers closing price on 12 June 2001 of US$21.86, the offer valued Howard Smith at US$11.14 per share:

$$[\$12.00 + (2 \times \$21.86)]/5 = \$11.14$$

By the following day, Wesfarmers shares had risen to US$24.30, valuing the offer at US$12.12 per Howard Smith share. On 11 July 2001, Wesfarmers increased its offer to US$13.25 cash and two Wesfarmers shares for every five Howard Smith shares. Based on the Wesfarmers closing price on 11 July 2001 of US$26.85, the revised offer valued Howard Smith at US$13.39 per share:

$$[\$13.25 + (2 \times \$26.85)]/5 = \$13.39$$

Howard Smith's share price of US$9.75 prior to the announcement of the initial Wesfarmers offer reflected market speculation of a takeover and a

Table 3.1 Wesfarmers offer

	Howard Smith ($)	Offer value 11/7/01 ($)	Premium (%)
Pre buy-back price	8.85	13.39	51.3
Buy-back tender midpoint	9.10	13.39	47.1
Closing price 12/6/01	9.75	13.39	37.3

US$250 million share buy-back proposed by Howard Smith on 16 May 1991. The volume-weighted average price for Howard Smith shares over the month prior to the announcement of the details of the proposed buy-back tender was US$8.85.

Based on Wesfarmers share price of US$26.85 on 11 July 2001, the Wesfarmers offer incorporated a substantial premium to Howard Smith shareholders (see Table 3.1). Howard Smith Directors accepted the revised offer of US$13.25 cash and two Wesfarmers shares for every five Howard Smith shares, and recommended that Howard Smith shareholders accept the Wesfarmers offer, in the absence of any higher offer.

On 21 August 2001, Wesfarmers had received acceptances from Howard Smith shareholders entitling it to more than 90 percent of the shares in Howard Smith Limited. Having achieved the threshold, it proceeded to acquire the remaining Howard Smith shares compulsorily. Howard Smith Limited was suspended from trading on the Australian Stock Exchange. In the next section we conduct a financial analysis of the transaction.

3.4 FINANCIAL ANALYSIS

Our analysis of the transaction involves a four-step process. First, using discounted cash flow analysis of our estimates of the free cash flows accruing to equity investors, we value both the bidding firm and target firm prior to the announcement of the offer. We then use the same approach to value the target under control of the management of bidding firm, but prior to the businesses combining. We then value the combined entity prior to the realization of synergies. Finally, we value the combined entity with expected synergies in place. The basis for each step is described below. Supporting data is presented in Table 3.2.

3.4.1 Step 1: Value each company prior to the announcement of the takeover offer

The objective of this step is value each entity – buyer and seller – under its existing investment, capital structure and dividend policies in order to

Table 3.2 Financial analysis of Wesfarmers Ltd acquisition of Howard Smith Ltd

$ million	Acquirer Pre-deal	Target Pre-deal	Target Control	Entity Pre-synergy	Entity Post-synergy
Key drivers					
Revenue growth	5%	2%	4%		
Asset utilization	141%	174%	180%		
Cost margin	85%	91%	89%		
Dividend payout	90%	60%	60%		
Cost of equity	11.62%	13.51%	13.51%		
Weighted average cost of equity	8.91%	10.64%	10.64%	9.30%[a]	9.30%
Debt/equity	50%	50%	50%		50%
LT growth estimate	5.5%	6%	6%		5.6%
Free-cash forecasts					
Free-cash flow: Year 1	$303	$47	$114	$417	$417
Free-cash flow: Year 2	$453	$147	$154	$607	$574
Free-cash flow: Year 3	$485	$150	$160	$645	$619
Free-cash flow: Year 4	$350	$153	$166	$516	$553
Free-cash flow: Year 5	$421	$156	$173	$594	$631
Terminal value	$13,139	$3,565	$3,958	$17,097	$18,128
Valuation					
Enterprise value	$10,134	$2,620	$2,950	$13,084	$13,746
Equity value	$8,196	$1,736			
Shares in issue	375 m	196 m			
Share price	$21.86	$8.85			
Analysis					
Value of target pre-deal					$1,736
Value of control					$330
Value of synergies					$662
Value of target in deal					$2,727

Notes: [a] Equates to internal rate of return given enterprise value and free cash flow forecasts.
Source: Wesfarmers Annual Report.

provide a base to estimate control value and synergy value, where the former arises from improved management of the existing business and the latter from a combination of the assets and operations of the two entities.

To remove any bias from our analysis, and to eliminate noise, we valued both firms at their actual close-of-business prices on 12 June 2001 (their pre-announcement market capitalizations). This enabled us to assess key financial and operational drivers, as implied by actual share prices immediately prior to the takeover offer. The results are presented in columns 2 and 3 of Table 3.2.

3.4.2 Step 2: Estimate the value of control in the target

In this step, we value Howard Smith under the assumption that it is managed by Wesfarmers, but prior to the firms combining. The incremental increase in value in the target firm represents the value of control to Wesfarmers. We deliberately exclude synergies from this step in order to isolate any incremental impact arising from the supposed superior management of the target firm.

'Wesfarmers advised that it could improve the operating performance of BBC Hardware substantially by utilising its management expertise and operating approach. As noted by market analysts, Bunnings had achieved a significantly better performance record than Howard Smith's hardware division, as measured by sales and margins. Based on results to June 2000, average sales per Bunnings Warehouse store were approximately 60 percent higher than the corresponding average for BBC's Hardwarehouse stores. On a whole-of-business basis, Bunnings' EBIT margins were about 50 percent higher than BBC Hardware's.[7']

To incorporate conservative estimates of the value of Howard Smith under the control of Wesfarmer's management, revenue growth projections in our discounted cash flow model for the target were increased by two percentage points, costs margins reduced by two percentage points, and asset utilization increased by six percentage points. These changes are considered conservative and place the target firm closer, but still below, the bidding firm in terms of operational benchmarks. The results are presented in column 4 of Table 3.2. These changes result in an increase in value of US$330 million for Howard Smith.

3.4.3 Step 3: Value combined entity before synergies but with target under optimal management

In this step we combine the free cash flow projections of Wesfarmers pre-acquisition and Howard Smith under optimal control. This step provides two main advantages. First, it allows us to derive key operational and financial drivers arising from the combination of the entities, which in turn gives a basis for incorporating expected synergies arising from the combination. Second, we can use the combined free cash figures and asset valuation figure to calculate the internal rate of return on the combined entity before synergies. We use this figure as the basis of for the discount rate of the combined entity when synergies are incorporated in the cash flows estimates. The results are presented in column 5 of Table 3.2.

3.4.4 Step 4: Value the combined entity with synergies and optimal control of target

The forecast synergies of US$40 million per year (later revised to US$60 million) were reported to arise from operating gains in "store administration, merchandising and advertising, and overhead synergies in information technology, administration, store development and corporate services. More specifically: the amalgamation of merchandising teams and improved terms with suppliers that will reduce costs and increase gross margins; the reduction of advertising costs as a result of the promotion of only one brand in each market; the ability to access a larger customer and supplier base from which to develop and leverage on-line and business-to-business opportunities."

In addition there are the centralization of head office functions; and the closure of approximately forty-five of Howard Smith's under-performing smaller traditional stores.

Offset against the expected annual synergy benefits of us US$40–60 million are costs of store upgrades and rationalization costs. The CEO of Wesfarmers stated that these costs would be in the range of US$80–US$90 million. Using this information, our discounted cash flow valuation assumes a reduction in operating costs of us US$30 million in Year 2, US$40 million in Year 3, and US$50 million in Years 4 and 5. The terminal value was based on the free cash flow forecast as at the end of Year 5. Further, rationalization/store upgrade costs of US$50 million were added to each of Years 2 and 3, in line with projections released by the CEO of Wesfarmers.

The results are presented in column 6 of Table 3.2. These changes result in a change in value of the combined firm of US$662 million.

3.5 ASSESSMENT OF THE TRANSACTION

Our analysis values Howard Smith in the hands of Wesfarmers at US$2,727 million, comprising the pre-acquisition value of the target plus the present value of control and synergistic benefits (Table 3.3). Based on data at the time the takeover offer was announced, we can estimate the value of the acquisition to Wesfarmers. Recall that the offer was structured as US$12.00 cash and two Wesfarmers shares for every five Howard Smith shares. Based on the then Wesfarmers share price of US$21.86, the offer valued Howard Smith at US$11.14 per share:

$$[\$12.00 + (2 \times \$21.86)]/5 = \$11.14$$

Table 3.3 Howard Smith to Wesfarmers

Value of target to the acquirer	$m
Pre-acquisition valuation of Howard Smith	1,735
Value of control	330
Value of synergies	662
Value of the Howard Smith to Wesfarmers	2,727

Our US$2,727 million estimate of the value of Howard Smith in the hands of Wesfarmers is equal to US$13.92 per target share.[8] The gain to Wesfarmers from the acquisition at these prices (excluding legal and other transaction costs) is US$544.9 million:

$$(\$13.92 - \$11.14) \times 196\,m \text{ shares} = \$544.9 \text{ million}$$

On 11 July 2001 the offer was revised to US$13.25 cash and two Wesfarmers shares for every five Howard Smith shares. Based on the then Wesfarmers share price of US$26.85, the offer now values Howard Smith at us US$13.39 per share:

$$[\$13.25 + (2 \times \$26.85)]/5 = \$13.39$$

At these prices, our estimate of the gain to Wesfarmers from the acquisition drops substantially, from US$544.9 million to US$103.9 million:

$$(\$13.92 - \$13.39) \times 196\,m \text{ shares} = \$103.9 \text{ million}$$

On 21 August 2001, Wesfarmers received acceptances from Howard Smith shareholders entitling it to more than 90 percent of the shares in Howard Smith Limited. Having achieved the minimum threshold, Wesfarmers proceeded to acquire compulsory the remaining Howard Smith shares. Based on the Wesfarmers closing share price of US$29.80 on 21 August 2001, the offer now values Howard Smith at US$14.57 per share:

$$[\$13.25 + (2 \times \$29.80)]/5 = \$14.57$$

At these prices, the value of the consideration paid to Howard Smith shareholders now exceeds our estimate of the value of the target in the hands of Wesfarmers by approximately US$127 million:

$$(\$13.92 - \$14.57) \times 196\,m \text{ shares} = -\$127.4 \text{ million}$$

We find it highly probable that the strong positive share price movement for Wesfarmers over the offer period resulted in the firm overpaying for Howard Smith.[9]

3.6 CONCLUSION

Share exchanges are becoming increasingly common as a form of consideration in corporate acquisitions. Under a fixed share-exchange ratio the value of acquisition to shareholders in the bidding firm varies as the share price of the bidding firm changes over the course of the offer period. In this regard, the focus of much of the literature on transaction risk in acquisitions is directed to the adverse consequences of a falling share price for the bidding firm. This focus may be stimulated by the empirical observation that the share prices of bidding firms, more often than not, tend to fall on the announcement of share-financed acquisitions. Falling share prices reduce the value of the transaction to target shareholders and, as such, reduce the likelihood that the offer will be accepted in the absence of any offsetting increase in the consideration.

When share prices of bidding firms rise over the offer period, this may be viewed as a positive reaction to the transaction. Specifically, rising prices suggest that the present value of synergies and other benefits, net of integration and transaction costs, is expected to exceed the premium offered in the transaction. It seems overlooked by some commentators, however, that rising share prices on the part of the bidding firm also act to reduce any surplus on the deal that may be accruing to bidding shareholders. If the market overestimates the value of synergies in the transaction, it is possible that the transaction will destroy value for bidding shareholders, in the sense that the payment for the target firm exceeds the value of the benefits arising from the integration of the businesses.

In this chapter we examined the impact of a positive market reaction to an acquisition within the context of a large deal in Australia – the acquisition of Howard Smith Limited by Wesfarmers Limited. Using publicly available information on the transaction – released over the time of the offer – and conservative assumptions, we estimate that the deal destroyed value for Wesfarmers shareholders.

NOTES

1. See Bruner (2004) for a detailed summary.
2. See Travlos (1987), Fishman (1989) and Loughran and Vijh (1997).
3. This school of thought argues that it is arbitrary to characterize either entity in a share-exchange acquisition as "acquirer" or "target". See Hamermesh (2003).
4. Ibid., p. 888.
5. For example, the managing director of UBS Warburg commented: "The value of the bid consideration – which consisted mostly of shares in Wesfarmers – increased significantly as the offer period progressed and the market became more acutely aware of the high level of synergies which are expected to flow post merger" (INSTO, January 2002, p. 200).
6. Australian Financial Review, 8 January 2002, p. 15.

7. Wesfarmers Press Release, 13 June 2001.
8. This is based on 196 million Howard Smith shares on issue at the time of the takeover announcement.
9. Notably, the average annual share price to year-end May for Wesfarmers following the transaction was US$29.76, US$26.53 and US$27.54 for 2002, 2003 and 2004, respectively. The return of shareholder funds, pre-goodwill amortization, was 18.5 percent in 2001, 15.7 percent in 2002 and 15.8 percent in 2003.

REFERENCES

Amihud, Y., Lev, B. and N. Travlos (1990) "Corporate Control and the Choice of Investment Financing: The Case of Corporate Acquisition", *Journal of Finance*, 44: 41–57.

Bishop, S. R., Crapp, H. R., Faff, R. W. and Twite, G. J. (2004) *Corporate finance*, 5th edn (Frenchs Forest, Sydney: Prentice-Hall).

Bruner, R. (2004) *Applied Mergers and Acquisitions* (Hobohen, NJ: Wiley Finance).

Fishman, M. (1989) "Pre-emptive Bidding and the Role of the Medium of Exchange in Acquisitions", *Journal of Finance*, 44(1): 41–57.

Ghosh, A. and W. Ruland (1998) "Managerial Ownership, the Method of Payment in Acquisitions and Executive Job Retention", *Journal of Finance*, 53: 785–98.

Hamermesh, L. (2003) "Premiums in Stock-for-Stock Mergers and Some Consequences in the Law of Director Fiduciary Duties", *University of Pennsylvania Law Review*, 152: 881–916.

Hansen, R. (1987) "A Theory of the Choice of the Exchange Mechanism in Mergers and Acquisitions", *Journal of Business*, 60: 75–95.

Loughran, T. and A. Vijh (1997) "Do Long-term Shareholders Benefit from Corporate Acquisitions?", *Journal of Finance*, 52: 1765–90.

Modigliani, F. and Miller, M. (1958) "The Cost of Capital, Corporation Finance, and the Theory of Investment", *American Economic Review*, 48: 261–97.

Stulz, R. (1988) "Managerial Control and Voting Rights: Financing Policies and the Market for Corporate Control", *Journal of Financial Economics*, 20: 25–55.

Sudarsanam, S. (2003) *Creating Value from Mergers and Acquisitions* (London: Prentice-Hall).

Travlos, N. (1987) "Corporate Takeover Bids, Methods of Payment and Bidding Firms' Stock Returns", *Journal of Finance*, 42: 943–63.

Wesfarmers Ltd (2001) *Bidder Statement: Takeover of Howard Smith Limited* (Sydney, Australia).

CHAPTER 4

An Essay on the History of a Merger: The Case of the National Bank of Canada

Raymond Théoret and François-Éric Racicot

4.1 INTRODUCTION

At the end of the 1970s, the Canadian National Bank merged with the Provincial Bank to form the National Bank of Canada. The activities of these two banks were concentrated in Quebec, Canada. These banks fell on hard times at the beginning of the second half of the 1970s: following the world exchange crisis of 1973 and the concomitant jump in inflation, there was a rise in interest rates, and this event was very damaging for the financial results of the two banks, whose duration of assets was much longer than the duration of liabilities, especially deposits. These banks had also great difficulty in controlling their operating costs, which were too high relative to net interest income, their major revenue source. The situation degenerated so much that the financial regulating institutions pressed for a merger of the two banks. The fiscal year 1979–1980 was the first for the National Bank of Canada.

It is rare to have a case of a pure merger. In fact, it was the Provincial Bank that acquired the Canadian National bank. Following this acquisition, the directors of the Provincial Bank took the lead in the new bank, and the directors of the Canadian National Bank were dismissed or downgraded. New employees were hired to change the image of the bank, some being high flyers from other banks. But instability remained in the new bank for some time because its directors had difficulty in controlling operating costs and because the start of the 1980s was marked by the first oil crisis, which propelled interest rates to new highs, and by the repudiation of many sovereign debts, in which the two banks were very involved.

In this chapter, we shall question the merger of the two Canadian banks. As we shall see, these banks had similar financial problems at the time of the merger, and were both too concentrated on Quebec. The structure of their loan portfolios was also very similar. In this context, it was very difficult to produce synergy effects. Diversification effects were also almost impossible because of the similarities between the two banks. The return to profit at the National Bank seems not to be a result of the beneficial effects that a merger is considered to produce. In fact, the stock of the National bank was doomed to remain undervalued for some time. Its book value was high relative to its market value. This source of concern for the new direction of National Bank was caused by the low growth prospects of the new bank. The return of prosperity at the National Bank is more a result of special circumstances, such as the amendment of the Canadian Bank Act in 1987, which allowed banks to buy brokers, but its bricks and mortar network has never been very profitable.

4.2 THE STRUCTURES OF THE TWO MERGED BANKS

Figure 4.1 gives the evolution of the net interest income per $100 of assets, or net interest spread, of the two merged banks, and for all Canadian banks from 1967 to 1983. We notice that the two merged banks initially had an interest spread that was much higher than those of other Canadian banks. These two banks were more involved in residential mortgages and personal loans, which are retail activities, than their counterparts. These categories of loans have a high interest spread when interest rates are low and stable, as was the case at the end of the 1960s and the beginning of the 1970s. These two banks also invested more in sovereign loans in proportion to assets than did the other banks. These loans obviously have a higher spread than the "average" loan because of their greater credit risk. The Provincial Bank had the highest spread of the two, exceeding 3 percent at the end of the 1960s, quite high compared to a mean spread of less than 2 percent at the time of writing. But these spreads, which were a source of wealth at the beginning of the 1970s, were to become a source of distress by the end of the decade.

But the rising of interest rates which began after the world exchange crisis in 1973, and the following explosion of inflation, caused a general decrease in the interest rate spread of Canadian banks. This decrease was not limited to the two merged banks, but was also shared by other Canadian banks. Mortgages and personal loans, which were of long duration, were financed by short-term deposits, leaving a high-duration gap between loans and

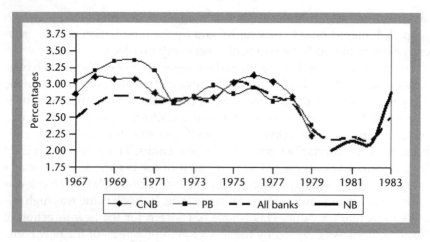

Figure 4.1 Interest rate spread of Canadian banks, 1967–83 (percentages)
Notes: CNB – Canadian National Bank; PB – Provincial Bank; NB – National Bank.
Sources: Bank of Canada statistics, A. E. Ames, banks' annual reports.

deposits. Today, this gap can be hedged by derivatives,[1] but in the 1970s, the derivatives market was only just beginning in Canada and it was not possible to use this market to hedge the crumbling gap.

What was dramatic for the two banks was that the interest rate spread relied on an expenses ratio that was higher than that of other banks. As we have already noted, this higher interest rate spread was caused by a greater involvement of these banks in retail activities compared to other banks, which concentrated more on banking activities such as commercial loans, for which the interest rate spread is quite low. But it is well known that retail activities require a greater network of branches, and this is expensive, to say the least. These activities also require more employees in term of assets. The two banks also had more branches across the regions than did the other Canadian banks, which was another explanation of their higher ratio of operating costs. For example, at the beginning of the 1970s, the ratio of operating costs was 2.87 percent at the Canadian National Bank and 2.89 percent at the Provincial Bank compared to 2.35 percent for all Canadian banks. This ratio was therefore comparatively high at the two analyzed banks. Note that these operating cost ratios included provisions for loan losses at this time, which is no longer the case today.

In Figure 4.2, we notice that the two banks had problems controlling their costs after the crisis of 1973. The swell of inflation wrote off preceding efforts to control costs in these banks. The ratios of operating costs of the Canadian National Bank and the Provincial Bank resume their climb, which was not the case in the other Canadian banks. These banks cut back on

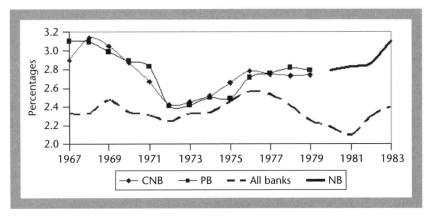

Figure 4.2 Ratio of operating costs of Canadian banks, 1967–83 (percentages)
Notes: As Figure 4.1.
Source: Bank of Canada *Annual Report*.

expenses and their operating costs ratio decreased a great deal as we see in Figure 4.2. They dismissed employees and shut down branches. This compensated for the contraction of the interest rate spread, but our two banks delayed this skimming process too long, with the consequence that their cost ratio was propelled to new highs, and the merger of the two banks did not stop this process, as the ratio increased even more after the date of the merger. A merging process is costly: it takes time to rationalize operations.

Being more involved in retail activities than the other Canadian banks, our two merging banks had a higher ratio of other income per $100 of assets in the 1960s and at the beginning of the 1970s. They had a higher income from financial services fees. In Figure 4.3, we observe that the ratio of other income exceeded 1 percent at the two banks at the end of the 1960s, but was around 0.8 percent at other banks. But this ratio followed the interest rate spread in the 1970s, perhaps because competition for services fees emanating from the other banks was activated. There was also some reduction of this ratio for the other banks, but it was less severe.

The decrease in the other income ratio was greatly detrimental to our two banks, because the gap between the interest rate spread and the operating costs ratio was so low in the 1970s. The other income ratio was difficult to manage because it depends mainly on the demand for financial services fees. Today, this ratio is much higher for Canadian banks because the revision of the Bank Act in 1987 allowed banks to indulge in brokerage activities, therefore the ratio of other income is nearly 2 percent today. But, in the 1970s, other income represented a smaller source of cash-flows for the banks. As we said earlier, it was very important to compensate for the small gap between the interest rate spread and operating costs of the

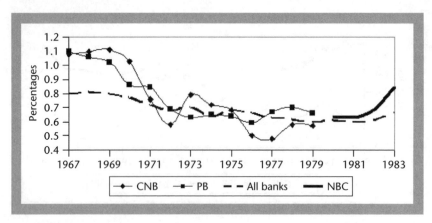

Figure 4.3 Ratio of other income of Canadian banks, 1967–83 (percentages)
Notes: As Figure 4.1.
Sources: As Figure 4.2.

Canadian National Bank and the Provincial Bank. But, in the 1970s, this source of profit was decreasing rapidly, and that was an important factor causing headaches for the two banks.

The evolution of the financial ratios of the Canadian National Bank and the Provincial Bank in the 1970s was forcing these two banks to fail. Figure 4.4 shows the severe deterioration in their net income ratio from 1973. This decrease was very important for these two banks, because the ratio was quite stable at other Canadian banks. As we said earlier, the other banks dealt with the bad financial climate of the time by reducing their operating costs drastically – the most adjustable component of the balance sheet in the short term. Our two banks delayed carrying out this operation, which was an error. At the end of the fiscal year 1978–9, the net income ratio collapsed to 0.17 percent at the Canadian National Bank but, at 0.32 percent, it was higher at the Provincial Bank, which put the Canadian National Bank in position of weakness in the merger, which took place in the fiscal year 1979–80.

The average net income ratio observed at the two banks in the second half of the 1970s was obviously insufficient to keep these banks in business. The net income ratio of the Canadian banks follows a stochastic mean-reverting process which is perhaps not obvious in Figure 4.4 because the reported period was very unstable for Canadian banks. A mean reverting process has the following form:

$$dR = \eta\left(\bar{R} - R\right)dt + \sigma\,dz \tag{4.1}$$

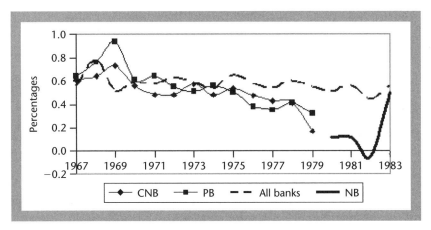

Figure 4.4 Net income ratio of Canadian banks, 1967–83 (percentages)
Notes: As Figure 4.1.
Sources: As Figure 4.1.

In this equation, $\bar{R}$ is the mean level to which the ratio R returns in the long term; η is the speed at which R returns to $\bar{R}$; σ is the volatility of the process; dt is a small time increment; and dz is a Wiener process – that is, $dz = \varepsilon\sqrt{dt}$, with $\varepsilon \sim N(0,1)$. The expectation of dz is equal to 0, and its variance is dt. A mean reverting process is estimated by the following equation if we choose as our estimation method the ordinary least squares (OLS):

$$R_t - R_{t-1} = \beta_0 + \beta_1 R_{t-1} + \varepsilon_t \qquad (4.2)$$

The parameters of Equation (4.1) are estimated by Equation (4.2). These parameters of the mean reverting process are retrieved as follows:[2]

$$\bar{R} = -\frac{\hat{\beta}_0}{\hat{\beta}_1} \qquad (4.3)$$

$$\hat{\eta} = -\ln(1 + \hat{\beta}_1) \qquad (4.4)$$

with $\hat{\beta} > -1$

$$\hat{\sigma} = \hat{\sigma}_\varepsilon \sqrt{\frac{2\ln(1 + \hat{\beta}_1)}{(1 + \hat{\beta}_1)^2 - 1}} \qquad (4.5)$$

We can also choose as an estimation method the maximum likelihood estimator (MLE). Let us suppose that the dependent variable of the regression is labelled y and that the explicative variable is named x. The maximum likelihood function, designated by l, is written as follows:

$$l(c, \beta, \sigma) = -\frac{T}{2}\ln(2\pi \times \sigma^2) - \left\{\left(\frac{1}{2\sigma^2}\right)\sum_{t=1}^{T}(y_t - c - \beta x_t)^2\right\} \quad (4.6)$$

with $(y_t - c - \beta x_t)$, the residuals of the regression, which we designate ε_t. We maximize this function with respect to c, β and σ to obtain the estimated values of these three parameters.

We must compute the conditional expectation of R_t and its conditional variance in order to proceed with the MLE method. For a mean reverting process, the conditional expectation of R_t is:

$$E(R_t) = e^{-\eta}R_{t-1} + \bar{R}(1 - e^{-\eta}) \quad (4.7)$$

The residuals that enter the likelihood function directly are therefore:

$$R_t - E(R_t) = R_t - e^{-\eta}R_{t-1} - \bar{R}(1 - e^{-\eta}) \quad (4.8)$$

Otherwise, the conditional variance of R_t is:

$$Var(R_t) = \frac{\sigma^2}{2\eta}(1 - e^{-2\eta}) \quad (4.9)$$

By using these equations, we obtain the MLE specification of a mean reverting process in EViews code, which is shown in Table 4.1.

We estimated the mean reverting process of the net income ratio of the National Bank over the period 1988–2003, because this was quieter than the period 1967–83 which was used to analyze the merger of the National Bank. Table 4.2 gives the result of this MLE estimation.

The data used were expressed on a quarterly basis. The estimated annualized long-term level of the net income ratio of the National Bank is equal to 0.52 (0.13 × 4). This coefficient is significant at a 95 percent confidence level according to Table 4.2. The speed of return of this ratio to its long-term level is estimated at 3.29, which is fairly fast. Table 4.3 gives the estimated parameters of the mean reverting process of the net income ratio of some Canadian big banks by the two methods explained earlier: OLS and MLE

We notice from Table 4.3 that we obtain almost identical coefficients by using the two different regression methods for the long-term level of the net income ratio and for the coefficient of speed of adjustment. The National Bank of Canada has a relatively low long-term net income ratio with regard

Table 4.1 EViews code to estimate a mean reverting process by the MLE method

@logl logl1

res1=rabnc-exp(-c(3))*rabnc(-1)-c(1)*(1-exp(-c(3)))

var=(c(2)/2*c(3))*(1-exp(-2*c(3)))

@param c(2) 0.5 c(3) 3

logl1=log(@dnorm(res1/@sqrt(var)))-log(var)/2

Note: *rabnc: net income ratio of the National Bank of Canada.
Source: Racicot and Théoret (2006).

Table 4.2 Estimation of the mean reverting process of the net income ratio of the National Bank of Canada using the MLE method

LogL: LOGL02TRIM

Method: Maximum Likelihood (Marquardt)

Date: 06/25/05 Time: 21:26

Sample: 2 64

Included observations: 63

Evaluation order: By observation

Convergence achieved after 102 iterations

	Coefficient	Std. Error	z-statistic	Prob.
C(3)	3.287950	4.436734	0.741074	0.4586
C(1)	0.130160	0.031761	4.098187	0.0000
C(2)	0.007138	0.010090	0.707501	0.4793
Log likelihood	50.61653	Akaike info criterion		1.511636
Avg. log likelihood	0.803437	Schwarz criterion		1.409582
Number of coefficients	3	Hannan-Quinn criteriom		1.471497

Source: Eviews (5.1).

to its competitors. We shall return to this point in the next section. Otherwise, the coefficient of speed of adjustment of the Toronto Dominion Bank (TD) bank is very low compared to other banks. The attraction exerted by the long-term level of its net income ratio is quite weak with regard to other banks.

We said earlier that the average net income ratio observed at the Canadian National Bank and the Provincial Bank in the second half of the 1970s was insufficient to keep these banks in business. In fact, there is a minimum average net income ratio that is the norm for Canadian banks: 0.55 percent. Table 4.3 shows that the long-term ratio was higher than that over the

Table 4.3 Estimation of the mean reverting process of the net income ratio of some Canadian Banks, by OLS and MLE, 1988–2003

	Long term ratio		η		σ	
	OLS	MLE	OLS	MLE	OLS	MLE
Total banks	0.61	0.61	3.22	3.22	0.31	0.097
	(6.97)	(11.45)	(7.49)	(0.98)		(0.91)
RBC	0.67	0.67	2.63	2.66	0.37	0.14
	(6.57)	(5.33)	(7.27)	(1.36)		(1.36)
TD	0.68	0.68	0.6	0.6	0.24	0.4
	(3.51)	(5.33)	(4.24)	(2.56)		(1.73)
NBC	0.52	0.52	3.29	3.29	0.57	0.17
	(4.09)	(5.80)	(7.50)	(0.74)		(0.70)

Notes: RBC: Royal Bank of Canada; TD: Toronto Dominion Bank; NBC: National Bank of Canada.
t statistics are in parentheses.
Sources: Eviews (5.1).

period 1988–2003 for the group of all banks. In the second half of the 1970s, the ratios observed for the two banks under discussion were much lower than the norm: the Canadian National Bank was heading for failure, while the Provincial Bank was slightly less weak. This caused great concern to the regulating authorities, because bank failures are very rare in Canada. The regulating authorities feared that the failure of such a large bank would create chaos in the Canadian financial system and therefore pressed for a merging of the two banks at the end of the 1970s. But could this merger succeed?

4.3 THE NEW MERGED BANK

As was stated earlier, it was the Provincial Bank that acquired the Canadian National Bank at the end of the 1970s. Therefore this was not a "pure" merger. The Canadian National Bank was in a weak position in this merger, so it was the former directors of the Provincial Bank who took the lead in the merging process. As noted earlier, the former directors of the Canadian National Bank were dismissed or downgraded. The previous Provincial Bank directors also wanted to revamp the image of the former banks by hiring "dynamic" new employees. But the new bank inherited the problems of the two old banks, which led to some incoherence in the merging process. It seemed to be a gamble, and the first years of the new bank were very difficult, with an air of depression.

The first problem with this merger was that the two banks shared similar weaknesses. They had a similar structure of assets and liabilities, and both were very exposed to escalating interest rates. Following the oil crisis at the

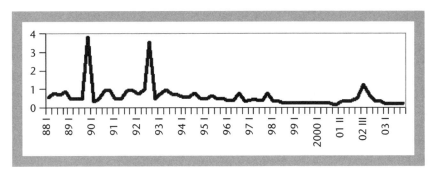

Figure 4.5 Ratio of provision for credit losses, National Bank of Canada, 1988–2003
Source: Canadian Bankers Association.

beginning of the 1980s, interest rates rocketed and the net income ratio of National Bank became negative – a situation even worse than before the merger. The situation was so serious at this time that the new directors reacted by cutting expenses drastically, notably by closing branches in their hundreds in Quebec over a very short space of time. Cash flow had to be restored at any cost if the bank was to survive.

Another problem for the two merging banks was that their operations were concentrated in Quebec. Consequently, diversification effects were not possible for these two banks, which had many more retail operations than the other Canadian banks. Based in Quebec, they were far from the Canadian financial center, which was located in Toronto, and not in Montreal, where the two banks had their head offices. This was a problem when the National Bank needed funds because it was not well-known outside the province of Quebec and could only obtain such funds at a higher risk premium than its competitors were offered.

The provision for credit losses also tended to be larger at the National Bank than for the five largest banks of Canada. They followed the business conditions of the province of Quebec, which is still the case at the time of writing. When there was a slowing down of economic activity in Quebec, provision for credit losses per $100 of assets of the National Bank increased sensibly. There were at this time many commercial and personal financial failures, and the increase in this ratio was such that it might have erased a greater part of the revenues of the National Bank.

We can judge the unstable character of the ratio of provision for credit losses of the National Bank by looking at Figure 4.5, which reports this ratio from 1988 to 2003. The peaks are associated with major credit events such as a writing-down of bad loans done to less-developed countries, or losses caused by a major real estate loan. We notice that this ratio deteriorated substantially during the recession at the beginning of the 1990s and during

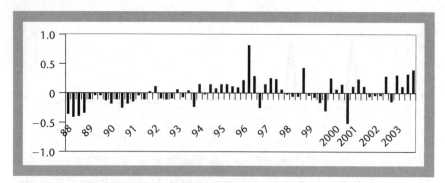

Figure 4.6 Spread between the operating expenses ratio of the National Bank and all banks, 1988–2003 (percentages)
Source: as Figure 4.5.

the economic slowdown that was observed at the start of the twenty-first century. The countercyclical movement of this ratio is related to the geographical concentration of the retail operations of the National Bank. This movement is less pronounced for the other banks, whose branch networks are distributed more evenly across Canada: poor economic conditions in one province may be hedged by better economic conditions in another. For example, if a province suffers from an oil crisis, this may be compensated by banking activities in another province – for example, Alberta, a good producer of "black gold".

The new merged bank also has a lot of trouble controlling its operating costs, as can be seen in Figure 4.6. To understand the spread between the operating expenses per $100 of assets of the National Bank and of all banks, we must realize that the ratio of net interest income is now lower at the National Bank than at the other banks. Therefore, the National Bank tends to have lower operating costs by $100 of assets than its competitors. But Figure 4.6 reveals that the spread of the ratios fluctuates greatly and is often positive, especially since the beginning of the twenty-first century. This is bad for the bank and indicates difficulties in controlling costs.

What really saved the bank was its growing involvement in broking activities with the foundation of its subsidiary, "Financière Banque Nationale", after the revision of the Bank Act in 1987. Following this advent, revenues other than interest rocketed, as can be seen from Figure 4.7, which gives the evolution of the spread between the ratios of other income of the National Bank and all banks. The spread has most often been positive since 1992, and it increased greatly since 2000. The National Bank has a competitive advantage on this front. It should be noticed that this spread now allows the operating costs of the National Bank to be more prominent without damaging the financial results of the bank too much. This gives the bank some leeway. In fact, there is evidence that the operating costs

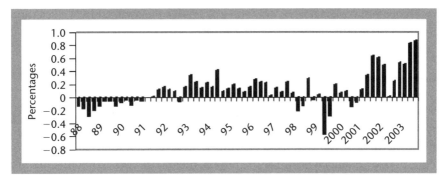

Figure 4.7 Spread between the ratio of other income, the National Bank and all banks, 1988–2003
Source: as Figure 4.5.

(per $100 of assets) of the bank are correlated positively with its other income. That is quite justifiable.

4.4 A LOW P/E RATIO FOR THE STOCK OF NATIONAL BANK

The low P/E ratio of the stock of National Bank, which has tended to persist following the merger, was an important source of concern for the directors of the National Bank of Canada. It was bad for its image. Typically, a low P/E ratio for a stock might be explained by the level of risk of the stock,[3] which was high at the time of the merger of the National Bank, but also depends on poor growth prospects and low dividends. All these factors were at play to explain the weakness of the P/E ratio of the bank and might justify why the price of its stock remained low for such a long time.

The stock of the National Bank was certainly not a *"valeur sûre"* in the first years after the merger of the banks. Profits continued to plunge before giving some indications of recuperation. The growth prospects were low for the bank because it remained concentrated in Quebec. Its international activities became more important, but they were slowed by the increasing risk from the debts of less developed countries. The dividend of the bank's stock was cut numerous times, signalling to financial markets that the bank was facing important cash-flow problems. A firm normally hesitates before cutting its dividend, because that sends a danger signal to the markets and may compromise the recovery of its stock. In addition, the memory of markets is such that investors remain suspicious after a dividend cut, even if the bank shows signs of strengthening. This delayed the recovery of National Bank stock on the financial markets. But the good results of its subsidiary "Financière Banque Nationale" restored the National Bank stock. However, its branch network is not a good source of profits: the ownership of bricks and mortar is a disadvantage in a virtual world.

4.5 CONCLUSION

The merger of National Bank of Canada was similar to a lottery: everything was possible but the chances of success were quite limited. As stated earlier, the structures of the two banks involved were very similar and they were both in poor financial health at the time of the merger. So, would the merger of two weak institutions give birth to a strong one?

An investment project like a merger often has real options[4] attached to it, but they were difficult to identify in the case of the merger of the Provincial Bank and the Canadian National Bank. Real options increase the net present value (NPV) of a project by adding flexibility to it. But it was quite difficult to imagine a growth option at the date of the merger, because the two banks had too many branches. Often, before this merger, there was a Provincial Bank branch located near a branch of the Canadian National Bank. There was the option of contraction, but the question was: is it easier to contract when we are two than when we are one? The answer to this question was not obvious. It appears consequently that the classical NPV of the merger of the two banks was negative and that its augmented NPV – that is., the classical NPV augmented by the value of real options – was not much higher.

What saved the National Bank was the opening of a financial subsidiary: "Financière Banque Nationale". The Canadian Bank Act in 1987, which authorized, among others things, brokerage activities by banks so far as they were separated from the banks, was a lifesaver for the National Bank. Prosperity returned. However, its branch network remained in the red. But what will happen to the bank if there is a collapse of the world stock markets? Will its profits plunge? Will that make the financial situation of the bank very precarious?

Even if it is now profitable, the National Bank must confront the imperative of the growth of its assets in the coming years, an imperative which appears necessary for its survival. The five largest Canadian banks have experienced a remarkable growth in their assets during recent years, but this was not the case with the National Bank.

In the past, the National Bank might have contemplated a merger with the Toronto Dominion Bank, which would have allowed the bank to extend its branch network in Ontario. The Toronto Dominion Bank would also have benefited from this merger, because its presence in Quebec is limited. Alternatively, like the Toronto Dominion Bank, the National Bank might make acquisitions that would exert a leverage effect on its assets, as, for example, the acquisition of a large trust or an important broker. Or it might by itself extend its network in Ontario and New Brunswick in order to develop its operations.

Nevertheless, it remains difficult for the National Bank to put such strategies quickly into action, because the bank had always trouble with the management of its operating costs, even though it made numerous efforts to control them in the past. In a world where globalization is synonymous with big financial institutions, the only solution to its growth problem seems to be another merger. Mouvement Desjardins, a financial cooperative movement also based in Quebec, has been confronted by a similar problem over many years. The problems of these two largest banking institutions in Quebec should be approached jointly.

NOTES

1. It could be hedged by a swap, where long assets are swapped for short ones.
2. More details on the estimation of the mean reverting process of the net income ratio of Canadian banks can be found in: Coën and Théoret (2004) and Racicot and Théoret (2006).
3. The financial leverage of the new National Bank was greater than this one of its competitors, which tends to increase the beta of the stock of the National Bank.
4. On the theory of real options, see: Trigeorgis (1996); Dixit and Pindyck (1994); Copeland and Antikarov (2001).

REFERENCES

Coën, A. and R. Théoret (2004), "Vers une vision probabiliste du choix d'investissement: une application à la performance du secteur bancaire", *Banque & marchés*, 72: 32–43.

Copeland, T. and Antikarov, V. (2001) *Real Options: A Practitioner's Guide* (New York: Texere).

Dixit, A. K. and Pindyck, R. S. (1994) *Investment under Uncertainty* (Princeton, NJ: Princeton University Press).

Gouriéroux, C. and Monfort, A. (1996) *Simulation-Based Econometric Methods* (Oxford University Press).

Racicot, F. -É. and Théoret, R. (2001) *Traité d'économétrie financière* (Lévy: Presses de l'Université du Québec).

Racicot, F. -É. and R. Théoret (2006) *Finance computationnelle et gestion des risques* (Lévy: Presses de l'Université du Québec).

Théoret, R. (2000) *Traité de gestion bancaire* (Lévy: Presses de l'Université du Québec).

Trigeorgis, L. (1996) *Real Options: Managerial Flexibility and Strategy in Resource Allocation* (Cambridge, Mass.: MIT Press).

CHAPTER 5

Corporate Diversification: The Costs and Benefits of Synergy

Felipe Balmaceda

5.1 INTRODUCTION

In this chapter I take up the question of why some firms pursue diversification strategies that are value-decreasing while others engage in strategies that are value-increasing. Two basic diversification strategies are contrasted: the first is a focused strategy in which each firm is run as a stand-alone firm; and the second is a diversified strategy in which two firms are merged and become different divisions of the same firm. The main goal is to understand why some value-decreasing mergers occur, and why some value-increasing mergers do not take place.

This question has very concrete motivation. There is a vast empirical literature – and a lot of casual observation – suggesting that diversification or merging is value-maximizing for some firms and value-destroying for others[1]. For example, in 1978, IT&T was involved in twelve different industries (at the 3-digit SIC code level), and had an average Tobin's Q of 0.570, which was lower than the average in all twelve industries. In contrast, 3 M was involved in eleven different industries, with a Q ratio of 2.02. Another well-known example of a highly diversified and successful company is General Electric, while a recent example of a failure is the AOL–Time Warner merger – at the time of writing, the company's stocks have fallen 66 percent since the merger closed in January 2001[2].

In order to provide an answer to the question posited in this chapter, I investigate the interaction between synergies and private benefits arising from the delegation of decision rights. In the simple set-up proposed, the CEO's decision rights allow him to choose between two non-contractible strategies – diversification or focused – and to select a non-contractible ex-ante and ex-post project in each unit. In addition, they enable the CEO to capture private benefits that are positively related to the gross cash flows generated by any project he or she oversees. Project choice requires the CEO to learn project payoffs in advance, which in turn implies that s/he has to spend time and effort on researching projects.

The model's crucial assumptions are as follows: first, there is an agency problem captured by the fact that the CEO's preferred project is different from the shareholders' preferred project; second, a merger creates synergies that increase expected cash flows only when project coordination across divisions takes place; and third, a merger creates a multi-tasking problem since the CEO has to investigate projects in more than one unit. These assumptions imply that the CEO has an incentive to research and to favor better projects, yet s/he always picks the best projects from his/her point of view. In addition, the multi-tasking problem faced by the CEO in a diversified firm implies that, in the absence of synergies, the CEO's incentives to investigate projects are smaller in a diversified firm than in a focused firm (hereafter, the initiative effect).

In this setting, it is shown that a CEO chooses to pursue value-increasing diversification when synergies are high, and value-increasing focus when synergies are low. When synergies are neither high nor low, depending on the parameterization, the CEO may pursue value-decreasing diversification or value-decreasing focus – that is, a focused strategy is adopted despite the fact that diversification maximizes firm value. The economics behind this can be grasped from the following simple example. Let S be the synergy gain from merging; bS be the CEO's private benefits from merging; C the CEO's private costs from merging; and K the costs paid by shareholders. The CEO will choose to merge if $bS > C$, and merging is value-increasing when $S > K$. It follows from this that the CEO does not merge when synergy is sufficiently low $S < C/b$, and this decision is value-increasing for a sufficiently low synergy ($S < K$), and value decreasing for a "moderate" S, namely $K < S < C/b$. If s/he does merge, the merger is value-increasing for sufficiently high synergy, $S > K$, and value reducing for a "moderate" synergy S, namely $C/b < S < K$ In our setup, merging is value-maximizing when the gains from synergies outweigh the initiative effect and coordination costs, while merging is the CEO's preferred strategy when synergies plus the extra private benefits from running a larger firm (empire-building preferences) balance the initiative effect, the coordination costs and the difference in the CEO's private cost of research between strategies.

As regards the result that value-decreasing mergers take place; that is, $C/b < S < K$, some robustness issues arise. First, it is shown that a CEO pursuing a merger strategy, that is value-destroying is robust for the introduction of optimally designed incentive contracts, and that aligning the CEO's interest is more expensive as the synergy level rises. Second, when the CEO's rights allow him/her only to make merger proposals to the Board and this decides whether to merge or not, it is shown that the Board will use an optimally designed acceptance rule in which value-decreasing mergers are approved with positive probability under different parameter configurations. This means that, under certain parameterization, the adoption of value-decreasing strategies is ex-ante optimal from the shareholders' point of view.

The model yields several empirical implications such as: (i) in a sample of firms equal in all parameters except the synergy level and expected cash-flows as stand-alone firms: (a) mergers of high-value stand-alone firms that yield synergies that are neither high nor low are traded at a discount, while those that yield high synergies are traded at a premium; (b) mergers of low-value stand-alone firms that yield synergies that are neither high nor low are traded at a discount, while those that yield high synergies are traded at a premium; and (c) potentially profitable mergers of low-value stand-alone firms that yield synergies that are neither high nor low may not take place. And (ii) an announcement of a corporate merger is associated with a positive stock price reaction and an announcement of a corporate divestiture is also associated with a positive stock price reaction.

The remainder of this chapter is as follows. In section 5.2 the related literature is discussed. Section 5.3 presents the basic model and preliminary results. In section 5.4, the benefits and costs of synergies for diversifying firms are studied. In particular, it is shown that the CEO may pursue value-decreasing diversification. This section also discusses the main empirical predictions of the model. In section 5.5, it is shown that value-decreasing diversification is robust to monetary incentives, and that when the decision right to choose the strategy stays in the hands of the Board, this will allow the CEO, under certain parameter configurations, to pursue value-decreasing diversification with positive probability. In section 5.6 concluding remarks are presented.

5.2 RELATED LITERATURE

The related literature is vast, and discussing it *in extenso* would take a chapter in its own right. Fortunately, most papers can be classified into one of the following three categories: (i) those in which diversification is always value-maximizing – for example Williamson (1975), formalized by Stein (1997), who suggests that managers possess monitoring and information advantages over external capital markets; (ii) those in which diversification is always value-decreasing – for example, Jensen and Meckling (1976), who suggest that managers make decisions that increase their personal benefits while potentially decreasing firm value because they are not full residual claimants;[3] and (iii) those that are consistent with the observation of both value-increasing and value-decreasing diversification, and usually suggest that there is an optimal level of diversification for each firm and/or time period.

From an economic standpoint, however, it is difficult to rationalize why, if diversified firms are always relatively inefficient, they continue to play such an important role in economic activity, or why, if they are always relatively efficient, stand-alone firms are commonly observed. Because of this, and since this chapter belongs to the third group, only papers belonging to that group will be discussed.

The resource-based theory of diversification argues that this emerges from firms' excess capacity in valuable resources and capabilities that are transferable across industries, but subject to market imperfections. Under these circumstances, economies of scope arise, and diversified firm's become the most efficient form of organizing economic activity (Penrose (1959), Panzar and Willig (1979)). If those conditions are not met, either because the firm diversifies into unrelated industries where the firm's resources are of little use (Rumelt, 1974) or because no transaction costs prevent the firm from profitably exploiting its resources in the market (Teece, 1980, 1982), diversification becomes sub-optimal. Similarly, Rotemberg and Saloner (1995) argue that firms may wish to avoid being too broad in scope, and conclude that innovative firms must remain narrow, while less innovative firms can be broad. Other theories indicate that the optimal level of diversification differs both across firms and over time – that is, depending on the life-cycle stage of the firm. In this vein, Matsusaka (2001) develops a model revolving around the notion of organizational capabilities in which diversification is a matching/search process. He shows that diversified firms may trade at a discount despite the fact that diversification is value-maximizing. The reason is that a poor match between organizational capabilities and divisions generates a discount at the same time as it induces firms to diversify in search of better matches. This suggests that the diversification discount may cause diversification, and not the other way around. Matsusaka and Nanda (1999) develop a model based on the costs and benefits of internal capital markets, where the key assumptions are that the transaction cost of raising external funds is larger than the cost of raising them internally, and managers have empire-building preferences. Finally, Fulghieri and Hodrick (2002) investigate the interaction between synergy and influence activities. Mainly, they show that synergy and influence activities are related in a non-monotonic way, such that synergies may decrease divisional managers' incentives to engage in influence activities. That paper is the closest to this chapter, and it is complementary, since it focuses on synergies and influence activities, while this chapter focuses on the link between synergies and the allocation of decision rights.[4] In addition, this chapter is intended to explain why value-decreasing mergers are undertaken, while Fulghieri and Hodrick (2002) offer an explanation for cross-sectional variation in post-merger performance.

Last, but not least, this chapter extends the predictions of agency theory beyond those currently existing in a way that is consistent with many empirical regularities concerning the ex-ante decision to diversify.

5.3 THE MODEL

5.3.1 Basic structure

Two divisions or units, denoted by, $i = 1, 2$, that can be operated either as stand-alone firms or as an integrated firm, are considered. Each firm is run by a risk-neutral CEO, and within each firm (division) there is the need to implement a non-contractible ex-ante and ex-post project or strategic decision.

The CEO is endowed with decision rights that allow him/her to choose a non-contractible diversification strategy and to select a project for each unit. For the sake of simplicity, only two strategies are considered: diversification, which means that the two units are operated as an integrated firm; and focus, which means that each unit is operated as a stand-alone firm. The delegation of these decision rights can be justified in several ways. For example, there is no major shareholder or block-holder that has the power to oppose to the CEO's decision,[5] the property is so diluted that shareholders have no incentive to monitor the CEO's decisions or, as in Shleifer and Vishny (1989), shareholders have no knowledge of the nuts and bolts of the new business and therefore cannot evaluate ex-ante whether it is optimal to pursue a given strategy.[6] In addition, the delegation of the right to choose projects can be justified by the fact that it is unlikely that shareholders or board members have better information than the CEO about the precise characteristics of each project.

It is assumed that each firm faces $N > 3$ unknown projects, $n \in \{1, 2, 3, \ldots, N\}$ and one known project, called the default project, that yields zero private benefits and cash flows. Of the remaining N projects, only two of them, projects α and β, yield positive cash flows and private benefits, while the rest yield negative cash flows and private benefits. Although project choice is ex-post observable, it is non-verifiable and thus non-contractible.

In order to make the CEO's project implementation decision non-trivial, it is assumed that the N projects cannot be distinguished from each other without further investigation. Mainly, the CEO has to engage in research to learn projects' payoffs. In particular, the CEO of a focused firm can choose a non-verifiable research effort or intensity $e_i \in \{0, 1\}$, $i = 1, 2$, at a private cost k_{e_i}, with $k_1 > k_0 = 0$, that enables him/her to learn the payoffs of all projects available to firm i with probability r_{e_i} and to learn nothing with probability $1 - r_{e_i}$, with $1 > r_1 > r_0 \geq 0$. More generally, the research effort can be thought of as any non-contractible firm-specific human capital investment, which may increase firm value under certain circumstances. The CEO of a diversified firm chooses non-verifiable research efforts $(e_i, e_j) \in \{0, 1\}^2$ at a private cost $k_{e_i + e_j}$ that enable him/her to learn the payoffs of all projects available to divisions i and j with probability $r_e r_j$, to learn the payoff of the projects available to division i and to learn nothing in division j with probability $r_{e_i}(1 - r_{e_j})$, $i = 1, 2$, and to learn nothing in both divisions with probability $(1 - r_{e_i})(1 - r_{e_j})$.

The following assumptions are made:

(A1): If the CEO's research fails, s/he is better off choosing the default project than randomly choosing a project.[7]

(A2): In the no-diversification case, the CEO of firm i prefers project α over project β.

(A3): In the no-diversification case, the preference of the CEO and owners are always opposed; that is, the owner prefers project β over α.

(A4): The private benefits of each project $n \in N$ are a share ε_n of the project gross cash flows.

(A5): The CEO's reservation utility is zero and he has a limited liability that is normalized to zero.

(A6): $k_2 = 2k_1 > k_0 = 0$.

Assumption (A1) is needed to make the problem non-trivial. Assumptions (A2) and (A3) are intended to capture the conflicts of interest between the manager and the owners; and assumptions (A4) and (A5) are standard in the literature. Assumption (A6) implies that there are no dis-economies of scope when a CEO oversees multiple projects.[8]

When a diversified strategy or a merger takes place – each firm becomes a division of a new firm managed by one of the merging CEOs – positive synergies are created when project coordination across divisions take place, while negative synergies are created when no coordination takes place.

The timing of decisions is as follows. First, the CEO chooses whether to merge or remain focused. Second, s/he chooses effort. Then nature decides whether research is successful or not. Finally, the CEO decides which project(s) to carry out.

In order to make the analysis as simple and transparent as possible, I will focus on a particular payoff structure consistent with the assumptions made above. When a focused strategy is adopted, project α yields a cash flow equal to λ with probability π, nothing with probability $1 - \pi$, and a share $\varepsilon_\beta = \varepsilon$ of cash flows as private benefits, while project β yields a cash

Table 5.1 Expected payoffs

Project	α	β
Cash flows	$\lambda\pi$	π
Private benefits	$\varepsilon\lambda\pi$	0

Table 5.2 Expected payoffs

Projects	(α, α)	(β, β)	(α, β)	(β, α)
Cash flows	$2\lambda\phi S$	$2\pi S$	0	0
Private benefits	$2\varepsilon\lambda\pi S$	0	0	0

flow equal to 1 with probability π, nothing with probability $1 - \pi$, and a share $\varepsilon_\beta = 0$ of cash flows as private benefits. These expected payoffs are summarized in Table 5.1.

(A7): $\lambda \in [0, 1]$.

Note that, λ captures the congruence of interests between shareholders and the CEO, and $1 - \lambda$ represents the dead-weight loss because of the CEO's private benefits. This, for example, arises when the CEO buys inputs from an inefficient supplier related to him/her, or hires a friend with inadequate qualifications to work on the project.

The payoff structure when a diversified strategy is adopted is as follows. When project α (β) is implemented in both divisions, it yields in division i, $i = 1, 2$, a cash flow equal to λS (S) with probability π and produces nothing with probability $1 - \pi$, while when project α (β) is implemented in one division and a project different from α (β) is implemented in the other division, projects yields zero cash flows. This assumes that negative synergies fully destroyed cash flows.[9] These payoffs are summarized in Table 5.2.

The payoff structure in Table 5.2 implies that the CEO prefers coordination in project α, while shareholders prefer coordination in project β, and thus merging neither solves nor aggravates the agency problem.

While the assumption that private benefits are a share of project cash flows is standard in the literature, it is worth commenting on the fact that this implies that private benefits increase with synergies. When cash flows decrease with synergies, showing that mergers are bad for shareholders, is trivial. Whereas showing that mergers are good for shareholders and bad for the CEO is trivial when cash flows increase with synergies, and private benefits decrease with it. This leaves the case analyzed in this chapter as the most interesting, since it is not at all obvious that mergers may destroy value when both cash flows and private benefits increase with synergies.

5.3.2 A focused strategy

The first – and simplest – strategy to be considered is a focused one. When research is successful, the CEO implements project α, while, when research fails, s/he picks the default project. Thus the CEO chooses a high research intensity when $r_1 \varepsilon \lambda \pi - k_1 \geq r_0 \varepsilon \lambda \pi$. It follows readily from this that the CEO's optimal research intensity, denoted by e^s, is as follows:

$$e^s = \begin{cases} 1 & \text{if } \varepsilon \lambda \pi \Delta r \geq k_1, \\ 0 & \text{if } \varepsilon \lambda \pi \Delta r < k_1, \end{cases}$$

where $\Delta r \equiv r_1 - r_0$.

The CEO's utility when a focused strategy is adopted is then given by:

$$U(\lambda) \equiv r_{e^s} \varepsilon \lambda \pi - k_{e^s} \tag{5.1}$$

and a stand-alone firm's value given by:

$$\Pi(\lambda) = r_{e^s} \lambda \pi \tag{5.2}$$

5.3.3 A diversified strategy

The next strategy is one in which the two firms are combined and they become two different divisions of the same firm. When research is successful in both divisions, the CEO implements project α in both divisions, while when research is successful in one division only, project types become irrelevant, since each project yields 0 cash flow, and when research fails in both divisions, the default project is implemented in both divisions.

The CEO's optimal research effort or initiative, denoted b, is given in the next lemma. The proof of all lemmas and propositions are presented in the Appendix on page 74.

Lemma 1 $(e_1^d, e_2^d) = (1,1)$ if $S > \tilde{S} \equiv \dfrac{k_1}{\varepsilon \lambda \pi (r_i + r_0) \Delta r}$ and $(e_1^d, e_2^d) = (0,0)$ otherwise.[10]

Because there are no dis-economies of scope, the CEO's research intensities are both high when synergies are high, and both low when synergies are low. The reason is that private benefits increase with synergies, and the CEO's cost of exerting a high research in one division is independent of the effort he exerts in the other division.

The CEO's utility when s/he adopts a diversified strategy is then given by:

$$U(S, \lambda) = 2 r_{e^d}^2 \varepsilon \lambda \pi S - (e_1^d + e_2^d) k_1 \tag{5.3}$$

and a diversified firm's value is given by:

$$\Pi(S, \lambda) = 2r_{e^d}^2 \lambda \pi S \tag{5.4}$$

It is clear from Equations 5.3 and 5.4 that both the CEO's utility and firm value increase with synergies, since cash flows as well as the CEO's research intensities increase with them.

From hereinafter, it is assumed that, in the absence of positive synergies, that is, $S = 1$, the CEO chooses a low initiative in both divisions, and prefers a focused strategy to a diversified one. That is,

(A8): $k_1 > \varepsilon \lambda \pi (r_1 + r_0) \Delta r$ and $2r_1 \leq 1$

5.4 THE ANALYSIS

5.4.1 The costs and benefits of synergies

In this section, we analyze the choice between merging and remaining focused. To determine the optimality of a merger, firm value under diversification is compared to that under a focused strategy, and to determine when a merger takes place, the CEO's utility under diversification is contrasted with that under a focused strategy.

The CEO pursues diversification when a diversified strategy yields a larger expected utility than a focused strategy; that is, when $\Delta U(S, \lambda) \equiv U(S, \lambda) - U(\lambda)$ is positive, while diversification is value-maximizing when it yields a larger firm value than a *pool* of two stand-alone firms; that is, when $\Delta \Pi(S, \lambda) \equiv \Pi(S, \lambda) - 2\Pi(\lambda)$ is positive. A pool of stand-alone firms – instead of a single stand-alone firm – is considered because, when a diversifying CEO acquires a new division, s/he must pay that unit at least its opportunity cost as a stand-alone firm. The CEO, however, does not internalize this opportunity cost, since the money to pay for a new unit comes from shareholders' pockets.

It follows readily from Equations (5.1) and (5.3) that the CEO chooses diversification when the following holds:

$$\Delta U(S, \lambda) = \left[2r_{e^d}^2(S-1)\varepsilon + 2(r_{e^d} - r_{e^s})\varepsilon - 2r_{e^d}(1-r_{e^d})\varepsilon + r_{e^s}\varepsilon\right]\lambda\pi \\ -(2e^d - e^s)k_1 > 0 \tag{5.5}$$

and it also follows readily from Equations (5.2) and (5.4) that diversification is value-maximizing when the following holds:

$$\Delta \Pi(S, \lambda) = \left[2r_{e^d}^2(S-1) + 2(r_{e^d} - r_{e^s}) - 2r_{e^d}(1-r_{e^d})\right]\lambda\pi > 0 \tag{5.6}$$

The first term in Equation (5.5) corresponds to the CEO's gains from synergies resulting from a given research effort level; while the second term, called the initiative effect, measures the difference between the CEO's initiative when diversification is pursued and that when a focused strategy is adopted. The third term, called coordination costs, captures the fact that when diversification is pursued, a unit yields positive expected cash flows only when research is successful in both units; while, when focus is pursued, a unit yields positive expected cash flows regardless of whether research is successful in the other unit. The fourth term indicates the extra private benefits from running a larger firm, and the last term is the difference between the CEO's private cost of effort when diversification is pursued, and when focus is pursued.

The terms in Equation (5.6) are equivalent to the first three terms in Equation (5.5). It readily follows from this that, in the absence of synergies, diversification is value-decreasing because the gains from synergies are zero, the initiative effect term is negative when $e^s = 1$ and zero otherwise, and coordination costs are always positive. It also follows that as synergies rise, synergy gains become positive, the initiative effect goes from being non-positive to being non-negative and coordination costs rise, since $r_1(1 - r_1) > r_0(1 - r_0)$. Thus, from the shareholders' standpoint, merging is value-maximizing when synergy gains outweigh the initiative effect and coordination costs. However, from the CEO's standpoint, this is not the case. On the one hand, synergies have to compensate not only the initiative effect and the coordination costs, but also the extra private cost that results from the multi-tasking nature of research under diversification, $(2e^d - e^s)k_1$. On the other hand, everything else being constant, merging implies larger private benefits even in the absence of synergies, since the CEO's private benefits are a positive share of a project's gross cash flows.

When private benefits from empire-building preferences outweigh the costs from multi-tasking, the CEO pursues value-decreasing diversification, while otherwise the opposite occurs. This is formally shown in the next proposition.

Proposition 2

(1) *Suppose that the optimal effort in a focused firm is $e^s = 1$. Then, value-increasing focus is pursued for all $S \leq \frac{1}{2r_1}$, value-decreasing diversification is pursued for all $\frac{1}{r_1} \geq S > \frac{1}{2r_1}$, and value-increasing diversification is pursued otherwise.*

(2) *Suppose the optimal effort in a focused firm is $e^s = 0$. (i) If $\tilde{S} > \frac{1}{r_0}$, then value-increasing focus is pursued for all $S \leq \frac{1}{2r_0}$, value-decreasing diversification is pursued for all $\frac{1}{r_0} \geq S > \frac{1}{2r_0}$, and value-increasing diversification is pursued*

otherwise; (ii) if $\frac{1}{r_0} \geq \tilde{S} > \frac{1}{2r_0}$, *then value-increasing focus is pursued for all* $S \leq \frac{1}{2r_0}$, *value-decreasing diversification is pursued for all* $\frac{1}{r_1} \geq S > \frac{1}{2r_0}$, *and value-increasing diversification is pursued otherwise; and (iii) if* $\tilde{S} \leq \frac{1}{2r_0}$, *then value-increasing focus is pursued for all* $S \leq \tilde{S}$, *value-decreasing focus is pursued for all* $\frac{\varepsilon \pi \lambda r_0 + 2k_1}{2\varepsilon \lambda \pi r_1^2} \geq S > \tilde{S}$, *and value-increasing diversification is pursued otherwise.*

This proposition shows that, regardless of a stand-alone firm value, value-increasing focus is pursued when the synergy level is sufficiently low, while value-increasing diversification is pursued when the synergy is sufficiently high. When synergies are neither high nor low, either value-increasing diversification or value-decreasing focus may be pursued. When the value of stand-alone firm is high, value-decreasing diversification is more likely to be pursued, while, when it is low, value-decreasing focus is more likely to be adopted.

5.4.2 Empirical implications

As mentioned earlier, the evidence on the consequences of diversification on firm value is, for the most part, mixed. The first wave of studies reported that, on average, there is a diversification discount, while the latest studies suggest that, on average, diversification does not destroy value, or at least not as much as the first wave of studies suggested. In fact, some even suggest that, on average, diversification may create value. Overall, the only robust conclusion across all studies is that diversification (focus) creates value for some firms and destroys value for others. Our model suggests – consistent with the evidence in Chevalier (2000), Lamont and Polk (2001) and Villalonga (2003), that the underlying characteristics of integrated firms are different from those of stand-alone firms. Since the choice of a diversification strategy is endogenous, merging firms have different characteristics from stand-alone firms. In this section, we discuss when endogenous selection results in a discount *vis-à-vis* a premium for conglomerate firms.

- *Implication 1*: In a sample of firms equal in all parameters apart from the synergy level S, and for a given expected cash flow as stand-alone firm, $\lambda \pi$:

    (i) Suppose that $e_s = 1$. Then a merging firm composed of high-value stand-alone firms is traded at a discount when synergies are neither high nor low, while it is traded at a premium when synergies are high.

(ii) Suppose that $\tilde{S} > \frac{1}{2r_0}$. Then a merging firm composed of low-value stand-alone firms is traded at a discount when synergies are neither high nor low, while it is traded at a premium when synergies are high.

(iii) Suppose that $\tilde{S} \leq \frac{1}{2r_0}$. Then potentially profitable mergers of low-value stand-alone firms that result in synergies that are neither high nor low do not take place.

The empirical evidence showing that there are some firms that benefit as well as some that do not from diversification is vast. For example, Rajan et al. (2000) report that around 40 percent of the firms they studied traded at a premium, but on average they traded at a discount;[11] and Chevalier (2000), Campa and Kedia (1999) and Villalonga (2004), among others, show that the discount is the result of uncontrolled endogeneity arising because firms differ systematically in multiple characteristics.

The model assumes that the diversification decision is a static phenomenon. However, the choice of a strategy evolves over time through mergers, divestitures and takeovers. A dynamic analysis of mergers and divestitures is beyond the scope of this chapter. None the less, the result enables us to study the effect of a one-time announcement of a merger on stock price reactions.

■ *Implication 2:* An announcement of a corporate merger is associated with a positive stock price reaction for the acquiring firm, and the announcement of a corporate divestiture is also associated with a positive stock price reaction for the divesting firm.

Consistent with this prediction, event studies show that the stock market reacts positively to refocusing spin-offs and divestitures (see Comment and Jarrell, 1995; John and Ofek, 1995; and Berger and Ofek, 1999). However, the evidence from event studies also shows that there is a positive reaction to diversifying mergers or acquisitions (see Matsusaka, 1993; Hyland, 1997; Hubbard and Palia, 1999; and Chevalier, 2000).

5.5 ROBUSTNESS

5.5.1 CEO's monetary incentives

In this section, I study the robustness of the result for the introduction of monetary incentives. In what follows it is assumed that owners always provide monetary incentives to ensure that the CEO exerts a high level of research effort. In addition, it is assumed that contracts can be conditioned only on projects' realized cash flows, and therefore when diversification is pursued, the contract can neither distinguish between a success in division

i and a failure in division j from a success in i and a failure in j, nor it can distinguish between a failure to implement a project and a failure in an implemented project.

Let us consider first the case of a focused firm. The optimal contract pays b_1 when the project yields 1, b_λ when it yields λ, and b_0 when it yields 0. Because of limited liability, setting $b_0 = 0$ is optimal. Thus the CEO implements project β when $\pi b_1 \geq \pi(\varepsilon\lambda + b_\lambda)$ – that is, when $b_1 - b_\lambda > \varepsilon\lambda$ – and project α otherwise.

The next lemma obtains the optimal incentive contract:

Lemma 3 *(i) Suppose that $\lambda\pi > \frac{k_1}{\varepsilon\Delta r}$. If $\lambda > \frac{1}{1+\varepsilon}$, then $b_\lambda = \frac{k_1}{\pi\Delta r} - \varepsilon\lambda$ and the CEO implements project α, while if $\lambda \leq \frac{1}{1+\varepsilon}$, then $b_1 = \frac{k_1}{\pi\Delta r}$ and the CEO implements project β; and (ii) suppose that $\lambda\pi \leq \frac{k_1}{\varepsilon\Delta r}$. If $\lambda > \frac{1}{1+\varepsilon}$, then $b\lambda = 0$ and the CEO implements project α, while if $\lambda \leq \frac{1}{1+\varepsilon}$, then $b_1 = \varepsilon\lambda$ and the CEO implements project β.*

The CEO's compensation disciplines him/her along two dimensions: effort choice and project choice. First, compensation increases his/her expected payoff and induces him/her to exert more effort. Second, when $b_1 - b_\lambda > \varepsilon\lambda$, the CEO selects the shareholders' preferred project. For low private benefits, aligning the CEO's interests can be achieved at a low cost, and it will be optimal to set $b_1 - b_\lambda > \varepsilon\lambda$. For high private benefits, the opposite occurs, since inducing the CEO to work hard when project α is implemented can be achieved at a low cost relative to inducing him/her to work hard when project β is implemented.

Suppose now that the CEO runs a diversified firm. Let us define the contract $B = (b_{11}, b_{10}, b_{\lambda\lambda}, b_{\lambda 0}, b_{00})$, where b_{11} ($b_{\lambda\lambda}$) is the bonus when both divisions succeed and each yields S (λS); b_{10} when one division succeeds and yields S (λS) and the other fails and yields 0; and b_{00} when both fail. Because of limited liability, it is optimal to set $b_{00} = 0$, and it is easy to show that it is also optimal to set $b_{10} = b_{\lambda 0} = 0$.[12] Then, the CEO's expected payoff when s/he implements project α in both divisions is $2\varepsilon\pi S\lambda + \pi^2 b_{\lambda\lambda}$, and when s/he implements project β in both of them it is $\pi^2 b_{11}$. Thus the CEO implements project β in each division when $b_{11} - b_{\lambda\lambda} \geq \frac{2\varepsilon\lambda S}{\pi}$.

The optimal incentive contract is obtained in the next lemma:

Lemma 4 *(i) Suppose that $S \leq \frac{k_1}{\varepsilon\lambda\pi(r_1+r_0)\Delta r}$. If $\lambda > \frac{1}{1+\varepsilon}$, then $b_{\lambda\lambda} = \frac{2}{\pi}\left(\frac{k_1}{\pi(r_1+r_0)\Delta r} - \varepsilon\lambda S\right)$, $b_{11} = 0$, and the CEO implements project S in both divisions, while if $\lambda \leq \frac{1}{1+\varepsilon}$, then $b_{11} = \frac{2k_1}{\pi^2(r_1+r_0)\Delta r}$, $b_{\lambda\lambda} = 0$, and the CEO implements project β in both divisions; and (ii) suppose that $S > \frac{k_1}{\varepsilon\lambda\pi(r_1+r_0)\Delta r}$. If $\lambda > \frac{1}{1+\varepsilon}$, then*

$b_{11} = b_{\lambda\lambda} = 0$ and the CEO implements project α in both divisions, while if $\lambda \leq \frac{1}{1+\varepsilon}$, then $b_{11} = \frac{2\varepsilon\lambda S}{\pi}$, $b_{\lambda\lambda} = 0$ and the CEO implements project β in both divisions.

As in a stand-alone firm, the CEO's compensation disciplines him/her along two dimensions: effort choice and project choice. This implies that the intuition is the same as above. The main difference stands for the effect of the synergy level. As the synergy level increases, aligning the CEO's interests can be achieved at a higher cost, since the CEO's private benefits from project α increase with S. In addition, the monetary payoff needed to induce the CEO to exert a high research effort level when project α is implemented decreases with the synergy level. Thus synergies make it more difficult to align the CEO's interests.

The next proposition obtains conditions under which the CEO adopts a value-increasing (decreasing) strategy for each possible parameterization, assuming that the owners want to implement a high research effort level under either strategy.

Proposition 5

(1) Suppose that $\lambda \pi > \frac{k_1}{\varepsilon \Delta r}$. Then value-increasing focus is pursued for all $S \leq \frac{1}{2r_1}$, value-decreasing diversification is pursued for all $\frac{1}{r_1} \geq S > \frac{1}{2r_1}$, and value-increasing diversification is pursued otherwise;

(2) Suppose that $\lambda \pi \leq \frac{k_1}{\varepsilon \Delta r}$ and $\lambda > \frac{1}{1+\varepsilon}$ (i) If $\lambda \pi \leq \frac{[\varepsilon r_0 + r_1(1+\varepsilon)]k_1}{\varepsilon(r_1+r_0)\Delta r(1+\varepsilon)}$, then value-increasing focus is pursued for all $S \leq \frac{r_1 \lambda \pi \Delta r (r_1+r_0)(1+\varepsilon) - k_1 r_0}{r_1 \lambda \pi (r_1+r_0) \Delta r (1+\varepsilon)}$, value-decreasing focus is pursued for all $\frac{(2r_1-r_0)k_1}{2r_1^2 \varepsilon \lambda \pi \Delta r} \geq S > \frac{r_1 \lambda \pi \Delta r (r_1+r_0)(1+\varepsilon) - k_1 r_0}{r_1 \lambda \pi (r_1+r_0) \Delta r (1+\varepsilon)}$, and value-increasing diversification is pursued otherwise; (ii) if $\frac{[2r_1(1+\varepsilon)-r_0]k_1}{2r_1 \Delta r \varepsilon (1+\varepsilon)} \geq \pi \lambda > \frac{[\varepsilon r_0 + r_1(1+\varepsilon)]k_1}{\varepsilon(r_1+r_0)\Delta r(1+\varepsilon)}$, then value-increasing focus is pursued if $S \leq \frac{\lambda \pi \Delta r(1+\varepsilon) - k_1}{\lambda \pi r_1 \Delta r}$, value-decreasing focus is pursued if $\frac{(2r_1-r_0)k_1}{2r_1^2 \varepsilon \lambda \pi \Delta r} \geq S > \frac{\lambda \pi \Delta r(1+\varepsilon) - k_1}{\lambda \pi r_1 \Delta r}$, and value-increasing diversification is pursued otherwise; and (iii) if $\pi \lambda > \frac{[2r_1(1+\varepsilon) - r_0]k_1}{2r_1 \Delta r \varepsilon (1+\varepsilon)}$, then value-increasing focus is pursued if $S \leq \frac{2r_1-r_0}{2r_1^2 \varepsilon \pi \lambda \Delta r} k_1$, value-decreasing diversification is pursued if $\frac{\lambda \pi \Delta r(1+\varepsilon) - k_1}{\lambda \pi r_1 \Delta r} \geq S > \frac{2r_1-r_0}{2r_1^2 \varepsilon \pi \lambda \Delta r} k_1$, and value-increasing diversification is pursued otherwise; and

(3) Suppose that $\lambda \pi \leq \frac{k_1}{\varepsilon \Delta r}$ and $\lambda \leq \frac{1}{1+\varepsilon}$. If $\lambda \pi \leq \frac{[\varepsilon \lambda r_0 + r_1]k_1}{\varepsilon(r_1+r_0)\Delta r}$, then value-increasing focus is pursued for all $S \leq \frac{\pi(r_1+r_0)\Delta r - r_0 k_1}{r_1 \pi (r_1+r_0) \Delta r}$, value-decreasing focus is pursued for

all $\frac{(2r_1-r_0)k_1}{2r_1^2\varepsilon\pi\lambda\Delta r} \geq S > \frac{\pi(r_1+r_0)\Delta r - r_0 k_1}{r_1\pi(r_1+r_0)\Delta r}$, and value-increasing diversification is pursued otherwise; (ii) if $\frac{[2r_1-r_0(1-\varepsilon\lambda)]k_1}{2r_1\Delta r\varepsilon} \geq \lambda\pi > \frac{[\varepsilon\lambda r_0+r_1]k_1}{\varepsilon(r_1+r_0)\Delta r}$, then value-increasing focus is pursued if $S \leq \frac{\pi\Delta r - k_1}{r_1\pi\Delta r(1-\varepsilon\lambda)}$, value-decreasing focus is pursued if $\frac{(2r_1-r_0)k_1}{2r_1^2\varepsilon\pi\lambda\Delta r} \geq S > \frac{\pi\Delta r - k_1}{r_1\pi\Delta r(1-\varepsilon\lambda)}$, and value-increasing diversification is pursued otherwise; and (iii) if $\pi\lambda > \frac{[2r_1-r_0(1-\varepsilon\lambda)]k_1}{2r_1\Delta r\varepsilon}$, then value-increasing focus is pursued if $S \leq \frac{(2r_1-r_0)k_1}{2r_1^2\varepsilon\pi\lambda\Delta r}$, value-decreasing diversification is pursued if $\frac{\pi\Delta r - k_1}{r_1\pi\Delta r(1-\varepsilon\lambda)} \geq S > \frac{(2r_1-r_0)k_1}{2r_1^2\varepsilon\pi\lambda\Delta r}$, and value-increasing diversification is pursued otherwise.

This proposition shows that monetary incentives do not change the result obtained in proposition when $\lambda\pi \geq \frac{k_1}{\varepsilon\Delta r}$. That is, when synergies are "moderate", value-decreasing diversification takes place. When $\lambda\pi < \frac{k_1}{\varepsilon\Delta r}$, the results change, yet value-reducing diversification is still observed. Thus monetary incentives are not capable of fully aligning the CEO's interests, and in many cases they have no effect on the interval where inefficient mergers takes place.

5.5.2 Board's monitoring

It has been assumed so far that the CEO is endowed with the decision right to select the firm's diversification strategy. In this section, it is assumed that the CEO has to present a proposal for merging to the Board, and this has to be approved in order to go forward. To do so, it is assumed that the CEO knows the synergy level that will be created by merging, but the Board members do not know it.

Let us define the following cutoffs for the synergy level: S^c is the minimum synergy level under which the CEO is better off merging than remaining focused, and S^f is the minimum synergy level under which a diversified firm's value is higher than that for a pool of focused firms. I shall restrict the analysis to those cases in which value-decreasing diversification would take place with positive probability if the Board were to rubber-stamp the CEO's choice of strategy. That is, $S^c > S^f$.

In addition, it is assumed that the Board believes that, with probability q_1, the merger yields a synergy level $S \leq S^c$; with probability q_2 it yields a synergy level $S \in (S^c, S^f]$; and with probability q_3 yields a synergy level $S \in I_3$.

When making a merger proposal to the Board, the CEO chooses a report to submit from the set of possible reports. That is, s/he can either report that the synergy is sufficiently small so that it is optimal for both shareholders and the CEO to remain focused, or that the synergy level is such that the CEO is better off by merging, but shareholders prefer to remain focused, or that the synergy level is such that both the firm and shareholders are better off by merging. In this scenario, the Board establishes an acceptance rule that maximizes shareholder value under the incentive compatibility constraint that the CEO reports truthfully the interval where the synergy level lies. This rule determines a proposal for merging acceptance as follows: p_1 = the probability of accepting a merger when the CEO reports that the synergy level is lower than S^c, p_2 = the probability of accepting a merger when the CEO reports that the synergy level is lower than S^f but larger than S^c; and p_3 = the probability of accepting a merger when the CEO reports that the synergy level is larger than S^f. In addition, when the CEO reports that the synergy level is larger than S^f, the Board instructs the CEO to prepare a report that explains carefully why he asserts that the synergy is larger than S^f. In writing the report, the CEO incurs a private cost of $m > 0$.

For the sake of brevity, let us denote the interval $[1, S^c]$ by I_1 $(S^c, S^f]$, by I_2, and $(S^f, \bar{S}]$ by I_3.

Given the definitions above, the Board's problem is to choose the acceptance probabilities $\{p_j\}_{j=1}^3$ that maximize shareholder value, as follows:

$$\max_{\{p_j\}_{j=1}^3} \sum_{j=1}^3 q_j[p_j\Pi(I_j, \phi, \lambda) + (1-p_j)\Pi(\lambda)]$$

subject to

$$p_j U(I_j, \phi, \lambda) + (1-p_j)U(\lambda) - m_j \geq p_k U(I_j, \phi, \lambda)$$
$$+ (1-p_k)U(\lambda) - m_k \text{ for all } j,k = 1,2,3 \text{ and } j \neq k, \{p_1, p_2, p_3\} \in [0,1]^3$$

where $m_1 = m_2 = 0$, and $m_3 = m$.

The objective function in the equation is the expected shareholder value, given the Board's acceptance policy, and the inequalities are the incentive compatibility constraints that induce the CEO to reveal truthfully the interval in which the synergy level lies. The latter restriction guarantees that the acceptance probabilities lie between zero and one.

The two incentive compatibility constraints which ensure that the CEO tells the truth when $S \in I_1$ are satisfied for all $p_1 \leq p_3$ and $p_1 \leq p_2$, since $U(I_1, \phi, \lambda) \leq U(\lambda)$. The two incentive compatibility constraints that ensure that the CEO tells the truth when $S \in I_2$ are satisfied when $(p_2 - p_3)$ $[U(I_2, \phi, \lambda) - U(\lambda)] \geq -m$ and $(p_2 - p_1)[U(I_2, \phi, \lambda) - U(\lambda)] \geq 0$. Finally, the two incentive compatibility constraints that ensure that the CEO tells the truth when $S \in I_3$ are satisfied when $(p_2 - p_3)[U(I_3, \phi, \lambda) - U(\lambda)] \leq -m$ and

$(p_3 - p_1)[U(I_3, \phi, \lambda) - U(\lambda)] \geq m$. It follows readily from this that a necessary condition for the incentive compatibility constraints to be satisfied is the following: $p_3 \geq p_2 \geq p_1$.

Notice that setting $p_1 = 0$ is always optimal, since a merger that yields a synergy level lower than S^c is value-decreasing, and thus the CEO as well as shareholders prefer to remain focused.

The next proposition derives the optimal acceptance policy. To save on notation, let us define $\tilde{q}_2$ by $(1 - q_1) \frac{\Pi(I_3, \phi, \lambda) - \Pi(\lambda)}{\Pi(I_3, \phi, \lambda) - \Pi(I_2, \phi, \lambda)}$.

Proposition 6 *(i) If $U(I_3, \phi, \lambda) - U(\lambda) \geq m > U(I_2, \phi, \lambda) - U(\lambda)$, then $p_3 = 1$ and $p_2 = 1$ – that is, value-increasing mergers are always accepted and value-decreasing mergers are never accepted; (ii) if $m > U(I_3, \phi, \lambda) - U(\lambda)$, then $p_3 = p_2 = 1$ if $q_2 \leq \tilde{q}_2$ – that is, all merger proposal are accepted – and $p_3 = p_2 = 0$ otherwise – that is, no merger proposal is accepted; and (iii) if $m \leq U(I_2, \phi, \lambda) - U(\lambda)$, then $p_3 = \frac{m}{U(I_2, \phi, \lambda) - U(\lambda)}$ and $p_2 = 0$ if $q_2 > \tilde{q}_2$ – that is, value-increasing mergers are sometimes accepted and value-decreasing mergers are never accepted – and $p_3 = 1$ and $p_2 = 1 - \frac{m}{U(I_2, \phi, \lambda) - U(\lambda)}$ otherwise – that is, value-increasing mergers are always accepted and value-decreasing mergers are sometimes accepted.*

To understand this result it is useful to have in mind that, when the incentive compatibility constraints are ignored, the Board will choose an acceptance policy that accepts all merger proposals that result in value-increasing diversification – that is, $p_3 = 1$, and rejects all proposals that result in value-decreasing diversification – $p_2 = 0$. This solution is incentive-compatible only when the cost of writing a report is neither too high nor too low. Because the cost of claiming that the synergy is such that diversification is value-increasing is neither too high nor too low, by accepting all value-increasing merger proposals and by rejecting all value-decreasing merger proposals, the Board elicits the truth from the CEO. When m is high, claiming that the synergy level is such that diversification is value-increasing is too expensive for the CEO, and therefore whenever $S \in I_3$, s/he has an incentive to claim that it belongs to I_2. Thus, the Board cannot induce the CEO to tell the truth, and as a result the Board accepts all proposals when the probability that the synergy level lies in I_2 is low, and rejects all of them otherwise. The opposite occurs when the probability that the synergy level lies in I_2 is high. Finally, when m is low, the CEO's incentive to claim that the synergy level lies in I_3 is high. Thus, the Board can induce the CEO to tell the truth either by rejecting some value-increasing mergers and rejecting all value-decreasing ones, or by accepting all value-increasing mergers and some value-decreasing ones. The former strategy is adopted when the probability that the synergy level lies in I_2 is low, and the latter when the opposite occurs.

This section shows, then, that in order to provide the CEO with incentives to reveal the real benefits from a merger, in most cases the Board has to adopt an acceptance rule in which value-decreasing mergers are accepted with positive probability. In fact, there is a parameterization in which all value-decreasing merger proposals are accepted.

5.6 CONCLUSION

It is usually believed that diversification can destroy value along three dimensions. First, a firm can destroy value by overpaying for an acquisition. Holding the value of a target constant, the acquirer simply pays too much. Second, a firm can destroy value by making the wrong internal investment decisions when it is diversified. Third, a firm can destroy value by unrealized synergies – ex-ante synergies are thought to be larger than they really are, or their materialization requires levels of coordination that are hard to achieve. The evidence on the average discount provides some support for the first two, but, as mentioned earlier, the evidence is mixed. This suggests that, instead of focusing on the average discount, it is more important to understand what are the characteristics of the firms that operate successfully as diversified firms and those that do not. This chapter contributes precisely in the latter direction by providing a fourth dimension along which value can be destroyed, and the particular characteristics of the firms that may engage in the adoption of value-decreasing diversification. In fact, the model predicts that the existence of synergies cannot be taken as evidence of potentially successful mergers, since synergies and agency conflicts are intertwined in ways that may result in the adoption of value-decreasing diversification or value-decreasing focus. In particular, when the synergies created by merging are neither high nor low, firms are more likely to engage in value-decreasing diversification.

In the future, it would be interesting to test the predictions of the model by incorporating measures of synergy, conflicts of interest, and the interaction between them, to isolate the portion of a merger that is a result of synergies and the portion motivated by private benefits.

APPENDIX

Proof of Lemma 1:
Proof This follows immediately from that the CEO's expected payoff is given by: $2r_{e_i^d} r_{e_j^d} \varepsilon \pi S \lambda - k_{e_1^d + e_2^d}$, and that the local and global incentive compatibility constraints are given by:

$$2\varepsilon \pi S \lambda \geq \frac{k_1}{r_1 \Delta r}$$

$$2\varepsilon \pi S \lambda \geq \frac{k_1}{r_0 \Delta r}$$

$$2\varepsilon \pi S \lambda \geq \frac{2k_1}{(r_1 + r_0)\Delta r}$$

Finally, notice that $\frac{k_1}{r_1 \Delta r} < \frac{k_1}{r_0 \Delta r}$, $\frac{k_1}{r_0 \Delta r} > \frac{2k_1}{(r_1 + r_0)\Delta r}$ and $\frac{k_1}{r_1 \Delta r} < \frac{2k_1}{(r_1 + r_0)\Delta r}$.

Proof of Proposition 2:
Proof Suppose that $k_1 \leq \varepsilon \lambda \pi \Delta r$, then $r_{e^s} = r_1$.

$$\Delta U(S, \lambda) = \begin{cases} r_1(r_1 2S - 1)\varepsilon \pi \lambda - k_1 & \text{if } S > \frac{k_1}{\varepsilon \pi \lambda (r_1 + r_0)\Delta r} \\ (r_0^2 2S - r_1)\varepsilon \pi \lambda + k_1 < 0 & \text{if } S \leq \frac{k_1}{\varepsilon \pi \lambda (r_1 + r_0)\Delta r} \end{cases}$$

and

$$\Delta \Pi(S, \lambda) = \begin{cases} 2r_1(r_1 S - 1)\pi \lambda & \text{if } S > \frac{k_1}{\varepsilon \pi \lambda (r_1 + r_0)\Delta r} \\ 2(r_0^2 S - r_1)\pi \lambda < 0 & \text{if } S \leq \frac{k_1}{\varepsilon \pi \lambda (r_1 + r_0)\Delta r} \end{cases}$$

Notice that $r_0^2 S - r_1$ evaluated at $S = \frac{k_1}{\varepsilon \pi \lambda (r_1 + r_0)\Delta r}$ is positive if and only if $k_1 > \frac{r_1(r_1 + r_0)\varepsilon \pi \lambda \Delta r}{r_0^2}$ and that $r_1 S - 1$ evaluated at $S = \frac{k_1}{\varepsilon \pi \lambda (r_1 + r_0)\Delta r}$ is positive if and only if $k_1 < \frac{(r_1 + r_0)\varepsilon \pi \lambda \Delta r}{r_1}$. Because $k_1 \leq \varepsilon \lambda \pi \Delta r$, then it must be true that $k_1 < \frac{r_1(r_1 + r_0)\varepsilon \pi \lambda \Delta r}{r_0^2}$ and therefore $r_0^2 S - r_1 < 0$ for all $S \leq \frac{k_1}{\varepsilon \pi \lambda (r_1 + r_0)\Delta r}$. This implies that $\Delta \Pi(S, \lambda) > 0$ if and only if $S > \frac{1}{r_1}$.

Note $r_1(r_1 2S - 1)\varepsilon \pi \lambda - k_1$ evaluated at $S = \frac{k_1}{\varepsilon \pi \lambda (r_1 + r_0)\Delta r}$ is positive if and only if $k_1 > \frac{r_1(r_1 + r_0)\varepsilon \pi \lambda \Delta r}{r_1^2 + r_0^2}$, while $(r_0^2 2S - r_1)\varepsilon \pi \lambda + k_1$ evaluated at $S = \frac{k_1}{\varepsilon \pi \lambda (r_1 + r_0)\Delta r}$ is positive if and only $k_1 > \frac{r_1(r_1 + r_0)\varepsilon \pi \lambda \Delta r}{r_1^2 + r_0^2}$. Notice that $k_1 \leq \varepsilon \lambda \pi \Delta r$ and since $\frac{r_1(r_1 + r_0)}{r_1^2 + r_0^2} > 1$, $k_1 < \frac{r_1(r_1 + r_0)\varepsilon \pi \lambda \Delta r}{r_1^2 + r_0^2}$. This implies that $\Delta U(S, \lambda) > 0$ if and only if $S > \frac{1}{2r_1}$.

Suppose that $k_1 > \varepsilon \lambda \pi \Delta r$, then $r_{e^s} = r_0$. Then

$$\Delta U(S, \lambda) = \begin{cases} (r_1^2 2S - r_0)\varepsilon \pi \lambda - 2k_1 & \text{if } S > \frac{k_1}{\varepsilon \pi \lambda (r_1 + r_0)\Delta r} \\ r_0(r_0 2S - 1)\varepsilon \pi \lambda & \text{if } S \leq \frac{k_1}{\varepsilon \pi \lambda (r_1 + r_0)\Delta r} \end{cases}$$

and

$$\Delta \Pi(S, \lambda) = \begin{cases} 2(r_1^2 S - r_0)\pi \lambda > 0 & \text{if } S > \frac{k_1}{\varepsilon \pi \lambda (r_1 + r_0)\Delta r} \\ 2r_0(r_0 S - 1)\pi \lambda & \text{if } S \leq \frac{k_1}{\varepsilon \pi \lambda (r_1 + r_0)\Delta r} \end{cases}$$

Notice that $r_0 S - 1$ evaluated at $S = \frac{k_1}{\varepsilon \pi \lambda (r_1 + r_0)\Delta r}$ is positive if and only if $k_1 > \frac{(r_1 + r_0)\varepsilon \pi \lambda \Delta r}{r_0}$ while $r_0 2S - 1$ evaluated at $S = \frac{k_1}{\varepsilon \pi \lambda (r_1 + r_0)\Delta r}$ is positive if and only if $k_1 > \frac{(r_1 + r_0)\varepsilon \pi \lambda \Delta r}{2r_0}$. In addition, $r_1^2 S - r_0$ evaluated at $S = \frac{k_1}{\varepsilon\pi\lambda(r_1+r_0)\Delta r}$ is positive if and only if $k_1 > \frac{r_0(r_1+r_0)\varepsilon\pi\lambda\Delta r}{r_1^2}$. Because $k_1 > \varepsilon\pi\lambda(r_1+r_0)\Delta r$ then $k_1 > \frac{r_0(r_1+r_0)\varepsilon\pi\lambda\Delta r}{r_1^2}$.

Note also that $(r_1^2 2S - r_0)\varepsilon\pi\lambda - 2k_1$ evaluated at $S = \frac{k_1}{\varepsilon\pi\lambda(r_1+r_0)\Delta r}$ is positive if and only if $k_1 > \frac{(r_1+r_0)\varepsilon\pi\lambda\Delta r}{2r_0}$.

Proof of Lemma 3:
Proof Notice that implementation of high research effort level when project α is implemented requires the following to hold: $r_1\pi(\varepsilon\lambda + b_\lambda) - k_1 \geq r_0\pi(\varepsilon\lambda + b_\lambda)$, and thus $\tilde{b}_\lambda = \max\left\{\frac{k_1}{\pi\Delta r} - \varepsilon\lambda, 0\right\}$. Whereas implementation of high research-effort level when project β is implemented requires the following to hold: $r_1\pi b_1 - k_1 \geq r_0\pi b_1$, and thus $\tilde{b}_1 = \frac{k_1}{\pi\Delta r}$.

Inducing the CEO to implement project β requires $\pi(\varepsilon\lambda + b_\lambda) \leq \pi b_1$, and thus the following must hold, $b_1 - b_\lambda \geq \varepsilon\lambda$. Note that $\tilde{b}_1 \geq \lambda\varepsilon$ and $\tilde{b}_\lambda = 0$ if and only if $k_1 > \varepsilon\lambda\pi\Delta r$. Consider first the case in which $k_1 > \varepsilon\lambda\pi\Delta r$. Then $\tilde{b}_1^s - \tilde{b}_\lambda \geq \varepsilon\lambda$. This implies that whenever the CEO is induced to exert a high research-effort level irrespective of the implemented project, she picks project β. Thus the Board sets $b_1 = \tilde{b}_1$ and $b_\lambda = 0$, when $r_1\pi\left(1 - \frac{k_1}{\pi\Delta r}\right) > r_1\pi\left(\lambda - \left(\frac{k_1}{\pi\Delta r} - \lambda\varepsilon\right)\right)$ and it sets $b_1 = 0$ and $b_\lambda = \tilde{b}_\lambda$ otherwise. This condition reduces to the following condition: $\lambda < \frac{1}{1+\varepsilon}$.

Consider next the case in which $k_1 \leq \varepsilon\lambda\pi\Delta r$. That is, $\tilde{b}_\lambda = 0$. Thus, the board sets $b_1 = \varepsilon\lambda$ and $b_\lambda = 0$, when $r_1\pi(1 - \lambda\varepsilon) > r_1\pi\lambda$ and it sets $b_1 = 0$ and $b_\lambda = 0$ otherwise. This condition reduces to the following condition: $\lambda < \frac{1}{1+\varepsilon}$.

Proof of Lemma 4:
Proof If project α is implemented in both divisions, the incentive compatibility constraints are given by:

$$2\varepsilon\pi\lambda S + \pi^2 b_{\lambda\lambda} \geq \frac{k_1}{r_1\Delta r}$$
$$2\varepsilon\pi\lambda S + \pi^2 b_{\lambda\lambda} \geq \frac{2k_1}{(r_1+r_0)\Delta r}$$

where the first incentive constraint guarantees that the CEO prefers $(1, 1)$ to $(1, 0)$ and $(0, 1)$ – the local incentive compatibility constraint, and the second ensures that the CEO prefers $(1, 1)$ to $(0, 0)$ – the global incentive compatibility constraint. Because $\frac{k_1}{r_1\Delta r} < \frac{2k_1}{(r_1+r_0)\Delta r}$, the global incentive compatibility constraint is the more constraining of the two. Thus it is optimal to set $b_{\lambda\lambda} = \tilde{b}_{\lambda\lambda} \equiv \max\left\{\frac{2}{\pi}\left(\frac{k_1}{\pi(r_1+r_0)\Delta r} - \varepsilon\lambda S\right), 0\right\}$.

If project β is implemented in both divisions, the incentive compatibility constraints are given by:

$$\pi^2 b_{11} \geq \frac{k_1}{r_1\Delta r}$$
$$\pi^2 b_{11} \geq \frac{2k_1}{(r_1+r_0)\Delta r}$$

Because $\frac{k_1}{r_1 \Delta r} < \frac{2k_1}{(r_1+r_0)\Delta r}$, the global incentive compatibility constraint is the more constraining of the two. Thus it is optimal to set $b_{11} = \tilde{b}_{11} \equiv \frac{2k_1}{\pi^2(r_1+r_0)\Delta r}$.

Finally, inducing the CEO to implement project β requires $\tilde{b}_{11} - \tilde{b}_{\lambda\lambda} \geq \frac{2\varepsilon\lambda S}{\pi}$. Notice that $\tilde{b}_{11} \geq \frac{2\varepsilon\lambda S}{\pi}$ and $\tilde{b}_{\lambda\lambda} \geq 0$ if and only if $S \leq \frac{k_1}{\varepsilon\pi\lambda(r_1+r_0)\Delta r}$.

Consider first the case in which $S \leq \frac{k_1}{\varepsilon\pi\lambda(r_1+r_0)\Delta r}$, then $\tilde{b}_{11} - \tilde{b}_{\lambda\lambda} = \frac{2\varepsilon\lambda S}{\pi}$. This implies that whenever the CEO is induced to exert a high research-effort level in both divisions irrespective of the project implemented, she is also induced to implement project β. Thus the Board sets $b_{11} = \tilde{b}_{11}$ and $b_{\lambda\lambda} = 0$, when $2r_1^2\pi\left(S - \frac{k_1}{\pi(r_1+r_0)\Delta r}\right) > 2r_1^2\pi\left(\lambda S - \left(\frac{k_1}{\pi(r_1+r_0)\Delta r} - \varepsilon\lambda S\right)\right)$, while it sets $b_{11} = 0$ and $b_{\lambda\lambda} = \tilde{b}_{\lambda\lambda}$ otherwise. This condition reduces to the following condition: $\lambda < \frac{1}{1+\varepsilon}$. Suppose, next, that $S > \frac{k_1}{\varepsilon\pi\lambda(r_1+r_0)\Delta r}$. Then, $\tilde{b}_{\lambda\lambda} = 0$ and $\tilde{b}_{11} = \frac{2\varepsilon\lambda S}{\pi}$. In this case, the Board sets $\tilde{b}_{11} = \frac{2\varepsilon\lambda S}{\pi}$ and $b_{\lambda\lambda} = 0$ when $2r_1^2\pi(S - \varepsilon\lambda S) > 2r_1^2\pi S\lambda$, while it sets $b_{11} = b_{\lambda\lambda} = 0$ otherwise. This condition reduces to the following condition: $\lambda < \frac{1}{1+\varepsilon}$.

Proof of Proposition 5:

Proof Suppose that $k_1 \leq \varepsilon\lambda\pi\Delta r$ and $\lambda > \frac{1}{1+\varepsilon}$. Then, $r_{e^s} = r_1$, $b_\lambda = 0$, and the CEO implements project α. In addition, if $S \leq \frac{k_1}{\pi\varepsilon\lambda(r_1+r_0)\Delta r}$, then $b_{\lambda\lambda} = \frac{2}{\pi}\left(\frac{k_1}{\pi(r_1+r_0)\Delta r} - \varepsilon\lambda S\right)$, $b_{11} = 0$, and the CEO implements project α in both divisions, while if $S > \frac{k_1}{\pi\varepsilon\lambda(r_1+r_0)\Delta r}$, then $b_{11} = b_{\lambda\lambda} = 0$ and the CEO implements project α in both divisions. This implies the following:

$$\Delta U(S, \lambda, B) = \begin{cases} r_1(r_1 2S - 1)\varepsilon\pi\lambda - k_1 & \text{if } S > \frac{k_1}{\varepsilon\pi\lambda(r_1+r_0)\Delta r} \\ r_0^2 \frac{2k_1}{(r_1+r_0)\Delta r} - r_1\varepsilon\pi\lambda + k_1 < 0 & \text{if } S \leq \frac{k_1}{\varepsilon\pi\lambda(r_1+r_0)\Delta r} \end{cases}$$

and

$$\Delta\Pi(S, \lambda, B) = \begin{cases} 2r_1(r_1 S - 1)\pi\lambda & \text{if } S > \frac{k_1}{\varepsilon\pi\lambda(r_1+r_0)\Delta r} \\ 2r_1(r_1 S - 1)\pi\lambda - 2r_1^2\pi\left(\frac{k_1}{\pi(r_1+r_0)\Delta r} - \varepsilon\lambda S\right) < 0 & \text{if } S \leq \frac{k_1}{\varepsilon\pi\lambda(r_1+r_0)\Delta r} \end{cases}$$

Notice that if $S > \frac{k_1}{\varepsilon\pi\lambda(r_1+r_0)\Delta r}$, we are in the case in which there is no incentive contract, and thus by proposition $\Delta U(S, \lambda) > 0$ if and only if $S > \frac{1}{2r_1}$ and $\Delta\Pi(S, \lambda, B) > 0$ if and only if $S > \frac{1}{r_1}$. Whereas if $S \leq \frac{k_1}{\varepsilon\pi\lambda(r_1+r_0)\Delta r}$, $\Delta\Pi(S, \lambda, B) > 0$ if and only if $S \geq \frac{\pi\lambda\Delta r(r_1+r_0)+r_1 k_1}{r_1\pi\lambda\Delta r(r_1+r_0)(1+\varepsilon)} > \frac{k_1}{\varepsilon\pi\lambda(r_1+r_0)\Delta r}$, where the last inequality follows from that $k_1 \leq \varepsilon\lambda\pi\Delta r$.

Suppose, next, that $k_1 \leq \varepsilon\lambda\pi\Delta r$ and $\lambda \leq \frac{1}{1+\varepsilon}$. Then $r_{e^s} = r_1$, $b_1 = \varepsilon\lambda$, and the CEO implements project β. In addition, if $S \leq \frac{k_1}{\pi\varepsilon\lambda(r_1+r_0)\Delta r}$, then $b_{11} = \frac{2k_1}{\pi^2(r_1+r_0)\Delta r}$, $b_{\lambda\lambda} = 0$, and the CEO implements project β in both divisions, while if $S > \frac{k_1}{\pi\varepsilon\lambda(r_1+r_0)\Delta r}$, then $b_{11} = \frac{2\varepsilon\lambda S}{\pi}$ and $b_{\lambda\lambda} = 0$, and the CEO implements project β in both divisions. In this case:

$$\Delta U(S, \lambda, B, b) = \begin{cases} r_1(r_1 2S - 1)\varepsilon\lambda - k_1 & \text{if } S > \frac{k_1}{\varepsilon\pi\lambda(r_1+r_0)\Delta r} \\ r_0^2 \frac{2k_1}{(r_1+r_0)\Delta r} - r_1\varepsilon\pi\lambda + k_1 < 0 & \text{if } S \leq \frac{k_1}{\varepsilon\pi\lambda(r_1+r_0)\Delta r} \end{cases}$$

and

$$\Delta\Pi(S, \lambda, B, b) = \begin{cases} 2r_1(r_1 S - 1)\pi(1-\varepsilon) & \text{if } S > \frac{k_1}{\varepsilon\pi\lambda(r_1+r_0)\Delta r} \\ 2r_1^2(r_1 S - 1)\pi - r_1^2 \frac{2k_1}{(r_1+r_0)\Delta r} + r_1 2\varepsilon\pi\lambda < 0 & \text{if } S \leq \frac{k_1}{\varepsilon\pi\lambda(r_1+r_0)\Delta r} \end{cases}$$

If $S > \frac{k_1}{\varepsilon\pi\lambda(r_1+r_0)\Delta r}$, by proposition $\Delta U(S, \lambda) > 0$ if and only if $S > \frac{1}{2r_1}$ and $\Delta\Pi(S, \lambda, B, b) > 0$ if and only if $S > \frac{1}{r_1}$. While if $S \leq \frac{k_1}{\varepsilon\pi\lambda(r_1+r_0)\Delta r}$, $\Delta\Pi(S, \lambda, B, b) > 0$ if and only if $S > \frac{\pi(r_1+r_0)\Delta r(1-\varepsilon\lambda)+r_1 k_1}{\pi r_1(r_1+r_0)\Delta r} > \frac{k_1}{\varepsilon\pi\lambda(r_1+r_0)\Delta r}$ since $k_1 \leq \varepsilon\lambda\pi\Delta r$.

Suppose, next, that $k_1 > \varepsilon\lambda\pi\Delta r$ and $\lambda > \frac{1}{1+\varepsilon}$. Then $r_{e^s} = r_1$, $b_\lambda = \frac{k_1}{\pi\Delta r} - \varepsilon\lambda$ and the CEO implements project α. In addition, if $S \leq \frac{k_1}{\pi\varepsilon\lambda(r_1+r_0)\Delta r}$, then $b_{\lambda\lambda} = \frac{2}{\pi}\left(\frac{k_1}{\pi(r_1+r_0)\Delta r} - \varepsilon\lambda S\right)$, $b_{11} = 0$, and the CEO implements project α in both divisions, while if $S > \frac{k_1}{\pi\varepsilon\lambda(r_1+r_0)\Delta r}$, then $b_{11} = b_{\lambda\lambda} = 0$ and the CEO implements project α in both divisions. This implies the following:

$$\Delta U(S, \lambda, B, b) = \begin{cases} r_1^2 2\varepsilon\pi\lambda S - 2k_1 - r_0 \frac{k_1}{\Delta r} & \text{if } S > \frac{k_1}{\varepsilon\pi\lambda(r_1+r_0)\Delta r} \\ r_0^2 \frac{2k_1}{(r_1+r_0)\Delta r} - r_0 \frac{k_1}{\Delta r} < 0 & \text{if } S \leq \frac{k_1}{\varepsilon\pi\lambda(r_1+r_0)\Delta r} \end{cases}$$

and

$$\Delta\Pi(S, \lambda, B, b) = \begin{cases} 2r_1\pi\left[(r_1 S - 1)\lambda + \frac{k_1}{\pi\Delta r} - \varepsilon\lambda\right] & \text{if } S > \frac{k_1}{\varepsilon\pi\lambda(r_1+r_0)\Delta r} \\ 2r_1\pi\left[(r_1 S - 1)\lambda(1+\varepsilon) + \frac{k_1}{\pi\Delta r} \frac{r_0}{(r_1+r_0)}\right] & \text{if } S \leq \frac{k_1}{\varepsilon\pi\lambda(r_1+r_0)\Delta r} \end{cases}$$

If $S \leq \frac{k_1}{\varepsilon\pi\lambda(r_1+r_0)\Delta r}$, then $\Delta\Pi(S, \lambda, B, b) > 0$ if and only if $S > \frac{r_1\lambda\pi\Delta r(r_1+r_0)(1+\varepsilon)-k_1 r_0}{r_1\lambda\pi(r_1+r_0)\Delta r(1+\varepsilon)}$ where $\frac{r_1\lambda\pi\Delta r(r_1+r_0)(1+\varepsilon)-k_1 r_0}{r_1\lambda\pi(r_1+r_0)\Delta r(1+\varepsilon)} < \frac{k_1}{\varepsilon\pi\lambda(r_1+r_0)\Delta r}$ if and only if $k_1 > \frac{\varepsilon\pi\lambda(r_1+r_0)\Delta r(1+\varepsilon)}{\varepsilon r_0 + r_1(1+\varepsilon)}$. If $S > \frac{k_1}{\varepsilon\pi\lambda(r_1+r_0)\Delta r}$, then diversification is value-maximizing if $S > \frac{\lambda\Delta r(1+\varepsilon)-k_1}{\lambda\pi r_1\Delta r}$, where $\frac{\lambda\Delta r(1+\varepsilon)-k_1}{\lambda\pi r_1\Delta r} > \frac{k_1}{\varepsilon\pi\lambda(r_1+r_0)\Delta r}$ if and only if $k_1 > \frac{\varepsilon\pi\lambda(r_1+r_0)\Delta r(1+\varepsilon)}{\varepsilon r_0 + r_1(1+\varepsilon)}$, while the CEO pursues diversification whenever $S \geq \frac{2r_1-r_0}{2r_1^2\varepsilon\pi\lambda\Delta r} k_1 > \frac{k_1}{\varepsilon\pi\lambda(r_1+r_0)\Delta r}$. Note that $\frac{\lambda\Delta r(1+\varepsilon)-k_1}{\lambda\pi r_1\Delta r} - \frac{2r_1-r_0}{2r_1^2\varepsilon\pi\lambda\Delta r} k_1 > 0$ if and only if $k_1 < \frac{2r_1\pi\Delta r\varepsilon\lambda(1+\varepsilon)}{2r_1(1+\varepsilon)-r_0}$.

Finally, suppose next that $k_1 > \varepsilon\lambda\pi\Delta r$ and $\lambda \leq \frac{1}{1+\varepsilon}$. Then $r_{e^s} = r_1$, $b_1 = \frac{k_1}{\pi\Delta r}$ and the CEO implements project β. In addition, if $S \leq \frac{k_1}{\pi\varepsilon\lambda(r_1+r_0)\Delta r}$, then $b_{11} = \frac{2k_1}{\pi^2(r_1+r_0)\Delta r}$ $b_{\lambda\lambda} = 0$, and the CEO implements project β in both divisions, while if $S > \frac{k_1}{\pi\varepsilon\lambda(r_1+r_0)\Delta r}$, then $b_{11} = \frac{2\varepsilon\lambda S}{\pi}$ and $b_{\lambda\lambda} = 0$ and the CEO implements project β in both divisions. In this case,

$$\Delta U(S, \lambda, B, b) = \begin{cases} r_1^2 2\varepsilon\pi\lambda S - 2k_1 - r_0 \frac{k_1}{\Delta r} & \text{if } S > \frac{k_1}{\varepsilon\pi\lambda(r_1+r_0)\Delta r} \\ r_0^2 \frac{2k_1}{(r_1+r_0)\Delta r} - r_0 \frac{k_1}{\Delta r} < 0 & \text{if } S \leq \frac{k_1}{\varepsilon\pi\lambda(r_1+r_0)\Delta r} \end{cases}$$

and

$$\Delta\Pi(S, \lambda, B, b) = \begin{cases} 2r_1\pi\left[r_1 S(1-\varepsilon\lambda) - 1 + \frac{k_1}{\pi\Delta r}\right] & \text{if } S > \frac{k_1}{\varepsilon\pi\lambda(r_1+r_0)\Delta r} \\ 2r_1\pi\left[r_1 S - 1 + \frac{k_1}{\pi\Delta r}\frac{r_0}{(r_1+r_0)}\right] & \text{if } S \leq \frac{k_1}{\varepsilon\pi\lambda(r_1+r_0)\Delta r} \end{cases}$$

Suppose that $S \leq \frac{k_1}{\pi\varepsilon\lambda(r_1+r_0)\Delta r}$. Then diversification is value-maximizing when $S \geq \frac{\pi(r_1+r_0)\Delta r - r_0 k_1}{r_1 \pi(r_1+r_0)\Delta r}$. This is lower than $\frac{k_1}{\varepsilon\pi\lambda(r_1+r_0)\Delta r}$ for all $k_1 > \frac{\varepsilon\pi\lambda(r_1+r_0)\Delta r}{\varepsilon\lambda r_0+r_1}$. Suppose now that $S > \frac{k_1}{\varepsilon\pi\lambda(r_1+r_0)\Delta r}$, then diversification is value maximizing whenever $S > \frac{\pi\Delta r - k_1}{r_1\pi\Delta r(1-\varepsilon\lambda)}$, where $\frac{\pi\Delta r - k_1}{r_1\pi\Delta r(1-\varepsilon\lambda)} > \frac{k_1}{\varepsilon\pi\lambda(r_1+r_0)\Delta r}$ if and only if $k_1 > \frac{\varepsilon\pi\lambda(r_1+r_0)\Delta r}{\varepsilon\lambda r_0+r_1}$, while the CEO pursues diversification whenever $S \geq \frac{2r_1-r_0}{2r_1^2 \varepsilon\pi\lambda\Delta r} k_1$. Notice that $\frac{\pi\Delta r - k_1}{r_1\pi\Delta r(1-\varepsilon\lambda)} - \frac{2r_1-r_0}{2r_1^2 \varepsilon\pi\lambda\Delta r} k_1 > 0$ if and only if $k_1 < \frac{2r_1\pi\Delta r\varepsilon\lambda}{2r_1-r_0(1-\varepsilon\lambda)}$.

Proof of Proposition 6:
Proof If the incentive compatibility constraints are ignored, it follows from the objective function that it is optimal to set $p_3 = 1$ and $p_2 = 0$. This solution is incentive compatible if and only if the following holds:

$$U(I_3, \phi, \lambda) - U(\lambda) \geq m \geq U(I_2, \phi, \lambda) - U(\lambda)$$

Consider next the case in which $U(I_3, \phi, \lambda) - U(\lambda) < m$. In this case, the constraints $p_3[U(I_3, \phi, \lambda) - U(\lambda)] \geq m$ and $(p_3 - p_2)[U(I_3, \phi, \lambda) - U(\lambda)] \geq m$ can never be satisfied, and thus there is no incentive-compatible acceptable rule. Therefore, the Board either accepts all proposals, or rejects of all them. The Board accepts all proposals when the following holds:

$$q_2[\Pi(I_2, \phi, \lambda) - \Pi(\lambda)] + q_3[\Pi(I_3, \phi, \lambda) - \Pi(\lambda)] \geq 0$$

and rejects all of them otherwise.

Finally, consider the case in which $U(I_2, \phi, \lambda) - U(\lambda) > m$. In this case, p_2 and p_3 have to be chosen to satisfy the following:

$$(p_3 - p_2)[U(I_3, \phi, \lambda) - U(\lambda)] \geq m \geq (p_3 - p_2)[U(I_2, \phi, \lambda) - U(\lambda)]$$

and $p_3[U(I_3, \phi, \lambda) - U(\lambda)] \geq m$. There are possible cases: (i) $p_2 = 0$ and $p_3 = \frac{m}{U(I_2, \phi, \lambda) - U(\lambda)} < 1$; and (ii) $p_3 = 1$ and $p_2 = 1 - \frac{m}{U(I_2, \phi, \lambda) - U(\lambda)}$. The former is optimal when the following holds:

$$\frac{m}{U(I_2, \phi, \lambda) - U(\lambda)} q_3[\Pi(I_3, \phi, \lambda) - \Pi(\lambda)] \geq$$
$$\left[1 - \frac{m}{U(I_2, \phi, \lambda) - U(\lambda)}\right] q_2[\Pi(I_2, \phi, \lambda) - \Pi(\lambda)] + q_3[\Pi(I_3, \phi, \lambda) - \Pi(\lambda)]$$

After a few steps of simple algebra, this reduces to condition $q_2 > \tilde{q}_2$.

ACKNOWLEDGMENTS

Special thanks go to Alexander Galetovic for his useful comments on an earlier version of this chapter and to participants at the regular seminars at the University of Chile. All errors are my own responsibility.

NOTES

1. On average there is a diversification discount; that is, on average, diversified firms trade at a discount relative to a portfolio of stand-alone firms in the same business segments. For example, Berger and Ofek (1995) find that diversified firms are valued 13 percent to 15 percent below the sum of the imputed values of their segments. Rajan et al. (2000) reports that around 40 percent of the firms they studied traded at a premium, but on average they were traded at a discount. Similar evidence can be found in Wernerfelt and Montgomery (1988), Lang and Stultz (1994), Comment and Jarrell (1995), and Servaes (1996). However, a number of recent papers (Campa and Kedia, 1999; Hyland, 1999; Chevalier, 2000; and Whited, 2001) have shown that the average discount is the result of uncontrolled endogeneity, because firms with poor returns as stand-alone firms are the ones most likely to diversify. Yet Lamont and Polk (2002) have challenged this conclusion, and have shown, after carefully controlling for endogeneity, that diversification is on average value-decreasing.
2. Merrill Lynch analysts estimated the potential synergies for this merger at US $1 billion.
3. In this context, there are three different types of agency problems that provide explanations for why a conglomeration strategy is adopted. First, Amihud and Lev (1981) postulate that managers diversify their idiosyncratic risk resulting from having undiversified positions in their own firms. Second, managers derive private benefits of control from managing more diversified firms (Jensen, 1986; Stulz, 1990). Reasons for this range from prestige for managing larger firms, entrenchment through specific human capital investments (see Shleifer and Vishny, 1989) to the idea that larger firms provide larger pay, power and prestige (Jensen and Murphy, 1990). Third, divisional managers' rent-seeking incentives cause investment distortions (see Scharfstein and Stein, 2000) or influence costs that may lead to inefficient transfers from divisions with high-growth opportunities to those with lower ones (see Meyer et al., 1992 and Rajan et al., 2000).
4. Fulghieri and Hodrick (2002) assume that diversification and divestiture decisions are made by the Board to maximize firm value.

5. There is plenty of agreement that managers of large public corporations are subject to loose scrutiny. Boards of Directors give managers considerable leeway to choose investment projects and they usually do not use the immediate effect on firm value of acquisitions or investment as a measure of the long-run optimality of managerial decisions (see Morck et al. (1990) for evidence on managerial objectives driving acquisitions).
6. Later, it will be shown that, under certain parameterization, it is optimal for the Board to accept any merger proposal made by the CEO.
7. See Aghion and Tirole (1997) and Burkart et al. (1997) for the same assumption.
8. The results are robust to the existence of dis-economies of scope.
9. The fact that the lack of coordination fully destroys cash flows is made for the sake of simplicity, and is not needed for the results to hold.
10. The fact that the CEO never chooses a high research intensity in one division and a low one in the other is because there are no dis-economies of scope. This result holds when the dis-economies of scope are not too severe – that is, when $k_2 \leq \frac{(r_1+r_0)}{r_0} k_1$. When $k_2 > \frac{(r_1+r_0)}{r_0} k_1$, an asymmetric research effort choice across divisions is possible. The chapter's results are robust to this, yet the number of cases to analyze increases considerable and there is no gain from intuition.
11. Similar evidence can be found in Wernerfelt and Montgomery (1988), Lang and Stultz (1994), Comment and Jarrell (1995) and Servaes (1996).
12. This is a standard result in the literature.

REFERENCES

Aghion, P. and Tirole, J. (1997) "Formal and Real Authority in Organization", *Journal of Political Economy*, 105(11): 1–29.

Amihud, Y. and Baruch, Lev, (1981) "Risk Reduction as a Managerial Motive for Conglomerate Mergers", *Bell Journal of Economics*, 12: 605–17.

Anderson, R. C., Bates, T. W., Bizjak, J. M. and Lemmon, M. L. (1998) "Corporate Governance and Firm Diversification" (August 23, 1998). Available at SSRN: http://ssrn.com/abstract=121013 or DOI: 10.2139/ssrn.121013(www.ssrn.com)

Argyres, N. S. (1995) "Technology Strategy, Governance Structure and Interdivisional Coordination", *Journal of Economic Behavior and Organization*, 28: 337–358.

Berger, P. G. and Ofek, E. (1995) "Diversification Effect on Firm Value", *Journal of Financial Economics*, 37(1): 39–65.

Berger, P. G. and Ofek, E. (1999) "Causes and Effects of Corporate Refocusing Programs", *Review of Financial Studies* 12(2): 311–45.

Burkart, M., Gromb, D. and Panunzi, F. (1997) "Large Shareholders, Monitoring and the Value of the Firm", *Quarterly Journal of Economics*, August: 693–728.

Campa, J. M. and Kedia, S. "Is There a Diversification Discount", (1994) *Journal of Finance*.

Chevalier, J. (2000) "What Do We Know About Cross-Subsidization: Evidence from the Investment Policies of Merging Firms", GSB working paper, University of Chicago.

Comment, R. and Jarrel, G. (1995) "Corporate Focus and Stock Return", *Journal of Financial Economics*, 37(1): 67–87.

Copeland, T. E. and F. J. Weston (1988) *Financial Theory and Corporate Policy*, 3rd edn (New York: Addison-Wesley).

Dennis, D. J., D. K. Denis and A. Sarin (1997) "Agency Problems, Equity Ownership, and Corporate Diversification", *Journal of Finance*, 52(1), March: 135–60.

Fulghieri, P. and Hodrick, L. S. (2002) "Synergies and Internal Agency Conflicts: The Double-edged Sword of Mergers", Working paper, Columbia University.

Graham, John R., Michael Lemmon and Jack Wolf (2002) "Does Corporate Diversification Destroy Value?", *Journal of Finance*, 57: 695–720.
Hart, O. and Holmstrom, B. (2002) "Vision and Firm Scope", Working paper, Harvard University, Cambridge, Mass.
Hubbard, R. G. and Palia, D. (1999) "A Reexamination of the Conglomerate Merger Wave in the 1960s: An Internal Capital Market View", *Journal of Finance*, 54(1):1131–52.
Hyland, D. C. (1997) "Why Firms Diversify: An Empirical Examination", unpublished doctoral dissertation, Ohio State University, Columbus, Ohio.
Hyland, D. (1999) "Why Do Firms Diversify? An Empirical Examination", Working paper, University of Texas, Arlington.
Jensen, M. C. (1986) "Agency Cost of Free Cash Flow, Corporate Finance, and Takeovers", *American Economic Review*, 76(2), May: 328–9.
Jensen, M. C. and Meckling, W. H. (1976) "Theory of the Firm: Managerial Behavior, Agency Costs and Ownership Structure", *Journal of Financial Economics*, 3(4): 305–60.
Jensen, M. C. and Murphy, K. J. (1990) "Performance Pay and Top Management Incentives", *Journal of Political Economy*, 98(2): 225–65.
John, K. and Ofek, E. (1995) "Asset Sales and Increase in Focus", *Journal of Financial Economics*, 37(1): 105–26.
Kaplan, S. N. and Weisbach, M. S. (1992) "The Success of Acquisitions: Evidence from Divestitures", *Journal of Finance*, 47(1): 107–39.
Lamont, O. and Polk, V. (2001) "The Diversification Discount: Cash Flows vs. Returns", *Journal of Finance*, 52: 83–111.
Lamont, O. and Polk, V. (2002) "Does Diversification Destroy Value? Evidence from Industry Shocks", *Journal of Financial Economics*, January: 51–77.
Lang, L. and Stulz, R. M. (1994) "Tobin's q, Corporate Diversification, and Firm Performance", *Journal of Political Economy*, 102(6): 1248–80.
Martin, John D. and Akin Sayrak (2003) "Corporate Diversification and Shareholder Value", *Journal of Corporate Finance*, 9: 37–57.
Matsusaka, J. G. (1993) "Takeover Motives during the Conglomerate Merger Wave", *Rand Journal of Economics*, 24(3), pp. 357–79.
Matsusaka, J. G. (2001) "Corporate Diversification, Value Maximization and Organizational Capabilities", *Journal of Business*, 74(3): 409–31.
Matsusaka, J. G. and Nanda, V. (1999) "Internal Capital Markets and Corporate Refocusing" Working paper, University of Southern California.
May, D. O. (1995) "Do Managerial Motives Influence Firm Risk Reduction Strategies", *Journal of Finance*, 50: 1291–308.
Meyer, M., Milgrom, P. and Roberts, J. (1992) "Organizational Prospects, Influence Costs and Ownership Changes", *Journal of Management Strategy*, 1: 9–35.
Morck, R., Shleifer, A. and Vishny, R. (1990) "Do Managerial Objectives Drive Bad Acquisitions?", *Journal of Finance*, 45: 31–48.
Palia, D. (1999) "Corporate Governance and the Diversification Discount: Evidence from Panel Data" Unpublished manuscript, University of Chicago.
Panzar, J. C. and Willig, R. D. (1979), "Economies of Scale and the Profitability of Marginal-Cost Pricing: Reply", *Quarterly Journal of Economics*, 93(4): 743–44.
Panzar, John C. and Willig, Robert D. (1981) "Economies of Scope", *American Economic Review*, 71, 268–72.
Penrose, Edith T. (1959) *The Theory of the Growth of the Firm* (New York: Wiley).
Prahalad, C. K., and Hamel, G. (1990) "The Core Competence of the Corporation", *Harvard Business Review*, May–June,: 79–93.
Rajan, R., Servaes, H. and Zingales, L. (2000) "The Cost of Diversity: The Diversification Discount and Inefficient Investment", *Journal of Finance*, 55: 35–80.

Rotemberg, J. and Saloner, G. (1995) "Benefits of Narrow Business Strategy", *American Economic Review*, 84(2), May: 1330–49.

Rumelt, Richard P. (1974) "Strategy, Structure, and Economic Performance", Division of Research, Harvard Business School, Boston, Mass.

Scharfstein, D. S. and Stein, J. C. (2000) "The Dark Side of Internal Capital Markets: Divisional Rent Seeking and Inefficient Investment", *Journal of Finance*, 55: 2537–64.

Servaes, H. (1996) "The Value of Diversification During the Conglomerate Merger Wave", *Journal of Finance*, 51: 1201–25.

Shleifer, A. and Vishny, R. (1989) "Managerial Entrenchment: The Case of Manager-Specific Investments", *Journal of Financial Economics*, 25: 123–39.

Stein, J. C. (1997) "Internal Capital Markets and the Competition for Corporate Resources", *Journal of Finance*, 52: 111–13.

Stulz, R. M. (1990) "Managerial Discretion and Optimal Financing Policies", *Journal of Financial Economics*, 26: 3–27.

Teece, David J. (1980) "Economies of Scope and the Scope of the Enterprise", *Journal of Economic Behavior and Organization*, 1: 223–47.

Teece, David J. (1982) "Toward an Economic Theory of the Multiproduct Firm", *Journal of Economic Behavior and Organization*, 3: 39–63.

Villalonga, B. (2003) "Research Roundtable Dicussion: The Diversification Discount", Mimeo, Harvard Business School.

Villalonga, Belén (2004) "Diversification discount or premium? New evidence from BITS Establishment-level Data", *Journal of Finance*, 59(2): 475–502.

Wernerfelt, B. and Montgomery, C. A. (1988) "Tobin's q and the Importance of Focus in Firm Performance", *American Economic Review*, 78(2), May: 246–50.

Whited, T. (2001) "Is It Inefficient Investment That Causes the Diversification Discount?", *Journal of Finance*, 56:(5) 1667–91.

Williamson, O. E. (1975) *Markets and Hierarchies: Analysis and Antitrust Implications* (New York: Free Press).

CHAPTER 6

The Influence of M&As on Firm Value: The Turkish Experience

M. Nihat Solakoğlu and Mehmet Orhan

6.1 INTRODUCTION

World economies were exposed to several merger and acquisition waves within the last century. Moreover, more recently, a shift of M&A activities from regional to more global nature has been observed (Gugler *et al.* 2003). These waves, as discussed in the literature, can occur either because of some type of industry shocks or because of market timing Harford (2005)[1]. Up until the last decade, though, Turkish economy did not have a significant experience with mergers and acquisitions, either domestic or cross-country. More global nature of M&A activities and the emergence of the Istanbul Stock Exchange (ISE) played an important role in this change. In particular, it became less costly for Turkish firms to raise capital and consider strategies to acquire or merge with other firms. In addition, it can be argued that existence of the stock exchange has caused information and monitoring costs to fall with improved regulations and laws. As a result, it became easier for acquirer and target firms to evaluate costs and benefits of merging or acquisition strategies.

As discussed by previous studies, there are several reasons that explain why M&A activity leads to an improvement on firm value. These reasons mainly fall under two groups that are linked to managerial motivations: reasons that reflect self-serving motivations or that not. When the motivations are not related to self-interest of managers, M&A activity should lead to a positive impact on shareholder wealth and hence on firm value.

The increase in shareholder wealth may be caused by cost reduction (due to expense reduction or lower adverse selection costs), efficiency improvements, risk reduction (due to diversification), or increased market power (if firms operate in the same sector)[2]. On the other hand, when the motivation is related to self-interest of managers[3], one should not expect to observe an increase in firm value (e.g., Peristiani, 1997; Cheng et al., 2004)[4]. Previous research also indicates that source of financing, cash or stock, can be an important determinant of M&A impact on firm value (e.g., Andrade et al., 2001).

One group of studies focus on the short-run impact of M&As on target and acquiring firms by using an event-study analysis. An evaluation of stock returns relative to the expected levels around the announcement date is expected to reveal investor expectations about the value change as a result of merger or acquisition. In other words, these studies show how investors appraise the M&A activity. In addition, most studies form a consensus that target firm returns show a positive abnormal return while acquiring firm returns do not change significantly (e.g., Cheng et al., 2004; DeLong, 2001; Scholtens and de Wit, 2004; Kıymaz, 2004; Amihud et al., 2002).

Traditional approach to test the long-run effects of M&A includes the comparison of pre- and post-merger accounting data. Mainly, studies show that short-run improvements are not realized in the long-run (e.g., Cheng et al., 2004). Other measures of long-run performance are also used in the literature to evaluate the long-run impact of M&A activity on firm value. Some alternatives are X-efficiency and scale efficiency. It can be argued that these are better measures for cost efficiency than financial ratios and they can be more effective to examine long-run effects of mergers (e.g., Peristiani, 1997)[5]. It is also possible to argue that innovative performance of the firm after the merger should be higher due to improved post-merger knowledge base (e.g., Cloodt, 2006)[6].

There is also a large and growing literature on the effects of cross-border mergers and acquisitions on firm value[7]. Cross-border M&As do not only cause a reallocation of resources within/across an industry and national borders, but also between nations and even regions. Research reveals that both geographic concentration and activity focus are important for cross-border M&A to be value increasing (DeLong, 2001). In addition, differences in laws and regulations and investor protection are also important factors to determine the cross-border merger patterns and success rate (Rossi and Volpin, 2004; Buck and DeLong, 2004)[8]. Although there are some differences in findings, as in domestic M&As, research indicates that wealth gains mostly accrue to target firms rather than acquiring firms for cross-border M&As (e.g., Kıymaz, 2004; Gugler et al., 2003; Bessler and Murtagh, 2002; Kıymaz and Mukherjee, 2001).

As indicated earlier, the low volume of M&A activity, both in numbers and in value, including a Turkish firm either as a target or a bidder has prevented researchers in the past evaluating the M&A impacts on firm value. Within the last decade but in particular within the last couple of years, this situation has changed significantly. For instance, while there were only five completed mergers and acquisitions in 1997, we can find 164 announced cases in 2005[9]. Although the number of M&A activity looked somewhat higher since 1998, a close examination of the transaction value of M&A activity indicates that 2005 was different than earlier years[10]. While the total transaction value was US $613.7 million in 2002, for 2005 the transaction value rose to US $30.4 billion. Even in 2004, the announced value was much lower and it was around US $2.5 billion. Clearly, the role and significance of M&As for Turkish economy started to change dramatically around 2005 (*Aydın*, 2004; Ernst & Young 2005 M&A report).

The majority of M&A activity over the last decade in Turkey can be considered domestic rather than cross-border. However, along with growing M&A activity in 2005, we also observe growing importance of cross-border acquisitions and mergers. For example, share of cross-border activity was around twenty percent in 2003. In 2005, however, about thirty-nine percent of total activity was cross-border. Moreover, European firms lead the foreign firms, either as bidder or target, in the cross-border M&A list (Ernst & Young 2005 M&A report).

This study investigates the impact of mergers and acquisitions on firm value for the Turkish target and acquiring firms. Given the recent nature of M&A activity in Turkey, firm value is evaluated in the short-run through an event-study analysis. In other words, we consider a positive return over expected around the announcement date as an increase in firm value. Additionally, we examine the role of firm-specific and merger-specific factors on the sign of the M&A impact on firm value. In other words, we try to identify the factors that significantly impact the probability of observing a positive abnormal return by utilizing logistic regression approach[11]. The remainder of the paper is organized as follows. Section II discusses data sources, and the methodology to analyze short-term impact of M&A on firm value. Discussion of results is left to section III. Last section presents our main conclusions and suggestions for further research.

6.2 DATA AND METHODOLOGY

Our analysis is performed using merger and acquisition data obtained from Bloomberg through a local investment firm. Dataset covers most of the announced activity between late 2003 and middle of 2006. Although the Turkish economy experienced a total of 389 M&As between 2003 and 2005, we could only identify 38 activities that includes at least one firm that is traded in the Istanbul Stock Exchange. For 2006, we identified an additional 14 firms, providing us a total of 52 acquirer and target information, with 30 being for the target[12]. Consistent with the observed trend in M&A activity in Turkey, the majority of transactions were also between Turkish firms in this sample. In addition, about 42% of the transactions could be categorized as cross-border, with mostly foreign firms bidding for Turkish firms. Moreover, about 57% of the M&A activity included firms operating in the same industry. Particularly for cross-border activity, 73% of the acquirer and target firms were operating in the same industry. Within this sample, M&A activity seems to concentrate in financial and consumer goods sectors.

Daily data of securities traded at the Istanbul Stock Exchange (ISE) and market index[13] are obtained from *www.analiz.com* for the acquirer and bidder firms in our sample. The following specification of the market model is used to determine the expected returns in our analysis:

$$R_{it} = \alpha_i + \beta_i R_{mt} + \varepsilon_{it} \tag{6.1}$$

where R_{it} is the daily return of security i, and R_{mt} is the market return at time t. ε_{it} is the disturbance term satisfying the classical assumptions. We estimate the model above with 80 observations dating over $[-90, -11]$ days before the announcement. The event window includes 20 days around the announcement date. The abnormal returns are the OLS residuals over the subperiod defined as:

$$AR_{it} = R_{it} - (\hat{\alpha}_i + \hat{\beta}_i R_{mt}) \tag{6.2}$$

The abnormal returns for each day of the event window over the firms are calculated and reported in Table 6.1 and Table 6.2 to present some characteristics of these returns for different days of the event window for target and acquiring firms, respectively. Although the mean of abnormal returns are oscillating around zero throughout the event window, there is a slight decrease in the trend. The dispersion also has such a trend, which is somewhat smaller in magnitude, but the more striking characteristic of the dispersion indicated by the standard deviation is the peak it attains in the immediate neighborhood of the announcement day. The lowest minimum is at the exact date of the announcement with -21.4%, and the maximum is incidentally attained just before that day with the same percentage.

A crucial point of interest is whether the population mean of the abnormal returns is significantly different than zero or not. More formally; the null of $H_0: AAR = 0$ is to be tested against the alternative of $H_1: AAR \neq 0$ at various significance levels for both acquiring and target firms. The corresponding test statistic is the ratio of the mean to the standard deviation of the sample mean, i.e. $t = (\bar{x} - \mu_0)/(s/\sqrt{n})$ where $\bar{x}$ is the sample mean, s is the sample standard deviation and n is the sample size. This test statistic follows the Student's t-distribution with $n-1$ degrees of freedom. Last columns of Tables 6.1 and 6.2 are the t-statistics where (***), (**), and (*) denote significances at 1%, 5%, and 10% levels, respectively. The abnormal returns prove to be significantly different than zero for the majority of the days belonging to the event window for the target firms.

Table 6.1 Descriptive statistics belonging to target firms

Day	Mean	Med.	St. Dev.	Kurt.	Skew.	Range	Min.	Max.	t-stat.
−10	0.89	−0.01	3.13	8.81	2.62	16.16	−2.64	13.50	1.55(**)
−9	0.94	−0.00	3.34	0.00	0.50	14.01	−6.50	7.51	1.54(**)
−8	1.16	0.22	2.63	2.07	1.30	12.36	−3.59	8.76	2.42(***)
−7	−0.13	−0.27	2.62	5.34	1.54	14.14	−4.76	9.38	−0.28
−6	−0.07	−0.15	3.14	9.31	2.02	19.46	−6.81	12.70	−0.11
−5	0.62	0.29	2.68	0.09	−0.10	11.93	−5.35	6.58	1.27(*)
−4	0.27	0.11	2.53	2.62	0.53	13.73	−5.64	8.09	0.58
−3	0.88	−0.34	4.02	1.86	−0.49	19.01	−11.5	7.49	1.20(*)
−2	1.05	1.04	3.56	3.77	−0.68	20.13	−10.6	9.54	1.62(**)
−1	0.94	0.43	7.22	2.17	0.62	35.59	−14.1	21.40	0.71(*)
0	−1.24	0.32	7.01	2.90	−0.64	38.75	−21.4	17.30	−0.97(*)
1	−0.15	−0.88	5.02	4.47	1.58	26.24	−8.61	17.60	−0.16
2	0.54	−0.29	2.94	2.28	1.28	14.25	−4.59	9.66	1.00(*)
3	−0.60	−0.32	2.98	3.59	−1.40	15.40	−10.3	5.09	−1.11(*)
4	−0.46	−0.39	2.32	0.37	−0.52	10.22	−6.04	4.18	−1.10(*)
5	0.16	−0.34	2.39	2.34	1.47	10.72	−3.41	7.31	0.36
6	−0.31	−0.68	3.00	7.64	1.91	16.75	−5.36	11.40	−0.56
7	−0.83	−0.51	2.18	1.18	−1.11	9.20	−6.64	2.56	−2.08(***)
8	0.41	−0.15	3.47	8.11	2.38	18.72	−4.55	14.20	0.64
9	−0.04	−0.07	2.63	0.48	0.06	11.58	−5.95	5.63	−0.09
10	−0.78	−1.07	2.25	0.96	−0.01	11.12	−6.68	4.43	−1.87(***)

Source: www.analiz.com

We observe less significance in average abnormal returns being other than zero for the acquiring firms as displayed in the last column of Table 6.2. Furthermore, days with significant average abnormal returns are smaller (11 out of 23) as well.

6.3 DISCUSSION OF RESULTS

Another point of interest is how the Cumulative Abnormal Returns (CAR) are changing over the event window. We define the CAR for any day t (inside the event window from −10 to 10) as the sum of the average abnormal returns up to that day as $CAR(t) = \sum_{i=-10}^{t} AAR_i$. Figure 6.1 displays how the CAR changes throughout the event window for the target firms. The CAR

Table 6.2 Descriptive statistics belonging to acquiring firms

Day	Mean	Med.	St. Dev.	Kurt.	Skew.	Range	Min.	Max.	t-stat.
−10	−0.29	−0.26	2.45	−0.03	0.70	9.03	−3.60	5.43	−0.56
−9	−0.25	−0.13	1.55	0.18	0.13	6.24	−3.54	2.71	−0.76(*)
−8	0.10	0.14	2.06	3.62	1.04	9.93	−3.51	6.42	0.23
−7	−0.14	−0.42	2.00	1.14	0.21	9.17	−4.77	4.40	−0.32
−6	0.43	0.13	2.28	−1.12	0.05	7.59	−3.49	4.10	0.88(*)
−5	0.15	0.21	2.12	3.73	0.28	11.46	−5.33	6.13	0.33
−4	0.88	0.26	2.90	−0.12	0.74	10.63	−3.10	7.53	1.42(**)
−3	−0.35	−0.72	3.16	7.04	1.87	15.74	−4.96	10.78	−0.52
−2	0.41	0.66	1.60	1.61	−1.07	6.91	−3.98	2.93	1.19(*)
−1	−0.32	−0.81	3.80	3.18	1.28	17.96	−7.78	10.18	−0.39
0	0.30	0.88	2.26	0.92	−0.46	10.17	−5.06	5.11	0.62
1	−0.53	−0.08	2.31	0.09	−0.05	9.62	−5.05	4.57	−1.07(*)
2	−0.48	−0.81	1.48	−0.67	0.47	5.20	−2.64	2.56	−1.53(**)
3	−0.11	−0.22	2.03	0.16	0.10	8.34	−4.39	3.95	−0.24
4	0.24	0.08	1.19	−0.90	0.42	4.17	−1.55	2.62	0.95(*)
5	−0.76	−1.36	2.10	−0.14	0.80	7.42	−3.71	3.71	−1.69(***)
6	−0.91	−0.88	1.49	−0.52	0.02	5.44	−3.46	1.97	−2.88(****)
7	0.53	−0.01	1.59	3.77	1.68	7.33	−1.75	5.57	1.57(***)
8	0.20	−0.14	1.54	−1.05	0.48	5.01	−1.94	3.07	0.60
9	0.11	0.47	1.65	1.51	−0.43	7.58	−3.62	3.96	0.31
10	−0.34	−0.35	1.49	0.00	0.33	5.87	−2.94	2.93	−1.07(**)

Source: www.analiz.com

increases until about the announcement day and then starts to decrease due to the abnormal returns being positive until the announcement day and then being negative, on the average. The investor is expected to get additional cumulative return of 7% should he be invested in the M&As traded on the ISE.

The situation is similar for the bidder firms but the picture is a bit more mixed and the returns are somewhat smaller than the target firm returns. The same investor's additional cumulative return is less than 1% should he be invested in the acquiring firms. This CAR would not be maintained as positive if the investor kept on investing in the same firms following the announcement date and the loss would become more if the investor remained with the same securities.

We furthermore analyze whether there have been structural changes in the behaviors of the returns represented by the market model regression equation. We advance a version of the Chow test (1960) to conclude in the existence of a structural change. The null hypothesis this time claims that there is no structural change in the regression line, H_0: *No structural change*, against the alternative of the structural change. More formally, what is meant by the structural change in the regression equation is that there is

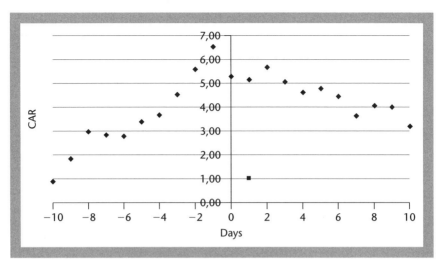

Figure 6.1 CAR for target firms
Source: www.analiz.com

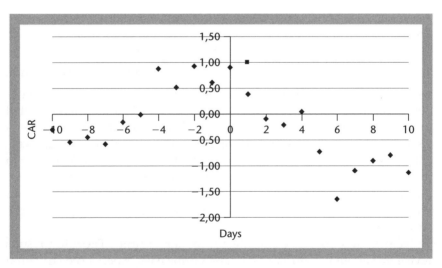

Figure 6.2 CAR for bidder firms
Source: www.analiz.com

change in at least one of the parameters in the regression equation of the market model. That is, either α or β or both in Equation [1] for the firm must be significantly different in pre- and post- periods.

The whole period of 120 day observations are separated to the pre-and post-periods with the pivot day of the announcement time. There are 90 observations in the pre-period ($n_1 = 90$) and 30 observations in the post-period ($n_2 = 30$) adding up to a total of 120 observations ($n = 120$). The residual sum of squares are calculated for all these three periods and called

Table 6.3 F-statistics for testing the structural change, acquiring firms

Firm	F-stat.	Firm	F-stat.
1	2.11(*)	12	3.19(***)
2	2.77(**)	13	0.66
3	2.29(*)	14	1.30
4	1.29	15	1.58(*)
5	1.18	16	2.92(**)
6	0.24	17	1.30
7	0.22	18	0.08
8	3.18(***)	19	2.43(**)
9	0.39	20	1.06
10	3.23(***)	21	0.16
11	2.65(**)	22	0.32

Source: www.analiz.com

RSS_{pre}, RSS_{post}, and RSS_{whole}, respectively after the calculation of the OLS parameter estimates for these three periods one by one.

The test statistic: $F = \frac{(RSS_{whole} - RSS_{pre} - RSS_{post})/k}{(RSS_{pre} + RSS_{post})/(n_1 + n_2 - 2k)}$ follows the F-distribution with (k) numerator degrees of freedom and $(n_1 + n_2 - 2k)$ denominator degrees of freedom. This statistic is calculated for all bidder firms and listed in Table 6.3. The F-critical values for 1%, 5%, 10%, and 25% significant levels for (2,116) numerator and denominator degrees of freedom are 4.80, 3.08, 2.35, and 1.40 respectively. All test statistics are evaluated according to these critical values and the rejections based on these significance levels are indicated by (*), (**), (***), and (****) for 25%, 10%, 5%, and 1% significance levels. Test results conclude that 10 out of 22 acquiring firms experience the structural change.

Table 6.4 reports the test results for the target firms. These test results reveal that about two thirds of the target firms have experienced structural changes around the announcement date with about one third being highly significant. The structural changes are observed more for the target firms than the acquiring firms. 23 out of 30 target firms experience the structural changes. The significance levels are larger for the target firms as well.

Average abnormal returns between days −10 and +10 around announcement date are provided in Table 6.5 for several firm- and M&A-specific factors. It appears that AAR is larger for cross-border than domestic M&As. Particularly for target firms, we notice a large and positive average abnormal return. On the other hand, for acquirer firms, AAR indicates a larger decline in firm value for cross-border than domestic activity. Similar result can be

Table 6.4 F-statistics for testing the structural change, target firms

Firm	F-stat.	Firm	F-stat.
1	0.82	16	1.45(*)
2	7.30(*)	17	2.09(*)
3	2.53(**)	18	2.94(**)
4	0.82	19	1.77(*)
5	1.61(*)	20	0.73
6	7.91(****)	21	4.71(***)
7	11.20(****)	22	2.61(**)
8	5.05(****)	23	4.38(***)
9	0.78	24	3.56(***)
10	1.15	25	1.73(*)
11	4.48(****)	26	2.27(**)
12	0.30	27	3.23(***)
13	3.26(***)	28	4.11(***)
14	1.55(*)	29	3.63(***)
15	0.97	30	4.84(*)

Source: www.analiz.com

Table 6.5 Firm and M&A Specific Factors and AAR

			Acquirer Firm		Target Firm	
	No	Yes	No	Yes	No	Yes
Cross-border M&A	1.7%	13.3%	−1.3%	−30.9%	6.9%	20.2%
Same-industry M&A	−1.5%	12.5%	−14.3%	0.8%	7.3%	21.5%
Foreign Partners[a]	12.4%	−11.2%	−3.4%	−24.1%	26.7%	−7.3%
Family Ownership[b]	−15.5%	21.5%	−40.0%	4.8%	−7.8%	41.8%
International Activity[c]	−1.0%	16.1%	−25.8%	19.2%	24.1%	10.9%
Larger firm[d]	2.0%	11.2%	8.5%	−25.4%	−4.5%	30.5%

(a) Foreign Partners indicates existence of pre-M&A partnership with foreign firms or investors.

(b) Family Ownership indicates that acquirer or target firms have at least one family/individual as a major shareholder.

(c) International Activity shows that firms have positive levels of exports or imports.

(d) Larger Firm shows the size of the firm through number of employees. Firms with employees more than the median level (1833) are assumed to be large. Average number was 6519 for large firms, while it was 470 for others.

Sources: Istanbul Stock Exchange (www.imkb.gov.tr), www.analiz.com, Bloomberg.

seen for the same-industry transactions, with 21.5% increase in the stock return above the expected level for target firms if acquirer and target firms are in the same industry.

Existence of foreign partnership before the announcement date, surprisingly, indicates a lower post-M&A abnormal return[14]. Contrary to our expectations, family ownership leads to a higher post-merger return. As discussed in the literature, family ownership and control is expected to be positively associated with better performance and higher firm value (e.g., Maury, 2006; Maury and Pajuste, 2005; Barth et al., 2005; Davies et al., 2005). Accordingly, investors should expect moderate gains in performance and firm value post-M&A since these firms are expected to operate close to their efficiency frontier. We also notice that both the level of international activity, measured either by the non-negative levels of exports or imports, and the size of the firm, measured by the pre-merger number of employees, lead to a larger increase in post-M&A returns. In general, consistent with the earlier findings, Table 6.5 shows that target firms exhibit larger increase in firm value around the announcement date as measured by cumulative average abnormal returns.

The relationship between firm- and merger-specific factors and likelihood of observing positive abnormal return is analyzed by estimating the following equation.

$$P(AAR)_i = \mu + X_i\beta + \varepsilon_i \qquad (6.3)$$

In this equation, $P(AAR)_i$ is a binary variable taking a value of one for firm i when average abnormal return of this firm is greater than zero. Otherwise, it takes a value of zero. The matrix X_i includes a measure of firm size, an indicator variable for cross-country mergers and acquisitions, an indicator for target firms, indicators for ownership structures (namely for the existence of major foreign and family shareholders), an indicator for the same industry transactions, and finally an indicator for the existence of international transactions[15]. As a link function, we use logistic distribution[16]. With this analysis, our objective is to identify the factors that significantly impact the likelihood of positive average abnormal returns at the M&A level[17]. Results are presented in Table 6.6.

Based on % concordant and c-value, we can decide that model fit is acceptable. Signs of the coefficients are consistent with Table 6.5 presentations. However, out of seven variables, only three of them are statistically significant. Not surprisingly, Table 6.6 shows that being a target rather than acquirer increases the probability of realizing a positive abnormal return around the announcement date. Moreover, existence of international transactions also positively impacts the likelihood of positive abnormal returns. As discussed earlier, family ownership seems to have a positive impact on this probability as well.

Table 6.6 Firm and M&A specific factors and likelihood of observing abnormal returns

Cross-border	Same Industry	Foreign	Family	International Activity	Size	Target
0.0925	0.4850	−1.1719	1.4196*	1.2144*	0.0585	1.4532*
(.8457)	(.7192)	(.8483)	(.7474)	(.7226)	(.165)	(.874)
% concordant: 77.2						
c-value: 0.775						

Standard errors are provided in parantheses.
***, **, and * represent significance at 1%, 5% and 10% levels, respectively.
Size is measured by the log of number of employees. All the other variables are binary variables with a value of one representing the variable definition.
Sources: Istanbul Stock Exchange (www.imkb.gov.tr), www.analiz.com, Bloomberg.

6.4 CONCLUSION

This study examines the short-term impacts of merger and acquisitions on firm value for Turkish acquirer and target firms through an event-study approach. Given the recent increase in the number and value of M&A activity in Turkey, it becomes more important to understand the size and direction of change in firm value. Consistent with the existing literature, we find that target firms realize larger increases in firm value than acquirer firms. The observed increase in the CAAR before the announcement date indicates the existence of information spillover. An application of Chow test reveals that target firm returns have more structural changes than acquirer firm returns. Furthermore, the null of "no structural change" is more significantly rejected for target firms.

By investigating firm-specific and M&A-specific factors separately, we also find that larger firms, firms with a major family shareholder, and firms with international transactions realize a larger positive abnormal return. In addition, cross-border and same-industry M&A activity leads to a larger positive abnormal return. Pre-M&A existence of foreign major shareholders, on the other hand, causes a decrease in firm value post-M&A. An examination of the relationship between these factors and the likelihood of observing an increase in firm value show that only family ownership, existence of international transactions and being a target firm significantly impacts the probability.

Given the increasing number of mergers and acquisitions in Turkey, there is room for further research to investigate the relationship between macroeconomic factors and M&As. In addition, more recent announcements of bank mergers in Turkey provide an opportunity to investigate efficiency gains in the future.

NOTES

1. Industry shocks can be economic, regulatory or technological. Harford (2005) shows that industry shocks are the main drivers for merger waves but sufficient capital liquidity is required.
2. Some sources of firm value can be more important at certain times and be correlated with the reasons for the merger wave to start (Andrade et al., 2001).
3. Such as size of the firm, growth of the firm,etc.
4. Epstein (2005) examines the factors for mergers to be succesful and discusses six determinants: strategic vision and fit, deal structure, due diligence, premerger planning, post-merger integration, and external factors. This study also indicates that merger of equals will be more likely to cause power struggles within the merged company to be unsuccesful in terms of wealth gains.
5. Peristiani (1997) finds that mergers do not create value for banking sector when X-efficiency is used as the measure. However, there does seem to be a moderate improvement when scale efficiency is used, which is mostly caused by the lower scale-efficiency of the target firms.
6. Coodth et al. (2006), using a panel data set, find that size of the knowledge base improves the post-M&A performance in the mid-run.
7. Most studies concentrate on the banking or financial services. For example, Amihud et al. (2002) investigate the effect of mergers on risk for banking sector. They find that the risk of the acquiring bank do not change after the merger.
8. Differences in laws, regulations, language and geographical distance will increase the information and monitoring costs (Amihud et al., 2002; Buck and DeLong, 2004).
9. In fact, we observe an increasing M&A activity before 2001 crisis in Turkey with some decline during the crisis. Since 2002, the level of activity shows an increasing trend. The number of M&A activity between 1997 and 2005 are: 5, 52, 76, 101, 82, 54, 80, 91, and 164 (Aydın, 2004; Ada et al., (2006), Ernst & Young 2005 M&A report).
10. Based on the announced transaction values.
11. As shown by Kıymaz (2004), macrovariables also play significant roles in explaining wealth gains. Given that our sample mostly includes announcements in 2004 and 2005, we were not able to incorporate this line of research into our analysis.
12. Given that currently there are 261 firms traded on the ISE, this should not be too surprising.
13. Index includes 100 firms traded in the Istanbul Stock Exchange.
14. Foreign partnership is defined as the existence of major foreign shareholder in the previous accounting year of the announcement year.
15. Variable descriptions are provided under table 6.5 and table 6.6.
16. Instead of using logistic regression which uses logistic distribution as the link function, one can also use probit regression which uses normal distribution as the link function for estimation. In most cases, as in this one, results should not be different from each other. For details on logistic/probit regression, see Greene (1997, chapter 19).
17. Given that the size differences in abnormal returns might not be different from each other significantly, through this approach, we are hoping to see which factors causes positive abnormal returns.

REFERENCES

Ada, E., Demirhan, D. and Gökalp, F. (2006) "Şirket, birleşme ve satınalmalarının stratejik önemi ve işletmelerin piyasa değeri üerine etkisi", *Analiz*, 6(15): 29–38.

Amihud, Y., DeLong, G.L. and Saunders, A. (2002) "The Effects of Cross-border Bank Mergers on Bank Risk and Value", *Journal of International Money and Finance*, 21: 857–77.

Andrade, G., Mitchell, M. and Stafford, E. (2001) "New Evidence and Perspectives on Mergers", *Journal of Economic Perspectives*, 15(2): 103–20.

Aydın, N. (2004) "Birleşme ve satınalmalarda işletme değrlemesi", in *Şirket Birleşmeleri*, (ed.), by H. Sumer and H. Pernsteiner, 193–211.

Barth, E., Gulbrandsen, T. and Schone, P. (2005) "Family Ownership and Productivity: The Role of Owner-management", *Journal of Corporate Finance*, 11: 107–27.

Bessler, W. and Murtagh, J.P. (2002) "The Stock Market Reaction to Cross-border Acquisitions of Financial Services Firms: An Analysis of Canadian Banks", *Journal of International Financial Markets, Institutions and Money*, 12: 419–40.

Buck, C.M. and DeLong, G. (2004) "Cross-border Bank Mergers: What Lures the Rare Animal?", *Journal of Banking & Finance*, 28: 2077–102.

Cheng, L.T.W. and Leung, T.Y. (2004) "A Comparative Analysis of the Market-based and Accounting-based Performance of Diversifying and Non-diversifying Acquisitions in Hong Kong", *International Business Review*, 13: 763–89.

Chow, G.C. (1960). "Tests of Equality between Sets of Coefficients in Two Linear Regressions", *Econometrica*, 28(3): 591–605.

Cloodt, M., Hagedoorn, J. and Van Kranenburg, H. (2006) "Mergers and Acquisitions: Their Effect on the Innovative Performance of Companies in High-tech Industries", *Research Policy*, 35: 642–54.

Davies, J.R., Hillier, D. and McColgan P. (2005) "Ownership Structure, Managerial Behavior and Corporate Value", *Journal of Corporate Finance*, 11: 645–60.

DeLong, G.L. (2001) "Stockholder Gains from Focusing Versus Diversifying Bank Mergers", *Journal of Financial Economics*, 59: 221–52.

Epstein, M.J. (2005) "The Determinants and Evaluation of Merger Success", *Business Horizons*, 48: 37–46.

Greene, W.H. (1997) *Econometric Analysis*, 3rd edition, Englewood Cliff, NJ: Prentice-Hall.

Gugler, K., Mueller, D.C., Yurtoglu, B.B. and Zulehner, C. (2003) "The Effects of Mergers: An International Comparison", *International Journal of Industrial Organization*, 21: 625–53.

Harford, J. (2005) "What Drives Merger Waves?", *Journal of Financial Economics*, 77: 529–60.

Kıymaz, H. (2004) "Cross-border Acquisitions of US Financial Institutions: Impact of macroeconomic factors", *Journal of Banking & Finance*, 28: 1413–39.

Kıymaz, H. and Mukherjee, T.K. (2001) "Parameter Shifts when Measuring Wealth Effects in Cross-border Mergers", *Global Finance Journal*, 12: 249–66.

Maury, B. (2006). "Family Ownership and Firm Performance: Empirical Evidence from Western European Corporations," *Journal of Corporate Finance*, 12: 321–41.

Maury, B. and Pajuste, A. (2005) "Multiple Large Shareholders and Firm Value", *Journal of Banking & Finance*, 29: 1813–34.

Peristiani, S. (1997). "Do Mergers Improve the X-efficiency and Scale Efficiency of US Banks? Evidence from the 1980s", *Journal of Money, Credit and Banking*, 29(3) 326–37.

Rossi, S. and Volpin, P.F. (2004) "Cross-country Determinants of Mergers and Acquisitions", *Journal of Financial Economics*, 74: 277–304.

Scholtens, B., de Wit, R., (2004) "Announcement Effects of Bank Mergers in Europe and the US", *Research in International Business and Finance*, 18: 217–28.

CHAPTER 7

Price Volatility in Stocks Subject to Tender Offers

Elaine Hutson

7.1 INTRODUCTION

Enduring interest in the market for corporate control stems from its importance in ensuring that assets are managed as efficiently as possible to generate output from the economy's stock of productive resources. A plethora of empirical studies examining the efficiency of this market in many countries has provided evidence that firms subject to takeover bids experience substantial revaluation. The emphasis of this research has been on the behavior of the level of prices around the announcement of takeover offers, with very few studies examining the price volatility of target companies, and fewer still investigating what happens to trading volume around takeover announcements.

We examine the daily price volatility and trading volume of 154 targets of tender offers from one year before the takeover announcement and during the 'bid period' following the offer until the outcome of the offer is known. Using unconditional and conditional approaches to estimating volatility, we find that it falls dramatically for most takeover targets after the takeover announcement. Trading volume does not fall commensurately, and it in fact rises in cases where there would be considerable doubt about the takeover bid's outcome, such as bids that are ultimately unsuccessful, and those that are opposed by target management. We also find, contrary to expectations, that trading volume increases after the takeover announcement for targets of non-cash bids.

The chapter is structured as follows. Section 7.2 reviews the literature and presents the theoretical rationale for the empirical analysis. Section 7.3

discusses the econometric approach to be used and describes the hypotheses relating to volatility. Section 7.4 introduces the data set and presents preliminary results, including summary statistics and betas for the sample of target stocks. Section 7.5 presents the results of the econometric modelling, while section 7.6 examines the findings on volume. The final section summarizes the main arguments of the chapter and draws together the conclusions.

7.2 PREVIOUS RESEARCH AND THEORETICAL BACKGROUND

There is a large body of evidence demonstrating that target company shareholders earn substantial excess returns around takeover announcements.[1] Most of this excess return is earned on the announcement day, and several studies have found evidence of higher volatility associated with takeover announcements. Levy and Yoder (1993) found significantly higher option-implied standard deviations for target stocks from three days before the announcement up to and including, but not after, the announcement day. Lee *et al.* (1994) and Smith *et al.* (1997) found that intra-day trading volume and unconditional stock price volatility is abnormally high, but decreasing, on the day of a takeover announcement.

Several more recent studies have documented substantial excess returns to target shareholders during the "bid period"[2] – usually measured from the day after the announcement to the time of the resolution of the bid. Investors who attempt to profit from this apparent anomaly are engaging in what is popularly known as "risk arbitrage" or "merger arbitrage", and a growing interest in this area relates to its increasing use as a technique employed by hedge fund managers. These "abnormal" returns earned by merger arbitrageurs raise an important question that has attracted comparatively little attention in the literature: do target shareholders experience a significantly higher risk commensurate with the higher returns they earn? Bhagat *et al.* (1987) found that the unconditional standard deviation of post-announcement target returns is in fact lower than during the pre-bid period. They explained this reduction in risk in terms of the target stock becoming a portfolio of the share plus a put option on the bidding firm. Hutson and Kearney (2001) used a version of the autoregressive conditional heteroscedastic (ARCH) model on a sample of 112 Australian target stocks and found a significant reduction in conditional price volatility after the takeover announcement. They explained this phenomenon with reference to the mixture of distributions model (MDM) of speculative trading, whereby the reduction in volatility is caused by convergence of trader opinion as to target value as the bid progresses. It appears, therefore, that, after an initial increase, target stock price volatility – and hence risk – is lower than before the takeover announcement.

Hutson and Kearney (2001) also found that the effect of the market on targets of successful takeover bids diminished after the takeover announcement. This did not occur to the same extent, however, for targets of failed bids. This finding received some corroboration by Mitchell and Pulvino (2001), who found that the beta on a risk arbitrage portfolio was a very low but significant 0.11. In bear markets, however, the portfolio beta increased substantially, to approximately 0.5. Their explanation for this is that in falling markets there is a greater likelihood of bid failure.

7.2.1 Target price volatility

In examining the likely effect of a takeover offer on target price volatility, we follow Hutson and Kearney (2001), and explore the second-moment implications of the target pricing model of Brown and Raymond (1986), and Samuelson and Rosenthal (1986). (The model has also been applied by Larcker and Lys (1987) and Barone-Adesi et al. (1994)). This model[3] assumes that given a bid price, p_t^b, the price of a target stock on any day during the bid period, p_t, is determined by the market's assessment of the probability of success of the bid, π_t, and by the price to which it is expected to revert if the bid fails, p_t^f:

$$P_t = \pi_t P_t^b + (1-\pi_t)p_t^f \qquad (7.1)$$

During the course of a takeover bid that is ultimately successful, traders will revise upward their estimate of the bid's likelihood of success, π_t. As the conclusion of the bid approaches, π_t will therefore tend towards unity as traders increasingly agree on its outcome, the second term in Equation (7.1) will tend to zero, and the target share price p_t will converge to the bid price, p_t^b.[4] The model implies that the stock pricing process simplifies to a system whereby, given a bid price, the value of target stocks is determined largely by the likelihood of success of the bid.

For targets of takeover bids that ultimately fail, the simplified pricing model still holds, but the variable π_t in Equation (7.1) does not converge to unity as for targets of successful bids,[5] and the variable fallback price, p_t^f, has a larger role in the price determination process. We therefore argue that, for failed bids, there will be a reduction in price volatility for targets after the takeover announcement, but this will not be as great as for targets of successful bids.

Another factor that may contribute to failed targets having higher price volatility during the bid period relative to targets of bids that succeed, is that during the course of the bid there may be greater uncertainty as to the takeover offer's outcome. The variable π_t will therefore be more volatile.

Several studies (for example, Walkling, 1985; Walkling and Long, 1986) have found that takeover bids that are opposed by target management are significantly more likely to fail than those for which management is supportive or neutral. In common with targets of failed takeover bids, it is likely, therefore, that targets of hostile bids experience a lesser reduction in price volatility than targets of friendly bids.

Finally, a crucial factor affecting post-announcement target volatility is the nature of the consideration offered by the bidder. If the offer is cash, one of the three variables in Equation (7.1) – p_t^b – becomes a constant. As the conclusion of the bid approaches and π_t tends to unity, the target share price will converge to the fixed bid price. In share-exchange bids, p_t^b is a variable that is equal to the bidder's share price multiplied by the exchange ratio. Because the offer price varies with the bidder's share price, there should be a smaller reduction in the target's price volatility than in the case of cash bids.[6]

7.2.2 Target trading volume

The model of Brown and Raymond (1986) and Samuelson and Rosenthal (1986) examines target price levels only. Our application of this model to target stocks looks at its second-moment implications. It does not, however, provide any insight into the expected effect on trading volume. To provide a framework for examining the volume effects of takeover bids on targets, and to provide additional insights into price volatility, we use the model of speculative trading that has become known as the mixture of distributions model (MDM). In an early version of the MDM, Epps and Epps (1976) argued that the intra-day price changes reflect the average of changes in traders' "reservation" prices. An increase in the extent to which traders disagree is associated with a larger absolute price change. The positive volatility–volume relation arises because the volume of trading is related positively to the degree of dispersion in traders' reservation prices. Subsequent models of the price volatility–volume relation have similar implications; see, *inter alia*, Jang and Ro (1989), Holthausen and Verrechia (1990), Harris and Raviv (1993), Shalen (1993) and Wang (1993, 1994).

We use Tauchen and Pitts' (1983) version of the MDM (which extends the work of Epps and Epps (1976)) to provide a framework for examining the volume–volatility relationship for target stocks. Tauchen and Pitts (1983) specify two components of informational events: those common to all traders (common informational events) and those specific to individual traders (trader-specific informational events). The model predicts that price volatility is influenced by both components, but trading volume is determined only by the dispersion in trader-specific information. This delineation between common informational events and trader-specific information enables a deeper examination of the speculative trading process for target stocks. A brief exposition of this model follows.

Tauchen and Pitts' (1983) model of speculative trading assumes that an asset with price p is traded by $j = 1\ldots J$ traders who transact at irregular intervals of time. The intra-day demand for this asset by trader j at time i is written as:

$$Q_i^{D^j} = \alpha \left[p_i^j - p_i \right] \tag{7.2}$$

where $Q_i^{D^j}$ is the trader's demand for the asset, p_i^j is his/her reservation price, p_i is the current market price, $\alpha > 0$ and $Q_i^{D^j}$ can be positive or negative, depending on whether a long or short position is required. Traders possess different reservation prices because they differ in their expectations about the future prospects of the asset. Equilibrium is reached in the market at each point in time when the market's price is the average of the traders' reservation prices. It follows that price changes and trading volume are written as in Equations (7.3) and (7.4) below:

$$\Delta p_i = \frac{1}{J} \sum_{j=1}^{J} \Delta p_i^j \tag{7.3}$$

$$V_i \equiv \frac{1}{2} \sum_{j=1}^{J} \left| Q_i^{D^j} - Q_{i-1}^{D^j} \right| = \frac{\alpha}{2} \sum_{j=1}^{j} \left| \Delta p_i^j - \Delta p_i \right| \tag{7.4}$$

A variance components model describes the change at time i in trader j's reservation price for the asset, Δp_i^j as:

$$\Delta p_i^j = \phi_i + \varphi_i^j \tag{7.5}$$

where ϕ_i and φ_i^j denote, respectively, common informational events and trader-specific informational events, with $E(\phi_i) = E(\varphi_i^j) = 0$, $Var(\phi_i) = \sigma_\phi^2$ and $Var(\varphi_i^j) = \sigma_\varphi^2$. The expressions for the change in price and volume at time i consequently become:

$$\Delta p_i = \phi_i + \overline{\varphi_i}, \quad \overline{\varphi_i} = \frac{1}{J} \sum_{j=1}^{J} \varphi_i^j \tag{7.6}$$

$$V_i = \frac{\alpha}{2} \sum_{j=1}^{J} \left| \Delta p_i^j - \Delta p_i \right| = \frac{\alpha}{2} \sum_{j=1}^{J} \left| \varphi_i^j - \overline{\varphi_i} \right| \tag{7.7}$$

In Equations (7.6) and (7.7), price volatility is determined by the common informational component, ϕ_i, and by the average change in price resulting from trader-specific information, $\overline{\varphi_i^j}$. Volume is determined by the dispersion of traders' opinion around the average of trader-specific informational events. In Tauchen and Pitts' model, both common informational events and the average of trader-specific events affect price volatility but not volume. If an informational event is common to all traders, or if traders largely agree on a piece of information's effect on value, then it is possible that a large effect on stock value may be accompanied by little or no effect on trading volume.

We argue that the bid price, p_t^b in Equation (7.1), can be seen as a common informational component, ϕ_i in Equation (7.6), and the likelihood of the bid's success, π_t in Equation (7.1), is the trader-specific informational component, φ_i^j (Equations 7.5–7.7). Extending the discussion in section 2.1, we argue that, for ultimately successful bids, the trader-specific component π_t converges to 1 as the bid progresses. There is both less trader-specific information affecting the stock, and reduced opinion as to its value (reduced trader-specific dispersion). Both volatility and volume should therefore decline for ultimately successful bids. Continuing uncertainty about the likelihood of success of bids that ultimately fail or that are opposed by target management implies that, while volatility should decline for these cases, volume may not. Finally, because the only difference between cash and non-cash bids is that the common informational component p_t^b for the latter is variable, we hypothesize that the volume behavior should be the same for these two sub-samples.

Four predictions flow from this discussion. First, the conditional price volatility and volume of targets of successful bids should be significantly lower than their pre-bid values. Second, for targets of failed and hostile bids, conditional price volatility should decline by less than that of the targets of successful and friendly bids, respectively, but volume should be insignificantly different post-announcement *vis-à-vis* pre-announcement. Third, the reduction in price volatility should be greater for targets of cash bids than non-cash bids, but there should be no difference in post-announcement volume between these two sub-samples.

7.3 THE ECONOMETRIC ANALYSIS: MARKET EFFECT AND VOLATILITY

We specify a two-equation model for the mean and standard deviation of target stocks, following the procedure of Davidian and Carroll (1987) and Schwert (1989). The model is specified in Equations (7.8) and (7.9) below. The return on the asset, Δp_t, is defined as the log difference between p_t and p_{t-1}; Δm_t denotes the return on the market, and LV_t denotes the log of trading volumes:

$$\Delta p_t = \alpha_0 + \sum_{i=1}^{5} \alpha_1^i \Delta p_{t-i} + \alpha_2 \Delta m_t \times DUMPRE_t + a_3 \Delta m_t \\ \times DUMPOST_t + \alpha_4 ANNOU_t + \varepsilon_t \tag{7.8}$$

$$\sigma_t = \gamma_0 + \sum_{i=1}^{5} \gamma_1^i \sigma_{t-i} + \sum_{i=0}^{5} \gamma_2^i LV_{t-i} + \gamma_3 \, DUMPOST_t + u_t \tag{7.9}$$

The mean Equation (7.8) is a generally specified autoregressive model in which the target return is related to a constant, itself lagged up to five times (given that daily data is being used), the market return, and two dummy variables. The return on the market, Δm_t, is separated into pre-announcement and post-announcement components by means of two dummy variables, $DUMPRE$, which is set to unity before the takeover announcement and zero after; and $DUMPOST$, which is set to zero before the announcement and to unity after. This approach is preferable to calculating excess returns in advance of the econometric modeling because it allows us to examine whether the role of the market in the target price formation process changes after the takeover announcement. If the estimated values of α_2 and α_3 are significantly different, it will lend support to our proposition that target stocks undergo a change in their price formation process when they are "in play". The dummy variable $ANNOU$ is set to unity on the day of the announcement and to zero at all other times. It captures any spike in the return series that might occur on announcement of a takeover bid.

The dependent variable in the conditional variance Equation (7.9) is obtained as the absolute value of the residuals from the mean Equation (7.8), ($\sigma_t = /\varepsilon_t/$). It is related to a constant, itself lagged five times, and the current and five lags of the log of trading volumes. The dummy variable $DUMPOST$ is included to examine whether there is a post-announcement change in the conditional price volatility of target stocks. If the estimated value of γ_3 is significantly negative, it will support our hypothesis that target stocks exhibit lower conditional price volatility when they are "in play".

In order to account appropriately for the non-zero cross-equation covariances that arise from the generated regressors problem (see, *inter alia*, Pagan, 1984, 1986; McAleer and McKenzie, 1991; and Oxley and McAleer, 1993), Equations (7.8) and (7.9) are estimated jointly for each target stock using the generalized least squares (GLS) estimation procedure. This is done by estimating the mean Equation (7.8), using the absolute value of the residuals as the dependent variable in Equation (7.9), and sequentially restricting the use of the general-to-specific estimation strategy until the parsimonious version is obtained for each target stock in our sample.

7.4 DATA AND PRELIMINARY RESULTS

The dataset for this study consists of 154 US tender offers during the period January 1995 to December 1998. Daily closing prices, volumes (number of shares traded per day) and closing market values were obtained from

Datastream. The takeover information is drawn from the Thompson Financial Securities Data takeover database, which provides the announcement date, the conclusion date, the method of payment, the outcome of the bid, and target management's attitude to the offer. Success is defined as either (a) the bidder meeting its minimum acceptance conditions, or (b) the bidder declaring the bid unconditional and receiving acceptances from at least 50 percent of shareholders. In estimating our models, the pre-announcement period begins 250 days before the takeover announcement and ends at the close of business the day before the announcement. The post-announcement period begins at close of business on the day of the announcement and runs until the formal conclusion of the bid.

The data requested from Thompson Financial Securities data were tender offers during the period 1995–8 in which both bidder and target were US-based companies. Targets not listed, or not listed for the full year prior to the takeover announcement were removed. Table 7.1 summarizes the data. The sample comprises 141 targets of successful bids and the remaining thirteen are targets of unsuccessful bids. It includes 133 targets of cash bids and twenty-one targets of non-cash bids. Of the 154 cases, 128 can be described as friendly (target directors recommended acceptance of the offer or were neutral) and the remaining twenty-six can be considered hostile (target directors opposed the bid). As can be seen from Table 7.1, all the non-cash bids were acquired successfully by the bidder, while thirteen of the 133 cash takeover offers failed. Consistent with previous research, there is a strong correlation between management's attitude to the bid and its outcome, with only three friendly bids out of 128 failing, while ten out of twenty-six (38 percent) of the hostile bids failed.

Table 7.1 Frequency table of outcome by consideration and management attitude

	Success	Failure	Total
Consideration			
Cash	120	13	133
Non-cash	21	0	21
Total	141	13	154
Management attitude			
Friendly	125	3	128
Hostile	16	10	26
Total	141	13	154

Sources: Thompson Finance Securities Database and Datastream.

Figure 7.1 plots the cumulative average abnormal return (CAAR) for the 154 target companies, from 200 days before the announcement to eighty days subsequently. The graph clearly shows a "spike" at announcement, with the CAAR increasing about 25 percent. An interesting feature of the CAAR is the apparent decline in market-adjusted performance of this sample of target firms, which is consistent with the theory that poorly performing firms become takeover targets.

Table 7.2 provides summary statistics of target returns, divided into the pre-announcement and post-announcement periods. In calculating these statistics, the pre-announcement period is defined to exclude the contaminating effects of the so-called "runup" period (of twenty days), during which there is an observed tendency for target stock prices to rise prior to the public announcement of the bid. The post-announcement period excludes the day of the announcement in order to eliminate the one-off hike in price volatility and trading volumes associated with the announcement itself. In each case, the results are further divided by outcome of the bid (successes and failures), by consideration (cash and non-cash), and by management's attitude (friendly and hostile).

The summary statistic of most relevance to this chapter is the standard deviation of target returns. The average unconditional standard deviation for the full sample declines by a highly significant 53 percent, from 0.036 pre-announcement to 0.017 post-bid. This is a much larger decline than reported for Australian target stocks in Hutson and Kearney (2001), of 34 percent.

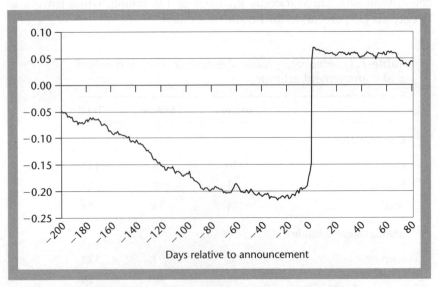

Figure 7.1 Cumulative average abnormal returns
Sources: Thompson Financial Securities Database and Datastream.

Table 7.2 Summary statistics for target returns

	Sample size	Mean	Standard deviation	Percentage decline in standard deviation (p-value)
Pre-bid period				
Total	154	0.000	0.036	
By outcome				
Successes	141	0.000	0.036	
Failures	13	0.000	0.032	
By consideration				
Cash	133	0.000	0.037	
Non-cash	21	0.001	0.025	
By management attitude				
Friendly	128	0.000	0.036	
Hostile	26	0.000	0.033	
Post-bid period				
Total	154	0.001	0.017	53 (0.00)
By outcome				
Successes	141	0.001	0.016	56 (0.00)
Failures	13	0.002	0.027	16 (0.22)
By consideration				
Cash	133	0.001	0.017	54 (0.00)
Non-cash	21	0.001	0.021	16 (0.14)
By management attitude				
Friendly	128	0.001	0.015	58 (0.00)
Hostile	26	0.002	0.026	21 (0.04)

Notes: The pre-bid period runs from 250 to 20 days prior to the takeover announcement. The post-bid period starts 1 day after the takeover announcement and runs until the conclusion of the bid. These figures are cross-sectional averages of the statistics calculated for each target company in time-series. The column headed "Percentage decline in standard deviation (p-value)" reports the results for the test that pre- and post-announcement unconditional standard deviations are equal against the alternative that the pre-announcement standard deviation exceeds the post-announcement standard deviation, using a one-tailed t-test with unequal variances.
Sources: Thompson Financial Securities Database and Datasteam.

For successfully targeted stocks, the decline is greater at 56 percent, from a pre-bid average of 0.036 to 0.016 post-bid. For targets of failed bids, the reduction in volatility is only 16 percent, and this is not statistically significant (p = 0.22). The reduction in target price volatility from the pre-bid to the post-bid period is significant for cash bids at 54 percent, but insignificant for non-cash bids at 16 percent (p = 0.14). For targets subject to friendly bids, the decline is a highly significant 58 percent (p = 0.00), while for hostile bids the decline is smaller at 21 percent, although this is still significant at standard levels (p = 0.04).

These results are qualitatively consistent with Bhagat *et al.* (1987), who reported that the unconditional standard deviation for a sample of 295 targets subject to tender offer during the period 1962 to 1980 declined by 16 percent, from an average of 0.025 pre-bid to 0.021 post-bid. The reduction in risk reported here is considerably greater. This is probably explained by our sample being dominated by targets of full bids, whereas over two-thirds of Bhagat *et al's* (1987) sample comprised partial bids.

7.5 ECONOMETRIC RESULTS

The model described in Equations (7.8) and (7.9) has been estimated using the procedure described in the previous section for each of the 154 target stocks in the sample. Tables 7.3 and 7.4 present summaries of the important findings from the modeling process. Table 7.3 focuses on the role played by the market coefficients in the mean equations, and Table 7.4 summarizes the results regarding the effect of the takeover announcement in the conditional standard deviation equations.

7.5.1 The mean equations

The return on the market, Δm_t, in the mean Equation (7.8) is separated into its pre- and post-bid components using the dummy variables *DUMPRE* and *DUMPOST*. If the estimated coefficients on these variables are significantly different (if $\alpha_2 \neq \alpha_3$), it will support our proposition that target stocks undergo a change in their price formation process after the announcement of the takeover bid. Columns 1 and 3 of Table 7.3 report the average values of the market coefficients before (α_2) and after (α_3) the announcement of the takeover bid. Columns 2 and 4 report the proportion of each group for which the market variable is statistically significant at the 10 percent level or better. Column 5 reports the percentage change in the average market coefficient after the announcement, and the p-value for the test that pre- and post-announcement market effects are equal against the alternative that the pre-announcement market effect exceeds the post-announcement market effect,

Table 7.3 Market coefficients in the mean equations

	Pre-bid		Post-bid		
	Average value α_2 [1]	Proportion significant [2]	Average value α_3 [3]	Proportion significant [4]	Percent change (p-value) [5]
Full sample	0.540	94/154 (61%)	0.236	22/154 (14%)	−56% (0.00)
By consideration					
Cash	0.543	81/133 (61%)	0.201	15/133 (11%)	−63% (0.00)
Non-cash	0.513	13/21 (64%)	0.558	8/21 (36%)	+9% (0.41)
By outcome					
Success	0.538	85/141 (60%)	0.210	14/141 (10%)	−61% (0.00)
Failures	0.564	10/13 (75%)	0.523	6/13 (46%)	−7% (0.44)
By management attitude					
Friendly	0.521	78/128 (61%)	0.175	14/128 (11%)	−66% (0.00)
Hostile	0.623	15/26 (59%)	0.502	7/26 (26%)	−19% (0.26)

Notes: This table summarizes the results of the market coefficients (α_2 and α_3 in the mean Equations (7.8) for 112 target stocks, delineated by outcome and by method of payment. The columns headed proportion significant report the percentage of the sample where a significant value for α_2 or α_3 was obtained. The last column reports the percentage reduction in market effect after the announcement, and the p-values for the test that pre- and post-announcement market effects are equal against the alternative that the pre-announcement market effect exceeds the post-announcement market effect, using a one-tailed t-test with unequal variances.
Sources: Thompson Financial Securities Database and Datastream.

using a one-tailed t-test with unequal variances. The figures are first presented for the whole sample, followed by the sample delineated by consideration, outcome and method of payment.

It is clear that after a takeover announcement there is a reduction in both the average value of the market coefficient and the number of cases in which the return on the market is found to be significant. The average value of the pre-bid market coefficients (α_2) for the full sample is 0.540, and it is significant at the 10 percent level or better in 61 percent of cases (94/154). The average value of the market coefficients after the announcement (α_3) is 0.236, and this is significant at the 10 percent level or better in only 14 percent (22/154) of cases. This represents a highly significant decline of 56 percent in the effect of the market on the pricing of target stocks after the takeover announcement.

For targets of successful bids, the average value for α_2 is 0.538 (with 60 percent being significant), and the average value for α_3 is 0.210 (with 10 percent significant). This decline of 61 percent in the effect of the market after the takeover announcement is statistically significant at the 1 percent level.

Table 7.4 Effects of takeover announcements in the target volatility equations

	Average value γ_3	Average normalized value γ_3	Number of γ_3s significantly negative
Full sample	−0.012	−0.550 (0.307)	129/154 (84%)
By consideration			
Cash	−0.013	−0.573 (0.292)	114/133 (86%)
Non-cash	−0.005	−0.337 (0.372)	13/21 (62%)
By Outcome			
Success	−0.013	−0.571 (0.293)	120/141 (85%)
Failure	−0.006	−0.320 (0.376)	8/13 (62%)
By management attitude			
Friendly	−0.013	−0.583 (0.280)	110/128 (86%)
Hostile	−0.009	−0.406 (0.377)	19/26 (73%)

Notes: This table reports summary results for the bid dummy coefficient, γ_3 in Equation (7.9). This dummy is set at zero for the pre-announcement period, and unity for the post-announcement period. "Average normalized value" is γ_3 for each target divided by its mean volatility, averaged over the group. The standard errors for the average normalized returns are reported in parentheses. The column headed "Percentage for γ_3s significantly negative" reports the percentage of the sample where significantly (at the 10 percent level or better) negative values for γ_3 where obtained.
Sources: Thompson Financial Securities Database and Datastream.

The findings for targets of failed bids are very different. There is a reduction in the average value of the market coefficient of only 7 percent, and this is not significant. This finding is not consistent with Hutson and Kearney (2001), who found that the reduction in market effect for targets of successful and failed bids was similar. For this group of thirteen failed US tender offers, unlike for targets of successful bids, the market still plays an important part in bid period target price determination. When the sample is delineated by consideration, however, the results are consistent with Hutson and Kearney (2001). The average market effect for non-cash bids in fact rises by 9 percent after the takeover announcement, although this change is not significant at standard levels. For targets of cash bids, there is a significant reduction in market effect of 63 percent.

Finally, the targets of friendly bids exhibit the greatest reduction in market effect – a highly significant 66 percent, with the number of cases recording significant market effects declining from 61 percent of the sample pre-bid to 11 percent post-announcement. Targets of hostile bids, however, experience an insignificant decline in market effect of 19 percent. This is probably explained by the fact that hostile bids are more likely to fail, and so the variable fallback price, p_t^b, in Equation (7.7) plays a larger part in the price determination process. Indeed, as can be seen in Table 7.1, 10/26 (38 percent) of the hostile bids failed, whereas the figure for friendly bids is 3/128 (2 percent).

7.5.2 The conditional volatility equations

Our primary interest in the volatility equations concerns whether the conditional price volatility of target stocks declines when they are "in play". This question is addressed by examining the behavior of the coefficient γ_3 in Equation (7.9); if γ_3 is significantly negative, then volatility is lower in the bid period vis-à-vis the year pre-bid. Table 7.4 summarizes our findings. It gives the mean value for γ_3 and the proportion of cases in which γ_3 is significantly negative. These figures are presented for the total sample, and for the sample delineated by outcome, consideration and management attitude. Table 7.4 also includes mean values for "normalized" γ_3s, which have been calculated for each target stock by dividing γ_3 by the absolute value of the mean of the dependent variable (MDV). This is necessary because the values for γ_3 are not strictly comparable to the extent that the magnitudes of the estimated conditional volatilities differ across the sample. The table includes the results for both the unadjusted and the normalized values for γ_3, with standard errors for the latter reported in parentheses. In the following discussion, we focus on the normalized values of γ_3.

The mean normalized value of γ_3 for successful takeovers is -0.571, and 85 percent (120/141) of the cases are significantly negative at the 10 percent level or better. This is a much stronger reduction in conditional volatility than found by Hutson and Kearney (2001), where the comparable figures are -0.374 and 69 percent. The average normalized value of γ_3 for failed bids, at -0.320, is almost half that of successes. A smaller proportion, but still a majority – eight out of thirteen (62 percent) – are significantly negative at the 10 percent level or better.

For the targets of cash bids, 86 percent are significantly negative; for non-cash the proportion is 62 percent. The average normalized γ_3s are, respectively, -0.573 for cash and -0.337 for non-cash cases. For friendly bids, 86 percent had significant reductions in volatility, with a normalized value for γ_3 of -0.583, while a lesser 73 percent of hostile bids had significant γ_3s, with a mean normalized value of -0.406.

These findings are largely consistent with the predictions discussed in sections 7.2 and 7.3, which follow from our application of the MDM to the case of target stocks. When a stock becomes a takeover target, there is a shift in the pricing regime to one where the most important determinant, given a certain bid price, is the likelihood of success of the bid. The MDM implies that price volatility is positively related to the divergence of investor opinion regarding stock value. With target stocks, we see a reduction in volatility after the announcement of the takeover that is consistent with the convergence of investor opinion regarding value. The result is most dramatic for targets of ultimately successful bids, and this can be explained by the probability of success converging to 1 toward the end of the bid period as diversity of investor opinion regarding the outcome of the bid collapses. The volatility reduction post-bid is stronger for targets of cash bids than for non-cash bids, because of a volatile bid price in stock-swap bids. Targets of friendly bids experience a greater volatility reduction than targets of hostile bids, and we argue that this is because there is a greater divergence of investor opinion on the likelihood of success of the bid in hostile takeovers, resulting in higher price volatility relative to friendly bids.

The volume–volatility models imply that price volatility and trading volume move together – that "it takes volume to move markets". In the next section we examine what happens to trading volumes during the bid period.

7.6 TRADING VOLUMES

Figures 7.2 to 7.5 depict trading volumes for the period 200 days before to 80 days after the takeover announcement. In order to calculate cross-sectional summary statistics, volume is calculated as the percentage of shares outstanding traded each day. Figure 7.2 is the average (Panel A) and median (Panel B) percentages traded for the full sample. The vertical axes for each plot have been trimmed because the volume "spike" on the day of announcement is several times larger than normal trading volumes. As seen in Panel A, in 'normal' pre-bid trading, these stocks trade on average about 0.5 of 1 percent of their total shares outstanding each day. After the dramatic spike in average trading volume on announcement day to 14.23 percent, the average volume drops to 5.36 percent on day +1, and it gradually falls back to 'normal' by about day +20. After this, however, trading levels settle down to a level that appears to be lower than pre-bid. Panel B shows that the median volume traded is considerably lower than the mean. The "normal" pre-bid median is approximately 0.25 of 1 percent. This increases to a spike of 9.2 percent on announcement day, and similarly to the pattern shown in the mean, median volumes appear to drop down to a lower figure after about day +20. It is clear from observing the plot of average volumes versus medians, volume is heavily right-skewed. The remaining volume data are therefore summarized by median plots only. Figure 7.3 presents the sample delineated by outcome, and Figure 7.4 divides the sample by consideration into cash and non-cash bids. Figure 7.5 separates the sample by management attitude to the bid – friendly (Panel A) and hostile (Panel B).

Panel A of Figure 7.3 shows a rather dramatic reduction in trading volume after about day +20 for targets of successful bids. This is consistent with

Panel A: Average

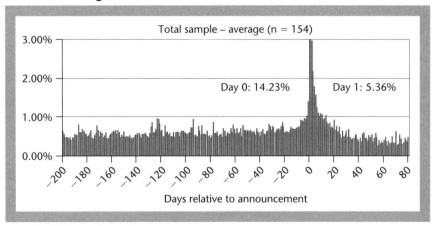

Panel B: Median

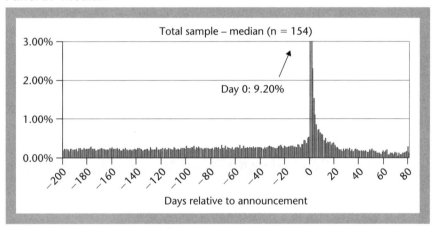

Figure 7.2 Proportion of stock trading each day, full sample
Sources: Thompson Financial Securities Database and Datastream.

our prediction that both volatility and volume for targets of successful bids should fall. Panel B shows that, for targets of failed bids, trading activity does not appear to diminish. This is consistent with our hypothesis regarding the trading volume of targets of ultimately unsuccessful bids, although it is difficult to make strong inferences because of the small sample size.

Figure 7.4, Panel A shows that volumes for targets of cash bids behave as predicted, showing a very dramatic reduction in trading levels after about day +20. For non-cash bids, however, volume appears to be higher

Panel A: Successful

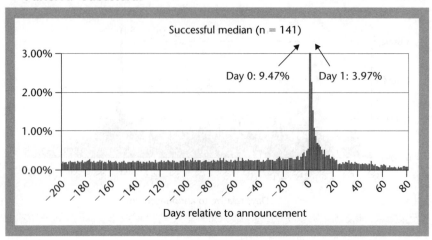

Panel B: Failed

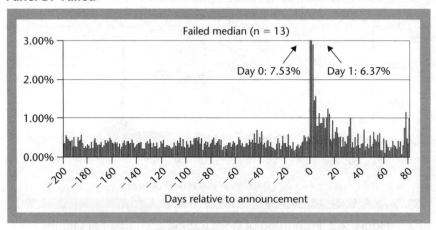

Figure 7.3 Proportion of stock trading each day, by outcome
Sources: Thompson Financial Securities Database and Datastream.

post-announcement. This result is surprising, and does not support our hypothesis that there should be no difference in post-announcement volume between the cash and non-cash sub-samples. One possible explanation is that some of the trading activity in the bidder's stock is transferred to the target's during the course of the takeover bid, as purchasing the target stock in a share-exchange bid would an alternative method of buying the bidder's stock.

Figure 7.5 shows that volumes in the friendly and hostile sub-samples behave in a similar way to that of the successful and failed sub-samples.

Panel A: Cash

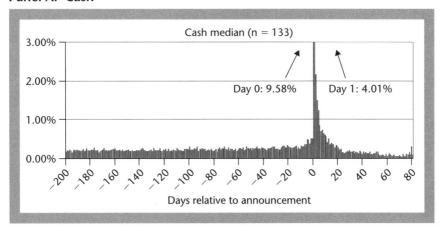

Panel B: Non-cash

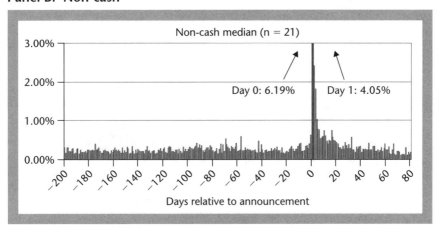

Figure 7.4 Proportion of stock trading each day, by consideration
Sources: Thompson Financial Securities Database and Datastream.

The friendly sub-sample (Panel A) shows a substantial reduction in trading volume after about day +20, while the graph for the hostile subsample shows that trading volume appears to settle at a higher level than pre-bid.

While we have found that there is a greater reduction in volatility in targets of US tender offers across all sub-samples when compared with Australian takeover targets, this reduction in volatility is not associated as strongly with falling volumes as was found by Hutson and Kearney (2001). Australia is a relatively thinly traded market, but this may also be explained by greater risk arbitrage activity in the USA.

Panel A: Friendly

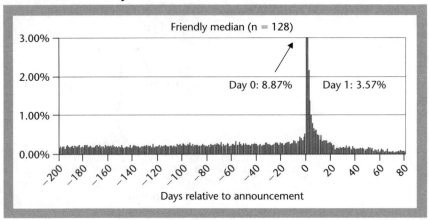

Panel B: Hostile

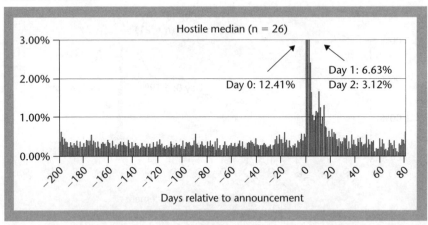

Figure 7.5 Proportion of stock trading each day, by management attitude
Sources: Thompson Financial Securities Database and Datastream.

7.7 CONCLUSION

The price volatility of stocks subject to takeover bids has received little academic attention. The literature is dominated by studies examining the level of prices around takeover announcements, which have found consistently that target tocks are subject to substantial revaluation, and that risk arbitrageurs earn significant abnormal returns. What explains these excess returns? It is certainly not an increase in risk. For a sample of Australian target stocks, Hutson and Kearney (2001) found a reduction in price volatility after the takeover announcement. Our results for a sample of 154 US tender offers confirm that this is not simply an artifact of thinly traded markets. Also consistent with Hutson and Kearney (2001), targets of tender offers experience a dramatic reduction in the effect of the market after a takeover announcement. In an examination of trading volume, we find that in successful, friendly and cash sub-samples, trading volume follows price volatility downward. However, for targets of failed, hostile and non-cash bids, volume either stays the same or increases after the takeover announcement.

Our findings have two important implications. First, event studies that examine the gains to target shareholders assume unchanged risk after the takeover announcement. Our results show that this assumption is not valid, and that target shareholders tend to earn even greater risk-adjusted abnormal returns than has previously been estimated. Further, our results show that shareholders of companies subject to share-exchange bids face a different level of risk from those subject to cash bids, which is different again from those subject to mixed bids. Future research on value creation in corporate takeovers should include not only the effect of time-varying risk on target excess returns, but also the differential effects caused by differences in bid consideration. Second, our results have implications for appropriate regulation of the market for corporate control. The regulation of acquisitions in many countries imposes excessive cost burdens on bidding firms, which may inhibit the efficient working of the market. These regulations are often justified on the grounds of "protecting" target shareholders. It is well recognized that target shareholders almost always earn abnormal returns, and our results show that this occurs alongside a strong tendency for their risk to decline. Regulatory reform should recognize that target shareholders are the major "winners" in control transactions, and focus more on improving the efficient operation of the market for corporate control.

NOTES

1. See Jensen and Ruback (1983) for a review of the US evidence.
2. For example, Dukes et al. (1992), Baker and Savasoglu (2001), Mitchell and Pulvino (2001), Jindra and Walkling (2004).
3. Brown and Raymond (1986) and Samuelson and Rosenthal (1986) applied their model to unrevised cash bids only. We extend the model to include non-cash bids.
4. This model is an imperfect representation of the target pricing process. It appears to work well when applied to targets of takeover bids that are ultimately successful, but it tends to overestimate the likelihood of success for targets of failed bids (see Zissu, 1989; Hutson, 2000). This is probably because the likelihood of a subsequent bid is an important additional determinant of the price of stocks subject to takeover bids that fail (see Bradley, 1980; Bradley et al., 1983; Fabozzi et al., 1988).
5. Samuelson and Rosenthal (1986), Brown and Raymond (1986) and Barone-Adesi et al. (1994), found that π_t is significantly lower than for targets of successful bids.

6. There are certain circumstances in which volatility could rise instead of fall; for example, in cases where the likelihood of success is high and the price volatility of the bidder is higher than that of the target.

REFERENCES

Baker, M. and Savasoglu, S. (2002) "Limited arbitrage in mergers and acquisitions" *Journal of Financial Economics*, 64: 91–115.

Barone-Adesi, G., Brown, K. and Harlow, W. (1994) "On the Use of Implied Volatilities in the Prediction of Successful Corporate Takeovers", *Advances in Futures and Options Research*, 7: 147–65.

Bhagat, S., Brickley, J. and Loewenstein, U. (1987) "The Pricing Effects of Interfirm Cash Tender Offers", *Journal of Finance*, 42(4): 965–86.

Bradley, M. (1980) "Interfirm Tender Offers and the Market for Corporate Control", *Journal of Business*, 53(4): 345–76.

Bradley, M., Desai, A. and Kim, E. H. (1983) "The Rationale Behind Interfirm Tender Offers", *Journal of Financial Economics*, 11: 183–206.

Brown, K. C. and Raymond, M. V. (1986) "Risk Arbitrage and the Prediction of Successful Corporate Takeovers", *Financial Management*, Autumn: 54–63.

Davidian, M. and Carroll, R. (1987) "Variance Function Estimation", *Journal of the American Statistical Association*, 82: 1079–91.

Dukes, W. P., Frolich, C. J. and Ma, C. K. (1992) "Risk Arbitrage in Tender Offers", *Journal of Portfolio Management*, Summer: 47–55.

Epps, T. W. and Epps, M. L. (1976) "The Stochastic Dependence of Security Price Changes and Transaction Volumes: Implications for the Mixture of Distributions Hypothsesis", *Econometrica*, 44(2): 305–21.

Fabozzi, F. J., Ferri, M. G., Fabozzi, T. D. and Tucker, J. (1988) "A Note on Unsuccessful Tender Offers and Stockholder Returns", *Journal of Finance*, 43(5): 1275–83.

Harris, M. and Raviv, A. (1993) "Differences of Opinion Make a Horse Race", *Review of Financial Studies*, 6(3): 473–506.

Holthausen, R. W. and Verrecchia, R. E. (1990) "The Effect of Informedness and Consensus on Price and Volume Behavior", *The Accounting Review*, 65(1): 191–208.

Hutson, E. (2000) "Takeover Targets and the Probability of Bid Success: Evidence from the Australian Market", *International Review of Financial Analysis*, 9(1): 45–65.

Hutson, E. and Kearney, C. (2001) "Volume and Volatility in Stocks Subject to Takeover Bids: Australian Evidence Using Daily Data", *Journal of Empirical Finance*, 8(3): 273–96.

Jang, H. J. and Ro, B. T. (1989) "Trading Volume Theories and Their Implications for Empirical Information Content Studies", *Contemporary Accounting Research*, 6(1), 242–62.

Jensen, M. and Ruback, R. S. (1983) "The Market for Corporate Control: The Scientific Evidence", *Journal of Financial Economics*, 11: 5–50.

Jindra, J. and Walkling, R. (2004) "Speculation Spreads and the Market Pricing of Proposed Acquisitions, *Journal of Corporate Finance*, 10: 495–526.

Larcker, D. F. and Lys, T. (1987) "An Empirical Analysis of the Incentives to Engage in Costly Information Acquisition", *Journal of Financial Economics*, 18: 111–26.

Lee, C. M. C., Ready, M. J. and Seguin, P. J. (1994) "Volume, Volatility, and New York Stock Exchange Trading Halts", *Journal of Finance*, 49(1): 183–214.

Levy, H. and Yoder, J. A. (1993) "The Behaviour of Option Implied Standard Deviations Around Merger and Acquisition Announcements", *The Financial Review*, 29(2): 261–72.

McAleer, M. and McKenzie, C. R. (1991) "When Are Two Step Estimators Efficient?", *Econometric Reviews*, 10: 235–52.

Mitchell, M. and Pulvino, T. (2001) "Characteristics of Risk and Return in Risk Arbitrage", *Journal of Finance*, 61(6): 2135–75.

Oxley, L. and McAleer, M. (1993) "Econometric Issues in Macroeconomic Models with Generated Regressors", *Journal of Economic Surveys*, 7: 1–40.

Pagan, A. (1984) "Econometric Issues in the Analysis of Regressions with Generated Regressors", *International Economic Review*, 25: 221–47.

Pagan, A. (1986) "Two Stage and Related Estimators and their Applications", *Review of Economic Studies*, 53: 517–38.

Samuelson, W. and Rosenthal, L. (1986) "Price Movements as Indicators of Tender Offer Success", *Journal of Finance*, 41(2): 481–99.

Schwert, G. W. (1989) "Why Does Stock Market Volatility Change Over Time?", *Journal of Finance*, 54: 1115–51.

Shalen, C. T. (1993) "Volume, Volatility, and the Dispersion of Beliefs", *The Review of Financial Studies*, 6(2): 405–34.

Smith, B. F., White, R., Robinson, M. and Nason, R. (1997) "Intraday Volatility and Trading Volume After Takeover Announcements", *Journal of Banking and Finance*, 21(3): 337–68.

Tauchen, G. E. and Pitts, M. (1983) "The Price Variability–Volume Relationship in Speculative Markets", *Econometrica*, 51(2): 485–505.

Walkling, R. A. (1985) "Predicting Tender Offer Success: A Logistic Analysis", *Journal of Financial and Quantitative Analysis*, 20(4): 461–78.

Walkling, R. A. and Long, M. S. (1986) "Strategic Issues in Cash Tender Offers: Predicting Bid Premiums, Probability of Success, and Target Management's Response", *Midland Corporate Finance Journal*, 4: 57–65.

Wang, J. (1993) "A Model of Intertemporal Asset Prices Under Asymmetric Information", *Review of Economic Studies*, 60: 249–82.

Wang, J. (1994) "A Model of Competitive Stock Trading Volume", *Journal of Political Economy*, 102(1): 127–68.

Zissu, A. (1989) "The Information Content of Post Tender Offer Movement in the Price of Target Shares", *Economics Letters*, 29: 253–5.

CHAPTER 8

Merger Arbitrage: An Introduction

Greg N. Gregoriou and François-Serge Lhabitant

8.1 INTRODUCTION

Merger arbitrage is not a new strategy. It was described explicitly in the third edition of Benjamin Graham's classic text, *Security Analysis*, and it has been an important contributor to the success of some of Wall Street's most well-known players. For example, Warren Buffett, "the Oracle of Omaha", practiced merger arbitrage extensively during the early part of his career – see, for example, the 1988 Berkshire Hathaway letter to investors. Later, the risk arbitrage desk at Goldman Sachs became legendary in the 1980s and brought in huge profits. And last, but not least, merger arbitrage also underlies many of the deals made by Ivan Boesky, the arbitrageur who made the term "insider trading" famous.

In spite of all the publicity it has received over the years, merger arbitrage has generated little academic attention. Most of the traditional merger literature seems to have focused exclusively on determining the impact of mergers on the prices of the underlying companies. For instance, accounting analyses have examined the accounting data such as, profit margins, or expense ratios for firms before and after acquisitions, to determine how things have changed after the merger. They have also compared the financial performance in post-merger acquisition versus the typical average in the industry. In contrast, time series analyses have usually relied on the assumption of efficient financial markets with the value of a company's stock already incorporates all the available information influencing its future profitability. These types of analyses compare stock prices to their "normal" behaviour to determine how much of their return is attributable to the merger (the acquirer's stock typically drops and the target's stock typically rises).

It is only recently that the financial literature has started addressing topics such as the profitability of merger arbitrage as a strategy. Moore, Lai and Oppenheimer (2006), "the success of takeovers ... [depend upon] the position held by arbitrageurs, the supply of arbitrage capital, and the overall role of arbitrageurs in the takeover process". However, very few papers have analyzed the fundamental ideas behind the strategy, which explains why merger arbitrage remains largely misunderstood by the general public. It has even become synonymous with speculation, extraordinary profits, greed, and spectacular company implosions. In this chapter, we aim at correcting this perception by revisiting merger arbitrage and explaining its sources of profit, as well as its risks.

8.2 MERGER ARBITRAGE: THE STRATEGY

Merger arbitrage as a strategy relies heavily on the price inefficiencies that arise when a merger or an acquisition is announced. To understand these inefficiencies and their associated strategies, we shall consider the example of a takeover and distinguish three distinct cases, based on the methods of payment used by the acquirer: (i) cash transactions; (ii) stock exchanged at a fixed rate; and (iii) stock exchanged at a variable rate.

8.2.1 Cash transactions

In a cash transaction, the acquirer offers to buy shares of the target company at a fixed price paid in cash. To convince shareholders to accept the offer, the bid price is normally set higher than the market price of the target company just prior to the announcement of the takeover offer. The difference between, the pre-merger price and the bid price is called the "merger premium".

Invariably, following the announcement and filing of the acquisition bid, the market price of the target firm's shares adjusts upward. However, even after this adjustment, shares of the target typically still trade at a discount to the expected final per share value of the target's shares upon successful completion of the deal. This discrepancy, which is often referred to as "money left on the table", is called the *arbitrage spread*.

In theory, the arbitrage spread can easily be captured by purchasing the target company's shares immediately after the announcement, and holding them until the merger is complete. However, this assumes implicitly that the bid will be successful at the bid price, and that all the shares of the arbitrageurs will be tendered and accepted. In reality, this implies taking several risks. For example, the bid may fail as a result of a shareholder vote or a regulatory problem (for example, General Electric's (GE) failed bid for Honeywell, a case we shall discuss in more detail later). In such a case, the target company's stock will typically fall back to, or even below, its pre-offer value, resulting in large losses for the arbitrageurs.[1] In addition, arbitrageurs also need to be prepared for their funds to be tied up for months while the transaction is completed. The longer the acquisition process and the higher the interest rate, the higher the carrying costs of the funds involved, and the lower the profitability of the trade.

The outcome of a merger arbitrage deal can therefore be seen as a binary situation. If the merger closes successfully, the arbitrageur will incur a profit based on the net spread, but if it fails, the arbitrageur will suffer a loss, which is generally substantially more than the potential profits had the merger been successful. Arbitrageurs must gauge carefully all the possible pros and cons of a deal, with probability of success being perhaps the element that is the most crucial, and the most difficult to assess (see Table 8.1).

Arbitrageurs typically infer the market-implied probability of completion for the deal, and compare it to their own estimated probability. For example, assume an arbitrageur has estimated that a deal will lead to a profit of \$G or a loss of \$L. We can obtain the market-implied probability π that would make the expected return equal to zero:[2]

$$\pi \times (\$G) + (1 - \pi) \times (\$L) = 0$$

Thus:

$$\pi = -\frac{\$L}{\$G - \$L}$$

The absolute dollar gain \$G and loss \$L are keys to identifying correctly individual arbitrage risks, and to estimating the market-implied probability. \$G is easily obtained from the arbitrage spread, but the estimation of \$L is more subjective and involves a mix of fundamental and technical estimates, as well as the target and/or acquirer's stock price before the announcement or transaction rumors. Constant monitoring and reassessment of the deal parameters is also essential.

From this perspective, in a sense, merger arbitrage becomes a bet on the distribution of future share prices. Merger arbitrageurs think that the market-"implied" distribution, which is used for calculating the *current* market price, is biased or incorrect. They think they can forecast this distribution better than the market, because of their experience, analysis, access to information, knowledge of the company, shareholders, regulators and so on.

8.2.2 Cash transaction example

Let us now consider a real-life cash transaction to illustrate the process. We have selected the case of First Data Corp. versus Paymentech Inc., two

Table 8.1 Factors to consider when assessing a merger arbitrage investment opportunity

Company considerations	Transaction considerations
• Target and acquirer business performance	• Initial shareholder reaction
• Valuation, corporate finance	• Deal type: friendly versus hostile
• Market conditions	• Negotiation: auction versus exclusive
• Industry dynamics, competition	• Consideration: all-stock, all-cash, cash and stock, cash or stock
• Relative size of target versus acquirer	• Financing issues
• Acquirer ownership in target	• Antitrust: regulatory issues (HSR)
• Institutional ownership in target	• Lawsuits: shareholders, customers, competitors, governments
• Corporate governance structures	• Walk-away provisions: MAC, performance and market tests, termination dates, break-up fees
	• Additional requirements to close: shareholder votes, asset sales
	• Takeover defenses available
	• Management support
	• Experience of financial adviser(s)
	• Tax approval
Return considerations	**Trading considerations**
• Net spread (and annualized return)	• Liquidity of target and acquirer
• Expected timing until close	• Stock loan availability to short acquirer shares
• Premium offered and target and acquirer break prices if deal fails	• Collar average pricing period
• Dividends received/paid until close	• Pro-rata election period
• Presence of other potential bidders	• Alternative investment opportunities: swaps, options, convertibles
• Value of options embedded in collar	
• Uncertain final pro-rata factor	
• Implied probability of completion	
• Risk/return multiple	
• Comparable precedent transactions (industry, size, type, consideration)	

companies involved in the business of e-commerce payment solutions. On 22 March 1999, First Data announced an offer to purchase all publicly-held shares of Paymentech at a price of US$25.50 for each share. Although not yet approved by regulators, the transaction was rapidly considered to be carrying a relatively low risk, because Banc One was at the same time the major shareholder of Paymentech (52.5 percent) and the merchant processor for First Data.

Figure 8.1 plots Paymentech's share price during the year 1999. On March 22, the shares closed at US$24; on March 23, they closed at US$23.25. Arbitrageurs would have been able to buy shares at US$24 just after the deal announcement, at a discount to the bid price. And indeed, as Figure 8.1 shows, there was a peak in trading activity between March 22, the day the deal was announced, and March 24.

The Department of Justice approved the transaction on May 13, and Paymentech's share price immediately headed toward US$25.50. The deal closed on July 27, with First Data acquiring all of Paymentech's publicly-traded shares, and Paymentech becoming a limited liability company. Paymentech then merged with Banc One Payment Services, First Data's merchant bank alliance with Banc One Corp. The result for arbitrageurs who bought shares at US$24 and then sold them at US$25.50 was a 6.25 percent gain over four months.

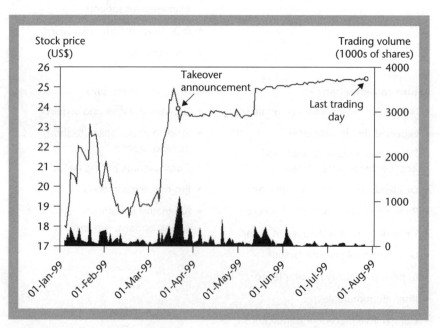

Figure 8.1 Movement of Paymentech share price (top) and trading volume (bottom), January–August 1999

8.2.3 Stock transactions with fixed exchange rates

Let us now consider the case of a plain vanilla stock transaction – that is, the acquirer offers a quantity q_A of its common shares against the delivery of a quantity q_T of the target company's common shares. The quantities q_A and q_T are typically fixed, and will be revealed publicly when the merger offer is announced. For simplicity, we fix $q_T = 1$ for the remainder of this chapter.

After the bid announcement, the target company's stock will, on average, typically trade at a discount to the offered price – that is, the value of q_A shares of the acquiring company. This discount is called the arbitrage spread. Note that this spread now depends on *two* variable prices.

Once again, it appears, we can easily capture this spread by going long on one share of the target company (which sells at a discount with respect to the offered value), and shorting q_A shares of the acquiring company (which is expected to decrease in value). This is designed to isolate the expected spread, while removing other sources of variability, notably market risk. Note that since this is a long/short position, the arbitrageur no longer cares about the *absolute* price variations of the target and bidder shares – s/he is only interested in their *relative* evolution, and more specifically in their convergence.

Ignoring transaction costs, the arbitrageur's P&L can then be split into three components:

- *The arbitrage spread*, which is expected to shrink to zero if the offer is successful. The merger arbitrageur is in essence short this spread and will profit if it narrows.

- The dividend spread, i.e., the difference between the dividends cashed in by the arbitrageur on the long investment in the target's stock, minus the dividends that the arbitrageur needs to pay back to the stock lender on q_A acquirer's stock.

- The interest paid by the arbitrageur's broker on the cash proceeds from the short sale. Most of the time, this interest rate should be relatively close to the Libor rate.

In a stock-for-stock offer, the actions of merger arbitrageurs are not neutral for the share prices of the underlying companies. Selling the acquiring company's stock short can lead to a significant decline in the share price, particularly for smaller companies. For an acquiring company, research has found that about half the average decline is attributable to this phenomenon. It represents typically 1–2 percent on the day of announcement – see Mitchell *et al.* (2004).

8.2.4 Example of a successful stock-for-stock transaction

The acquisition of Visio Corp. by Microsoft in 1999 provides an illuminating example of a successful stock-for-stock transaction. Microsoft Corp. announced it would acquire Visio, a supplier of technical drawing software, on September 15, 1999. Microsoft's terms were 0.45 shares of Microsoft for every Visio share. Any remaining fractional shares would be paid in cash, based on a formula incorporating Microsoft's average closing price for the twenty trading days ending on December 31, 1999. The acquisition required approval by both regulators and Visio shareholders.

Figure 8.2 plots the Visio share price from September 1999 to January 2000. On September 15, Visio closed at US$39.875, and Microsoft closed at US$92.625. According to the terms of the merger, a Visio share would be worth US$41.681, or a US$1.806 merger spread. Of course, this spread would have been irrelevant to Visio shareholders; to them, the price of Microsoft after the deal closed would have been far more important. But to a merger arbitrageur, capturing that spread while hedging the Microsoft risk away would have been vital. Thus a merger arbitrageur would have sold short 0.45 Microsoft shares for any Visio share s/he purchased. And his/her focus would have been on the narrowing or widening of the spread, the price difference between his/her long and short positions.

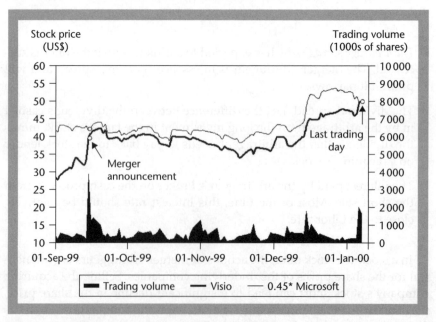

Figure 8.2 Movement of the share prices of Microsoft (top line) and Visio (middle line), and Visio trading volume (bottom), September 1999–January 2000

The deal, valued at US$1.5 billion, closed on January 10, 2000. The trading volume was again higher than usual around the announcement date and just before the exchange of securities.

8.2.5 More complex transactions

Collar offers, either fixed or floating, are more complex transactions than cash or stock-for-stock offers. In a collar offer, the target company's shareholders are offered a certain number of shares depending on the range of the acquirer's stock price over a specific time period (usually around the merger closing date). These shares may be fixed or floating.

In a fixed collar offer ("fixed exchange collar"), target shareholders receive a fixed number of shares of the bidder for each share of the target company as long as the bidder's stock price stays within a predefined range. If the bidder's stock price falls below the lower bound of the range, then a fixed dollar price is offered for each share of the target company (which is translated in a larger number of the bidder shares). Similarly, if the bidder's stock price rises above the higher bound of the range, then a fixed dollar price is also offered for each share of the target company (which is translated in a smaller number of the bidder shares). Alternatively, in some cases, the bidder and target shareholders may also have the option to cancel or renegotiate the deal if the bidder's stock price exists from the range. As explained by Fuller (2003). "a *fixed collar* is a useful way to lessen the chance that the bidder will overpay, or that the target will be underpaid".

As an illustration, consider the banking merger between First Union and BancFlorida Financial (Figure 8.3). The terms of the deal were the following:

BancFlorida's shareholders received 0.669 shares of First Union common stock for each share of BancFlorida common stock if First Union's common stock price was between $41.875 and $44.875 per share.[3] If First Union's common stock price went below $41.875, BancFlorida's shareholders would receive $28 or First Union common stock for each share of BancFlorida common stock. If First Union's common stock price was above $44.875, BancFlorida shareholders would receive $30 of First Union common stock for each share of BancFlorida common stock. (PR Newswire, Jan 17 1994 Issue)

A floating collar offer is a useful way to lessen the chance that the bidder will give away too large a percentage of ownership in the merged firm, or that the target will receive too small a percentage. In a *floating collar* offer, target shareholders receive a fixed price for each share of the target company as long as the bidder's stock price stays within some predefined range. If the bidder's stock price falls below the lower bound of the range, then a fixed number of shares of the bidder is offered for each share of the target company (which results in a lower payoff than with the fixed price).

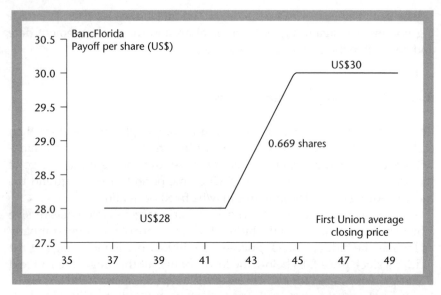

Figure 8.3 Fixed collar offer of First Union and BancFlorida

Similarly, if the bidder's stock price rises above the higher bound of the range, then another fixed number of shares of the bidder is also offered for each share of the target company (which results in a higher payoff than with the fixed price). Alternatively, in some cases, the bidder and target shareholders may also have the option to cancel or renegotiate the deal if the bidder's stock price exists from the range.

As an illustration, consider the banking merger between BioShield Technologies Inc. and AHT Corp. (Figure 8.4). The terms of the deal were the following:

- If the average closing trading price of BioShield was between US$6.00 and US$18.00 per share, AHT shareholders would receive US$1.75 worth of BioShield common stock.
- If BioShield was at US$6.00 or less, AHT shareholders would receive 0.29167 (=US$1.75/6) BioShield shares for each AHT share. If the price was at US$18.00 or above, they would receive 0.09722 (US$1.75/18) BioShield shares.

The main difference between the arbitrage on a stock-for-stock deal and on a collar merger is that the exchange ratio fluctuates continuously during a collar merger. The arbitrageur must therefore be prepared to adjust his/her long and short positions continuously, not only to adhere to the offer terms, but also to ensure that the correct hedge is in place. The adjustments are similar to those made when delta-hedging an option (see Figures 8.3 and 8.4).

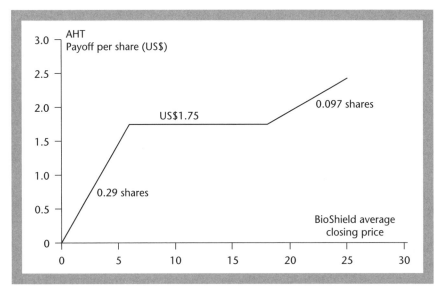

Figure 8.4 Floating collar offer of BioShield Technologies Inc. and AHT Corp.

Indeed, a collar can be seen as a portfolio of options on the bidding firm, whose time to maturity is expected to be equal to the deal duration. To hedge correctly, arbitrageurs must purchase the target share of stock and sell short Δ shares of the bidding firm (where Δ is the delta of the equivalent portfolio of options).

On the one hand, a fixed collar can be seen as a bullish spread, a long position in calls with a lower strike price, and a short position in calls with a higher strike price as can be seen in our first example. Consider that a share of BancFlorida was analogous to 0.669 calls on First Union with a strike price of US$41.875, and a short position of 0.669 calls with a strike price of US$44.875. The delta of the combined option portfolio was simply 0.669 times the delta of one call option, minus 0.669 times the delta of the put option. Similarly, a floating collar can be seen as a combination of a long position in call options and a short position in put options on the bidding firm.

On the other hand, as in our second example, a share of AHT Corp. was similar to 0.09722 shares of call options on BioShield Technologies Inc. with a strike price of US$18.00, and a short position of 0.29167 shares of puts with a strike price of US$6.00. The delta of the combined option portfolio was simply 0.09722 times the delta of the call option, minus 0.29167 times the delta of the put option.

Collar offers can have even more complexity, especially those where one of the parties retains the right to cancel. If one follows Fuller's (2003) suggestion and model, a simple merger offer as an exchange option – the option to exchange some of the bidder's stock for some of the target's stock – then collar offers can be analyzed and valued as barrier exchange options. In such a case, the barrier allows for cancellation if the bidder's stock price exits from a certain price range.

Theoretically, there is no problem as long as the bidder's stock price does not exceed the boundaries of the collar. If it does, and the deal needs to be cancelled or renegotiated, the spread may widen. In reality, however, the liquidity and the bid–ask spreads of the underlying securities must be monitored carefully and continuously. They can dramatically affect the readjustment of the hedge and therefore the final profitability of the arbitrage.

8.3 KEY SOURCES OF MERGER ARBITRAGE RISK

As mentioned above, there are two main types of risk inherent in merger arbitrage: *transaction risk* – the risk that the transaction will not proceed; and *calendar risk* – the risk that the length of time to completion will result in some of the merger terms becoming impractical for one or more of the parties. Ironically, the size of potential profits is not one of the key risks in merger arbitrage. Indeed, most arbitrageurs take their positions *after* the announcement of the merger terms, so the initial spread is known and they can ensure it corresponds to their maximum gain.

8.3.1 Transaction risk

The likelihood that any announced merger will be completed is usually high, but there are many factors that could affect the outcome. Empirically, deal success hinges on elements such as:

- *Acquirer attitude*. A hostile takeover attempt can lead to the use of takeover defense mechanisms that can dramatically reduce the chances of a successful bid. Research has found that friendly offers are twenty times more likely to succeed than hostile ones (see, for example, Branch and Yang, 2003).
- *Deal type*. Branch and Yang (2003) have also found that flexible stock-for-stock exchanges (93 percent) have slightly higher success rates; and cash and fixed stock-for-stock exchanges have slightly lower success rates (87 percent and 88 percent, respectively).
- *Takeover premium*. A higher premium usually improves the chances that the deal will gain shareholder acceptance.
- *Target company ownership structure*. If the target company's shareholders consist of merger arbitrageurs, the deal is more likely to go through, because they will likely vote in support of it to protect their own interests.[4]

- *Bidder influence* (see Betton and Eckbo, 2000).
- *Target management attitude* (see Schwert, 2000).
- The amount of *lock-up options* granted by the target managers (see Burch, 2001).
- *The number of arbitrageurs involved.* Note again that arbitrageurs, who all have long positions in the target company, will tend to vote for mergers to protect their own interests.[5]
- *Anti-trust issues.* In the USA, the Department of Justice may have issued preliminary approval prior to the announcement of the merger. However, Federal Trade Commission (FTC) approval is still required. In some cases, the FTC may impose conditions that make the merger less desirable or not feasible, such as the divestment of key holdings.
- *The economy.* The state of the economy matters: a robust economy tends to favor merger activity; a deteriorating economy is usually a discouraging factor.

8.3.2 Calendar risk

Calendar risk is the uncertainty about how much time will elapse between the official announcement of a deal to its conclusion (presuming that the deal occurs). This type of risk is not easily predictable. But research has found that deals with large premiums at the date of announcement tend to have longer time periods between announcement and consummation (see, for example, Mitchell and Pulvino, 2001). Additionally, high premiums are often found in deals with more issues to resolve, which tends to raise the level of uncertainty.

Market events sometimes also play a part in the delay or cancellation of pending mergers. For example, the September 2001 terrorist attacks caused delays or cancellations on deals between AT&T Broadband (targeted by Comcast), Brooks Brothers (a unit of Marks & Spencer), Hughes Electronics (owned by General Motors), Compaq Computer (targeted by Hewlett Packard), Tempus Group (targeted by Havas Advertising) and Telemundo Communications Group, among others. Merger arbitrageurs may attempt to spread their risk by holding diversified portfolios and using several arbitrage situations at the same time, preferably in different economic sectors.

8.3.3 Example of a failed arbitrage trade

As discussed by Lhabitant (2007), the case of General Electric and Honeywell provides a particularly illuminating example of a failed arbitrage. In October

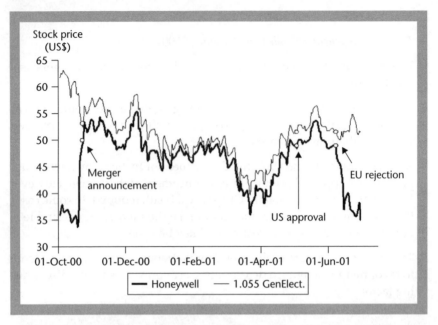

Figure 8.5 Evolution of the arbitrage spread between Honeywell and General Electric

2000, General Electric (GE) announced its intention to buy Honeywell International in a stock-for-stock transaction. The deal, valued at US$45 billion, immediately appeared on the radar screens of merger arbitrageurs.

General Electric offered 1.055 shares of their own stock for each share of Honeywell, whose share price had dropped dramatically in the year since they had been purchased by Allied Signal (who assumed the Honeywell name). In addition, United Technologies had been in competing discussions with GE to acquire Honeywell until just a few days earlier (GE's offer beat United Technologies's offer by 14.6 percent, based on pre-announcement closing prices).

Consider the two companies' stock performance (see Figure 8.5): Honeywell was trading at US$35–37 a share in early October, on a daily volume of 3 to 4 million shares (see Figure 8.6). Two days before the announcement, on October 20, the share price jumped to US$46 on a daily volume of 22 million shares. On October 23, it reached US$49.9375 with a daily volume of 39.3 million shares. GE was trading at US$58–59 at the beginning of October, with a daily volume of 9 to 10 million shares (see Figure 8.7). On October 20, their share price dropped to US$52.25 on a daily volume of 14.6 million shares, and on October 23, it dropped to US$49.75, with a daily volume of 50.2 million shares.

The US Department of Justice carefully scrutinized the deal for monopoly concerns in the areas of jet engine, automation control and industrial sensor

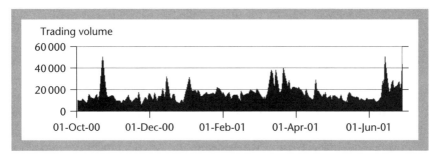

Figure 8.6 Trading volume of General Electric

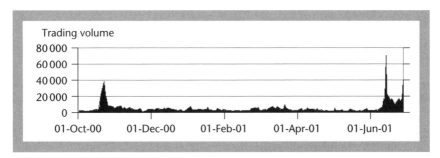

Figure 8.7 Trading volume of Honeywell

production. But on May 2, 2001, they approved the merger. On May 18, Honeywell peaked at US$53.25, and GE at US$52.99, an arbitrage spread of US$2.65 per share (with the 1.055 coefficient). Investors were short by 130 million GE shares, five times more than before the deal was announced. It was estimated that risk arbitrageurs held about US$1 billion of Honeywell shares.

There was still concern over regulatory approval, although arbitrageurs had initially thought the deal would sail through. But in early June 2001, reports surfaced of problems with the European Union (EU) review. On June 14, the EU's Competition Commissioner announced it would reject the proposed merger, despite GE's concession to divest US$2.2 billion in assets. The EU stated concerns over monopolization of the market for jet engines and aviation electronics.

The GE/Honeywell debacle marked the first time the EU had rejected a merger deal that the US had already tentatively approved. Honeywell's stock went from US$42.26 to US$37.10, with a record volume of 71 million shares, while GE gained US$1 at US$48.86, also with a record volume of 50 million shares.

The deal was not officially terminated until October 2, but the damage had been done and the firms reverted to trading on their own fundamental values. Everyone was hurt by the deal's collapse. Given the size of the companies involved, most arbitrageurs had included the trade in their portfolios. The collapse led to a climate of risk aversion, and diminished merger arbitrage activity for several months.

But it also caused merger spreads to become more sensitive to rumours, particularly regarding regulatory issues, and this has had a profound effect on how merger arbitrageurs conduct business. Since GE/Honeywell, several other high-profile deals have foundered during the approval process, notably Airtours/First Choice, Interbrew/Bass, and the Tesco/Sainsbury/Asda bids for Safeway. All of these failed deals went through a Phase I examination and a lengthy Phase II investigation, as well as several appeals, which has highlighted the importance of fully assessing any and all antitrust implications of deals involving competing companies.

8.4 HISTORICAL PERFORMANCE

From a historical perspective, merger arbitrage is a relatively low-risk hedge fund strategy with steady returns. To illustrate, consider the CS/Tremont Event-Driven/Risk Arbitrage Index. From January 1994 to August 2006, this index has generated an annualized return after fees of 7.67 percent, with 4.21 percent volatility. In comparison, over the same period, the S&P 500 delivered an average return of 8.46 percent p.a. with a volatility of 15.60 percent, and the Lehman Global Aggregate Bond Index delivered an average return of 6.39 percent p.a. with a volatility of 3.17 percent (see Figure 8.8).

The success of merger arbitrage depends on (i) the availability of a sufficient volume of mergers and takeovers in the market to permit the construction of a diversified merger arbitrage portfolio; and (ii) a sufficient spread on each successful transaction to compensate for failing transactions. Thus it is not unusual that the best years of merger arbitrage were during 1994–2000, the boom years for the media, telecom and technology sectors. The only exception was 1998, when the strategy was affected by the LTCM debacle.[6]

The years 2001 and 2002 saw relatively poor performance, primarily caused by the slump in merger activity and the tightness of merger spreads. The summer of 2002 was also affected by the loss of confidence following the rash of corporate implosions at Enron, WorldCom, Adelphia and Global Crossing, and the numerous earnings restatements.

Fortunately, the situation started improving again in 2003. Valuation multiples rose high enough to prod hesitant sellers into action, merger volume gradually increased, the lending community provided substantial liquidity at relatively low cost, and private equity firms became increasingly aggressive in leveraged buyout operations. As well as in the USA, this phenomenon extended to Europe and Asia,[7] and a large number of merger arbitrage

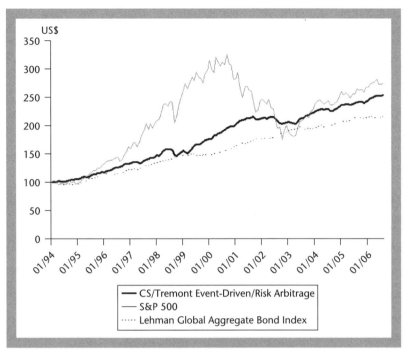

Figure 8.8 Historical performance of US$100 invested in January 1994 in the CS/Tremont Merger Arbitrage Index

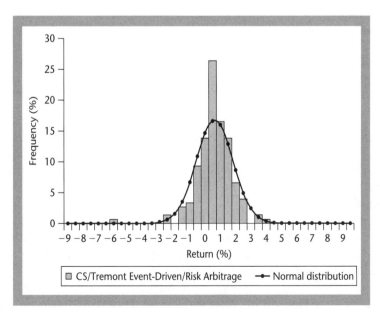

Figure 8.9 Return distribution of the CS/Tremont Merger Arbitrage Index

Table 8.2 Key statistics of the CS/Tremont Merger Arbitrage Index compared with those of the S&P 500 and the Lehman Global Aggregate Bond Index

	CS/Tremont Event-Driven/Risk Arbitrage	S&P 500	Lehman Global Aggregate Bond index
Return (% p.a.)	7.67	8.46	6.39
Volatility (% p.a.)	4.21	15.60	3.17
Skewness	−1.26	−0.59	−0.31
Kurtosis	6.80	0.75	0.53
Normally distributed?	No	No	Yes
Correlation with strategy		0.45	−0.04
Positive month frequency (%)	80	63	73
Best month performance (%)	3.81	9.67	3.49
Average positive month performance (%)	1.03	3.27	0.95
Upside participation (%)		72	150
Negative month frequency (%)	20	37	27
Worst month performance (%)	−6.15	−14.58	−2.06
Average negative month performance (%)	−1.02	−3.52	−0.64
Downside participation (%)		−162	−289
Maximum drawdown (%)	−7.60	−46.28	−5.43
Value at risk (one-month: 99%)	−2.69	−10.10	−1.89

funds expanded internationally. However, caution should accompany this return to optimism. Although the volume of mergers is rising, the average level of premiums paid is still relatively low historically, while the number of arbitrageurs keeps increasing. This translates into more competition for less profit.

The returns of the CS/Tremont Event-Driven/Risk Arbitrage Index are not normally distributed (see Figure 8.9), primarily because of extremely high excess kurtosis (6.8). This is essentially a result of the losses experienced in August 1998 (−6.15%) (see Table 8.2).

The drawdowns of the strategy are limited, but they coincide with equity drawdowns (see Figure 8.10). Note that the number of deals is closely linked to equity market performance and more generally to economic growth. Indeed, merger arbitrage returns generally lag corporate activity by one

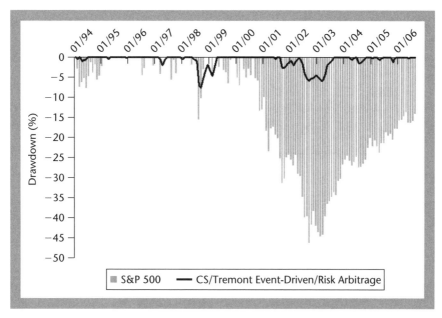

Figure 8.10 Maximum draw downs of the CS/Tremont Merger Arbitrage Index compared to those of the S&P 500 index

quarter, primarily because the average arbitrage deal takes so long to complete (100 days on average). Falling equity markets or an uncertain economic outlook can therefore throw a large number of transactions into jeopardy, particularly those linked to a stock merger (where the bidder offers to pay with shares).

This asymmetric behaviour of the merger arbitrage index between periods of falling and rising equity markets suggest the absence of a linear relationship between the strategy and standard market indices usually used as benchmarks (see Figure 8.11). Rather, merger arbitrage funds may exhibit an option-like pattern. Based on a sample of 4,750 US merger/acquisition events, Mitchell and Pulvino (2001) found that merger arbitrage strategies exhibit a similar pay-off to an uncovered call–put option on the equity market index. This can be explained intuitively as follows. When equity markets are rising, the merger deal flow is abundant, most mergers will be successful, and this therefore results in positive returns for merger arbitrageurs. However, their maximum profit is capped as they cannot capture more than the arbitrage spread. By contrast, in bearish markets, acquiring firms bid more carefully and are reluctant to make large bids that would significantly affect their balance sheets, the merger deal flow dries up, spreads are compressed and most mergers are cancelled or take longer than expected to be completed. This usually corresponds to difficult times for merger arbitrageurs. As a result, the strategy turns out to be highly cyclical,

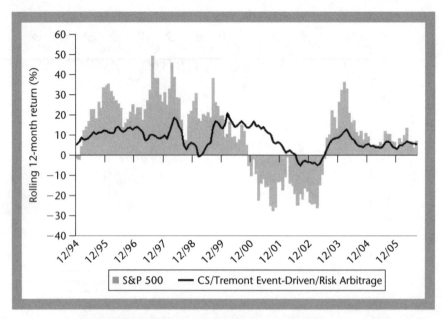

Figure 8.11 Rolling 12-month returns of the CS/Tremont Merger Arbitrage Index compared to those of the S&P 500 index

with positive limited profits in booming markets and almost unlimited losses during bearish markets. But this is another debate.

8.5 CONCLUSION

Over the recent years, merger arbitrage has reappeared as the logical side-effect of the record number of M&A deals. The strategy has changed very little since its early days – merger arbitrageurs are still essentially taking bets that an announced merger will be completed. In making such bets, arbitrageurs purchase the stocks of companies that are going to be acquired by another corporation, but are trading in the market at a price that is lower than the deal price. When a deal closes, arbitrageurs have netted a profit on the difference between the price at which they bought the stock and the price that is paid for that stock by the acquiring company.

As illustrated in this chapter, the strategy delivers attractive returns, but also conveys some risks. When a deal is announced, arbitrageurs therefore need to assess the potential benefits (the spread between the deal value and the current market price) and the potential risks (the non-consummation of the deal and how far the target stock will fall in such an event; and how long the deal will take and what happens if there are snags that stretch out the closing of the deal). In sum, arbitrage investing involves no magic, but a rather disciplined, research-intensive methodology in the purchase of announced mergers and acquisitions. Rigorous analysis and wise judgement comprise the science and art of successful merger arbitrage investing. This will be important to remember in the future, as there seem to be more and more players and all of them are competing for the same dollars.

NOTES

1. The bid price may also be revised upward or downward, leading to greater returns or to lower (or even negative) returns.
2. For the sake of simplicity, we ignore the time value of money in our calculations. In reality, the expected return should be positive.
3. To avoid market manipulation, we calculate First Union's common stock price based on the average closing price for the ten trading days prior to the effective acquisition date.
4. The instinctive clarification for the success of merger arbitrageurs is that they have a better understanding and possess superior information than the market regarding the likelihood of the deal is completed. Nevertheless, numerous theories today propose that arbitrageurs can achieve a major and important impact on the takeover process, in spite of their ability or inability to predict the outcome of the takeover. For instance, Cornelli and Li (2001) studied the role of arbitrageurs in takeovers and suggested that their information gain occurs from their own position rather than from their aptitude to predict outcomes.
5. This results in an asymmetry of information in favor of some arbitrageurs, if they know the exact number of shares they control. This also explains why, after a tender offer, the trading volume usually increases dramatically, in large part because of risk arbitrageurs accumulating shares.
6. Although most market participants were unaware of it, LTCM was running a large merger arbitrage book and was forced to liquidate it in a hurry, to reduce its exposure and to raise cash. All merger arbitrage funds plunged. Moreover, the subsequent debacle in the financial markets prompted the cancellation of a large number of pending mergers.
7. According to Thomson Financial, US mergers totaled more than $1.8 trillion in 2005 versus $1.4 trillion for European mergers, $446 billion for Asia and $64 billion for the rest of the world.

REFERENCES

Berkshire Hathaway (1988) *Annual Report to Investors*, Omaha, Nebraska.
Betton S. and Eckbo, B. E. (2000) "Toeholds, Bid-jumps and Expected Payoffs in Takeovers", *Review of Financial Studies*, 13: 841–82.
Branch B. and Yang, T. (2003) "Predicting Successful Takeovers and Risk Arbitrage", *Quarterly Journal of Business and Economics*, 42: 3–18.
Burch, T. R. (2001) "Locking Out Rival Bidders: The Use of Lockup Options in Corporate Mergers", *Journal of Financial Economics*, 60: 103–41.
Cornelli F. and Li, D. (2001) "Risk Arbitrage in Takeovers", Working paper, The Wharton School, University of Pennsylvania.

Fuller K. (2003) "Why Some Firms Use Collar Offers in Mergers", *Financial Review*, 38: 127–50.

Graham, B. and Dodd, D. (1934) *Security Analysis* (New York: McGraw-Hill), reprinted 1996.

Lhabitant, F. S. (2007) *The Handbook of Hedge Funds* (Hoboken, NJ: John Wiley).

Mitchell, M. and Pulvino, T. (2001) "Characteristics of Risk in Risk Arbitrage", *Journal of Finance*, 56: 213–75.

Mitchell, M., Pulvino, T. and Stafford, E. (2004) "Price Pressure around Mergers", *Journal of Finance*, 59: 1–31.

Moore, K. M., Lai, G. C. and Oppenheimer, H. R. (2006) "The Behavior of Risk Arbitrageurs in Mergers and Acquisitions", *Journal of Alternative Investments*, 9: 19–27.

PR Newswire (January 17, 1994) "First Union and BancFlorida Announce Merger", United Business Media, New York, NY.

Schwert G. W. (2000) "Hostility in Takeovers: In the Eyes of the Beholder?", *Journal of Finance*, 55: 2599–640.

CHAPTER 9

The Impact of Cross-Border Mergers and Acquisitions on Financial Analysts' Forecasts: Evidence from the Canadian Stock Market[1]

Alain Coën, Aurélie Desfleurs and Claude Francoeur

9.1 INTRODUCTION

The main objective of this chapter is to analyze the performance of financial analysts before and after cross-border mergers and acquisitions. We propose to focus on the evolution of financial analysts' forecast (hereafter FAF) accuracy and FAF bias. We compare the pre-merger and post-merger forecast accuracy of consensus analysts' forecasts two years after the merger on the Canadian stock market for the 1990–2004 period.

From the early 1990s, and following the Asian crisis, the crash of the technology bubble, and numerous financial scandals marked by Enron's bankruptcy and Arthur Andersen's liquidation in 2002, financial analysts have been strongly criticized. As acknowledged in the financial literature, they tend to be overly optimistic and reluctant to forecast bad news: losses and earnings decreases. It is striking to note in the literature that FAF errors are smaller for profits and earnings increases. Thus, the real utility and the independence of financial analysts may be questioned. Nevertheless, the accuracy of earnings forecasts made by financial analysts is crucial. The precision and the quality of FAF tend to reduce information asymmetries, influence market expectations, share prices and firm's cost of capital, and may have implications for disclosure policy.

Numerous studies have been devoted to the analysis of FAF errors. According to studies on the US markets, forecast errors may be related to many determinants. Among the most documented determinants, we find that earnings type – profits versus losses; increases versus decreases (Dowen, 1996; Ciccone, 2005); the business activities of the firm (Dunn and Nathan, 1998); the economic situation (Chopra, 1998); the forecast horizon (Richardson *et al.*, 1999), the industrial sector (Brown, 1997); the competence of analysts (Mikhail *et al.*, 1999); or the distance (Malloy, 2005) – analysts located closer to a firm seem to be more accurate. From an international perspective, Chang *et al.* (2000) underline significant differences in the quality of FAF errors among countries. According to Chang *et al.* (2000), Ang and Ciccone (2001), Black and Carnes (2002) and Hope (2003), earnings forecast errors may be related to macroeconomic factors, legal and institutional environments, financing structure, and in particular, accounting systems (Hope, 2003). Hope (2003) shows that the level of disclosure, the quality of norms and their application are relevant in explaining the differences in FAF errors among countries.

Following the studies led by Haw *et al.* (1994) and Erwin and Perry (2000), among others (see also Canina and Sinha, 2002), we propose to extend the analysis of FAF determinants to mergers. Our main contribution is to focus on cross-border mergers and acquisitions, and their impact on the accuracy and quality of FAF on Canadian stock markets for the 1990–2004 period. It is well-known in the literature that mergers may complicate significantly the task of financial analysts, and thus should induce an increase of FAF errors. As pointed out by Haw *et al.* (1994), mergers should lead to an increase in the variability in earnings. Therefore, in accordance with previous studies, we can reasonably anticipate a deterioration of FAF errors after mergers and thus address the following question: how long does it take for financial analysts to reach their pre-merger level of accuracy? Canadian and US stock markets are known to be correlated strongly, compared to other markets in the world. We observe that US targets are predominant for Canadian bidders, and it may be interesting to shed light on the time required to reach the pre-merger level and compare it with other studies. Periods shorter than the three or four years for foreign acquisitions on a worldwide basis can be interpreted as a sign of financial integration. Moreover, we take into account the main motivations for foreign mergers and acquisitions, and attempt to measure their impact on FAF errors, along with the disturbances induced by mergers.

We present and justify our conceptual framework for testing our hypotheses concerning the performance of analysts for cross-border mergers and acquisitions on the Canadian stock markets for the 1990–2004 period in section 9.2. The data source and forecast errors measures are described in section 9.3. We describe the methodology and analyze the results in section 9.4. Section 9.5 summarizes our main results and presents concluding comments.

9.2 CONCEPTUAL FRAMEWORK

As underlined by Haw *et al.* (1994), mergers tend to complicate forecasting activity. This phenomenon is known to modify sharply the variations in earnings, and may lead to interpretation problems. Haw *et al.* show that changes in the earnings stream, in leverage and in disclosure are the main elements to explain the increase of uncertainty and opacity. For international and cross-border mergers, the level of difficulties faced by financial analysts to make recommendations should increase significantly. According to Heath and Tversky (1991) and studies in psychological economics, the unknown may be considered as riskier. As mentioned by Solnik (1996): "Any unknown is perceived as risky; foreign capital markets are perceived as very risky by investors who are not familiar with them." Therefore, following Haw *et al.* (1994), we can reasonably anticipate a deterioration of post-merger FAF errors for our sample of cross-border mergers and acquisitions on the Canadian stock markets. Thus, we test the following hypothesis:

> H1: *The financial analysts' forecast errors deteriorate after cross-border mergers and acquisitions on the Canadian stock markets.*

To compare and analyze FAF errors before and after cross-border mergers, we introduce a measure defined as the difference between FAF errors one year after mergers and FAF errors one year before mergers. We then focus on the main determinants able to explain this difference. It is well known that errors related to consensus earnings forecasts tend to decline with analyst coverage (Alford and Berger, 1999). Following, Haw *et al.* (1994), we anticipate an increase in the number of analysts for important and larger post-mergers firms, and propose to test the following hypothesis:

> H2: *The difference between FAF errors one year after mergers and FAF errors one year before mergers should be negatively related with the analyst following increase.*

Erwin and Perry (2000) show that it is important to distinguish focus-preserving foreign acquisitions from focus-decreasing ones. For a sample of foreign acquisitions made by US firms during the 1985 to 1997 period, Erwin and Perry demonstrate that FAF errors are higher for firms choosing acquisitions outside their core business segment than for firms opting for expansion within their core business. Thus, we test:

> H3: *The difference between FAF errors one year after cross-border mergers and FAF errors one year before cross-border mergers may be negatively related with focus preserving mergers and acquisitions (M&As).*

As mentioned earlier, and confirmed by recent evidence, Canadian and US stock markets are highly correlated. This stylized fact may be considered an indicator of financial integration. In this case, we may anticipate that FAF errors after a cross-border involving a US target should be smaller.

> H4: *The difference between FAF errors one year after cross-border mergers and FAF errors one year before cross-border mergers should be negatively related with US target firms.*

Cross-border mergers involve public and non-public targets, and information disclosure is less significant for non-public firms and frequently neglected by financial analysts. Therefore, FAF errors for cross-border mergers involving non-public targets should be high compared to public targets.

> H5: *The difference between FAF errors one year after cross-border mergers and FAF errors one year before cross-border mergers should be negatively related with the public target firm.*

9.3 MEASURES OF FINANCIAL ANALYSTS' FORECAST ERRORS AND DATA

9.3.1 Measures of FAF errors

To measure the accuracy of financial analysts, we study the absolute mean of forecast errors defined as difference between the actual earnings and the mean forecast earnings, divided by the actual earnings because deflating by stock price causes forecast properties to be influenced by market conditions:

$$|FERE| = \left|\frac{e_{j,t}}{RE_{j,t}}\right| = \left|\frac{F_{j,t} - RE_{j,t}}{RE_{j,t}}\right| \qquad (9.1)$$

where
$FERE_t$ = forecast error for firm j divided by earnings per share for fiscal year t,
$e_{j,t}$ = forecast error for firm j earnings per share for fiscal year t,
$F_{j,t}$ = consensus forecast (*Forecast EPS*) for firm j and fiscal year t,
$RE_{j,t}$ = reported earnings per share (*Reported EPS*) for firm j and fiscal year t.

The quality of analysts' forecasts is dependent on their accuracy, and on the existence of a bias. Therefore we also inspect the descriptive statistics of forecast errors with their sign:

$$FERE = \frac{e_{j,t}}{|RE_{j,t}|} = \frac{F_{j,t} - RE_{j,t}}{|RE_{j,t}|} \qquad (9.2)$$

If *FERE* is positive, we conclude that the analysts' forecast is above reported earnings and the analysts are over-optimistic. But, if *FERE* is negative, the analysts' forecast is below reported earnings and we can conclude that financial analysts are pessimistic. Finally, if forecasts are not biased, the average forecast error might not be statistically different from zero.

9.3.2 Data

Our initial data set of cross-border Canadian M&A is obtained from the Securities Data Corporation (SDC) Worldwide M&A database owned by Thomson Financial. We use consensus earnings forecast data provided by the International Institutional Brokers Estimate System (IBES) from January 1990 to December 2005.

Our initial sample includes cross-border M&As for which all the following criteria apply:

(i) Acquisitions were completed during the period January 1990 to December 2003;

(ii) Only deal values of over US$10 million are considered, to ensure that M&As have a true impact on the variables that we examine;

(iii) Acquiring firms' forecasts for the year before and the two years after the merger are available on the IBES database;

(iv) No major acquisitions were made by the acquirer within three years of the merger under study; and

(v) Acquiring firms are not banks or utilities because they regulate businesses and have unique disclosure.

The initial sample includes 198 cross-border M&As carried out by 177 firms, but only 86 M&As for which acquiring firms realize no other major acquisitions within three years of the transactions under study. Table 9.1 describes the distribution of our sample by year, foreign target firm's geographic area and bidder's sector.

Forecasts for acquiring firms considered in the sample are the mean analysts' consensus annual earnings per share forecasts as reported on IBES

Table 9.1 Distribution of cross-border mergers and acquisitions by year of announcement, bidder's sector and target's geographic area

M&A year of announcement	Number of M&As
1990	2
1991	2
1992	2
1993	1
1994	6
1995	6
1996	7
1997	4
1998	6
1999	3
2000	16
2001	7
2002	15
2003	9
Target's geographic area	
Africa/Middle East	1
Americas	66
Central Asia/Asia	5
Europe	14
Bidder's sector	
Basic industries	26
Capital goods	8
Consumer durables	9
Consumer non-durables	5
Consumer services	7
Energy	10
Health care	4
Technologies	15
Transportation	2

Sources: Securities Data Corporation (SDC) Worldwide M&A database, Thomson Financial.

summary tape. We use forecasts released in the last month of the fiscal year to compute forecast errors. When errors exceed 200 percent, they are truncated at 200 percent to minimize small denominator and extreme data problems. Truncation was required for nine of the eighty-six forecast errors one year after the merger, and for three of the eighty-six forecast errors two years after the merger.

As in Erwin and Perry (2000), to study the characteristics of firms involved in foreign merger activity, we develop a measure of focus using the primary SIC codes of the acquiring and target firms. If the primary SIC code of the target matches the acquiring firm at the three-digit level, the cross-border merger is considered to be focus preserving (FP). Those that do not match at the three-digit level are considered to be focus decreasing (FD). We report forty-two focus preserving M&A and forty-four focus decreasing M&A.

9.4 EMPIRICAL RESULTS AND ANALYSIS

Table 9.2 displays descriptive statistics for absolute forecast errors |*FEREs*| and forecast errors with their signs, *FEREs*, for the eighty-six cross-border mergers on the Canadian stock markets for the 1990–2004 period. We observe that all means are statistically significant at the 1 percent level, highlighting the difficulties faced by financial analysts to provide accurate forecasts. One year before (0.244), one year (0.445) and two years (0.350) after cross-border mergers, all absolute forecast errors are highly statistically significant (see Table 9.2, panel A). This stylized fact sheds light on the relatively poor accuracy of FAF for cross-border mergers. If we focus on the bias, we see that for the three years, the FAF errors are statistically significant and positive. This result is an illustration of the over-optimism shown by financial analysts in their recommendations. To test our first hypothesis related to the deterioration of financial analysts' forecast accuracy, we analyze the difference between the measures of absolute forecast errors one year after and one year before cross-border mergers (Table 9.2, panel D). The difference, with a measure of 0.200, is statistically positive and can be interpreted as the illustration of the deterioration of financial analysts' accuracy. This result is confirmed by the difference in the sign of forecast errors for the same period, which is statistically significant at the 5 percent level (0.129) in Table 9.2, panel B. The measure is positive and reveals the over-optimism of financial analysts. They tend to be more optimistic after the cross-border mergers than before. The number of financial analysts increases after cross-border mergers. The difference shows a statistically measure of 0.919, as reported in Table 9.2, panel C. If we concentrate on the difference between one year before and two years after cross-border mergers and acquisitions, the difference in absolute forecast errors is positive but not statistically significant. This result reveals that it would take only two years for financial

Table 9.2 Descriptive statistics of forecast errors and analyst following before and after eighty-six cross-border M&As

A: Absolute forecast errors by financial analysts before and after cross-border M&As

	Mean	Median	Standard error
Year before M&A	0.244**	0.088	0.368
One year after M&A	0.445**	0.114	0.626
Two years after M&A	0.350**	0.153	0.479

B: Signed forecast errors by financial analysts before and after cross-border M&As

	Mean	Median	Standard error
Year before M&A	0.104**	−0.003	0.430
One year after M&A	0.233**	0.049	0.733
Two years after M&A	0.270**	0.048	0.529

C: Number of analysts following the merged firm before and after cross-border M&As

	Mean	Median	Standard error
Year before M&A	8.849**	8.000	6.352
One year after M&A	9.767**	8.000	7.056
Two years after M&A	9.291**	9.000	6.904

D: Difference in forecast errors and analyst following before and after cross-border M&As

Difference	Absolute forecast errors	Signed forecast errors	Number of analysts
Mean difference between one year before and one year after M&A	0.200**	0.129*	0.919**
Median difference between one year before and one year after M&A	0.019	0.075	0.000
Mean difference between one year before and two years after M&A	0.106	0.166*	0.442
Median difference between one year before and two years after M&A	0.010	0.059	0.000

Notes: For all panels in this table, ** Significant at 1 percent level; * Significant at 5 percent level. For median we use the Wilcoxon test statistic.

analysts to reach their pre-merger level of accuracy. This point can be viewed as an illustration of the financial integration between Canadian bidders and their foreign targets. We observe that the difference related to the number of financial analysts is not statistically significant two years after a cross-border M&A. On the other hand, it would take a longer time to reduce over-optimism. As we can see from Table 9.2, panel D, the measure of bias (0.166) is still statistically significant two years after the event.

We highlight two main features of cross-border M&A on Canadian stock markets. First, in Table 9.3, we separate focus-preserving M&As from focus-decreasing M&As. The results confirm our main observations and conclusions (Table 9.3, panels A, B and C), however, there is a striking difference. If we study the differences, we observe that absolute forecast errors tend to be higher for focus-decreasing M&As (Table 9.3, panel D). This point is quite logical, if we consider that a diversification outside the core business can increase uncertainty and opacity, and thus earnings variability. Any unknown may be perceived as riskier, and so a known environment is as less risky and can be confirmed by the results obtained for signed forecast errors (Table 9.3, panel D). Financial analysts are statistically more confident for focus-preserving M&As and show a real over-optimism one year after cross-border mergers. As we can see from Table 9.3, panel D, the pre-merger level of accuracy seems to be attained two years after the event, confirming our previous results.

Table 9.3 Descriptive statistics of forecast errors and analyst following before and after cross-border M&As: 42 focus-decreasing (FD) targets versus 44 focus-preserving (FP) targets

A: Absolute forecast errors by financial analysts before and after cross-border M&As

	Mean		Median		Standard error	
	FD	FP	FD	FP	FD	FP
Year before M&A	0.212**	0.275**	0.079	0.094	0.343	0.392
One year after M&A	0.494**	0.397**	0.124	0.114	0.693	0.559
Two years after M&A	0.360**	0.341**	0.199	0.121	0.481	0.482

B: Signed forecast errors by financial analysts before and after cross-border M&As

	Mean		Median		Standard error	
	FD	FP	FD	FP	FD	FP
Year before M&A	0.121	0.087	0.011	−0.012	0.386	0.472
One year after M&A	0.140	0.322**	0.034	0.075	0.843	0.606
Two years after M&A	0.295**	0.245**	0.076	0.040	0.525	0.538

(Continued)

Table 9.3 Continued

C: Number of analysts following the merged firm before and after cross-border M&As

	Mean		Median		Standard error	
	FD	FP	FD	FP	FD	FP
Year before M&A	8.357**	9.318**	8.000	7.500	5.552	7.064
One year after M&A	8.810**	10.682**	8.000	8.000	5.478	8.248
Two years after M&A	8.238**	10.295**	8.000	9.000	5.418	8.007

D: Difference in forecast errors and analyst following before and after cross-border M&As

Difference	Absolute forecast errors		Signed forecast errors		Number of analysts	
	FD	FP	FD	FP	FD	FP
Mean difference between one year before and one year after M&A	0.282**	0.122	0.018	0.235**	0.452	1.364*
Median difference between one year before and one year after M&A	0.018	0.027	0.014	0.129	0.000	1.000
Mean difference between one year before and two years after M&A	0.148	0.066	0.174	0.158	−0.119	0.977
Median difference between one year before and two years after M&A	0.030	−0.004	0.062	0.049	0.000	0.000

Notes: For all panels – ** Significant at 1 percent level; * Significant at 5 percent level. For median we use Wilcoxon test statistic.

Second, we distinguish US targets from non-US targets in Table 9.4, and compare the relative importance of fifty-eight US targets to twenty-eight foreign targets. Our results confirm (Table 9.4, panels A, B, and C) that financial analysts are, paradoxically, more accurate for non-US M&As. The differences pre- and post-mergers for absolute and signed forecast errors are not statistically significant one year after cross-border M&As for non-US targets (Table 9.4, panel D). On the other hand, financial analysts make significant errors in their predictions even two years after the event for US targets, which is interpreted as an illustration of over-confidence and/or

Table 9.4 Descriptive statistics of forecasted errors before and after a cross-border M&A: twenty-eight non-US targets versus fifty-eight US targets

A: Absolute forecast errors by financial analysts before and after cross-border M&A

	Mean		Median		Standard error	
	Non-US	US	Non-US	US	Non-US	US
Year before M&A	0.296**	0.219**	0.098	0.086	0.433	0.334
One year after M&A	0.303**	0.513**	0.086	0.154	0.432	0.694
Two years after M&A	0.280**	0.384**	0.064	0.193	0.441	0.497

B: Signed forecast errors by financial analysts before and after cross-border M&A

	Mean		Median		Standard error	
	Non-US	US	Non-US	US	Non-US	US
Year Before M&A	0.119*	0.096*	0.024	−0.009	0.513	0.389
One Year After M&A	0.069*	0.312**	0.023	0.058	0.526	0.806
Two Years After M&A	0.240**	0.284**	0.034	0.077	0.464	0.561

C: Number of analysts following the merged firm before and after cross-border M&A

	Mean		Median		Standard error	
	Non-US	US	Non-US	US	Non-US	US
Year Before M&A	10.536**	8.034**	10.500	6.500	6.274	6.280
One Year After M&A	11.643**	8.862**	11.000	7.000	6.243	7.294
Two Years After M&A	10.857**	8.534**	11.000	7.000	5.324	7.474

D: Difference in forecast errors and analyst following before and after cross-border M&A

Difference	Absolute forecast errors		Signed forecast errors		Number of analysts	
	Non-US	US	Non-US	US	Non-US	US
Mean difference between one year before and one year after M&A	0.006	0.294**	−0.051	0.216**	1.107	0.828

(Continued)

Table 9.4 Continued

D: Difference in forecast errors and analyst following before and after cross-border M&A

Difference	Absolute forecast errors		Signed forecast errors		Number of analysts	
	Non-US	US	Non-US	US	Non-US	US
Median difference between one year before and one year after M&A	−0.004	0.049	−0.010	0.106	1.000	0.000
Mean difference between one year before and two years after M&A	−0.017	0.165*	0.121	0.188**	0.321	0.500
Median difference between one year before and two years after M&A	−0.009	0.043	0.043	0.069	−0.500	0.000

Notes: For all panels in the table, ** Significant at 1 percent level; * Significant at 5 percent level. For median we use Wilcoxon test statistic.

over-optimism. The bias reaches a level of 0.188 two years after the mergers and is significant at the 1 percent level. The US informational environment and its level of disclosure should reduce FAF error; however, the opposite is observed. Over-confidence and over-optimism may seriously disturb and corrupt the accuracy and quality of financial analysts' forecasts.

We run regressions to explain the difference in FAF errors one year after and one before cross-border M&As. The results are reported in Table 9.5 for the absolute forecast error (accuracy), and in Table 9.6 for the signed forecast error (bias). As expected, the increase of analyst coverage is negatively related with the difference and is statistically significant (−0.349 and −0.372 in Table 9.5). We can confirm our second hypothesis. The focus-preserving M&A dummy is negative and coherent with our third hypothesis for absolute forecast errors as well for signed forecast errors.

Our fourth hypothesis is rejected. FAF errors for US targets are statistically significant, a finding both paradoxical and unexpected. Nevertheless, as shown earlier in the analysis of descriptive statistics, these results are not surprising if we admit that financial analysts are less accurate for US targets and show evidence of over-optimism for this environment. The results obtained for the dummy status confirms our expectations but are not statistically significant. Coefficients signs are negative and prove that it is easier to forecast earnings for public target firms than for non-public targets. Our fifth

Table 9.5 Difference in FAF errors: accuracy. Results from regression of the difference in *absolute* analysts' forecast errors one year before and after a cross-border M&A

Variable	Intercept	VarNumest	Focus	US	Adj. R²
Parameter estimate	0.352*	−0.349**	−0.179	0.267*	0.081
T statistic	1.941	−2.285	−1.267	1.758	
P-value	0.056	0.025	0.209	0.083	

Variable	Intercept	VarNumest	Focus	US	Status	Adj. R²
Parameter estimate	0.402*	−0.372**	−0.153	0.237	−0.159	0.076
T statistic	2.092	−2.387	−1.051	1.509	−0.801	
P-value	0.040	0.019	0.296	0.135	0.425	

Notes: $Diff_t = \alpha_0 + \alpha_1 \, VarNumest_t + \alpha_2 \, Focus_t + \alpha_3 \, US_t + (Status_t) + e_t$,

where $Diff_t$ = change in *absolute* forecast errors one year after the cross-border M&A = $(ABSFERE_{t+1} - ABSFERE_{t-1})$

$Focus_t$ = 1 for focus-preserving M&A; 0 for focus-decreasing M&A;
US_t = 1 for US target firm; 0 for target firms from other countries;
$VarNumest_t$ = 1 for analyst following increase; 0 for analyst following decrease or stability;
$Status_t$ = 1 for public target firm; 0 for non-public target;
e_t = error term;
t = M&A year.
** Significant at 5 percent level; * Significant at 10 percent level (*t* test).

hypothesis is not statistically verified by the data of our sample, and should be rejected. The results for FAF bias, reported in Table 9.6, are coherent but give a poor explanation of the differences.

9.5 CONCLUSION

In this chapter, we analyzed the impact of cross-border M&A on the accuracy and quality of financial analysts' forecast on the Canadian stock markets for the 1990–2004 period. Confirming previous studies focusing on the analysis of US and foreign bidders, we show that this event deteriorates the precision of financial analysts' forecast, and induces an increase of errors one year after the cross-border mergers. Interestingly, we have shed light on the relative rapidity of reaching the pre-merger level of accuracy. For numerous markets around the world, FAF accuracy tends to deteriorate during the three to four years after the mergers. It takes two years for financial analysts

Table 9.6 Difference in FAF errors: bias. Results from regression of the difference in *signed* analysts' forecast errors one year before and one years after a cross-border M&A

Variable	Intercept	VarNumest	Focus	US	Adj. R^2
Parameter estimate	−0.020	−0.165	0.201	0.237	0.019
T statistic	−0.095	−0.925	1.215	1.339	
P-value	0.924	0.358	0.228	0.184	

Variable	Intercept	VarNumest	Focus	US	Status	Adj. R^2
Parameter estimate	0.016	−0.181	0.220	0.215	−0.115	0.001
T statistic	0.072	−0.995	1.290	1.174	−0.497	
P-value	0.943	0.323	0.201	0.244	0.621	

Notes: $Diff_t = \alpha_0 + \alpha_1 \, VarNumest_t + \alpha_2 \, Focus_t + \alpha_3 \, US_t + (Status_t) + e_t$,
where

$Diff_t$	= change in *signed* forecast errors one year after the cross-border M&A
	= $(FERE_{t+1} - FERE_{t-1})$
$Focus_t$	= 1 for focus-preserving M&A; 0 for focus-decreasing M&A;
US_t	= 1 for US target firm; 0 for target firms from other countries;
$VarNumest_t$	= 1 for analyst following increase; 0 for analyst following decrease or stability;
$Status_t$	= 1 for public target firm; 0 for non-public target;
e_t	= error term;
t	= M&A year.

** Significant at 1 percent level; * Significant at 5 percent level (*t* test).

to improve their forecast and assimilate the flow of new earnings information. As expected, an increase of analyst coverage decreases financial analysts' forecast errors after cross-border M&As.

In our analysis we examine and separate preserving focus mergers from decreasing focus mergers, and US targets from non-US targets. Our results highlight the difficulties faced by financial analysts in forecasting mergers outside the core business of the bidders. On the other hand, we have shown that FAF errors are smaller for non-US targets. Financial analysts seem to be inclined to show over-optimism and over-confidence when they analyze US firms. The unknown is perceived as risky and any known or relative proximity is seen as less risky.

The role of financial analysts' recommendations is crucial to understand and analyze the consequence of M&As. Marked by an increase in earnings variability, our results show that the quality and accuracy of FAF are as important as behavioural puzzles.

NOTE

1. The authors thank Thomson Financial for providing the I/B/E/S database and Securities Data Corporation (SDC) Worldwide M&A database. We remain responsible for any errors.

REFERENCES

Alford, A. W. and Berger, P. G. (1999) "A Simultaneous Equations Analysis of Forecasts Accuracy, Analysts Following, and Trading Volume", *Journal of Accounting, Auditing & Finance*, 14: 219–46.

Ang, J. S. and Ciccone, S. J. (2001) "International Differences in Analyst Forecast Properties", Working paper, Florida State University and University of New Hampshire.

Black, E. L. and Carnes, T. A. (2002) "Analysts' Forecasts in Asian Markets: How Does the Accounting System Affect Accuracy?" *Journal of International Financial Management and Accounting*, 17(3): 208–27.

Brown, L. (1997) "Analysts Forecasts Errors: Additional Evidence", *Financial Analysts Journal*, 53: 81–8.

Brown, L., Richardson, G. and Schwager, S. (1987) "An Information Interpretation of Financial Analyst Superiority in Forecasting Earnings", *Journal of Accounting Research*, 25: 49–67.

Canina, L. and Sinha, P. (2002) "The Impact of Mergers and Acquisitions on Earnings Predictability: An Examination of the Lodging Industry", Working paper, Cornell University, New York, USA.

Chang, J. J., Khanna, T. and Palepu, K. G. (2000) "Analyst Activity Around the World", Working paper, The Wharton School and Harvard Business School, Cambridge, Mass., USA.

Chopra, V. K. (1998) "Why So Much Error in Analysts' Earnings Forecasts?", *Financial Analysts Journal*, 54: 35–42.

Ciccone, S. J., (2005) "Improvement in Forecasting Ability of Analysts", *International Review of Financial Analysis*, 14: 1–22.

Dowen, R. J. (1996) "Analyst Reaction to Negative Earnings for Large Well-Known Firms", *The Journal of Portfolio Management*, 21: 49–55.

Dunn, K. and Nathan, S. (1998) "The Effect of Industry Diversification on Consensus and Individual Analysts' Earnings Forecasts", Working paper, Baruch College and Georgia State University.

Erwin, G. R. and Perry, S. E. (2000) "The Effect of Foreign Diversification on Analysts' Prediction Errors", *International Review of Financial Analysis*, 9: 121–45.

Haw, I., Jung, K. and Ruland, W. (1994) "The Accuracy of Financial Analysts' Forecasts After Mergers", *Journal of Accounting, Auditing and Finance*, 9(2): 465–83.

Heath, C. and Tversky, D. (1991) "Preference and Belief: Ambiguity and Competence in Choice under Uncertainty", *Journal of Risk and Uncertainty*, 4(1): 5–28.

Hope, O.-K. (2003) "Disclosure Practices, Enforcement of Accounting Standards and Analysts' Forecast Accuracy: An International Study", *Journal of Accounting Research*, 41: 235–78.

Loree, D, Chen, C. C. and Guisinger, S. (2000) "International Acquisitions: Do Financial Analysts Take Note?", *Journal of World Business*, 35: 300–13.

Malloy, C. J. (2005) "The Geography of Equity Analysis", *Journal of Finance*, 60: 719–55.

Mikhail, M. B., Walther, B. R. and Willis, R. H. (1997) "Do Security Analysts Improve their Performance with Experience?", *Journal of Accounting Research*, 35: 131–66.

Richardson, S., Teoh, S. H. and Wysocki, P. (1999) "Tracking Analysts' Forecasts over The Annual Earnings Horizon: Are Analysts' Forecasts Optimistic or Pessimistic?", Working paper, University of Michigan Business School.

Solnik, B. H. (1996), *International Investments* (Reading, Mass.: Addison-Wesley).

CHAPTER 10

The Economic Analysis of US Antitrust Merger Law

Germán Coloma

10.1 INTRODUCTION

The aim of this chapter is to survey the basic economic literature concerning the antitrust analysis of mergers in the USA. That is a relatively difficult task, since the USA has a long history of antitrust merger law, and it is also the country where the economic analysis of mergers began.

The economic analysis of US antitrust merger law can be made using different perspectives. In this chapter I shall adopt three of them, which seem to be representative of three important branches in the literature on law and economics. One of these perspectives is the theoretical literature on welfare economics, whose aim is to analyze the effect that different kinds of mergers may have on profits and surpluses generated in the markets where the merging companies operate. This literature is dominated by the analysis of a fundamental trade-off that many mergers pose: the fact that they are able to generate cost reductions in the merging partners but at the same time can affect the profits or surpluses of other economic agents that do not take part in the mergers, such as consumers, suppliers or competitors of the merging parties.

A second line of analysis is the one followed by the literature that concentrates on the economic logic of the statute and case law that governs mergers in the USA. Beginning with the introduction of mergers as a possible anti-competitive practice in the Clayton Act (1914), mergers have been the main issue of two important Clayton Act amendments, introduced by the Celler–Kefauver Act (1950) and the Hart–Scott–Rodino Act (1976). All these statutes have generated different economic interpretations of the requirements that mergers have to fulfil to be considered anti-competitive, which materialized in a significant amount of case law concerning mergers. Another important source for the economic analysis of antitrust merger law has been the set of guidelines issued by the US antitrust agencies (Federal Trade Commission and Justice Department) that first appeared in 1968, adopted their present form in 1992, and were amended most recently in 1997.

The last strand of the economic literature concerning the antitrust analysis of mergers in the USA is the one comprising case studies of different mergers. The interest in this literature is twofold: on the one hand, it has generated results concerning the effects of particular mergers that occurred, or might have occurred in different markets and moments of time; and on the other, it has helped to develop a series of empirical methods to study these phenomena, mainly through the comparison of market results before and after the mergers took place.

10.2 THEORETICAL LITERATURE

The economic analysis of the antitrust effects of mergers is based strongly on a classification that divides mergers into three categories: horizontal, vertical and conglomerate. Horizontal mergers take place among firms that compete in the same market; vertical mergers are between a supplier and a customer; and conglomerate mergers, imply mergers that are neither horizontal nor vertical. Two important sub-categories in the latter group are the ones formed by product-extension mergers (these are mergers among firms that use similar production processes or marketing channels) and by market-extension mergers (mergers among firms that operate in the same industry but in different geographical markets).

This classification of mergers is useful to analyze the effect of a merger on the way that markets work. A horizontal merger, for example, implies an immediate modification of the structure of the markets on which it has an impact, since two or more firms that used to be competitors become a single economic entity, with a larger share in a market whose concentration indices increase. A vertical merger, in contrast, does not produce a change in the number of firms that supply or demand a product, but it means that some transactions that were made among independent economic units become internal transactions within the same economic group. Conglomerate mergers, finally, can only generate indirect effects in the way that markets work, which are normally limited to upstream markets in which the conglomerate buys certain production or distribution inputs.

The economic literature on the antitrust analysis of mergers distinguishes two main motives that may induce a merger process.[1] These are an increase of market power (which implies the possibility of rising prices) and an increase of productive efficiency (which implies the possibility of reducing costs). This distinction is extremely important for antitrust analysis, since the most widespread interpretation of the implicit logic of the enforcement of antitrust merger provisions is related to the idea that mergers that generate an increase in market power and raise prices should be prohibited, while mergers that increase productive efficiency and reduce costs should be authorized.

The market power/productive efficiency distinction is also related to the classification of mergers mentioned above (see page 156). A horizontal merger, for example, is the most likely to generate an increase in market power, since the suppression of competition among the merging parties is the most direct way to allow them to increase their prices. A vertical merger, conversely, can only increase market power indirectly, if it helps one of the merging parties to reinforce its dominance in a market. A conglomerate merger, finally, usually has no market power effects, unless it is able to reduce the "potential competition" of the merging parties in a market in which one of them is already operating and the other is able to enter.

The ways in which the different kinds of mergers can reduce costs are also different. A horizontal or market-extension merger typically helps to exploit economies of scale in the production or distribution of certain goods or services, while a product-extension merger is more likely to generate economies of scope (that is, cost reductions related to the joint provision of two products). Vertical mergers, in contrast, are usually able to reduce transaction costs (that is, the costs of using the market as a coordinating mechanism among economic units), while pure conglomerate mergers generally derive their main efficiency advantages from the fact that they imply a change in the management of one of the merging companies.

The first important economic analysis of the role of antitrust merger law is a paper by Williamson (1968), who first presented the fundamental trade-off between productive efficiency and market power that occurs in the evaluation of a horizontal merger. This trade-off is represented in Figure 10.1, in which we have depicted an initially competitive market where the industry's marginal cost is higher before a certain merger than after that merger (MC0 > MC1). If, as a consequence of the merger, the market goes on behaving in the same competitive fashion, then the operation generates an increase in productive efficiency, which induces a higher output level ($Qc_1 > Q_0$) and a lower price ($Pc_1 < P_0$). If, instead, the market becomes a monopoly, the increase in productive efficiency is partially or totally compensated by greater market power, which generates an output decrease ($Qm_1 < Q_0$) and a price increase ($Pm_1 > P_0$).

The trade-off between productive efficiency and market power associated with a horizontal merger can also appear in less extreme contexts, where market structure does not move from perfect competition to monopoly, but remains in an intermediate point. Farrell and Shapiro (1990), for example,

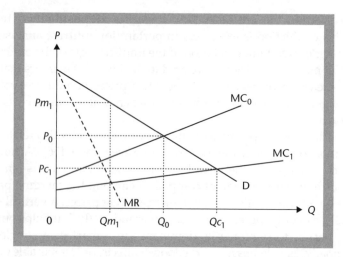

Figure 10.1 The trade-off between productive efficiency and market power in the evaluation of a horizontal merger

developed a model in which the market is a Cournot oligopoly (that is, a market where firms choose their output, taking their competitors' output as a given) and, consequently, market power exists both before and after the merger. In this case, a merger generates an increase in market concentration, and two basic results hold: (i) a horizontal merger can generate a reduction in price (and hence an increase in consumer surplus), but that is only possible if the merger induces a strong marginal cost reduction for the merging parties; and (ii) even if the marginal cost remains the same, a horizontal merger can generate an increase in total surplus (that is, in the sum of consumer surplus and firms' profits) if the market share of the merging parties is rather small and the rest of the industry is relatively concentrated.

When a horizontal merger occurs in a market with differentiated products, some new results appear concerning the productive efficiency/market power trade-off. These results depend on the kind of existing product differentiation, and on the impact of the merger on that differentiation. If, for example, a merger induces the suppression of one of the varieties provided, then the consumer surplus tends to be affected more severely (since the post-merger situation implies higher prices, smaller output levels and a reduction in variety). If, conversely, the merger reduces the number of suppliers but not the number of available varieties of the product, then the consumer surplus tends to be less severely affected, because the elimination of competition between the merging parties is less important than in the case where they both supply an identical same product.

The seminal paper about the antitrust effects of horizontal mergers in product-differentiated markets is by Deneckere and Davidson (1985), and shows that, in these markets, firms may have more incentives to merge, since the expected reaction of their competitors after a merger is to increase their own prices. This contrasts with the expected reaction of competitors in a homogeneous-product market, which is to increase output (and, consequently, to induce a counterbalancing reduction in prices).

Markets with product differentiation, however, may also allow for horizontal mergers that induce a reduction in market power rather than an increase. Norman and Pepall (2000), for example, developed a model in which a merger can result in an increase in variety, by transforming a market where many firms are located in fewer places into a market with fewer firms but a larger number of locations. A similar result can occur if, in a market with a dominant firm, there is a merger among non-dominant firms that operate in the competitive fringe. That merger is able to create a new firm that challenges the dominance of the previous market leader, and may therefore reduce its market power and generate an equilibrium with lower prices and a larger output level.

The antitrust analysis of vertical mergers is also a field where market power explanations coexist with productive efficiency motives. One of the most studied problems concerning this is the so-called "market power extension" hypothesis, which assumes that a vertical merger may help an upstream monopolist to extend its dominance to a downstream market, and vice versa. The first people who studied this effect analytically were Vernon and Graham (1971), who showed that the hypothesis could be true if the merger was able to stop the substitution of a monopolized input for other, less-monopolized alternatives. If this substitution was not possible before the merger (for example, because the production function of the output producers required fixed-input proportions), then a vertical merger would not be able to extend monopoly power from an upstream to a downstream market.

Another important idea that appears in the economic literature on vertical mergers is the concept of "raising rivals' costs". This concept, introduced by Salop and Scheffman (1987), implies that a vertical merger may "shrink" a certain input market, and this might make that market less competitive. If, for example, a vertical merger generates a reduction in the availability of a certain resource for the firms that compete with the ones that merge, then this might imply that the price of that resource will increase and its traded quantity decrease, generating a situation of "market foreclosure". Ordover *et al.* (1990) show that this situation of foreclosure may be an equilibrium in a context where there can be vertical mergers.

On the other hand, the basic efficiency explanations for vertical mergers are linked with the idea that they serve to reduce transaction costs among the merging parties. One of the most important theoretical papers that analyzes this problem is the one by Grossman and Hart (1986), who provide a general explanation for situations where vertical integration occurs, either backward or forward (that is, for situations in which a customer acquires a supplying firm, or a supplying firm acquires a customer). The basic explanation has to do with the importance of the externalities each firm generates on the other firm's profits (that is, how important are the other firm's activities to enhancing one's profits). If the supplying firm's activities are very important for the customer's profits, and not the reverse, then the model predicts that the customer will acquire the supplier; and in the same way, if the customer's activities are very important for the supplier's profits, then the expected integration occurs through the acquisition of the customer by the supplier.

The economic explanations for conglomerate mergers, finally, are also strongly related to efficiency phenomena. One of the first papers to analyze them was the one by Mueller (1969), who studied the idea that a conglomerate merger could increase the value of two companies by reducing their exposure to risk. This occurs if the returns of those companies are negatively correlated, and therefore the cost of capital for a firm that operates in both industries is smaller than the one that each industry faces individually. Another efficiency advantage of a conglomerate merger (especially when considering product-extension mergers) is the exploitation of economies of scope. This is the theme of another branch of the theoretical literature about mergers, whose first important example is a paper by Teece (1982).

10.3 STATUTE AND CASE LAW

The first antitrust statute passed by the US Congress was the so-called Sherman Act (1890), which does not consider mergers explicitly as anti-competitive behavior. However, the first antitrust cases objecting to mergers were analyzed as possible violations of the Sherman Act. One early example is "US v. *Northern Securities*" (1904), in which the US Supreme Court prohibited a merger between two railway companies that operated in the Northwestern area of the USA. That merger was considered to restrict trade and therefore to violate section 1 of the Sherman Act, since it was assimilated into a *per se* anti-competitive horizontal agreement.[2]

Although many early horizontal mergers were not challenged by the US antitrust authorities, the idea that they could constitute a manifestation of *per se* anti-competitive behavior remained important for many years. Vertical mergers, in contrast, were never considered as illegal *per se*, and were always analyzed by applying the so-called "rule of reason".[3] The first antitrust case concerning a vertical merger that reached the Supreme Court, for example, was favorable to the defendants, since the court considered that the merger under analysis was not illegal.[4]

The first antitrust statute that included mergers explicitly as a possible illegal behavior was the Clayton Act (1914), whose section 7 is precisely about mergers and acquisitions. Its enforcement, however, was notably rare, since that section only banned stock acquisitions, and not asset acquisitions. When the Clayton Act was amended in 1950 by the so-called Celler–Kefauver Act, this problem disappeared, and all kinds of mergers and acquisitions came to be considered as anti-competitive provided they "substantially lessen competition or tend to create a monopoly".

The enforcement of the Celler–Kefauver Act was considerably important in the 1960s, when several antitrust merger cases reached the US Supreme Court. The most notable of these was "*US v. Brown Shoe*" (1962), about a merger that was at the same time horizontal and vertical. The two merging parties were producers and distributors of shoes, but one of them (Brown Shoe) was more important as a producer and the other one (Kinney) was more important as a retailer. Although neither of them had a very large market share (Brown Shoe's was 4 percent and Kinney 1 percent, both at the national level), the Supreme Court understood that the merger was illegal, since it had taken place in a market with an important trend towards concentration.

Several other horizontal mergers were challenged in the 1960s, and that trend even reached some product-extension mergers. The most cited example of this last category is the merger challenged in the case "*FTC v. Procter & Gamble*" (1967), in which the acquisition of the main chlorine bleach producer (Clorox) by a company that did not produce chlorine bleach but was thought to be its main "potential competitor" (Procter & Gamble) was considered illegal.

The most important amendment to the Clayton Act concerning antitrust merger law was probably the one introduced by the so-called Hart–Scott–Rodino Act (1976), which created a pre-merger notification procedure. This procedure requires that the companies engaged in a merger must notify their intentions to one of the US antitrust agencies (either the Department of Justice or the Federal Trade Commission), and those agencies have a certain period to analyze the possibility of challenging that merger.[5]

With the introduction of this pre-merger notification procedure in 1976, the antitrust agencies began to analyze almost the whole universe of possibly anti-competitive mergers. Contrary to the expectation of some early commentators, this generated a change in the way those agencies analyzed mergers, making them challenge only the cases that implied very high market shares, very large increases in market concentration and markets with very important entry barriers. Vertical and conglomerate mergers, began correspondingly to be considered legal in their enormous majority, and almost all cases came to an end in their early judicial stages or were subject to agreements between the parties and the antitrust agencies.[6]

The experience of the US Department of Justice (DOJ) and the Federal Trade Commission (FTC) in analyzing mergers generated a number of published documents in which these agencies exposed their views concerning antitrust merger analysis. The first of these documents, published in 1968, outlined the US Department merger guidelines. These guidelines were amended several times, and in 1992 a new version of them was issued jointly by the DOJ and the FTC under the title *Horizontal Merger Guidelines*.[7] In these guidelines, the antitrust agencies expressed their main views concerning the definition of the relevant markets affected by a merger, the measurement of market shares and market concentration indices, the potential adverse effects of a merger on a market, and the possible merger defenses based on the relative absence of entry barriers, the existence of efficiency gains and the argument that one of the merging parties was in fact a "failing firm" that was leaving the market in any case.

The antitrust merger guidelines were applied in numerous cases, for both accepting and rejecting mergers. One interesting early application, concerning the joint analysis of two almost simultaneously proposed mergers, occurred in 1986, with the cases of "Coca-Cola/Dr. Pepper" and "Pepsi/Seven-Up". Both mergers were objected to by the FTC because they would have implied the disappearance of the third and fourth most important firms in the American carbonated soft drinks market, consolidating the industry into only two important companies: Coca-Cola and Pepsi.[8] This structural change would also have influenced the local bottling markets in many US states, since in the majority of them Coca-Cola and Pepsi had their own bottlers, and the remaining companies used a third, independent company. If Dr. Pepper and Seven-Up disappeared as independent firms, therefore, the structure of the bottling markets would have been likely to changed and become a two-firm oligopoly instead of a three-firm oligopoly, notably increasing the market power of the implied companies.

A relatively common feature in many important mergers decided in the Hart–Scott–Rodino Act era is their authorization subject to certain conditions imposed by the antitrust agencies. Those conditions are sometimes proposed by the merging parties, and are sometimes negotiated between those parties and the agencies. The negotiations generally occur before the cases get to court, but sometimes they happen when the case is analyzed at a judicial stage. One important example of these judicial agreements is the one that occurred in the case of "GTE/Bell Atlantic" (1999), in which the DOJ accepted the consolidation of two important telephone companies subject to the divestiture of several mobile telephone divisions the companies had. The merger under analysis was basically a market-extension merger, since the core business of the two companies was the local fixed telephone services provided under monopoly conditions in separated markets. Both companies, however, also provided mobile telephony in several urban areas, and in some of them they competed against each other. It was precisely in those areas where the largest competition problems arose, and the condition that the DOJ imposed was that the companies divested one mobile telephone division in each of the cities where their services overlapped.

10.4 EMPIRICAL STUDIES

The empirical economic literature on antitrust merger evaluation is diverse and has used a variety of techniques to study the effects of mergers on market structure, price levels, profits and welfare. In his survey of empirical studies of mergers and acquisitions, for example, Pautler (2001) distinguishes five basic approaches: stock market studies; large-scale econometric studies; clinical econometric case studies; structure–conduct–performance studies; and experimental economics studies.

Stock market studies typically use stock market data concerning the pre-merger price of the merging firms' shares to calculate the normal return of a stock as a function of the market's average return (generally measured by a certain index such as the Dow Jones). With that estimation, these studies calculate the "abnormal returns" (positive or negative) generated by the merger, using data from a few days before and after the merger is announced. Most studies use only data from the merging firms' stock, but others also use data from the merging parties' rivals, to find some evidence about the competitive implications of the merger.

One of the first studies on this topic, by Eckbo (1983), found that in many horizontal mergers there were large abnormal returns for shareholders of the rival firms, suggesting that the merger could effectively induce less competitive behavior in the relevant product markets. When some antitrust action against these mergers was announced, however, the effect on the rivals' returns seemed to be insignificant, pointing to some questions about the efficacy of those actions.

Although many stock market studies analyze mergers in different industries, some of them concentrate on mergers that occur in the same industry. Singal (1996), for example, studied a sample of fourteen US airline mergers, and found that positive returns appeared in the cases where mergers induced large market concentration increases, but that they tended to be negative when mergers were relatively small and likely to generate cost reductions because of the more efficient use of common airports.

The second approach to studying the antitrust effects of mergers is to do *large-scale econometric studies* based on accounting data for firms before and after an acquisition. One leading example of this literature is a book by Ravenscraft and Scherer (1987), which found that horizontal and market-extension mergers tended to be more profitable than vertical and pure conglomerate mergers. A similar conclusion is the one that appears in a more recent study by Maksimovic and Phillips (2001), which shows that mergers are generally less efficiency-enhancing than other asset transfers. To reach this conclusion, these authors used data from 35,000 US plants that were transferred between 1974 and 1992, through stock or direct asset acquisitions. They found that, in general, the asset buyers are the more productive firms, while stock buyers are in many cases conglomerate firms that tend to be more reticent to sell their less productive assets than are single division firms.

The third empirical approach mentioned by Pautler (2001) is the one formed by the so-called *"clinical econometric case studies"*, which focus on the effect of particular mergers in the product markets in which the merging firms operate. One prominent example of this kind of study is Werden et al. (1991), measuring the effects of two actual airline mergers on prices and service quality. The authors use a model that incorporates specific supply and demand variables, allowing them to obtain estimates of price and quality changes. However, they are not able to translate these numbers into estimates of changes in consumer and producer surpluses.

Another important study along the same lines is Baker and Bresnahan (1985), a study of the effects of a merger between two brewers that uses explicit demand and supply equations and is able to estimate both price and welfare changes resulting from that merger. Its main drawback, however, is that it analyzes a fictitious merger, and therefore uses only pre-merger data to make the estimations.

In a more recent example of a clinical merger study, Vita and Sacher (2001) applied a specific supply and demand framework to analyze the effect of an actual merger between two hospitals, using both pre-merger and post-merger data. Their approach uses a control group of hospitals that did not merge in order to contrast the results obtained for the hospitals that *did* merge, but once again the study only focuses on price changes and does not provide evidence on profit or welfare changes.

The three examples mentioned above evaluate mergers using a general market power approach, but they do not test alternative market behavior hypotheses before and after the merger. In general, the literature about oligopoly model testing has been developed to analyze market behavior in a context in which mergers may or may not happen,[9] but it is not common to find examples that deal with cases in which there is a question about which market structure existed before and after the merger.

Another line of the empirical literature related to the antitrust effect of mergers is the so-called *"structure–conduct–performance approach"*, a general way to analyze the effect of market concentration on prices and profits. Normally, this literature is not focused on the effects of mergers on market performance variables, but it helps to analyze the effects of increasing concentration on a variety of variables related to profits, margins and other variables. One leading example of this is Schmalensee (1985), who uses a dataset of 456 firms in 242 industries and decomposes profit variations into three components: industry level effects; market concentration; and firm's market share. His conclusions are that the effects at the level of the firm are quite small in comparison to industry level effects (related to efficiency) and market concentration effects (related to market power). These two effects, however, seem to be negatively correlated (that is, positive market concentration effects tend to appear in industries with smaller profit rates, and were insignificant in industries with higher profit rates).

Although the most traditional structure–conduct–performance studies tend to use inter-industry data, there are several more modern examples that concentrate on single industries, and look for relationships between concentration and prices (instead of concentration and profits). Weiss (1989) reviews several of these single-industry studies, and finds that, on average, a 10-point increase in market concentration induces a 3 percent increase in the prices of the products traded in the relevant markets. These results, in general, are imputed to market power phenomena, since other factors related to cost characteristics are controlled by using additional variables (input prices, production scales and so on).

The last source of empirical results related to the effect of mergers and market concentration on prices and profits comes from a relatively new line of research in economics, known as *experimental economics*. Studies that follow this approach are made using real people, who take on the roles of buyers and sellers, and are given financial incentives that try to mirror those that exist in actual markets. One important result appearing in these studies is the idea that, under conditions of price competition, a market that consists of four buyers and four sellers converges to the perfectly competitive outcome. This result, which appears in papers such as Dufwenberg and Gneezy (2000), is independent on the existence of potential entry, but seems to be dependent on the amount and timing of information that the market participants possess. Davis and Holt (1994), for example, have found that, if one of the four sellers has the possibility of announcing his/her price first, then supracompetitive prices tend to appear by means of tacit collusion devices, and the seller that moves first generally ends up with higher profits and a larger market share.

10.5 CONCLUSION

The economic literature on the antitrust effects of mergers, which has been developed mainly in the USA, has influenced (and, at the same time, been influenced by) the evolution of US antitrust merger law. If we look at the most relevant theoretical literature on the topic, we find that its most pervasive idea is that mergers can generate at the same time some efficiency (pro-competitive) effects and some market power (anti-competitive) effects. The balance of these effects differs according to the type of merger and the characteristics of the markets influenced by the merger.

The US antitrust merger law, through its combination of statute law, case law and antitrust agency opinions, has increasingly adopted the theoretical perspective mentioned above. At the same time, the emergence of new cases and agency guidelines has generated new theoretical and empirical economic literature that analyzes the effects of mergers and merger evaluation criteria. In general, both types of literature coincide in the idea that most mergers generate greater efficiency than market power effects, unless they occur in highly concentrated markets with large barriers to entry. This is also the predominant idea that the US antitrust agencies have spread since the passing of the Hart–Scott–Rodino Act in 1976, and can be considered as the basic antitrust standard for the current analysis of possibly anti-competitive mergers.

NOTES

1. For an excellent explanation of this literature, see Viscusi *et al.* (2005), ch. 7.
2. Section 1 of the Sherman Act declares illegal every "contract, combination in the form of trust ... or conspiracy, in restraint of trade".
3. The distinction between conduct that is *per se* illegal and conduct that has to be analyzed under a rule of reason is very important in US antitrust analysis. It first appeared in the sentence of the case "*US v. Addyston Pipe*" (1898).
4. That case was "*US v. Columbia Steel*" (1948).
5. In fact, the Hart–Scott–Rodino Act pre-merger notification procedure only applies to relatively large mergers. However, in practice, only these mergers are likely to pose any antitrust concern.
6. It is noticeable, for example, that, since the passing of the Hart–Scott–Rodino Act, no antitrust merger cases have reached the US Supreme Court.
7. These guidelines were amended again in 1997, by both the DOJ and the FTC.
8. The FTC's objections to these mergers triggered different reactions from Coca-Cola and Pepsi. While Pepsi abandoned its merger plans almost immediately, Coca-Cola did not accept the agency decision and the case was decided at a federal court (*Coca-Cola v. FTC*, 1986). The court's decision, however, was favorable to the FTC, and the acquisition did not take place. A few months later, Seven-Up and Dr. Pepper were acquired by a single economic group, unrelated to either Coca-Cola or Pepsi, and that acquisition was not objected to by the US antitrust agencies.
9. The leading example of those studies is Bresnahan (1987), which contrasts several alternative hypotheses (basically price competition and collusion) to analyze the behavior of the American automobile industry in different years of the 1950s. In this study, the analyzed event was not a merger but a possible price war that ended a period of tacit cartel behavior.

REFERENCES

Baker, J. and Bresnahan, T. (1985) "The Gains from Merger or Collusion in Product-Differentiated Industries", *Journal of Industrial Economics*, 33: 427–44.

Bresnahan, T. (1987) "Competition and Collusion in the American Automobile Industry: The 1955 Price War", *Journal of Industrial Economics*, 35: 457–82.

Davis, D. and Holt, C. (1994) "Market Power and Mergers in Laboratory Markets with Posted Prices", *Rand Journal of Economics*, 25: 467–87.

Deneckere, R. and Davidson, C. (1985) "Incentives to Form Coalitions with Bertrand Competition", *Rand Journal of Economics*, 16: 473–86.

Dufwenberg, M. and Gneezy, U. (2000) "Price Competition and Market Concentration: An Experimental Study", *International Journal of Industrial Organization*, 18: 7–22.

Eckbo, E. (1983) "Horizontal Mergers, Collusion and Stockholder Wealth", *Journal of Financial Economics*, 11: 241–74.
Farrell, J. and Shapiro, C. (1990) "Horizontal Mergers: An Equilibrium Analysis", *American Economic Review*, 80: 107–26.
Grossman, S. and Hart, O. (1986) "The Costs and Benefits of Ownership: A Theory of Vertical and Lateral Integration", *Journal of Political Economy*, 94: 691–719.
Maksimovic, V. and Phillips, G. (2001) "The Market for Corporate Assets: Who Engages in Mergers and Asset Sales and Are There Efficiency Gains?", *Journal of Finance*, 56: 2019–65.
Mueller, D. (1969) "A Theory of Conglomerate Mergers", *Quarterly Journal of Economics*, 83: 643–59.
Norman, G. and Pepall, L. (2000) "Spatial Competition and Location with Mergers and Product Licensing", *Urban Studies*, 37: 451–70.
Ordover, J., Saloner, G. and Salop, S. (1990) "Equilibrium Vertical Foreclosure", *American Economic Review*, 80: 127–42.
Pautler, P. (2001) "Evidence on Mergers and Acquisitions", Working paper No. 243, Washington, DC, Federal Trade Commission.
Ravenscraft, D. and Scherer, F. (1987) *Mergers, Sell-offs and Economic Efficiency* (Washington, DC: Brookings Institution).
Salop, S. and Scheffman, D. (1987) "Cost-Raising Strategies", *Journal of Industrial Economics*, 36: 19–34.
Schmalensee, R. (1985) "Do Markets Differ Much?", *American Economic Review*, 75: 341–51.
Singal, V. (1996) "Airline Mergers and Competition: An Integration of Stock and Product Price Effects", *Journal of Business*, 62: 233–68.
Teece, D. (1982) "Towards an Economic Theory of the Multiproduct Firm", *Journal of Economic Behavior and Organization*, 3: 39–63.
Vernon, J. and Graham, D. (1971) "Profitability of Monopolization by Vertical Integration", *Journal of Political Economy*, 79: 924–5.
Viscusi, K., Vernon, J. and Harrington, J. (2005) *Economics of Regulation and Antitrust*, 4th edn (Cambridge, Mass.: MIT Press).
Vita, M. and Sacher, S. (2001) "The Competitive Effects of Not-for-Profit Hospital Mergers: A Case Study", *Journal of Industrial Economics*, 49: 63–84.
Weiss, L. (1989) *Concentration and Prices* (Cambridge, Mass.: MIT Press).
Werden, G., Joskow, A. and Johnson, R. (1991) "The Effects of Mergers on Price and Output: Two Case Studies from the Airline Industry", *Managerial and Decision Economics*, 12: 341–52.
Williamson, O. (1968) "Economics as an Antitrust Defense: The Welfare Tradeoffs", *American Economic Review*, 58: 18–36.

List of cases

Coca-Cola/Dr. Pepper (*Coca-Cola* v. *FTC*), 641 FSupp 1128, 1986.
FTC v. *Procter & Gamble*, 386 US 568, 1967.
GTE/Bell Atlantic, DOJ 99-CIV-1119, 1999.
Pepsi/Seven-Up v. *FTC*, 6-23-1986.
US v. *Addyston Pipe*, 175 US 211, 1898.
US v. *Brown Shoe*, 370 US 294, 1962.
US v. *Columbia Steel*, 334 US 495, 1948.
US v. *Northern Securities*, 193 US 197, 1904.

CHAPTER 11

Ethical Issues in Mergers and Acquisitions

Robert W. McGee

11.1 INTRODUCTION

Acquisitions and mergers have been receiving bad press for decades. The media portrays images of greedy predators seeking weak or unfortunate companies to target for hostile acquisitions. If press accounts were believed, one might easily arrive at the conclusion that such activities are harmful to the economy and to the employees of the target, as well as to the local communities where the targeted company is located. Yet some studies (Jensen, 1988) have concluded that most acquisitions and mergers actually benefit the economy, thus meeting the utilitarian ethics test. Furthermore, any attempt to prevent a hostile takeover necessarily violates someone's property and contract rights. This chapter analyzes the topic of acquisitions and mergers from the perspectives of utilitarian ethics and rights theory, and discusses the ethical issues involving hostile takeovers and the attempts that have been made to prevent them.

11.2 ETHICAL APPROACHES

There are two basic ethical approaches that can be taken to examine acquisitions and mergers – utilitarian ethics and rights theory. Matters are complicated by the fact that there is more than one branch of utilitarian ethics: rule utilitarianism and act utilitarianism. But that is the least of our problems when we are applying utilitarian ethics to an acquisition and merger situation to determine whether a particular acquisition or merger includes unethical behavior.

There are several structural flaws inherent in any utilitarian approach. While the basic premise of utilitarian ethics is that something is considered ethical if the result offers the greatest good for the greatest number (Mill, 1993), or if the result is a positive-sum game (which is not quite the same), but it is not always easy, or even possible, to determine gains and losses, because they cannot always be measured (Rothbard, 2004). Estimates can be made, but reasonable people can disagree on outcomes. In close-call situations, reasonable people may even differ about whether the game is positive or negative.

The situation is complicated by the fact that there are winners and losers, and that those who have a lot to gain or lose tend to get the ear of the legislature and the regulators, whereas those with little to gain or lose do not. In many cases, they do not even know that they would gain or lose anything as a result of an acquisition or merger. The Public Choice School of Economics has been examining problems like this for decades (Rowley *et al.* 1988; Buchanan, *et al.* 1980). It presents a classic case where concentrated special interests can resort to rent-seeking (Tullock, 1970, 1989, 1993) to feather their nests at the expense of the general public or the constituency they are supposed to serve.

The utilitarian ethics approach might be illustrated by the flowchart in Figure 11.1. It really is a quite simple approach. If the act results in the greatest good for the greatest number, it passes the utilitarian ethics test. But what if a few individuals benefit a great deal, and a lot of people stand to lose just

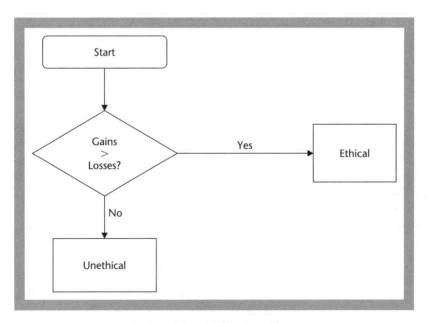

Figure 11.1 Utilitarian ethics
Source: McGee, 2006.

a little? There is no way to compare interpersonal utilities (Rothbard, 2004), so the equation becomes complicated, or even impossible to solve.

The individuals who are most likely to block attempts at a hostile takeover are the target company's management, since they are the ones most likely to lose if the takeover bid is successful, and at least some of them will lose their jobs. So the usual modus operandi is to do whatever they can to block the takeover bid, or at least to make it as expensive as possible, so that the predator will find the takeover is not worth pursuing.

One way that a company's management tries to prevent a hostile takeover is by the use of a "poison pill" (Datta and Iskandar-Datta, 1996), a maneuver that makes the company a less attractive takeover target. Another way is "greenmail" (Manry and Stangeland, 2001). In other words, they use corporate assets to buy off the predator. In exchange for a large cash payment, the predator promises to go away.

One ethical problem involved in this kind of behavior is that the corporate officers have a fiduciary duty to their shareholders to do things to increase shareholder wealth. Hostile takeovers are generally good for shareholders, yet the management of the target company often uses corporate assets in an attempt to thwart the takeover. In other words, they are breaching their fiduciary duty by using corporate assets to do things that are against the shareholders' interests. But what is worse is that politicians and regulators tend to be on the side of the target company's management. They also want to prevent hostile takeovers, which leaves no one to protect the shareholders.

The utilitarian flowchart can be revised to take into account the inclusion of the fiduciary duty problem, as in Figure 11.2. But not all utilitarians would agree with this flow of logic. Some of them would just include the breach of fiduciary duty as one of the negative factors to be considered in the utilitarian calculus, to be offset against gains. They would not consider a breach of fiduciary duty to be a deal killer, but other utilitarians would consider it so.

What is extremely curious from the perspective of economic philosophy is that the management team of the target company often uses utilitarian arguments to justify their actions. They argue that the shareholders will be worse off as a result of the acquisition if it is allowed to proceed. That may be the case sometimes, since not all mergers benefit shareholders in the long run. The problem is that it is not known whether the shareholders will be better or worse off until after the takeover. So target company management, regulators and legislators often begin from the premise that shareholders will be better off if the takeover is not allowed to take place. But why do they not simply let the shareholders decide for themselves? After all, it is the shareholders, not the management or regulators, who in fact own the shares that are to be traded.

Another problem with applying utilitarian ethics is trying to determine who will be affected by a particular transaction. The easy groups to identify are

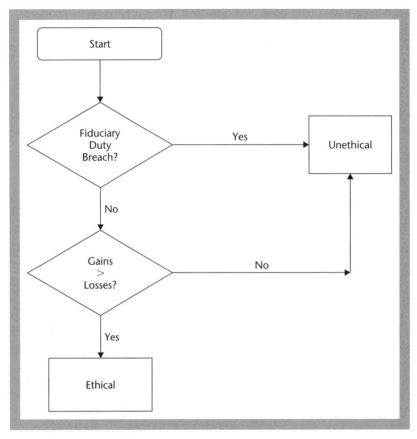

Figure 11.2 Revised flowchart
Source: McGee, 2006.

the shareholders and management of the target company. The shareholders will probably benefit, although this is not always true, and target company management will lose because they will lose their jobs, or at least some of them will.

Presumably, the predator company and its shareholders will also benefit. Otherwise they would not attempt the takeover in the first place. So it then becomes a question for utilitarians of whether the gains of the predator, the predator's shareholders and the shareholders of the target company more than offset the losses the target company management will incur. That is not an easy question to answer, since it is not possible to determine in advance with any kind of certitude what the gains and losses will be. It may not even be possible to determine who the winners and losers will be.

But that is not the end of the story. Other groups are also affected by a hostile takeover. The community where the target company is located is also affected. But whether it is affected adversely or benefited by the takeover is not always clear-cut. If the predator pours resources into the new acquisition, the community stands to benefit. But if the predator dissects the company, keeps (or sells) the best parts and disposes of the rest, the community stands to lose.

But there is another question that needs to be asked – should the effect on the local community even be considered? The community has not invested in the stock of the corporation, so why should the effects on the community even be considered? The community is, in effect, a parasite, a freeloader that wants to benefit even though it has not invested in the company's stock. They have invested nothing, so why should their views even be considered?

As a practical matter they are considered for purely political reasons. Politicians have votes to gain if they can show that they are concerned about the effects a takeover will have on the constituency that elects them. This is precisely why takeovers should be free and unregulated, so that such decisions cannot be influenced by politics, by people who have invested nothing in the target corporation (McGee, 1989).

This brings us to another flaw that is inherent in utilitarian ethics. It totally ignores rights (Frey, 1984; Brandt, 1992; McGee, 1994), a concept that Jeremy Bentham, one of the founders of utilitarianism, disdained (Waldron, 1987). To a utilitarian, the only thing that matters is gains and losses (Goodin, 1995; Shaw, 1999). If someone's rights must be violated on the path to a positive-sum game, or for the greatest good to accrue to the greatest number, that is fine, and that is where the rights approach differs from utilitarian ethics. It is also one of the reasons why a rights approach is morally superior to any utilitarian approach (McGee, 1994). In a rights approach, there is no need to measure gains and losses. There is no need to determine which groups should be included and which excluded from the equation. All that is necessary is to ask whether anyone's rights would be violated if the transaction were allowed to go forward. If the answer is "yes", then the transaction is unethical.

The rights approach can be illustrated by the flowchart shown in Figure 11.3. According to the rights approach, an act is automatically unethical if someone's rights are violated. Whether an act is ethical in cases where rights are not violated depends on the act. For example, acts of prostitution might be considered unethical by some people even though such acts do not result in rights violations. But it does not follow that they should be illegal, just as it does not follow that hostile takeovers should be illegal if they do not violate anyone's rights.

One thing is certain. If some target company executives use the force of government to prevent a hostile takeover, which is really nothing more than the transfer of shares from the people who have them to the people who want them, the target company executives are acting unethically because they are preventing shareholders and potential shareholders from exercising

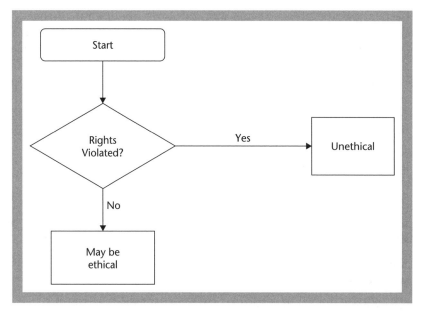

Figure 11.3 Rights-based ethics
Source: McGee, 2006.

their property and contract rights. The legislators who passed laws that allow them to engage in this kind of anti-takeover activity have also acted unethically, since they are preventing people from exercising their property and contract rights. So if anyone is acting unethically, it is the target company executives, and the lawmakers and regulators who support this kind of activity, not the predator companies.

11.3 REVIEW OF THE LITERATURE

Much has been written about various aspects of acquisitions and mergers. Space does not permit a full discussion here, but we can examine a few studies. The Woodstock Theological Center (1990) examined various ethical issues regarding hostile takeovers. One underlying premise in their study was that corporations are social institutions, not just private ones. Stated differently, this group believes that groups that have not bothered to invest in the corporation are in some way, perhaps mystically, entitled to a voice in decisions that affect it. The whole concept of social responsibility of corporations is a slippery slope. Once one starts assigning corporate responsibility to groups other than shareholders, there is no logical stopping point (Hessen, 1979; Berle and Means, 2002). Only shareholders have in fact invested in the corporation. What moral authority do other groups have to claim a share of the corporate pie?

Certainly, corporations have a moral duty to honor employment contracts, but employees do not have any right to a job that goes beyond the terms of their employment contract. Corporations have a moral obligation not to pollute the environment, because doing so constitutes a violation of someone's property rights. One of the problems with environmental economics is such property rights are not always clearly defined. But there is no duty to the community to continue employing members of the community if their services are no longer needed. Milton Friedman got it right when he stated that a corporation's only duty is to its shareholders (Friedman, 1970).

Jensen (1988) summarized the various effects of takeover activity as follows:

- Takeovers benefit target company shareholders. Share premiums exceed 30 percent on average, and can exceed 50 percent;
- Shareholders of acquiring firms gain about 4 percent from a hostile takeover;
- Takeovers increase efficiency by an average of 8 percent, and they do not waste resources;
- Actions by management to eliminate or prevent takeover offers are suspect as being harmful to shareholders;
- Golden parachutes generally do not harm shareholders;
- Predator activities tend to benefit shareholders;
- Acquisition and merger activity has not increased industrial concentration;
- Takeover gains do not come from monopoly power.

Jensen has done a good job of summarizing research in this area, so there is no need to repeat it here. The evidence he uncovers shows that takeovers generally benefit all groups except target company management, which meets the utilitarian ethics test.

One of the main problems, from an ethical perspective, is that corporate directors and managers control vast assets that they do not themselves own (Thompson and Smith, 2001). Since their jobs are on the line whenever a predator targets their company, there is tremendous pressure to use these corporate assets to protect themselves and their jobs at the expense of the shareholders they represent. They have a fiduciary duty to protect shareholder assets, but they sometimes use those assets to protect themselves instead. The court in *Unocal Corp.* v. *Mesa Petroleum* recognizes this potential conflict:

When a board addresses a pending takeover bid it has an obligation to determine whether the offer is in the best interests of the corporation and its shareholders.

In that respect a board's duty is no different from any other responsibility it shoulders, and its decisions should be no less entitled to the respect they otherwise would be accorded in the realm of business judgment. There are, however, certain caveats to a proper exercise of this function. Because of the omnipresent specter that a board may be acting primarily in its own interests, rather than in those of the corporation and its shareholders, there is an enhanced duty which calls for judicial examination at the threshold before the protections of the business judgment rule may be conferred.

The poison pill has been a tool of choice for corporate managers who want to prevent a hostile takeover, being used to increase the cost of a takeover, and thus make it less desirable. If a poison pill prevents the takeover of an inefficient firm, thus allowing inefficient managers to continue at the helm, the result will be continued sub-optimum profits. Since stock price is related to earnings, this means that the stock price will also be lower than would be the case if more efficient managers were allowed to come in and make the corporation more efficient. The mere announcement that a poison pill has been adopted can have an adverse effect on the stock price (Jarrell and Poulsen, 1987; Malatesta and Walkling, 1988; Ryngaert, 1988). Bondholders are also harmed by poison pills (Datta and Iskandar-Datta, 1996).

Poison pills have been shown to be a tool that can be used by entrenched management to protect their jobs at the expense of the shareholders they represent. Yet they continue to exist, with the full support of the legislatures and courts. Velasco (2002) discusses the reasons for their continued existence.

11.4 CONCLUSION

The main ethical issues involved in acquisitions and mergers revolve around property and contract rights, not whether they are good or bad for society or some sub-set thereof. It is difficult to measure gains and losses with any degree of accuracy, and it is impossible to measure them precisely. It is impossible to measure interpersonal utilities, which makes it difficult even to determine whether the result is a positive- or negative-sum game in close situations. Practically the only thing that can be measured is the effect that some antitakeover device such as a poison pill or greenmail has on stock price.

But all this measurement business should serve only as an academic exercise. The only important thing is whether an acquisition or merger, be it friendly or hostile, violates someone's rights. If it does not, then individuals should be able to trade the property they have for the property they want. They should be able to buy or sell shares of the corporation without interference from any individual or government. Any such interference in capitalist acts between consenting adults violates their contract and property rights and can never be justified. But nobody seems to be asking that question. Perhaps it is time they did.

REFERENCES

Berle, A. A. and Means, G. C. (2002) *The Modern Corporation and Private Property* (New Brunswick, NJ/London: Transaction Books).
Brandt, R. B. (1992) *Morality, Utilitarianism, and Rights* (New York: Cambridge University Press).
Buchanan, J. M., Tollison, R. and Tullock, G. (eds) (1980) *Towards a Theory of a Rent-Seeking Society* (College Station, Tex.: Texas A&M University Press).
Datta, S. and Iskandar-Datta, M. (1996) "Takeover Defenses and Wealth Effects on Securityholders: The Case of Poison Pill Adoptions", *Journal of Banking and Finance*, 20: 1231–50.
Frey, R. G. (ed.) (1984) *Utility and Rights* (Minneapolis: University of Minnesota Press).
Friedman, M. (1970) "The Social Responsibility of Business", *The New York Times Magazine*, September 13, pp. 33, 122–6; reprinted in many places, including K. R. Leube (ed.) (1987) *The Essence of Friedman* (Stanford, Calif.: Hoover Institution Press), pp. 36–42.
Goodin, R. E. (1995) *Utilitarianism as a Public Philosophy* (New York: Cambridge University Press).
Hessen, R. (1979) *In Defense of the Corporation* (Stanford, Calif.: Hoover Institution Press).
Jarrell, G. A. and Poulsen, A. (1987) "Shark Repellents and Stock Prices: The Effects of Antitakeover Amendments since 1980", *Journal of Financial Economics*, 19: 127–68.
Jensen, M. (1988) "Takeovers: Their Causes and Consequences", *Journal of Economic Perspectives*, 2(1): 21–48.
Malatesta, P. H. and Walkling, R. A. (1988) "Poison Pill Securities: Stockholder Wealth, Profitability, and Ownership Structure", *Journal of Financial Economics*, 20: 347–76.
Manry, D. and Stangeland, D. (2001) "Greenmail: A Brief History", *Stanford Journal of Law, Business and Finance*, 6: 217–38.
McGee, R. W. (1989) "The Economics of Mergers and Acquisitions", *The Mid-Atlantic Journal of Business*, 25(4): 45–55.
McGee, R. W. (1994) "The Fatal Flaw in NAFTA, GATT and All Other Trade Agreements", *Northwestern Journal of International Law and Business*, 14(3): 549–65.
McGee, R. W. (2006) "Why Is Insider Trading Unethical?", Andreas School of Business Working Paper, Barry University, October.
Mill, J. S. (1993) *On Liberty and Utilitarianism* (New York: Bantam Books).
Rothbard, M. N. (2004) *Man, Economy, and State* (Auburn, Ala: Ludwig von Mises Institute).
Rowley, C. K., Tollison, R. D. and Tullock, G. (eds) (1988) *The Political Economy of Rent-Seeking* (Boston/Dordrecht/Lancaster: Kluwer).
Ryngaert, M. (1988) "The Effect of Poison Pill Securities on Shareholder Wealth", *Journal of Financial Economics*, 20: 377–417.
Shaw, W. H. (1999) *Contemporary Ethics: Taking Account of Utilitarianism* (Oxford: Blackwell).
Thompson, R. B. and Smith, D. G. (2001) "Toward a New Theory of the Shareholder Role: Sacred Space in Corporate Takeovers", *Texas Law Review*, 80: 261–326.
Tullock, G. (1970) *Private Wants, Public Means: An Economic Analysis of the Desirable Scope of Government* (New York: Basic Books).
Tullock, G. (1989) *The Economics of Special Privilege and Rent Seeking* (Boston, Dordrecht, London: Kluwer).
Tullock, G. (1993) *Rent Seeking* (Brookfield, Vt: Edward Elgar).

Velasco, J. (2002) "The Enduring Illegitimacy of the Poison Pill", *Journal of Corporation Law*, 27: 381–423.

Waldron, J. (ed.) (1987) *Nonsense Upon Stilts: Bentham, Burke, and Marx on the Rights of Man*. (New York: Methuen).

Woodstock Theological Center (1990) *Ethical Considerations in Corporate Takeovers* (Washington, DC: Georgetown University Press).

List of Cases

Unocal Corp. v. Mesa Petroleum, 493 A.2d 946, 954 (Del. 1985).

CHAPTER 12

The Use of Equity Swaps in Mergers[1]

Paul U. Ali

12.1 INTRODUCTION

Cash-settled equity swaps are an integral part of any portfolio manager's toolkit. In their simplest form, an equity swap involves one party exchanging cash flows that mimic a fixed or floating interest rate for cash flows designed to replicate the income and capital return of a parcel of shares (Ali, 1999; Marshall and Yuyuenonwatana, 2000). Equity swaps can also be used to replicate the returns on a basket of different shares or an entire stock market. In this way, an investor is able to obtain economic exposure to the shares underlying the equity swap without having to purchase those shares. In addition, investors routinely make use of equity swaps to avoid transactional imposts (for example, stamp duty and capital gains tax on transfers of shares, and withholding taxes on dividends) and overcome legal impediments to dealings in shares (for example, limitations on the short-selling of shares, foreign ownership of shares, and cross-border remittances of dividends and sale proceeds).

A new use has now emerged for cash-settled equity swaps. While they continue to be used extensively to establish pure portfolio positions, increasingly, corporate raiders, arbitrageurs and hedge funds have begun to resort to equity swaps to influence the outcomes of takeover bids. The potentially negative consequences for market transparency – where shareholders in a target company and the market generally are unable to determine who has effective control of the target company's shares, and whether third parties who control significant parcels of the target company's shares may be assisting a bidder in its attempt to gain control of the target – have led regulators in the UK and Australia to treat cash-settled equity swaps as if they were physically settled (Falkner, 2005; Panel on Takeovers and Mergers, 2005b; Takeovers Panel, 2005b).

This regulatory intrusion runs counter to the single factor that differentiates cash-settled equity swaps from physically-settled ones. An investor who has used a cash-settled equity swap to create a long position in shares has only economic exposure to those shares and no entitlement, under the terms of the swap, to delivery of the shares on settlement. Instead, depending on the price performance of the shares during the term of the swap, the investor will either be entitled to receive from its counterparty a payment reflecting any increase in value during that time, or be required to make a payment to the counterparty reflecting any fall in the value of the shares. In contrast, an investor who holds a long position in shares under a physically-settled equity swap will, on settlement, be entitled to take delivery of those shares from its counterparty.

Regardless of the type of swap, it is likely that the investor's counterparty will acquire the underlying shares to hedge its exposure to the investor under the swap. If the counterparty does, in fact, own or control the underlying shares and has allocated those shares to the swap, it is uncontroversial that the investor, under a physically-settled equity swap, should be taken to have a similar control interest in the underlying shares to what its counterparty has, because of its contractual right to take delivery of those shares at some future date. However, it is difficult to see how, in the face of a cash-settled equity swap, a similar control interest in the underlying shares should be extended to the investor. Yet this conflation of a synthetic interest in shares with a control interest in those shares is effectively what the regulator of takeovers in the UK has accomplished, and what its counterpart in Australia has sought to achieve.

12.2 EQUITY SWAPS

Equity swaps are over-the-counter derivatives, designed to replicate the economic incidents of individual shares, baskets of different shares, or equity indices (Ali, 1999; Marshall and Yuyuenonwatana, 2000). They involve the exchange of equity-linked payments, and payments linked to some other asset. In a "vanilla" equity swap, the investor will receive cashflows equal to the dividends paid on a notional parcel of shares, and will make interest rate payments on a notional principal amount to its counterparty, the swap dealer. (The interest rate component is no different from the single leg of a vanilla interest rate swap.) Equity swaps are typically cash-settled. On the maturity or the earlier termination of the swap, the investor will be entitled to receive from its counterparty an amount calculated by reference to any increase in the capital value of the notional parcel of shares. If, instead, there has been a decline in the capital value of the underlying shares, the investor will be obligated to make a payment to its counterparty of an amount calculated by reference to that fall in value.

Equity swaps overlie notional, not actual, parcels of shares. Accordingly, the mere entry into a cash-settled equity swap will not result in the investor acquiring ownership or control of the shares underlying the swap. From the terms of the swap alone, there should thus be no question of the investor obtaining a control interest in those shares.

12.3 HEDGING OF SWAP EXPOSURE

Although an equity swap involves only a notional parcel of shares, there is a strong incentive for the counterparty (where the investor has used the equity swap to establish a long position in shares) to acquire the actual shares represented by that notional parcel (Ali, 1999). The acquisition of those shares at or about the inception of the swap enables the counterparty to hedge its exposure under the swap, by limiting its risk of loss in the event that there is a significant increase in the capital value of the notional parcel of shares during the term of the swap.

It is not, however, usual for the investor, under a cash-settled equity swap, to have a control interest in the shares held by the counterparty to hedge its exposure to the investor. The investor will not normally be in a position to direct how the counterparty should undertake any hedging activities (for example, it may be more expedient for the counterparty to hedge its exposure by using equity derivatives or some other asset as a proxy for the notional parcel of shares). Nor it is common for the terms of the swap to confer upon the investor the right to direct how any shares acquired by the counterparty are to be voted, or in what circumstances the counterparty may dispose of those shares. In many instances, while the counterparty may reserve the right to vote the shares in accordance with its own best interests, it may abstain from voting not only because of its relationship with the investor, but also because it has a wide range of clients and wishes to avoid taking sides among them (ISDA, 2005).

Thus neither the equity swap itself nor the ancillary hedging activities of the counterparty should cause the investor to be treated as having a control interest in any shares acquired by the counterparty for hedging purposes.

12.4 "FEAR AND LOATHING" IN TAKEOVER BATTLES

Despite an investor not having a formal control interest in the shares referenced by a cash-settled equity swap (in that, as seen above, the investor has neither title to the shares nor any legal right to control the counterparty's dealings with the shares), the investor may nonetheless be in a position to exert significant de facto control over the shares. Control of shares normally flows from a party having title to shares or otherwise holding legally enforceable rights over those shares (in particular, in relation to voting or disposal of the shares). In the case of a cash-settled equity swap, economic ownership is separated from title or legally enforceable rights over shares. However, the existence of de facto control linked to economic ownership may enable an investor or a bidder to circumvent the disclosure requirements that apply to substantial shareholders, and to significant dealings in shares during a takeover, as these disclosure requirements are normally triggered by the acquisition of title or some other formal control interest in shares.

This de facto control appears to be manifested in the mutual understanding of the investor and its counterparty to the swap (Panel on Takeovers and Mergers, 2005b). On the one hand, title to the shares acquired by the counterparty for hedging purposes will be retained by the counterparty for the term of the swap, and there will normally be nothing in the terms of the swap to suggest that the counterparty does not have full control over those shares. Yet it is often the case that the shares will be voted by the counterparty in a manner consistent with the wishes of the investor, whether for relationship reasons or because the counterparty is acting in concert with the investor (Panel on Takeovers and Mergers, 2005a). Also, as it is unlikely that the counterparty will wish to have naked exposure to the investor, both parties will be aware that any shares acquired for hedging purposes are likely to be held by the counterparty for the full term of the swap, and thus on the maturity or earlier termination of the swap those shares will be available for acquisition by the investor (Panel on Takeovers and Mergers, 2005a).

The concern that this de facto control might undermine the transparency of the market for corporate control has led to the bodies that regulate takeovers in the UK and Australia (the UK Panel on Takeovers and Mergers, and the Australian Takeovers Panel, respectively) extending to cash-settled equity swaps the disclosure requirements that apply to acquisitions of shares and physically-settled equity swaps in the context of takeovers (Lumsden and Laughland, 2005).

The potential of cash-settled equity swaps to influence the outcome of a takeover battle was explored in the extensive legal proceedings concerning the takeover of an Australian coal mining company, Austral Coal, by a similar Australian company, Centennial, in early 2005. Shortly after Austral Coal and Centennial announced that the latter would be making a friendly takeover bid for the former, Glencore, the international commodities trader, acquired 4.99 percent of the shares of Austral Coal (placing it just below the 5 percent trigger for disclosure of a substantial shareholding under the Australian companies legislation). This physical acquisition of shares was coupled with two cash-settled equity swaps involving 7.4 percent of Austral Coal shares. Glencore eventually disclosed its physical shareholding in and synthetic exposure to Austral Coal, some two weeks after its aggregate economic interest in Austral Coal shares reached 5 percent (however, as Glencore correctly noted in its disclosure statement, the Australian disclosure requirements did not extend to pure economic exposure). In fact, it is not market practice in Australia for investors with only economic exposure to shares created by a cash-settled equity swap to disclose that exposure to the market, regardless of the level of shareholding referenced by the swap (Federal Court, 2006).

Centennial was ultimately successful in obtaining majority control of Austral Coal (eventually reaching 85.76 percent ownership) but was not able to squeeze out the other shareholders by means of the compulsory acquisition procedure contained in the Australian companies legislation, since it was unable to satisfy the requisite 90 percent shareholding threshold, as neither Glencore nor its two swap counterparties were willing to accept Centennial's takeover bid. The Australian Takeovers Panel found that Glencore's conduct constituted "unacceptable circumstances" in relation to Austral Coal (Takeovers Panel, 2005a; Takeovers Panel, 2005b).

The Panel ordered Glencore to compensate those shareholders of Austral Coal who had sold their shares during the period between Glencore first obtaining an aggregate economic interest in 5 percent of the shares of Austral Coal, and its disclosure of that interest to the market two weeks later (on the basis that Glencore had been able, during this period, to establish its long position in Austral Coal shares more cheaply and sooner than if it had made an earlier disclosure of its 5 percent economic interest to the market) (Takeovers Panel, 2005b). Thus, had Glencore's disclosure been more timely, buyers and sellers in the market would have been better-informed as to the demand for Austral Coal shares, and the market would have operated more efficiently than it did as to the pricing and allocation of those shares (Takeovers Panel, 2005b).

The decisive factor in the Australian Takeover Panel's decision was the de facto control that Glencore was able to exert over the Austral Coal shares acquired by its two counterparties for hedging purposes. It was accepted that the cash-settled equity swaps did not, on their own, confer upon Glencore any ownership interest in the hedge shares or the legal right to call for delivery of the hedge shares or to require its counterparties to undertake any action involving those shares (Takeovers Panel, 2005b). In addition, the terms of the equity swaps made it clear, consistent with market practice, that Glencore had no formal control rights in respect of the hedge shares (Takeovers Panel, 2005b).

While the swap counterparties were free to hedge their exposure to Glencore under the swaps in any way they thought fit, it was likely that Glencore either knew or could reasonably assume that the counterparties had no practical alternative to using Austral Coal shares to hedge their exposure (Takeovers Panel, 2005a; Takeovers Panel, 2005b). There were no options or other exchange-traded derivatives in respect of Austral Coal shares. Shares in other mining companies were not a suitable proxy for Austral Coal shares (as Austral Coal operated only a single mine, produced a single product and, moreover, was experiencing significant operational and financial difficulties).

Nor were there available futures contracts or an index that could be used as a proxy. Austral Coal was also the subject of a takeover bid, which was likely to make the price performance of its shares more volatile and reduce their correlation with the shares of other coal-mining companies. Finally, both counterparties were aware of the possibility that Glencore might make a competing takeover bid for Austral Coal, and this only increased the economic incentive for them to hedge their exposure by acquiring Austral Coal shares.

The counterparties thus had a strong economic incentive not only to acquire Austral Coal shares to hedge their exposure under the swaps but also not to dispose of those shares during the term of the swaps. In fact, under the terms of the two swaps, the level of the exposure of the counterparties to Glencore never exceeded the value of the hedge shares that the counterparty was able to acquire (Federal Court, 2006).

This economic incentive was taken as conferring on Glencore a significant degree of negative de facto control over the shares. The Australian Takeovers Panel considered that Glencore could affect the counterparties' rights to dispose of the shares by agreeing or refusing to agree to an early termination of the swaps (Takeovers Panel, 2005b). However, the Panel did not consider that this control translated into a positive power to control the disposal of the hedge shares, or an ability to acquire the hedge shares from the counterparties on the maturity or earlier termination of the swaps (Takeovers Panel, 2005b).

Accordingly, even though a cash-settled equity swap creates only economic exposure to shares, the Australian Takeovers Panel was of the opinion that that economic exposure – because the counterparty had no practical alternative to acquiring Austral Coal shares, and to retaining those shares so that its exposure to Glencore under the swap would continue – could give rise to de facto control over the shares. That control was therefore sufficient to create a disclosable interest (under Australian companies' legislation) in respect of the shares underlying the swap. This was so even though the control was only negative control in the sense that the existence of the investor's economic exposure for as long as the swap was in place was sufficient to prevent the counterparty from disposing of the shares during the term of the swap (and that the investor, Glencore, could determine whether the swap should be terminated prior to maturity).

Despite Glencore having no ownership interest in the hedge shares, or there being any arrangement between Glencore and its counterparty conferring on Glencore a positive power to exercise or control the voting of the shares or a positive power to dispose of or control the disposition of the shares, the Australian Takeovers Panel found that Glencore's de facto negative control was sufficient to trigger the operation of the disclosure rules that apply to significant acquisitions of shares during a takeover bid (Takeovers Panel, 2005b). Furthermore, this negative control over the disposal of the hedge shares (despite it not amounting to positive control over a disposal or engendering an entitlement to delivery of the shares) was considered by the Australian Takeovers Panel as being a more effective means of exerting control over the shares than a consensual arrangement or mutual understanding as to the voting of the shares or the affairs of the target company, or where parties were acting in concert in relation to a target company. In the latter case, the parties were free to withdraw from the arrangement at any time but that was not a practical possibility for Glencore's swap counterparties: the economic incentive to hold Austral Coal shares for the term of the swaps and the absence of a suitable alternative hedge meant that Glencore could rely on the swap counterparties not disposing of the hedge shares unilaterally during the term of the swaps, and thus could utilize the swaps effectively to prevent Centennial acquiring 100 percent of Austral Coal (Takeovers Panel, 2005b).

The Australian Takeovers Panel's analysis of negative control giving rise to a disclosable interest was rejected emphatically by the Federal Court of Australia following Glencore's application to have the court review the Panel's decision. The Federal Court accepted the Panel's findings that the counterparties were unlikely to dispose of the hedge shares as long as they had exposure to the Glencore shares under the swaps, and that the only power Glencore had in relation to those shares was the power to consent to an early termination of the swaps (Federal Court, 2006). The Court, however, disagreed with the Panel that this negative control was, on its own, sufficient to trigger the application of the disclosure rules.

Thus, for there to be a disclosable interest in the hedge shares, Glencore had to have "something more than being in a position to release an entity from a contingent contractual obligation simply because that entity has protected itself from exposure to that contingent contractual obligation by acquiring shares in a company, being shares that it has no obligation to acquire and that it has no obligation to retain" (Federal Court, 2006). As there was no practical hedge available to the counterparties other than the hedge shares, there was a strong economic incentive – but no legal obligation – for them to acquire the hedge shares. Equally, there was a strong economic incentive for the counterparties to retain the shares during the term of the swaps, but there was no legal constraint on them selling or lending out the hedge shares during that time.

This does not mean that economic exposure to shares created by cash-settled equity swaps will never give rise to a disclosable interest in the hedge shares. The Federal Court clearly left open the possibility that the disclosure rules would apply (and, consequently, non-disclosure could lead to a valid finding of unacceptable circumstances by the Australian Takeovers Panel) where an investor has a positive power to exercise or control the exercise of votes attaching to the hedge shares, or a positive power to dispose or control the exercise of a power to dispose of the hedge shares, however ephemeral or unenforceable that power or control might be (Federal Court, 2006). A similar result would be likely to follow where the counterparty, having such a control interest in respect of the hedge shares, was acting in concert with the investor in relation to the voting or disposition of the shares or the affairs of the target company (Federal Court, 2006).

12.5 CONCLUSION

Cash-settled equity swaps can be used in mergers to affect the outcome of a takeover bid (either by facilitating a bidder's gaining of control of the target company or, as in the case of the Austral Coal takeover discussed above, creating a blocking stake), by concealing control of shares (Hu and Black, 2006). These swaps separate economic ownership from title to shares, and by doing so make it possible to circumvent the disclosure rules predicated on title or formal control rights, such as voting rights (Hu and Black, 2006).

Market consensus has been that a cash-settled equity swap, particularly one whose contractual terms made it explicit that the investor has no interest in any hedge shares and no positive power to control the voting or disposal of those shares, would not give rise to the investor having a disclosable interest in the shares (Price and Mant, 2005). Even the inevitability of the counterparty acquiring the shares referenced by the swap to hedge its exposure to the investor, or the inevitability of the hedge shares being available for purchase by the investor on the maturity or earlier termination of the swap, would not alter this result. Accordingly, in order for the investor to have a disclosable interest in the hedge shares, there has to be something more, such as an arrangement or understanding between the investor and its counterparty (beyond mutual expectations based on the circumstances surrounding the entry into the swap) as to the hedge shares or the affairs of the target company.

This comfortable assumption that cash-settled equity swaps and other cash-settled equity-linked derivatives are outside the scope of the disclosure requirements that apply to substantial shareholders and to significant dealings in shares during a takeover has been overturned by the UK Panel on Takeovers and Mergers. The changes to the Takeovers Code by the UK Panel on Takeovers and Mergers effectively conflate an economic interest in shares referenced by a swap with a control interest in those shares. A similar result was attempted by the Australian Takeovers Panel in relation to the recent takeover of Austral Coal by treating negative control (derived from the discretionary power of the investor to agree or not agree to an early termination of a cash-settled equity swap) as giving rise to a disclosable interest. That interpretation has been rejected by the Federal Court of Australia, but the court did not rule out positive control giving rise to a disclosable interest, despite that control being ephemeral in nature, or the fact that it might be grounded on an unenforceable arrangement.

The treatment of cash-settled equity swaps evinced by takeover regulators in the UK and Australia may have an adverse impact on investors who have used such swaps to establish pure portfolio positions and have no intention of acquiring or facilitating the acquisition of control of a target company (for example, where such a swap is being used to implement a merger arbitrage strategy) or where an investor with a long position under a cash-settled equity swap has offset that position (ISDA, 2006). There is also the risk that the regulatory re-characterization of cash-settled equity swaps might undermine or distort market transparency. Cash-settled equity swaps reference notional, rather than actual parcels of shares, and it is conceivable that the application of disclosure requirements to such swaps could lead to the disclosure of many multiples of the real share capital of particular companies (ISDA, 2005).

This is not to deny, however, the potential of cash-settled equity swaps to deliver or deny control in a takeover situation. The parties to the swap may have entered into the swap on the understanding that the counterparty will warehouse the hedge shares for the investor for the term of the swap and the investor will acquire the shares on the maturity of the swap, or that the counterparty will at the very least remove the hedge shares from the free float of shares available to competing bidders and arbitrageurs. In these circumstances, a properly informed and transparent market for corporate control may mandate disclosure by the investor of its control interest in the hedge shares.

NOTE

1. This research was supported by a grant from the Australian Research Council (DP0557673).

REFERENCES

Ali, P. U. (1999) "Mimicking Shares: The Nature and Regulation of Equity Swaps", *Company and Securities Law Journal*, 17: 436–52.
Falkner, R. (2005) "Contracts for Differences: The Case for Disclosure", *International Financial Law Review*, October: 1–4.
Federal Court of Australia (2006) *Glencore International AG v Takeovers Panel*, FCA 274, 22 March.
Hu, H. T. C. and Black, B. (2006) "Empty Voting and Hidden (Morphable) Ownership: Taxonomy, Implications and Reforms", *Business Lawyer*, 61(3): 1011–70.
International Swaps and Derivatives Association (ISDA) (2005) Letter to Panel on Takeovers and Mergers, 28 February.
International Swaps and Derivatives Association (ISDA) (2006) Letter to Panel on Takeovers and Mergers, 27 January.
Lumsden, A. and Laughland, I. (2005) "Derivatives in Takeovers: The New Battleground?", *Corrs Public Securities Group*, Corrs Chambers Westgarth, Melbourne, 21 April.

Marshall, J. F. and Yuyuenonwatana, R. P. (2000) "Equity Swaps: Structures, Uses and Pricing", in J. C. Francis, W. W. Toy and J. G. Whittaker, *The Handbook of Equity Derivatives* (New York: John Wiley).

Panel on Takeovers and Mergers (2005a) Consultation Paper Issued by the Code Committee of the Panel: Dealings in Derivatives and Options – Outline Proposals Relating to Amendments Proposed to be Made to the Takeovers Code and the SARS, PCP 2005/1, 7 January.

Panel on Takeovers and Mergers (2005b) Consultation Paper Issued by the Code Committee of the Panel: Dealings in Derivatives and Options – Detailed Proposals Relating to Amendments Proposed to be Made to the Takeovers Code, Part 1: Disclosure Issues, PCP 2005/2, 13 May.

Price, C. and Mant, J. (2005) "The Panel Rules on Cash-Settled Swaps", *Focus: Mergers & Acquisitions*, Allens Arthur Robinson, Melbourne, August.

Takeovers Panel (2005a) *In the Matter of Austral Coal Limited*, 02(R), ATP 16, 20 July.

Takeovers Panel (2005b) *In the Matter of Austral Coal Limited*, 02(RR), ATP 20, 15 November.

CHAPTER 13

Banking Performance in Domestic and Cross-Border Acquisitions

Sergio Sanfilippo Azofra, Belén Díaz Díaz, Myriam García Olalla and Carlos López Gutiérrez

13.1 INTRODUCTION

During the 1990s, the banking sector experienced an unprecedented process of consolidation in most developed countries, in which mergers and acquisitions between credit institutions reached previously unknown levels. Bank concentration became relevant in the 1980s in the USA, becoming a worldwide phenomenon with increasing intensity during the 1990s. In fact, the number of mergers and acquisitions (M&As) among financial institutions in Europe rose from 330 in 1990 to 1,072 in 2000, and those carried out by banks rose from 97 in 1990 to 269 in 2000 (Thomson Financial, 2001).

The important growth in the number of M&As has been regarded by several authors as the financial institutions' strategic answer to the greater competitive pressure caused by the development of financial markets, disintermediation, deregulation, financial innovation and the increase in technological possibilities (Calomiris and Karceski, 1998; Berger et al., 1999). In this sense, bank expansion has been promoted primarily by two factors: the ability of banks to make acquisitions in the 1990s; and the deregulation of the industry.

According to the first factor, the improvement in economic conditions may have made it easier to obtain high levels of capital and certain excess capacity, which would have contributed to accelerating the consolidation process. Furthermore, although the serious crisis starting in 2000 put a substantial brake on this process, the European banks began to take up positions once again after overcoming several years of difficulties with their results accounts. In this regard, banks are seeking opportunities that will allow them to diversify geographically in markets with potentially greater profits.

Also, the deregulation factor has promoted a significant part of the increase in cross-border consolidation operations in the financial sector (Berger et al., 1999; Boot, 1999).[1] In the European Union (EU), the effective elimination in 1992 of barriers to the movement of workers, goods, services and capital across the borders of member countries – the benefits of which had already been highlighted in the Cecchini Report in 1988[2] – and the introduction of the "Second Directive on Banking Coordination", which reduces restrictions on the expansion of financial institutions within the EU, should promote M&As among member countries. Moreover, the privatization programs of national banks in several Latin-American countries and in Eastern Europe provide a good opportunity to move into these markets.[3]

Despite the increased liberalization, since the mid-1990s, 67 percent of the mergers and acquisitions carried out by European banks were domestic, and 33 percent were cross-border. With regard to the latter operations, the number of mergers and acquisitions carried out between two banks in the EU (359) was less than those carried out with banks in other countries (464).

The small number of international operations has raised their relevance for discussion. On the one hand, domestic transactions in the EU are exhausting their ability to generate scale and scope economies and to reduce costs, and hence M&As, among banks from different countries could be a good opportunity to overcome this limitation. On the other hand, banks' managers may still expect greater profits from domestic operations, because of the lower cultural, language and regulation barriers, and this may be why they do not make cross-border transactions.[4]

In fact, although both types of operation share numerous reasons for being carried out, domestic and cross-border operations are affected by different factors, thus leading to different results. Some banks, such as the Santander Group, BBVA or Deutsche Bank, have begun to take positions in the European market. However, in some cases, national authorities have stopped foreign banks from taking over domestic ones, preventing profit gains from international M&As.[5] In this respect, the literature on M&As, although analyzing the reasons for carrying out international acquisitions,[6] has overlooked the comparison between the performance obtained in domestic and international operations.

In this context, it seems appropriate to analyze the acquirers' performance in financial consolidation operations, differentiating domestic from cross-border transactions. Our analysis – which will focus on acquisitions, since international mergers are less frequent – is carried out using panel data methodology for a sample of European banks during the period 1992–2000.

This chapter is structured as follows. Section 13.2 reviews the studies on this subject and proposes the hypotheses to test. Section 13.3 describes the sample, methodology and variables used in the study. Section 13.4 presents the main results obtained from the empirical analysis, and finally, we outline our main conclusions.

13.2 CROSS-BORDER M&As: A LITERATURE REVIEW

In general terms, both domestic and cross-border acquisitions allow financial institutions to achieve economies of scale and scope, increase market power, improve management and reduce risk through geographical or product diversification.[7] Empirical studies, however, mainly from the USA, show that acquirers' gains are generally small or non-existent (Berger and Humphrey, 1992; DeYoung, 1993; Linder and Crane, 1993; Fixler and Zieschang, 1993; Peristiani, 1997). The majority of these studies use data from the 1980s, so they are framed within a period of time with very different characteristics from those corresponding to more recent times. There are no cases that cover the technological progress and financial deregulation that occurred in the 1990s.[8] More recent studies, however, find substantial profits are earned from financial consolidation operations, although these are generally in the long term. In the early years after the acquisition, the integration process and restructuring of the banks led to cost increases (Akhavein *et al.*, 1997; Rhoades, 1998; Hughes *et al.*, 1999; Becher, 2000; Cyree *et al.*, 2000; Carbó and Humphrey, 2002).

Most of these studies have focused on the US market, but their conclusions, although relevant, cannot be extrapolated directly to their European counterparts, because of the differences between the two financial systems. Nevertheless, European works – which are not as numerous as North American studies–although falling short of drawing final conclusions, have found some profits deriving from financial concentration operations.[9]

Focusing on the differences between domestic and international acquisitions, it should be highlighted that, while these share some reasons for being carried out, they are sometimes affected in a special manner by different factors (described below). Logically, then, they are likely to have different results.

With regard to domestic transactions, empirical evidence shows that these operations, although failing to provide a high degree of diversification, can lead to appreciable improvements in efficiency and performance, mainly because of the elimination of redundant costs resulting from geographical overlapping (Berger and Humphrey, 1992; Pilloff, 1996). Furthermore, Berger (2000) considers that scale economy gains, deriving from the larger size achieved after the M&A, are more noticeable when the banks that join forces are in the same local market, since domestic operations allow the distribution systems of the participating institutions to be grouped together and management to be combined. Finally, domestic acquisitions allow profits to be obtained from the increase in market power, since a leading position in a market allows the banks to increase the interest rate charged for their loans and reduce the interest rate paid on deposits (Berger *et al.*, 2000).

Unlike domestic M&As, international operations make it possible to attain a high-risk diversification because of the low correlation between costs and income from different countries or regions,[10] while making a fast entry into new markets possible.[11] Nevertheless, the acquirers' efficiency in cross-border transactions may decline, because the management and control of companies that are far away becomes more difficult, or because there are barriers against incorporating foreign companies in domestic economies. First, these barriers may be a result of the restrictions normally imposed by governments on mergers and acquisitions made by foreign companies. Governments may even approve or ban specific operations and promote domestic acquisitions to prevent M&As being carried out by foreign companies[12] (Boot, 1999). Second, language, cultural and regulatory barriers appear. In this regard, it is noted that merger and acquisition operations beyond the borders of the country to which the acquirer belongs are less common in the banking sector than in any other. This may be because of the importance of information asymmetries in banking relations, as well as regulatory restrictions (Focarelli and Pozzolo, 2001). Despite the fact that regulatory barriers on international transactions tend to disappear, information costs are maintained.

In this sense, most of the previous research shows that international operations do not lead to important cost savings, nor are they beneficial for the banks involved or their shareholders, a result of the existence of several barriers against accomplishing the operation.[13] Furthermore, domestic banks are more efficient than the nationals owned by foreign companies, which question the benefits of international acquisitions.[14]

However, within the EU there are certain reasons that may make profit gains possible in consolidation operations between member countries. In the first place, the effective removal in 1992 of barriers to the movement of labor, goods, services and capital across borders, coupled with the introduction of the Second Directive on Banking Coordination, have created a particularly favorable regulatory environment for carrying out this type of operation within the EU. In fact, Berger *et al.* (2000) show that international consolidation occurs in response to deregulation. In the second place, problems with information do not appear to be important in this case, since a considerable number of mergers and acquisitions have taken place between countries with cultural links – such as Belgium and the Netherlands, or among the Scandinavian countries (Lindblom and Von Koch, 2002). Also, Vander Vennet (1996) finds some benefits in the consolidation operations between different EU countries.

In summary, although international consolidation implies greater diversification than domestic transactions,[15] the profits deriving from international operations are not generally sufficient to compensate for the costs derived from organizational problems and barriers involving regulations, language, information and so on. However, cross-border transactions within the EU may obtain benefits as a result of the regulatory changes since the mid-1990s. Unlike the situation in international operations, domestic consolidation, although lacking such a degree of diversification, may generate appreciable improvements in efficiency and performance, as well as a better use of scale economies, especially in the long term (Berger and Humphrey, 1992; Pilloff, 1996).

In this regard, the following hypotheses are proposed:

Hypothesis 1 *Domestic financial acquisitions and those where the acquired bank belongs to another EU country have a positive influence on the acquirer's performance.*

Hypothesis 2 *International (non-EU) financial acquisitions have no positive influence and may even have a negative influence on the acquirer's performance.*

13.3 EMPIRICAL ANALYSIS: DEFINITION OF SAMPLE, VARIABLES AND METHODOLOGY

13.3.1 Definition of sample

The empirical analysis is carried out for a sample of EU financial institutions during the period 1992–2000. We started with a sample of 4,187 European banks that supply data to the Bankscope database, and then refined the sample in the following way: we eliminated from the sample those banks for which we did not have all the necessary information to calculate the variables. Moreover, since the effect of acquisitions on acquirers' performance may be visible in the long term, we only considered the banks for which we have data for at least five consecutive years (with both adjustments, we eliminated 1,881 banks). The remaining banks accomplished 435 acquisitions (according to Thompson Financial Mergers database, 2001).

Pairs of banks that were involved in a merger during the sample period and became one bank after the acquisition were also eliminated, since the aim of our study is to analyze the effects of the acquisition on the bidders' returns. We also eliminated the banks that were targeted for acquisition; thus, in the sample, we have acquirers and non-acquirers that were not targeted by a bidder, because, as Jensen and Ruback (1983) note, acquisitions have a positive effect on the targets' performance. Thus, if we want to focus on bidders' returns, we should eliminate these banks from the sample, to avoid a bias in the results because the bank was acquired. In these adjustments, we eliminated 115 banks and 195 acquisitions.

Finally, the analysis was conducted on a sample of 2,191 EU banks, of which 105 carried out at least one acquisition in the period analyzed. The total number of acquisitions is 240. Table 13.1 shows the number of banks per year and country, as well as the number of acquisitions considered in the sample. As well as the databases mentioned above, we also used *World Development Indicators 2003* for macroeconomic information.

13.3.2 Variables

In this study we analyze whether acquirers improve their performance after the acquisition, differentiating among domestic transactions, operations within the EU, and international acquisitions (when the target is outside the EU). In order to carry out the analysis it is necessary to define the following variables.

Dependent variable

With regard to the dependent variable, we used both return on assets (*ROA*) and return on equity (*ROE*). Return on assets is calculated on the mean assets of the bank at the beginning and end of the year, and return on equity is calculated on the mean equity value.

Profitability can be measured taking into account the net profit generated (Focarelli and Pozzolo, 2001). Nevertheless, if the countries have different taxation systems and amortization rules, this measurement would include such differences, and the results obtained in the analysis may be biased because of the way that performance is measured. For this reason, we use two measures of performance, since performance can be influenced by the different tax systems in each country, and by differences in goodwill amortization among countries:[16]

- *ROApretax* and *ROEpretax* are calculated using profit before taxes, therefore eliminating any possible influence of the different tax systems on the results of our analyses (Dickerson *et al.*, 1997).

- *ROAadjusted* and *ROEadjusted* are calculated using profit before taxes plus provisions and amortizations, eliminating any possible influence of the different amortization rules on the results of our analyses (Houston *et al.*, 2001).

Independent variables

As far as independent variables are concerned, we distinguish between those referring to acquisition operations and control variables, as described below and summarized in Table 13.2.

Table 13.1 Sample: number of acquisitions and number of banks in the sample, classified by year, country and type of operation

	No. of acquisitions	No. of acquiring banks	Total no. of banks
1992	6	6	282
1993	18	16	1 597
1994	30	21	1 922
1995	31	19	2 112
1996	38	23	2 191
1997	34	24	2 191
1998	19	17	2 191
1999	29	21	2 191
2000	35	25	1 207
Total	**240**		
Austria	9	3	47
Belgium	9	3	48
Germany	50	20	1 282
Denmark	7	6	78
Spain	23	14	100
Finland	0	0	6
France	46	19	213
UK	2	2	50
Greece	8	2	4
Ireland	6	1	12
Italy	60	23	224
Luxembourg	11	7	92
Holland	1	1	23
Portugal	6	2	7
Sweden	2	2	5
Total	**240**	**105**	**2 191**

No. of domestic operations	No. of cross-border operations (EU)	No. of cross-border operations (Non-EU)	Total no. of operations
176	18	46	240

Source: Thompson Financial Database.

Table 13.2 Definition of the variables used in the empirical analysis

Dependent variables

Economic profitability: ROApretax_{it} = Profit before tax$_{it}$ /[(Assets$_{it-1}$ + Assets$_{it}$)/2]

ROAadjusted_{it} = Profit before tax$_{it}$ + provisions$_{it}$/ [(Assets$_{it-1}$ + Assets $_{it}$)/2]

Financial profitability: ROEpretax_{it} = Profit before tax$_{it}$ / [(equity$_{it-1}$ + equity$_{it}$)/2]

ROEadjusted_{it} = Profit before tax$_{it}$ + provisions$_{it}$/ [(equity$_{it-1}$ + equity$_{it}$)/2]

Independent variables

Analysis of domestic acquisitions, those performed within the EU and those performed outside the EU Hypotheses 1 and 2
(dummy variables take value 0 in the case contrary to the one mentioned above)

National$_{it}$ = 1 if bank i carries out an acquisition within its country in $t-1$ and from then on adopts the value 1

National0$_{it}$ = 1 if bank i carries out an acquisition within its country in year t

....

National4$_{it}$ = 1 if bank i has carried out an acquisition within its country in year $t-4$

EU$_{it}$ = 1 if bank i carries out an acquisition within the EU in $t-1$ and from then on adopts value 1

EU0$_{it}$ = 1 if bank i carries out an acquisition within the EU in year t

....

EU4$_{it}$ = 1 if bank i has carried out an acquisition within the EU in year $t-4$

Non-EU$_{it}$ = 1 if bank i carries out an acquisition outside the EU in $t-1$ and from then on adopts the value 1

Non-EU0$_{it}$ = 1 if bank i carries out an acquisition outside the EU in year t

....

Non-EU4$_{it}$ = 1 if bank i has carried out an acquisition outside the EU in year $t-4$

Control variables

GDP$_{it}$ = natural logarithm of the GDP per capita based on the purchase power parity

HERF = $\Sigma_i(\text{Deposits}_{it}/\Sigma_i \text{Deposits}_{it})^2$

SHARE$_{it}$ = Market share = Deposits$_{it}$/Σ_i Deposits$_{it}$

SIZE$_{it}$ = Natural logarithm of total Assets$_{it}$

EQUITY$_{it}$ = Equity$_{it}$ /Assets$_{it}$

DEP$_{it}$ = Deposits$_{it}$ /Assets$_{it}$

LOANSDEP$_{it}$ = Loans$_{it}$ /Deposits$_{it}$

Source: Thompson Financial Database and Bankscope.

Independent variables regarding acquisitions

The fact that a bank carried out an acquisition is considered in the empirical analysis introducing dummy variables, explained below. In general terms, for each kind of acquisition we analyze two issues. First, we study whether there is a permanent change in the bidders' performance as a result of the acquisition. In this regard, a dummy variable is introduced for each type of acquisition, distinguishing whether the operation is between banks in the same country (*National*), between banks belonging to different countries in the EU (*EU*) or outside the EU (*Non-EU*), respectively. These variables take the value 1 from the year following the acquisitions, and zero otherwise (Dickerson *et al.*, 1997). For example, with regard the National variable, this will take value 1 for the year following the acquisition made by a bank within its own country, and 0 otherwise. In any case, if a bank makes more than one acquisition in the same year this is considered to be a single operation for the purposes of the analysis.

However, the analysis of permanent change in performance might entail two problems. On the one hand, it does not take into account the fact that there can be a lag between acquisition activity and performance change. In fact, empirical studies have analyzed the period starting from the year of the acquisition to six years after it (Rhoades, 1994). On the other hand, it does not consider the possibility that a bank carried out several acquisitions during the sample period. To overcome these two limitations, we conducted a second analysis in which we studied when the change in performance is produced. To do this, five dummy variables were introduced for each operation category (*National*, *EU* or *Non-EU*), so that, for example, in the case of national M&As, we have the following variables: variable $National0_{it}$ takes value 1 in the acquisition year, $National1_{it}$ takes value 1 one year after the acquisition year, and so on until variable $National4_{it}$, which takes value 1 four years after the acquisition. The same definition of variables is applicable for M&As both within and outside the EU.

Control variables

The control variables used consider both the characteristics of each bank and the characteristics of the country to which it belongs. The development level of each bank's country is proxied by the variable natural logarithm of GDP (gross domestic product) per capita, based on purchasing power parity (GDP).

A variable that considers the level of concentration of the deposits in each country is also introduced, measured through the Herfindahl index.[17] We have one concentration index for each country and year of the sample. The index is calculated considering all the banks in each country for which we have the data on deposits in the Bankscope database. The mean number

Table 13.3 Average number of banks per country 1992–2000, used in the Herfindahl index calculation

Country	Average no. of banks	Country	Average no. of banks
Austria	98	Italy	321
Belgium	83	Luxembourg	113
Denmark	86	Netherlands	42
Finland	10	Portugal	27
France	364	Spain	139
Germany	1 533	Sweden	19
Greece	20	UK	185
Ireland	28		

of banks considered during the sample period to estimate the index is shown in Table 13.3:

$$HERF_{it} = \sum_{i=1}^{n} \left(\frac{Deposits_{it}}{\sum_{i=1}^{n} Deposits_{it}} \right)^2$$

i is each of the banks in a country

The control variables that consider specific characteristics of the bank are those traditionally used in studies on profitability and bank efficiency (Berger and Humphrey, 1992; Akhavein et al., 1997; Cyree et al., 2000).

- The size of the bank, measured by the natural logarithm of total assets ($SIZE$).
- Market share, measured by the proportion of the total deposits of a country that corresponds to a bank – that is, by the ratio $Deposits_{it}/\sum_i Deposits_{it}$, with i being each of the banks in a country ($SHARE$).
- Equity over total assets ($EQUITY$).
- Loans over deposits, to show the percentage of deposits that are returned to the banking activity through loans ($LOANSDEP$).
- Deposits over total assets (DEP).

Table 13.4 shows the descriptive statistics of the variables used in the empirical analysis (mean and standard deviation).

Table 13.4 Descriptive statistics of the variables used in the empirical analysis

Variable	Mean	Standard deviation	Variable	Mean	Standard deviation
GDP	10.0082	0.14300	DEP	0.8164	0.15908
HERF	0.0386	0.04289	LOANSDEP	1.0108	30.70046
SIZE (€ millions)	1963.2815	7882.25896	ROApretax	0.0098	0.01683
SIZE (LN)	6.4108	1.36941	ROAadjusted	0.0142	0.01682
SHARE	0.0027	0.01622	ROEpretax	0.1583	0.28243
EQUITY	0.0741	0.09471	ROEadjusted	0.2399	0.52577

13.3.3 Methodology

Previous studies that analyze the effect of acquisitions over accounting performance have some limitations that can be eliminated using panel data methodology.

First, as suggested by Dickerson et al. (1997), most studies do not consider the dynamic aspects of bank performance and, more specifically, the degree of persistence in profits. This problem is caused by the lack of a panel data sample, or even in the studies where such data are available, the methodology used is based on a cross-section analysis, which does not solve the problem. Profit persistence suggests the need to use a dynamic focus to capture completely the impact of acquisitions on performance.

There is a second limitation in previous studies derived from the selection of a control sample to compare those banks that carry out acquisitions with those that do not. The control sample is generally composed of banks of the same size and similar performance to the firms that are to be analyzed. However, the comparison between the two samples does not take into account the influence of other variables on profitability. Therefore, in our analysis with panel data, we have included acquirers and non-acquirers, and have considered control variables, with which take into account the different characteristics of the banks and the countries to which they belong.

Finally, the number of acquisitions can be concentrated in a specific period of time. Therefore, if we chose a year of high acquisition activity to analyze the performance of acquirers, the results might be biased, since in many cases acquisitions will be carried out to follow competitors and not because it is considered an efficient growth strategy for the firm. To avoid this problem, we consider a sample period of eight years.

For these reasons, the test of the hypotheses is carried out using panel data methodology for a sample of EU banks between 1992 and 2000.

The empirical analysis of the hypotheses is based on the Arellano and Bond estimator (1991). Specifically, we use the robust GMM estimator in one step, as recommended by Arellano and Bond, since several studies have found that the two-step standard errors tend to be biased downward in small samples. The estimation considers all the specific characteristics of the bank as predetermined variables,[18] with the control variables referring to the acquiring country being the exogenous variables.[19]

Panel data methodology has been used in recent studies of M&As, among which we find Focarelli and Pozzolo's (2001) analysis of the determining factors in international bank mergers, and Dickerson's *et al.* (1997) study focusing on acquisitions in the UK. In no case, however, is the Arellano and Bond estimator calculated. This would have made it possible to correct the bias arising from applying other estimators in dynamic models. In particular, the equations to test are the following:

(i) To analyze whether there is a permanent change in acquirers' profitability as result of acquisitions, the following equation is considered:

$$Profitability_{it} = \mu_0 + \beta_0 \ Profitability_{it-1} + \beta_1 \ GDP_{it} + \beta_2 \ HERF_{it} + \beta_3 \ SIZE_{it} + \beta_4 \ SHARE_{it} + \beta_5 \ EQUITY_{it} + \beta_6 \ LOANSDEP_{it} + \beta_7 \ DEP_{it} + \beta_8 \ National_{it} + \beta_9 \ EU_{it} + \beta_{10} \ Non \ EU_{it} + \alpha_i + \mu_t + u_{it}$$

(ii) To analyze the exact moment when a change occurs in acquirers' profitability resulting from acquisitions, the following equation is considered:

$$Profitability_{it} = \mu_0 + \beta_0 \ Profitability_{it-1} + \beta_1 \ GDP_{it} + \beta_2 \ HERF_{it} + \beta_3 \ SIZE_{it} + \beta_4 \ SHARE_{it} + \beta_5 \ EQUITY_{it} + \beta_6 \ LOANSDEP_{it} + \beta_7 \ DEP_{it} + \Sigma \gamma_j \ National \ j_{it} + \Sigma \eta_j \ EU \ j_{it} + \Sigma \lambda_j \ Non \ EU \ j_{it} + \alpha_i + \mu_t + u_{it}$$

α_i captures (unobserved) bank heterogeneity; and μ_t considers time-specific factors, such as any aggregate impact on bank performance from a macroeconomic event.

13.4 RESULTS FROM EMPIRICAL ANALYSIS

In this section we explain the main results obtained in the empirical tests of the hypotheses (see Tables 13.5 and 13.6). The analysis was conducted using the four measures of performance described in Section 13.3 above (*ROApretax, ROEpretax, ROAadjusted, ROEadjusted*) as dependent variables. In all the regressions accomplished, the results for m_i test show there is no serial correlation of second order, thus the estimations are consistent.

Table 13.5 Analysis of permanent change in acquirers' profitability resulting from acquisitions

	ROApretax	ROAadjusted	ROEpretax	ROEadjusted
Lag	−0.1251**	−0.1342***	0.1894***	−0.0399***
	(−2.19)	(−2.33)	(3.05)	(−2.62)
EQUITY	0.1546**	0.1203**	0.2845	−0.3129
	(2.49)	(2.32)	(0.87)	(−0.25)
DEP	0.0494	0.0223	1.060**	2.966
	(1.63)	(0.87)	(2.38)	(1.45)
LOANSDEP	0.0000	0.0000	0.0089	0.0131
	(0.75)	(1.04)	(1.08)	(1.05)
SIZE	0.002	0.0037	−0.11	−1.08
	(0.24)	(0.48)	(−0.91)	(−1.14)
SHARE	0.0305*	0.0332*	0.4810*	0.4726
	(1.73)	(1.78)	(1.84)	(0.83)
HERF	−0.0217	−0.0331**	−0.0581	0.4731
	(−1.29)	(−2.14)	(−0.23)	(0.66)
GDP	0.0305***	0.0259***	0.511***	0.7987**
	(3.66)	(3.72)	(4.69)	(2.36)
National	0.0029***	0.0024**	0.0596***	0.060*
	(2.72)	(2.52)	(3.45)	(1.7)
EU	0.0029	0.0076*	−0.0092	0.1326
	(0.62)	(1.66)	(−0.18)	(0.87)
Non-EU	0.0085*	0.0046*	0.0597	0.0865
	(1.87)	(1.84)	(1.31)	(0.77)
Constant	−0.011	−0.0015***	−0.0105	0.0168
	(−1.78)	(−2.6)	(−1.44)	(0.41)
m_1	−2.55	−2.29	−2.33	−1.09
m_2	−0.83	−0.80	1.01	−0.56
Sargan	285.69	291.26	316.58	338.78

Notes: Parameters estimation by GMM; z values are given in parentheses. m_1 is a serial correlation test of order i in using residuals in first differences, asymptotically distributed as $N(0,1)$ under the null of no serial correlation. Sargan is Sargan test. Time-dummy variables are also included in the estimations, although the results are not shown in the tables to focus on the main results obtained. *** significance at 1 percent, ** significance at 5 percent, * significance at 10 percent.

Table 13.6 Analysis of temporal change in acquirers' profitability resulting from acquisitions

	ROApretax	ROAadjusted	ROEpretax	ROEadjusted
Lag	−0.1283**	−0.1357***	0.184***	−0.0408***
	(−2.25)	(−2.36)	(2.97)	(−2.65)
EQUITY	0.151**	0.1185**	0.2329	−0.4668
	(2.46)	(2.29)	(0.7)	(−0.36)
DEP	0.0497*	0.0225	1.058**	2.938
	(1.64)	(0.88)	(2.35)	(1.45)
LOANSDEP	0.0000	0.0000	0.0088	0.0129
	(0.78)	(1.06)	(1.08)	(1.06)
SIZE	0.0011	0.0028	−0.1324	−1.118
	(0.12)	(0.37)	(−1.09)	(−1.15)
SHARE	0.0287*	0.0317*	0.4158*	0.3510
	(1.65)	(1.75)	(1.72)	(0.63)
HERF	−0.0204	−0.0321**	−0.0273	0.3870
	(−1.21)	(−2.06)	(−0.11)	(0.6)
GDP	0.0299***	0.0254***	0.5067***	0.7333**
	(3.66)	(3.68)	(4.61)	(2.25)
National0	−0.0012	−0.0007	−0.0052	0.1149
	(−1.19)	(−0.89)	(−0.32)	(1.05)
National1	−0.0005	−0.0001	0.0032	0.1749
	(−0.52)	(−0.17)	(0.18)	(1.11)
National2	0.0018*	0.0014*	0.0370*	0.1518
	(1.86)	(1.76)	(1.9)	(1.22)
National3	0.0028***	0.0018**	0.0621***	0.1267
	(3.03)	(2.29)	(3.05)	(1.32)
National4	0.0046***	0.0023**	0.0933***	0.0531
	(4.04)	(2.32)	(3.55)	(1.13)
EU0	0.0033	0.0021	0.0532	0.0324
	(1.04)	(0.9)	(1.34)	(0.63)
EU1	0.0039	0.0062*	0.0041	0.0068
	(1.08)	(1.65)	(0.13)	(0.11)
EU2	0.0074*	0.0067*	0.0431	0.1058
	(1.8)	(1.65)	(0.96)	(0.85)

Continued

Table 13.6 Continued

	ROApretax	ROAadjusted	ROEpretax	ROEadjusted
EU3	0.0080*	0.009**	0.0344	0.1899
	(1.83)	(2.26)	(0.75)	(0.92)
EU4	0.0092 **	0.0104 **	0.072	0.1834
	(1.69)	(2.1)	(1.15)	(0.83)
Non EU0	−0.00	−0.0008	−0.0033	0.1019
	(−0.65)	(−0.49)	(−0.15)	(0.98)
Non EU1	−0.0026	−0.0021	−0.0359	0.1131
	(−1.15)	(−1.1)	(−0.95)	(0.87)
Non EU2	−0.0017	−0.0010	−0.0124	0.2408
	(−0.6)	(−0.54)	(−0.28)	(1.09)
Non EU3	0.0026	0.0015	0.0207	0.2539
	(0.74)	(0.49)	(0.62)	(1.1)
Non EU4	0.0026	0.0025	0.0226	0.4565
	(0.79)	(0.93)	(0.48)	(1.19)
Constant	−0.0010 *	−0.0015 **	−0.0098	0.019
	(−1.71)	(−2.52)	(−1.37)	(0.45)
Wald(28)	123.66	219.95	176.64	170.29
m^1	−2.54	−2.29	−2.32	−1.09
m^2	−0.82	−0.80	0.99	−0.57
Sargan	265.30	274.41	312.58	335.53
Obs. N.	9302	9302	9302	9298

Notes: Parameters estimation by GMM; z values are given in parentheses. m_1 is a serial correlation test of order *i* in using residuals in first differences, asymptotically distributed as $N(0,1)$ under the null of no serial correlation. Sargan is Sargan test. Time-dummy variables are also included in the estimations, although the results are not shown in the tables to focus on the main results obtained. *** significance at 1 percent, ** significance at 5 percent, * significance at 10 percent.

First, the results for Hypothesis 1, which test whether there is an improvement in the acquirer's performance in domestic and EU internal acquisitions, show a positive and significant influence of the variable *National* in all the estimations. Therefore, domestic acquisitions improve the acquirer's performance. As Berger *et al.* (1999) point out for the US market, this kind of operation can generate gains because of the reduction in costs produced by bank branch closure, scale economies or the increase in competitiveness. It should be noted, however, that while the coefficients of the variable *National* are high (almost 6 percent) when explaining *ROE*, both before tax and adjusted, the coefficients are low when explaining *ROA* (between 0.2 percent and 0.3 percent).

With regard to acquisitions accomplished within EU borders, the estimations to analyze whether there is a permanent change in acquirers' performance after the acquisition do not show significant results. In fact, the variable *EU* is only significant (at the 10 percent level) when explaining *ROAadjusted*. This result shows that while there has been significant deregulation in Europe, there are still several barriers, especially those imposed by the EU member governments, that block or limit this kind of operation.

When analyzing when the change in acquirers' performance is produced, the results show an increase in *ROApretax*, *ROEpretax* and *ROAadjusted* for acquirers in domestic acquisitions two years after the operation. This result supports the idea that 50 percent of the earnings derived from bank acquisitions are obtained one year after the transaction, because of the cost of integration and restructuring derived from the operation (Rhoades, 1993). In fact, the integration of different enterprises is not an easy task, since it involves, among other aspects, internal restructuring, the adoption of new techniques and the renewal of the management team, as well as changes in contracts with suppliers and workers. In this situation, organizational problems and conflicts of interest probably appear during the first years after the acquisitions, even in some cases leading to the failure of the transaction (Buono and Bowditch, 1989).

The positive effect of national acquisitions on *ROE* is more important than on *ROA*. A detailed analysis of the coefficients shows, as we have already mentioned, that acquirers' improvement in performance is obtained in the long term. As can be seen in Table 13.6 on page 201, the value of the coefficients and their significance grow as time passes, being particularly high four years after the acquisition.

Acquirers involved in an EU internal acquisition only show an increase in *ROApretax* two years after the operation and in *ROAadjusted* one year after the operation, with no influence on *ROEpretax* and *ROEadjusted*. Thus it cannot be concluded that EU acquisitions improve acquirers' performance, according to the results obtained in the analysis of the permanent change in performance mentioned previously and the ones obtained in the analysis of the temporal change in performance.

In conclusion, Hypothesis 1 is only confirmed for domestic acquisitions. It cannot definitely be supported for international operations inside the EU.

The results obtained for Hypothesis 2, regarding the acquisition of banks outside the EU, show a permanent improvement only in *ROApretax* and *ROAadjusted*, since the variable *Non-EU* is positive and significant at the 10 percent level in both cases. This variable does not have any influence on *ROE*. In the same way, the results obtained for the analysis of the temporal change in performance show how this kind of transaction does not improve acquirers' performance, not even in the long term. This result confirms Hypothesis 2, and highlights the problems of international acquisitions, in which the difficulty of managing enterprises that are far away, added to cultural, linguistic, information and regulatory barriers, prevent gains from being made by the acquirer.

Finally, we carried out a complementary analysis to evaluate the influence of the legal system in our results. In this sense, Haynes and Thompson (1999) suggest that the legal and competitive environment where the bank operates has an important effect on the profitability generated by M&A. In those systems with higher investor protection measures, it is less probable to undertake an acquisition with the aim of maximizing managers' wealth. A weak regulation system can encourage managers' opportunist behavior; that is, managers only undertake M&A in order to increase the size of their companies, and in this way increase their prestige (Vander Vennet, 1996).

We classify countries according to the origin of their commercial laws and investors' protection. To do so, we use the classification developed by La Porta *et al.* (1998), in which countries are grouped into four systems: the Common legal system (the UK and Ireland); the French system (Belgium, France, Greece, Italy, the Netherlands, Luxembourg, Portugal and Spain); the German system (Austria and Germany); and the Scandinavian system (Denmark, Finland and Sweden).

The Common system has the highest protection measures for external investors, giving rise to a more developed financial system. The French system has the least protection for investors, and capital and credit markets are less developed. In the middle we can find the German and Scandinavian systems, although the first has a well-developed banking system because of the higher legal protection for creditors.

To distinguish the different systems we include four dummy variables to indicate to which system a given country belongs. The variables are called *Common*, *French*, *German* and *Scandinavian*, respectively.

Tables 13.7 and 13.8 show the results obtained from this analysis. The results do not allow us to observe a different behavior in banks' profitability under the different legal systems in use in Europe, contrary to the suggested hypothesis.[20] This may be because of the development of Governance Codes during the second half of the 1990s in all the countries in the EU.[21] The Codes establish recommendations to reach higher levels of effectiveness and transparency in firms' governance, and higher credibility and protection of investors' interests. Therefore, we continue to support the hypothesis that acquisitions affect banks' performance positively two years after the transaction, and this does not seem to be conditioned by the legal system of the acquirers' country.

Table 13.7 Analysis of permanent changes in acquirers' profitability resulting from acquisitions in each legal system

	ROA	ROE
Lag	−0.4347811*** (−7.44)	−0.1693039* (−1.79)
EQUITY	0.1099459** (2.34)	−0.0554125 (−0.11)
DEP	0.0515075** (2.08)	0.5754057* (1.84)
LOANSDEP	0.0000611 (1.59)	0.0013276 (1.04)
SIZE	−0.0016402 (−0.22)	−0.0818845 (−0.7)
SHARE	−0.0050295 (−0.26)	0.6847446 (0.76)
HERF	−0.0140751 (−0.7)	−0.0003745 (0)
GDP	0.0224013** (2.26)	0.1555794 (0.75)
COMMON	−0.0042551 (−0.56)	0.0019046 (0.03)
FRENCH	0.0022204 (1.34)	−0.0222519 (−0.31)
GERMAN	0.0006718 (0.24)	0.0071894 (0.25)
SCANDINAVIAN	0.0021135 (0.77)	−0.0279598 (−0.29)
m_1	−1.54	−1.15
m_2	−1.72	0.38
Sargan	291.13	324.68

Notes: Parameters estimation by GMM; z values are given in parentheses. m_1 is a serial correlation test of order *i* in using residuals in first differences, asymptotically distributed as $N(0,1)$ under the null of no serial correlation. Sargan is Sargan test. Time-dummy variables are also included in the estimations, although the results are not shown in the tables to focus on the main results obtained. *** significance at 1 percent, ** significance at 5 percent, * significance at 10 percent.

Table 13.8 Analysis of temporal changes in acquirers' profitability resulting from acquisitions in each legal system

	ROA	ROE
Lag	−0.4349413 (−7.45)	−0.1695479* (−1.79)
EQUITY	0.1094021** (2.33)	−0.0732945 (−0.15)
DEP	0.0495998** (2.03)	0.5898544* (1.76)
LOANSDEP	0.0000591 (1.58)	0.0013395 (1.04)
SIZE	−0.0012813 (−0.17)	−0.0903106 (−0.79)
SHARE	−0.0104863 (−0.55)	0.3448244 (0.61)
HERF	−0.0120199 (−0.61)	0.0134775 (0.05)
GDP	0.0219392** (2.25)	0.1365364 (0.64)
Common0	0.0018653 (0.53)	0.0057924 (0.11)
Common1	−0.000039 (−0.01)	−0.0180415 (−0.6)
Common2	−0.0089587*** (−2.63)	−0.1121013** (−2.01)
Common3	−0.0062928 (−1.51)	−0.0352525 (−0.53)
Common4	0.0108087 (1.35)	0.2299287 (1.26)
French0	0.0002388 (0.31)	−0.0367079 (−0.73)
French1	0.0004407 (0.38)	−0.0365393 (−0.7)
French2	0.001447 (1.17)	−0.0291609 (−0.45)

Continued

Table 13.8 Continued

	ROA	ROE
French3	0.0026298** (2.32)	−0.0142236 (−0.19)
French4	0.0036756*** (2.6)	−0.0309637 (−0.3)
German0	−0.0016747 (−1.42)	0.0227589 (0.63)
German1	−0.0011848 (−0.93)	0.0080403 (0.28)
German2	0.000135 (0.11)	0.0319908 (1.01)
German3	0.0008907 (0.54)	0.0251749 (1.08)
German4	0.0011557 (0.67)	−0.0281643 (−0.42)
Scandinavian0	−0.0036028 (−0.73)	−0.0355593 (−0.54)
Scandinavian1	−0.0019075 (−0.37)	0.0220922 (0.4)
Scandinavian2	−0.0019123 (−0.33)	−0.0697042 (−0.67)
Scandinavian3	−0.0052525 (−0.75)	−0.0831919 (−0.7)
Scandinavian4	−0.0080649 (−0.81)	0.0699828 (0.83)
m_1	−1.54	−1.15
m_2	−1.72	0.38
Sargan	255.23	311.87

Notes: Parameters estimation by GMM; z values are given in parentheses. m_1 is a serial correlation test of order i in using residuals in first differences, asymptotically distributed as $N(0,1)$ under the null of no serial correlation. Sargan is Sargan test. Time-dummy variables are also included in the estimations, although the results are not shown in the tables to focus on the main results obtained.
*** significance at 1 percent, ** significance at 5 percent, * significance at 10 percent.

13.5 CONCLUSIONS

This study analyzes the performance gains obtained by the acquirer in domestic and cross-border acquisitions of banks. In summary, our findings show that domestic acquisitions improve acquirers' performance, especially in the long term, while cross-border operations (both EU and non-EU) do not have a significant effect on acquirers' performance.

The eventual introduction of the new accounting standards (IAS) and the new capital agreement (Basel 2), as well as the recent entry of ten new countries into the EU, may boost acquisitions within the EU over the next few years. However, as our results show, to make this process successful, it would be appropriate to harmonize current European legislation on this matter. This would undoubtedly accelerate M&As between countries.

There are some aspects in the present European banking regulations that restrict financial sector consolidation. In fact, the Second Banking Directive allows member states to block mergers and acquisitions in the financial sector, justifying this decision in the consequences that a greater banking concentration might have for competitiveness. Moreover, this regulation allows national authorities to exercise the right of veto in international acquisitions. This has often been used to protect national banks and to avoid control of the financial system from being taken over by foreigners. In this context, the number of cross-border mergers and acquisitions in the banking industry has been low in Europe. Only 13 percent of banking mergers were cross-border, while there were 35 percent in non-financial industries. However, driven by the pressure to compete globally, and facilitated by deregulation and the growing liberalization of markets worldwide, banks are interested increasingly in making cross-border rather than domestic M&A deals. Indeed, cooperation between banks from different member states is an essential part of making Europe more competitive. In view of this situation, the European Commission has presented a proposal for a Directive to make cross-border mergers easier, by overcoming obstacles caused by the different national laws and reducing the costs of the operation. The Directive would set up a cross-border merger procedure, whereby mergers would be governed in each member state by the principles and rules applicable to domestic mergers. The present Directive on Takeover Bids (2004/25/EC), in an attempt to make takeover bids in Europe easier, sets out fundamental principles to govern takeovers, and provides a means of determining the competent authority to supervise a takeover, and which national law is applicable in the case of cross-border takeovers. However, this Directive has been criticized because it still maintains the freedom of the national authorities to stop M&As.

In conclusion, a greater effort should be made to facilitate cross-border takeovers within the EU, with the aim of freeing gains made possible from the operation, and ultimately making the European financial market more competitive.

NOTES

1. Regulation is particularly important in the banking sector since, because of its special influence on the economy, it is normally highly regulated and protected. This is one of the reasons that, according to Focarelli and Pozzolo (2001), justifies the scarcity of bank mergers and acquisitions at the international level, compared to those carried out in other sectors.
2. This report stresses the substantial fall in costs arising from the single market program. Two important effects were forecast: (i) a fall in prices as a result of cost rationalisation and the increase in scale economies; and (ii) an increase in productivity arising from the relocation of resources (human, financial and technological) and an industrial restructuring, where mergers and acquisitions play a fundamental role.
3. It is not only the removal of international barriers that has led to an increase in international consolidation, but internal deregulation in itself has also led to the same situation. Thus, Saunders (1999) shows how allowing commercial banks in the UK to acquire investment banks in 1986 led to many of these banks being acquired by foreign investment or commercial banks.
4. In fact, Beitel et al. (2004) find an increase in shareholder value of 1.5 percent in domestic bank mergers, while in cross-border ones value falls by 0.4 percent.
5. For example, in 1999, the Portuguese government blocked the agreement between Banco Santander Central Hispano and the Chamalimaud Group, and in 2005 the Italian Central Bank prevented the BBVA and BNL acquisition.
6. See Focarrelli and Pozzolo (2001) and Buch and DeLong (2004).
7. Berger et al. (1999), Pilloff and Santomero (1998) and Vander Vennet (1996), among others, review these reasons.
8. These changes have led to substantial profit gains from mergers and acquisitions, especially in terms of scale and scope economies. See Berger and Mester (1997), Cavallo and Rossi (2001) and Carbó and Humphrey (2002).
9. See, for example, Vander Vennet (1996, 2002), and Cybo-Ottone and Mugia (2000).
10. Berger et al. (2000) note how the correlation between the bank income in different countries (EU, USA and Japan) is very low – even among EU member countries.
11. See Focarelli and Pozzolo (2001).
12. In fact, deregulation in Europe at first led to an increase in mergers and acquisitions at the domestic level as a defensive measure against increased competition, putting off the increase in the number of operations between countries until the 1990s (ECB, 2000).
13. However, Waheed and Mathur (1995) show that some benefits can be noted in the expansion of banks from developed countries into developing countries.
14. For a review of the literature on this issue, see DeYoung and Nolle (1996), Hasan and Hunter (1996) and Berger et al. (2000).
15. Normally, due to the poor correlation between the activities carried out in different countries.
16. EU countries have during the last few years followed different methods to amortize goodwill (excess of purchase price over the tangible value of the target's assets). Thus it is necessary to adjust bank performance to avoid the potential for distortion caused by the different accounting rules.
17. See Corvoisier and Gropp (2002), Akhavein et al. (1997) and Perisitiani (1997).

18. $E[x_{it}, u_{is}] = 0$ if $s \leq t$, x_{it} being the independent variables and u_{is} the error term.
19. $E[x_{it}, u_{is}] = 0$ for all s and t, x_{it} being the independent variables and u_{is} the error term.
20. However, M&As affect banks' performance in a positive way three years after the transaction in the French system, while they affect performance in a negative way two years after the transaction in the Common system. Nevertheless, the values of these effects are very low, implying that the influence is not very important.
21. All the countries in the sample have a Governance Code apart from Austria, Finland and Luxembourg.

REFERENCES

Akhavein, J. D., Berger, A. N. and Humphrey, D. B. (1997) "The Effects of Bank Megamergers on Efficiency and Prices. Evidence from the Profit Function", *Review of Industrial Organization*, 12: 95–139.

Arellano, M. and Bond, S. (1991) "Some Tests of Specification for Panel Data. Monte Carlo Evidence and an Application to Employment Equations?", *Review of Economic Studies*, 58: 277–97.

Becher, D. A. (2000) "The Valuation Effects of Bank Mergers", *Journal of Corporate Finance*, 6:189–214.

Beitel, P., Schiereck, D. and Wahrenburg, M. (2004) "Explaining M&As' Success in European Banks", *European Financial Management*, 10: 106–39.

Berger, A. N. (2000) "The Integration of the Financial Services Industry, Where Are the Efficiencies?", Board of Governors of the Federal Reserve System-Finance and Economics Discussion Series, 1–38.

Berger, A. N. and Humphrey, D. B. (1992) "Megamergers in Banking and the Use of Cost Efficiency as an Antitrust Defence", *Antitrust Bulletin*, 37: 541–600.

Berger, A. N. and Mester, L. J. (1997) "Inside the Black Box. What Explains Differences in the Efficiencies of Financial Institutions?", *Journal of Banking and Finance*, 21: 895–947.

Berger, A. N., Demsetz, R. S. and Strahan, P. E. (1999) "The Consolidation of the Financial Services Industry. Causes, Consequences, and Implications for the Future", *Journal of Banking and Finance*, 23: 135–94.

Berger, A. N., DeYoung, R., Genay, H. and Udell, G. (2000) "Globalization of Financial Institutions. Evidence from Cross-Border Banking Performance", in R. E. Litan and A. M. Santomero (eds), *The Brookings-Wharton Papers on Financial Services*, 3 (Washington, DC: Brookings Institution Press), 23–158.

Boot, A. W. A. (1999) "European Lessons on Consolidation Banking", *Journal of Banking and Finance*, 23: 609–13.

Buch, C. M. and DeLong, G. (2004) "Cross-border Bank Mergers: What Lures the Rare Animal?", *Journal of Banking and Finance*, 28: 2077–102.

Buono, A. F. and Bowditch, J. L. (1989) *The Human Side of Mergers and Acquisitions – Managing Collisions between People, Cultures and Organizations* (San Francisco: Jossey-Bass).

Calomiris, C. W. and Karceski, J. (1998) "Is the Bank Mergers Wave of the 1990s Efficient? Lessons from Nine Case Studies", in S. N. Kaplan (ed.), *Mergers and Productivity* (Chicago: University of Chicago Press), 93–161.

Carbó, S. and Humphrey, D. B. (2002) "Nueva Evidencia Empírica Sobre las Economías de Escala en el Sector Bancario", *Papeles de Economía Española*, 94: 163–69.

Cavallo, L. and Rossi, S. P. S. (2001) "Scale and Scope Economies in the European Banking Systems", *Journal of Multinational Financial Management*, 11: 515–31.

Corvoisier, S. and Gropp, R. (2002) "Bank Concentration and Retail Interest Rates", *Journal of Banking and Finance*, 26: 2155–89.

Cybo-Ottone, A. and Murgia, M. (2000) "Mergers and Shareholder Wealth in European Banking", *Journal of Banking and Finance*, 2: 831–59.

Cyree, K. B., Wansley, J. W. and Black, H. A. (2000) "Bank Growth Choices and Changes in Market Performance", *The Financial Review*, 41: 49–66.

DeYoung, R. (1993) "Determinants of Cost Efficiencies in Bank Mergers, Economic and Policy Analysis", Working paper 93, Washington Office of the Comptroller of the Currency, 1–40.

DeYoung, R. and Nolle D. E. (1996) "Foreign-Owned Banks in the U.S. Earning Market Share or Buying It?", *Journal of Money, Credit and Banking*, 28: 622–36.

Dickerson, A. P., Gibson, H. D. and Tsakalotos, E. (1997) "The Impact of Acquisitions on Company Performance. Evidence from a Large Panel of UK Firms", *Oxford Economic Papers*, 49: 344–61.

ECB (2000) *ECB Mergers and Acquisitions Involving the EU Banking Industry* (Frankfurt: European Central Bank Publications on Financial Stability).

Fixler, D. J. and Zieschang, K. D. (1993) "An Index Number Approach to Measuring Bank Efficiency. An Application to Mergers", *Journal of Banking and Finance*, 17: 437–50.

Focarelli, D. and Pozzolo, A. F. (2001) "The Patterns of Cross-Border Bank Mergers and Shareholdings in OECD Countries", *Journal of Banking and Finance*, 25(12): 2305–37.

Hasan, I. and Hunter, W. C. (1996) "Efficiency of Japanese Multinational Banks in the United States", in Andrew H. (ed.), *Research in Finance*, 14 (Greenwich, Conn. and London: JAI Press), 157–73.

Haynes, M. and Thompson, S. (1999) "The Productivity Effects of Bank Mergers: Evidence from the UK Building Societies", *Journal of Banking and Finance*, 23: 825–46.

Houston, J. F., James, C. M. and Ryngaert, M. D. (2001) "Where Do Merger Gains Come From? Bank Mergers from the Perspective of Insiders and Outsiders", *Journal of Financial Economics*, 60: 285–331.

Hughes, J. P., Lang, W., Mester, L. and Moon, C. G. (1999) "The Dollars and Sense of Bank Consolidation", *Journal of Banking and Finance*, 23: 291–324.

Jensen, M. and Ruback, R. S. (1983) "The Market for Corporate Control. The Scientific Evidence", *Journal of Financial Economics*, 11: 5–50.

La Porta, R., Lopez-De-Silanes, F., Shleifer, A. and Vishny, R. (1999) "Investor Protection: Origins, Consequences, Reform", *Journal of Political Economy*, 106(6): 1113–55.

Lindblom, T. and von Koch, C. (2002) "Cross-boarder Bank Mergers and Acquisitions in the EU", *The Service Industries Journal*, 22: 41–72.

Linder, J. C. and Crane, D. B. (1993) "Bank Mergers. Integration and Profitability", *Journal of Financial Services Research*, 7: 35–55.

Peristiani, S. (1997) "Do Mergers Improve the X-Efficiency and Scale Efficiency of U.S. Banks? Evidence from the 1980s", *Journal of Money, Credit, and Banking*, 29(3): 326–37.

Pilloff, S. J. (1996) "Performance Changes and Shareholder Wealth Creation Associated with Mergers of Publicly Traded Banking Institution", *Journal of Money, Credit and Banking*, 28: 294–310.

Pilloff, S. J. and Santomero, A. M. (1998) "The Value Effects of Bank Mergers and Acquisitions", in Y. Amihud, and G. Miller (eds), *Bank Mergers and Acquisitions* (Dordrecht: Kluwer Academic), 59–78.

Rhoades, S. A. (1993) "The Efficiency Effects of Bank Mergers. Rationale for a Case Study Approach and Preliminary Findings", in *29th Annual Conference on Bank Structure and Competition* (Federal Reserve Bank of Chicago), 377–99.

Rhoades, S. A. (1994) "A Summary of Mergers Performance Studies in Banking, 1980–93, and an Assessment of the Operating Performance and Event Study Methodologies", *Board of Governors of the Federal Reserve System, Stuff Studies 1990–99*, (167): 1–37.

Rhoades, S. A. (1998) "The Efficiency Effects of Bank Mergers. An Overview of Cases Studies of Nine Mergers", *Journal of Banking and Finance*, 22, 273–91.

Saunders, A. (1999) "Consolidation and Universal Banking", *Journal of Banking and Finance*, 23: 693–5.

Vander Vennet, R. (1996) "The Effect of Mergers and Acquisitions on the Efficiency and Profitability of EC Credit Institutions", *Journal of Banking and Finance*, 20: 1531–58.

Vander Vennet, R. (2002) "Cost and Profit Efficiency of Financial Conglomerates and Universal Banks in Europe", *Journal of Money, Credit and Banking*, 34: 254–82.

Waheed, A. and Mathur, I. (1995) "Wealth Effects of Foreign Expansion by U.S. Banks", *Journal of Banking and Finance*, 19: 823–42.

CHAPTER 14

Mergers between European Energy Firms: National Champions and Markets

Francesc Trillas

14.1 INTRODUCTION

European Union electricity and gas directives, aimed at the creation of an internal energy market, have triggered a wave of mergers and acquisitions. National and European authorities, however, have taken a somewhat incoherent stance *vis-à-vis* such processes, at times promoting the transactions and at others opposing them. This chapter reviews a number of recent takeover bids (both successful and unsuccessful), and examines the winners and the losers in this process through an analysis of stock market (event study) and other data. Although the perspective adopted is European, the main examples are drawn from one specific European country – Spain – reflecting the author's own research interests. Such a focus is arguably a pertinent research strategy today, given that the market for corporate control at the European level is characterized by an ongoing wave of takeovers. This means some time will need to pass before researchers are able to undertake a full assessment. Hence, any conclusions proffered at this stage can only be provisional, and point to possible lines of future study.

National governments have not stood idly by and watched this wave of takeovers gather strength. For example, *The Economist* (September 1, 2006) reported that, in preparation for the full liberalization of Europe's energy markets, the Spanish government thought that it needed a national energy champion to rival the gigawatts of Electricité de France, and Germany's RWE. Thus it chose to back Gas Natural, a Spanish gas company based in Barcelona, the Catalan capital, in its launch of a hostile bid for Endesa in September 2005, while initially opposing a competing bid from E.On. At the same time, the French government was promoting the merger between Suez and Gaz de France to avoid a hostile approach from ENEL in the French energy markets. Other national governments, notably the British, were less eager to defend national champions.

The rest of this chapter is organized as follows. In section 14.2, an economic analysis is carried out of the issues at stake. Section 14.3 then explores the behavior of target firms and related stakeholders, focusing on the case of Spain, as all Spanish electricity firms have been recent targets for takeover bids. Section 14.4 explores the incentives encouraging firms to expand, focusing on the behavior of two of the firms that have recently undergone the most rapid growth in this sector: Endesa and E.On. Section 14.5 presents a brief discussion on the interaction between anti-trust or competition policy and "strategic" objectives; and Section 14.6 concludes.

14.2 THE ISSUES AT STAKE

This section examines the way in which academic research has analyzed the constraints that regulation imposes on corporate control. This should serve to contextualize the events that have taken place in European energy markets since the mid-1990s. Some thoughts are also presented on the ways in which the processes of liberalization and privatization may or may not impinge on this analysis.

Network industries subject to regulation, as is the case, for example, of the electricity industry, are characterized by large sunk and long-lived investments. To the extent that certain segments form natural monopolies (distribution, transmission and system operations; in the past, generation and retail were also deemed to be part of a vertically integrated natural monopoly), price regulation of these parts of industry becomes necessary, resulting in the well-known time inconsistency problem of regulation: the regulator is placed under considerable pressure not to remunerate investments sufficiently, once these have occurred, so investors lack incentives to fund such investments in the first place. The various mechanisms societies have developed over time to alleviate this problem have crucially affected the different forms of ownership of the electricity firms that have existed. Public-sector ownership of firms was over many decades the preferred approach for alleviating the problem, because in this way the firm could internalize the interests of consumers and investors alike in its objective function. The presence of ownership mechanisms other than private ownership in the energy sectors of many countries must be seen in this context: state-owned firms, municipal firms, firms owned by regional or provincial governments, cooperatives, firms owned by non-profit savings banks. Popular capitalism (selling shares in formerly state-owned companies to the public at large to spread stock ownership among the population, as promoted by the Conservative government in Britain in the 1980s and early 1990s) was similarly believed to internalize the problem, as voters/consumers also became investors. The rate of return regulation used to guarantee the value of investments and the supervisory role of regulatory agencies acted as a subsidy to the monitoring task of shareholders. The regulation of incentives ceased to guarantee profit levels, so that management decisions reacquired their central role, but again tensions arose in the form of a credibility problem, that of maintaining a fixed price. Finally, in countries such as Spain, where state-owned firms co-existed in the electricity sector with privately owned ones,[1] collusion between policy-makers and firms, and the presence of financial institutions among the stock owners,[2] were also, in practice, a way of alleviating the time inconsistency problem in regulation, at the expense of other inefficiencies and a serious problem of legitimacy and transparency.

The presence of private investors in large electricity firms gives rise to agency problems, compounded inevitably by problems of regulatory risk. There are a variety of well-known mechanisms, all of them costly and imperfect, for preventing managers from behaving in a non-profit-maximizing way: a direct monitoring role by owners or boards of directors, monetary incentives, product market competition, managers' labor market competition, and takeovers. There are significant difficulties, however, in applying some of these mechanisms in quoted firms when they are also regulated firms: product market competition does not exist in natural monopoly segments, monetary incentives are more controversial than in other sectors, and the "political" profile of managers reduces the intensity of labor market competition.

Takeovers in regulated sectors can, in theory, serve as a mechanism to control managers, though academic research reveals that takeovers have a lower success ratio, take considerable time to reach completion (if indeed they ever do), and are costlier in regulated sectors than in other sectors. Stakeholders use the regulatory game to mobilize themselves. Takeovers attract considerable attention to regulated sectors, which is usually detrimental to the bidding firms, since consumer activism increases, reducing in turn the discounted value of future profits. The newly acquired saliency of regulatory issues makes consumers aware of their ability to exploit the sunk-cost nature of regulated assets, as well as giving them an incentive to incur the costs of making their voice heard, because this time the media and the politicians are paying attention. The activism of other stakeholders, such as workers and local communities, is similarly affected.[3] Takeovers occur with the theoretical objective of replacing inefficient managers with others who can obtain more value from the firm's assets. However, takeovers may destroy value if the managers of the bidding firms over-estimate their abilities, or if they wish to expand beyond what is optimal for their shareholders. It is common to observe waves of takeovers associated with deregulation, given that, when rigid rules that associate a firm with a given territory disappear, managers articulate attack and defense strategies *vis-à-vis* other corporations. Although we would expect bad bidders to become good targets, in practice public ownership, golden shares and the like make this very difficult in some countries. Golden shares, for example, introduced in the UK in the 1980s, give the government the power of veto in strategic transactions such as ownership changes that alter the control structure of firms.

Deregulation, by introducing the possibility of competition in certain segments, induces changes in corporate control, probably so as to increase the value of more concentrated ownership structures. The marginal benefit of improved control over managers (whose discretional powers rise) is now higher, and the implicit regulatory subsidy diminishes. Deregulation increases the costs of monitoring managers' behavior, and injects the business environment with uncertainty and instability. In the midst of such instability, investors must determine the proportion of success or failure that can be attributed to the managers, and the proportion that can be attributed to factors beyond their control. Increased instability increases the costs of observing the managers' conduct, which also favors more concentrated structures.

With the introduction of processes of liberalization, the frontiers of firms cease to be fixed. The expansion of regulated firms[4] seeks to take advantage of new growth opportunities derived from the possibility of competing with incumbent firms in other segments or geographical areas (in new markets, mergers and acquisitions attract less attention from anti-trust authorities than they do in traditional markets). When the incumbent firm operates in another jurisdiction, it is seen as a credible rival, and this intensifies competition. Nevertheless, the optimal size from a manager's point of view is usually greater than what the shareholders' and society at large consider to be the optimal size (remember, that some of the greatest corporate control scandals in the world have been related to the uncontrolled expansion of firms – for example, Enron or Vivendi – that began operations in regulated sectors). Acquiring firms have the opportunity to diversify their revenue sources, and seek synergies with their traditional businesses, exploiting potential scale and scope economies. Countries that are the recipients of investments, typically (though not always) developing countries, wish to import technology and capital. Some acquirers, not necessarily the most efficient, can benefit from predatory capital subsidies from the country of origin because of generous regulations, or their managers can benefit from relaxed forms of control by their shareholders.

The fact that privatizations often coincide with deregulation processes makes it difficult to untangle the effects of deregulation, on the one hand, from the effects of privatization, and on the other, from productive efficiency. Moreover, it is debatable whether in some countries, and here Spain is a good example, the governance of privatized firms as a result of the new ownership structure has greater benefits for firms and industries that are in the middle of a deregulation process. However, it is true that some privatizations do succeed in improving productive efficiency, but ultimately this is an empirical question.

14.3 THE BEHAVIOR OF TARGET FIRMS

14.3.1 The case of Spain

Table 14.1 presents a chronology of the main corporate control transaction attempts undertaken in Spain since October 1996, from the expansion of Endesa, the country's leading electricity company, and its subsequent privatization. The events in the table are consistent with the hypothesis that liberalization processes are associated with substantial movements in the corporate control market. These transactions have affected the four main electricity firms in Spain, albeit to very different degrees. To add to the information in the table, at the time of writing there were rumors that E.On's takeover bid had been agreed with Endesa's management team, while the acceptance of Gas Natural's takeover of Endesa had been stopped by the Spanish Supreme Court, and E.On had withdrawn its takeover bid after Italian firm ENEL, after reaching an agreement with Spanish construction company Acciona (a large shareholder in Endesa itself), had itself announced another takeover. Finally, ACS, a construction firm, following its purchase of 22 percent of Unión Fenosa from Banco Santander, the largest Spanish bank, subsequently took a further 10 percent stake of its shares some months later.

As a result of these and other less major transactions, the internal ownership structure of Spanish electricity firms has changed substantially since the mid-1990s. Table 14.2 describes the shareholding structure of the main firms in 1996 and compares it with their structure in 2006. (Note, however, that the table does not include the transmission grid owner and operator, Red Eléctrica Española. Here, the public sector is still its main shareholder, although the firm is now quoted on the stock market, which was not the case in 1996.) The most notable trends since 1996 have been the emergence on the Spanish electricity market of foreign firms still dominated by the public sector (ENEL in Viesgo, and Electricidade de Portugal in Hidrocantábrico), and the increasing influence of agents that have enjoyed recent success in other Spanish industrial sectors, such as saving banks[5] and construction firms.

In common with the main large European energy firms, all of the companies resulting from these transactions operate in the gas and electricity markets, as well as in renewable energies. We can observe an increase in the shareholding concentration of two of the smaller firms in the sector

Table 14.1 Corporate control transactions in the electricity sector (Spain)

Announcement date	Firms involved	Mechanism	Outcome
October 1996	Endesa/FECSA, Sevillana	Takeover	Acceptance
July 1997	Endesa/Enersis (Chile)	Takeover	Acceptance May 1999
June 1998	Endesa	Initial public offer	Last phase in Endesa's privatization
March 2000	Unión Fenosa/Hidrocantábrico	Takeover	Spanish government veto
September 2000	Ferroatlántica-EnBW/Hidrocantábrico	Takeover	Accepted with a veto over political rights
September 2000	Endesa/Iberdrola	Merger	Spanish government veto
August 2001	ENEL/Viesgo	Acquisition	Direct sale from Endesa
March 2003	Gas Natural/Iberdrola	Takeover	Electricity regulator veto
July 2004	EDP/Hidrocantábrico	Acquisition	Direct sale from EnBW and Cajastur
September 2005	Gas Natural/Endesa	Takeover	Government acceptance subject to various conditions
September 2005	ACS/Unión Fenosa	Acquisition	Direct sale of Banco Santander
February 2006	E.On/Endesa	Takeover	Approved by the European Commission

Note: In the case of a takeover or acquisition, the firm mentioned first is the bidder or acquirer.
Source: Based on event information from the Lexis/Nexis database.

(Hidrocantábrico and Unión Fenosa), and the stabilization of shareholding dispersion in the two largest (Endesa, if we take into account that the percentage of the government holding SEPI was dispersed after privatization in the form of an initial public offer, and Iberdrola). This dispersion stability, which is currently subject to tensions because of the pending resolution of the Endesa takeovers and the possible implications for Iberdrola, may benefit from asset sales resulting from the conditions imposed on the acquirer.[6] Table 14.2 underestimates the participation of the main Spanish savings bank, "la Caixa", in the corporate control market. This institution is the main shareholder in another two large firms in the energy sector, the oil firm Repsol and the gas firm Gas Natural. The latter already participates in electricity generation and has made recent takeover bids for the two main Spanish electricity firms, Iberdrola and Endesa. Table 14.2 also shows that

Table 14.2 Largest equity stakes (percentage of each shareholder)

Iberdrola 1996		Iberdrola 2006		Endesa 1996		Endesa 2006	
BBV	10.01	Chase Nominees Ltd	8.359	SEPI	66.89	Caja Madrid	9.936
Cía. de Carteras e Inversiones, S.A.	9.971	State Street Bank & Trust Co.	5.929			Chase Nominees Ltd	5.732
Franklin Resources Inc. Delaware	5.678	Banco Bilbao Vizcaya Argentaria, S.A.	5.46			State Street Bank & Trust Co.	5.038
The Chase Manhatan Bank, N.A.	5.17	Bilbao Bizkaia Kutxa, Aurr. Kut. Bah.	5.01			Axa, S.A.	5.35

U. Fenosa 1996		U. Fenosa 2006		H.Cantábrico 96		H.Cantábrico 06	
Arbujuelo	14.995	ACS	34.506	"la Caixa"	10.51	EDP	95.7
Caja Ahorros Madrid	0.86	PR Pisa, S.A.	32.073	BCO Herrero	10.02	Cajastur	3.1
		Caja de Ahorros de Galicia	9.993	Caja Ahorros Asturias	10		
		Corporación Caixa Galicia, S.A.	9.993	Masaveu	5.3		

Source: Electricity regulator CNE.

foreign capital (through foreign electricity firms or through investment funds) has higher stakes in 2006 than it had in 1996.

14.3.2 Spanish firms as targets and the case of Hidrocantábrico

As can be seen from Table 14.1, the four largest Spanish electricity firms have all been take over targets in recent years. However, to date, the only successful takeovers (in the sense of having triggered a change in the company's control) have had the relatively smaller firms, Hidrocantábrico and Unión Fenosa, as their targets. The bids for Endesa and Iberdrola did not result in changes in control, although the current takeovers targeting Endesa could well change this. The purchase of Viesgo, a subsidiary of Endesa, saw the entry into the Spanish market of one of the largest European electricity companies, ENEL, which has the state as its main shareholder. Gas Natural's bid to takeover Iberdrola was vetoed by the energy regulator CNE, which used its power to stop transactions that endanger investments in regulated sectors. All attempts at changing the structure of ownership have been surrounded by considerable political debate.

The case of the change of ownership and control in Hidrocantábrico illustrates some of the more interesting aspects of Spain's corporate market, specifically the roles of different levels of government (European, Spanish, regional), the savings banks, state-owned firms and the target-firm managers. To the events summarized in Table 14.1, we should add that Hidrocantábrico made an unsuccessful bid to buy Viesgo when Endesa put it up for sale. Besides, the takeovers of Unión Fenosa and Ferroatlántica–EnBW meant the withdrawal of other takeovers that had been launched by the US firm Texas Utilities and the German firm RWE, respectively. Furthermore, the Spanish government lifted the veto on the political rights of foreign state-owned firms in Hidrocantábrico in September 2003 after receiving a warning from the European Commission.

Although Table 14.1 only reports three of the transactions that affected Hidrocantábrico, the company, based in Asturias, was the target of five takeovers in 2000 and 2001. These were launched by Texas Utilities, Unión Fenosa, Ferroatlántica-EnBW, RWE and Cajastur–EDP – that is, one US firm, two German firms (one of them with the state-owned French firm EDF as the main shareholder), one Portuguese firm and one Spanish firm. The Belgian firm Electrabel also participated in the takeover contest as a minority shareholder. The winning bid was that made by Ferroatlántica–EnBW, although Cajastur and EDP remained as minority shareholders. Eventually, EDP acquired, in a direct transaction completed in 2004, a share package from the rest of the shareholders to obtain 95 percent of the stock. In this way, Hidrocantábrico became a subsidiary of EDP, with a chairman proposed by the local minority shareholder, the savings bank, Cajastur. The successful foreign companies, first EnBW and later EDP, participated in the contest in alliance with local investors, in an attempt to overcome political resistance associated with the national shareholders' loss of control.

The contest to control Hidrocantábrico, the fourth-largest Spanish electricity firm, was drawn out for more than a year in 2000 and 2001, and, in practice, it was not concluded until 2004, with the assumption of total control by EDP.

One of the interesting aspects of this takeover battle was that the regional government of Asturias (one of Spain's Autonomous Communities, where the company headquarters and most of its assets are located) and the incumbent management team at the time invited the battle to take place, on condition that the firm maintained its headquarters in Asturias, and that the change of ownership was compatible with the region's industrial and employment objectives. The regional government went to the extreme of criticizing the Spanish government over the takeover battle, as the latter was against the introduction of firms controlled by foreign state-owned capital. Meanwhile, the regional government was willing to accept such a presence as long as it ensured a strong subsidiary with its headquarters in Asturias, and provided the foreign company was willing to cooperate in the region's industrial and employment goals. This particular incident is illustrative of the fact that not all governments support national or regional champions in the same way. The outcome of the battle demonstrated that the economic and social agents operating in Asturias were able to find a compatible solution whereby the shareholders enjoyed large gains (see Figure 14.1); a strong firm with the ambition to become a key player was able to enter the future Iberian electricity market alongside the largest Spanish electricity firms with all that this meant for consumer gains from product market competition and improved productive efficiency; and a guarantee could be obtained that the new owners would cooperate with the "strategic" objectives of the industrial and employment policy of the regional government in Asturias.

14.4 EXPANDING FIRMS

The largest Spanish electricity firm, Endesa, and its German counterpart, E.On, are two clear examples of firms that were first allowed by their governments to expand at the national level, and which subsequently used their financial muscle to expand internationally.

Spanish electricity firms have been leading players in a remarkable expansion process characterized by investments in Latin America, investments and alliances in the rest of Europe, and diversification investing in the telecommunications industry. The most significant of these have been the acquisitions in Latin America. Table 14.3 shows the magnitude of the investments of Spanish energy (not only electricity) firms in Latin America.

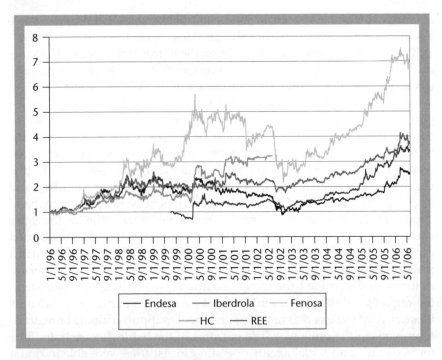

Figure 14.1 Stock prices, 1996–2006
Source: Thompson merger database 2001.

Table 14.3 Investments in Latin America (as at December 2002)

Company	Accounting value of investments (millions €)	Investments/Capitalization of consolidated group (%)
Repsol	12,375	80.4
Endesa	3,265	27.5
Iberdrola	1,450	12.0
Unión Fenosa	1,745	45.4
REE	52	4.0
Gas Natural	1,500	18.5

Source: Ontiveros *et al.* (2004).

The case of Endesa is of particular interest, as it is the largest Spanish electricity firm and one of the Spanish firms that has invested most heavily in Latin America (although it is also present in non-dominant firms in some European countries, including France and Italy). The expansion of Endesa in Latin America, like that of Telefónica, the Spanish incumbent telecommunications operator, began and gathered momentum when the company's largest shareholder was the state. The global result of expansion in Latin America was neutral for Endesa's shareholders, according to the event study technique, although the impact of its largest acquisition, the takeover of Chilean firm, Enersis, had negative results, according to two studies discussed below. Endesa also expanded into the telecommunications sector (Retevisión, Amena and Menta, later integrated under the company name, Auna), although it has recently abandoned this industry after the sale of Auna to Ono and France Telecom.[7] Both at Telefónica and at Endesa, there are reasons to believe that the main corporate control mechanisms did not work correctly. There were no shareholders with a controlling stake, there was no credible takeover threat at the time (either because of public ownership at the early stages of the expansions, or because of the government's threat to use the golden share), and product market and managerial labor market competition were scarce. The only factors acting as external discipline on manager conduct were the fact that the companies' stock was quoted on international markets, and the presence of institutional shareholders, as well as the slow and progressive introduction of product market competition (especially in mobile telephony in telecommunications and in the generation segment in electricity). The takeover of Enersis, the largest privatized electricity firm in Chile, took longer and was more costly than expected, and had negative consequences for (both bidder and target) shareholder wealth. It is also not clear whether Chilean consumers were better off after the takeover. On the one hand, the operation put pressure on the Chilean regulator to improve competition conditions in electricity, by triggering a debate on vertical integration. But Endesa won the takeover battle by defeating an offer from the American firm, Duke Energy, which was less willing to pay the high costs of a protracted and politicized battle, but it may well have had a better business plan for consumers. There is some consensus among experts, however, that the open attitude towards international competition from Chilean authorities and the quality of institutions have broadly benefited consumers.[8]

Actual events in the corporate control market of Spain's electricity firms in recent decades are consistent with predictions derived from academic research:

- Liberalization has triggered a wave of mergers and acquisitions, to the extent that all firms in the industry have been involved, and this has brought about an increase in shareholder concentration, which has so far mainly affected the relatively smaller firms.

- Takeovers in an industry where regulation still plays an important role are protracted, not always successful and have a high cost (at times excessively so) for shareholders in acquiring firms.

- The politicization of the control market in this industry is evident in the background of some of the managers involved, and in the reasons why some takeovers encounter obstacles or become the object of heated debates with little economic or financial content. The activism of a variety of interest groups (including managers, shareholders, and local and regional communities) confirms that collusion between policy-makers and lobbies[9] is an important factor in industries of this nature, and that the conduct of regulatory institutions is affected seriously by its presence.

- Resistance to ownership changes reveals the importance that society, through its political agents, attaches to the control of firms. Despite the effects of liberalization, the specificity and long-lived nature of investments still attract owners whose profiles differ form those of other capitalist private owners, especially state-owned firms and savings banks (which in Spain are more similar in nature to non-profit mutual firms). Liberalization (which only affects certain segments of the value chain) does not fundamentally alter the fact that long-lived specific investments are still subject to high regulatory, technological and market risks. The Spanish government consistently stopped mergers going ahead between national energy firms (Fenosa–Hidrocantábrico, Hidrocantábrico–Viesgo, and Endesa–Iberdrola) so as not to increase levels of concentration within the structure of the industry following the expansion of Endesa and prior to its full privatization in the late 1990s. However, the government failed to take advantage of the takeovers (for example, through the imposition of its own conditions) and the privatization of Endesa to achieve a less-concentrated industry structure.

Figure 14.1 describes the evolution in the stock prices of Endesa, Iberdrola, Hidrocantábrico, Red Eléctrica (REE) and Unión Fenosa between 1996 and 2006 (Hidrocantábrico ceased to be quoted as an independent value in 2002, and REE was first quoted in 1999). We observe that stock price increases coincide with periods of greatest activity in the market for corporate control. The Hidrocantábrico takeover clearly had a positive impact on the firm itself, as well as on Unión Fenosa, either because the latter was also seen as a potential target for a takeover bid, or because investors expected that the restructuring would increase market power, benefiting all firms in the market. Unión Fenosa's stock prices rose again when it was taken over by the construction firm, ACS. The firm that has perhaps fared worst on the stock market over this period has been Endesa, revealing that a company's shareholders do not necessarily come out on top when a strategy of consolidating and defending a national champion is adopted.

More precise quantitative data describing the effects of the expansion of Spanish firms can be obtained from event studies, which provide a measurement of the impact of particular events on shareholders' expectations (and, therefore, to the extent that financial markets are efficient, a quantification of the expected effect on the firm's discounted value). A study by López Duarte and García Canal[10] reports a positive and significant effect of foreign investments for all Spanish firms (not only in the electricity sector) on shareholder value. They also report that this is accompanied by a very high proportion – more than 45 percent – of investment announcements that have a negative impact on shareholders. Trillas (2001) concentrates on the Endesa case, paying special attention to the Enersis takeover, which is also studied by Parisi and Yáñez.[11] Both studies reveal a negative and significant impact on Endesa shareholders and on the minority shareholders of the target firm in Endesa's largest acquisition in Latin America. However, these event studies present either an overly broad picture, or an overly narrow one, without as yet seeking to quantify the effect on shareholders of all corporate control transactions in the electricity industry as a whole. The fact that the largest firms have been acquirers means, in all probability, that the global result will not be a net gain for shareholders (given that the bidder shareholders usually obtain worse results than those obtained by target shareholders), but the exact quantitative exercise has yet to be undertaken and, not unreasonably, will probably have to wait until the wave of takeovers comes to an end. The growing threats of takeover these large firm have to face can perhaps be seen, more recently, as a discipline mechanism for managers, who are possibly in the throes of learning how better to measure investment risks.

Table 14.4 shows the debt ratings of the largest European gas and electricity firms. The data report that two of the Spanish firms, those with the most aggressive expansion strategies, have relatively the worst ratings, although their solvency can still be qualified as strong or adequate. The data from the other main rating agency, Standard & Poor's (not reported here) confirm this pattern.

E.On emerged from the merger in the late 1990s of two large electricity firms in Germany, Veba and Viag. The new firm was involved very quickly in a number of international acquisitions, including Sydkraft in Sweden and Powergen in the UK, before it too was merged with the dominant German gas operator, Ruhrgas. In early 2006, E.On announced its next target, the takeover of the Spanish company, Endesa, in competition with an earlier bid launched by the Spanish gas firm, Gas Natural. Table 14.5 summarizes stock market reactions to E.On's acquisition announcements. Thus E.On can be seen to have followed the pattern of first establishing a strong national firm before setting out on an international process of expansion.

The Powergen and Endesa acquisitions were both presented as friendly – "white knight" – acquisitions. The two targets had both been created out of privatization processes and had subsequently begun to diversify their activities in other industries and parts of the globe – Powergen in the USA, and Endesa in Latin America.

E.On seems to typify the trend towards vertically integrated global utilities concentrating on both gas and electricity, but which have chosen to abandon investments in other sectors such as telecommunications.

Table 14.4 Debt ratings (Moody's, September 2005)

Company	Investment quality (degree of solvency)									
	Extreme	Very strong			Strong			Adequate		
	Aaa	Aa1	Aa2	Aa3	A1	A2	A3	Baa1	Baa2	Baa3
Centrica						A2				
E.On				Aa3						
Endesa							A3			
ENEL				Aa3						
EDP						A2				
ENI			Aa2							
G. Natural						A2				
G. France		Aa1								
Iberdrola						A2				
REE						A2				
RWE					A1					
Scottish Power						A2				
U. Fenosa									Baa2	
Vattenfall						A2				

Note: From left to right, the different ratings indicate declining rates of solvency, in line with the notation used by Moody's. For example, Baa1 indicates a first level of adequate investment quality, which is better than Baa2, which in turn is better than Baa3.
Source: Spanish electricity regulator CNE.

As can be seen from Table 14.5 (which reports abnormal returns on E.On stock prices), the only significant effect of the company's acquisition announcements was the positive abnormal return at the time of the Ruhrgas merger announcement. The effect on shareholder value of the announcement of the acquisitions of Powergen and Endesa did not differ significantly from zero, although the sign of the abnormal return in the case of Endesa was positive. This is consistent with theoretical and empirical research on takeovers, which expects shareholder gains to be captured by the target firm shareholders, and contrasts with the acquisition of Enersis by Endesa, in that the acquiring shareholders at least do not expect to make a loss on these acquisitions.

Figure 14.2 shows that since the year 2000 the stock market behavior of E.On has been much better than that of Endesa. We can conclude, therefore, that the performance of expanding firms on the stock market can vary markedly depending on the nature of their expansion plans, and that firms adopting expansion strategies that are not welcomed by shareholders (bad

Table 14.5 Stock market Reaction to E.On acquisition announcements

	3-day CAR (%)	$t = \dfrac{CAR}{\sqrt{3SD(AR)}}$
Powergen (January 17, 2001)	−3.2	−0.899
Ruhrgas (December 13, 2001)	6.5	2.09
Endesa (February 20, 2006)	2.7	1.55

Note: The cumulative abnormal returns (CAR) were computed using a market model over the observations of E.On and S&P 500 returns for a 1-year estimation window finishing one week before the event window. SD(AR) is the standard deviation of the difference between the actual returns and the predicted returns computed with this model over the estimation window.
Source: Based on stock prices from Yahoo Finance and event information from Lexis/Nexis.

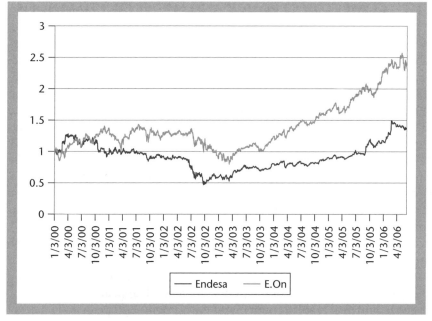

Figure 14.2 Endesa and E.On stock prices
Source: Spanish electricity regulator, CNE, Mahil, Spain.

bidders) risk being taken over by even stronger rivals (that is, they risk becoming good targets).

When E.On stepped in at the end of February 2006 with a bigger and better offer than that submitted by Gas Natural, the government did everything in its power to frustrate it. E.On offered €29.1 billion (US$34.7 billion) for Endesa – the biggest takeover bid in the history of the utilities industry – compared with Gas Natural's €22.5 billion cash-and-stock offer. However, after its own antitrust authority and the EU approved E.On's proposal in April, the government's obstructionism intensified. Eager to thwart the deal, the government invested special powers in CNE, Spain's energy regulator controlled by a board with close links to the government. At the end of July 2006, the CNE imposed nineteen conditions on E.On's bid for Endesa, including an undertaking to invest in gas transmission networks and the obligation to keep Endesa properly capitalized. Three of CNE's demands were highly controversial. First, E.On would have to sell the only nuclear-power plant wholly owned by Endesa. Next, it would also have to sell all of Endesa's coal-powered plants, because Spanish coal is subsidized and the government was concerned that the Germans would use cheaper imports. Third, E.On would have to divest itself of Endesa's operations in the Balearic and Canary Islands, and in northern Africa.

14.5 COMPETITION POLICY AND NATIONAL CHAMPIONS

In May 2006, the Spanish government repealed its golden shares regime, by which it had maintained for itself the sole option of vetoing control transactions involving privatized firms. At the time, the instrument was only available in the cases of Endesa and Telefónica, where it had been operative for more than ten years (in the UK, the golden shares of electricity distribution firms were operative for five years and, when they expired in 1995, this triggered a takeover wave that changed the ownership of all the firms affected).

The defense of public interest is usually cited as the reason for the existence of golden shares and other forms of restrictions on ownership changes. For example, in 1999, the Spanish government introduced a law by which the political rights of firms dominated by foreign status were restricted. This law was designed to prevent the French firm, Electricité de France (EDF), from taking control, through its German subsidiary EnBW, of the Spanish firm, Hidrocantábrico. Thus, unlike golden shares, this restriction vetoed not only changes in former state-owned firms, but also in those that had always been in the hands of the public. In general, appealing to the public or general interest is still a common practice among European politicians of many political persuasions as they seek to invoke restrictions on the free transfer of shares in electricity companies.

Strategies to protect the national identity of the owners of incumbent firms (popularly known as "national champion" strategies) seem to constitute part of the political equilibrium in many European countries. The argument is that it is desirable to protect large firms from external attacks on their ownership, (i) to defend "strategic" objectives (which my be related to industrial or labor policy measures, or, more recently, concern the security of supply in energy sectors, or the promotion of national inputs); and (ii) to turn them into strong competitors at the international level.[12]

The broad acceptance of such arguments means they cannot be ignored by research economists. The defense of strategic objectives has come to form part of the necessary vagueness of public objectives in democratic societies. When the objectives are many and not easily specified, existing legislation and contractual arrangements are necessarily incomplete, and so the only course of action open to the state is to exploit ownership instruments to achieve its objectives. As ownership is a residual decision-making instrument, these multiple and vague objectives can be achieved relatively efficiently. However, the obvious problem is that the very vagueness of these objectives makes accountability even more difficult,[13] while the monitoring of the costs for society of using certain ownership mechanisms or restrictions on ownership is not easily achieved. The same would be true if firms were not induced to maximize shareholder value but rather the value for all stakeholders: it would be considerably more challenging to match the incentives of managers with those of multiple stakeholders. Having said this, however, ownership clearly matters, in the sense that the location of the company headquarters and the closeness of decision-making units ensure a better adaptation to local preferences and may involve positive externalities and have bandwagon effects on the local economy. The problem is achieving these externalities with minimum costs in terms of efficiency while adhering to agreements on the free movement of capital to which a country has subscribed. Besides, ownership restrictions become more politically valuable in environments of increasing political concern and uncertainty derived from increasing fossil fuel prices, insecurity of supply because of dependence on conflict regions, or climate change (what the British economist Dieter Helm[14] has termed the typical concerns of the new paradigm in world energy after the year 2000, following two decades characterized by the paradigm of privatization and liberalization in a context of excess supply).

But in those cases in which the investor is foreign, and policy-makers and stakeholders believe there is a risk that the investor might abandon the country, what is important is that as long as the foreign investor remains as the owner, the latter has incentives to invest in assets which they will not be able to take with them when they leave. For example, in the electricity industry, the foreign firm should be encouraged to invest in specific physical assets, including networks and generation plants, which are the main assets in this industry. The risk that assets of this type might leave the country is zero. The physical assets of the electricity industry can continue to be used and have different owners over time, even if one particular investor might decide to abandon the country (indeed, this constitutes the main element in the regulators' bargaining power).

As for the second argument – namely, the need to support firms at the international level – the recent trend for operators to become subsidiaries of large multinational firms has experts predicting that in the not-too-distant future there will be no more than two or three large European companies controlling the European electricity market.[15] If a small number of firms end up competing against each other in all countries, we should not forget that multi-market contact is one of the factors facilitating collusion, which means instruments must be developed at the supranational level to take this phenomenon into consideration. The fact that, in practice, the market has yet to acquire a continental scale (because of insufficient transmission capacity and other constraints) does not mean that antitrust policy should not be used, or that legislation supporting a unified capital market across the EU should not be implemented.

Public or private asset ownership should not necessarily affect the nature of competition. Liberalization is possible with privatization (as has been the case in the UK) or without (as has occurred in Norway, where most electricity firms are municipal in origin) and can yield consumer benefits, as long as industry concentration in competitive segments is sufficiently low. Both in the UK and in Norway, concentration ratios in the wholesale electricity markets are clearly lower than those recorded in southern European countries.

European Union laws on antitrust policy do not distinguish between public and private capital, and many national governments, with the resistance of the European Commission – the executive body in Brussels, try to stop their leading companies from being bought by foreign (often, though not always, state-owned) firms. In order for such strategies to have any chance of overcoming the resistance of the European Commission, they have to be based on principles that are recognized by European norms, including restrictions on state aid, or predatory behavior. Several studies have analyzed the incentives for state-owned firms to adopt anti-competitive behavior, but it is difficult to see that the assumptions under which dominant state-owned firms in a particular country can abuse their dominant position can be applied to partially privatized firms operating in other countries.[16] Managers of partially privatized firms have a fiduciary duty to their minority shareholders, which means that they cannot depart from the profit-maximization objective, which makes predatory behavior very unlikely. Foreign firms that are dominant in their country of origin are in fact a guarantee that consumers will have credible rivals from among which to choose.[17] What should worry European authorities is that, if antitrust laws in the electricity industry are not harmonized, some operators may achieve competitive advantages from implicit subsidies in their local markets, with the consequence that the operators that end up providing the consumers with their service are not the most efficient, but rather the ones that are best-protected at home. However, individual countries need to analyze carefully the following reciprocity argument. If country A is protectionist, is it in country B's interests to be protectionist too? Reciprocity arguments in this field usually amount to impeding a welfare transfer from shareholders and consumers in country A to those in country B, as long as the original firm in country A is sufficiently more efficient than the firm in country B. Some countries (a minority) adhere, albeit to varying degrees, to this argument, depending on their political equilibrium, and legal and cultural traditions regarding state intervention and economic nationalism. In Chile and the UK, for example, there are no restrictions concerning the eligibility of acquiring firms – be they state-owned or otherwise – in their attempts to complete a takeover.[18] The new owners are simply asked to abide by the country's regulatory and labor laws (for example, the Spanish firm Endesa was state-controlled when it took over the Chilean firm, Enersis, and the French firm EDF was fully owned by the state when it took over London Electricity).

In terms of issues affecting regulation and antitrust, the diversified nature of firms is more problematic. In some countries (largely the case in Spain), the dominant regulatory practice is rate of return or cost-plus regulation, and there is no incentive regulation, so firms are interested[19] in practicing accounting and managerial cross-subsidies – in other words, in allocating high costs and relatively less able managers in segments where it is known that costs will be reimbursed no matter what their level.

14.6 CONCLUSION

As we have seen, the shareholders of acquiring firms do not usually benefit from the cross-border acquisitions of electricity companies in Europe. In most cases, such acquisitions benefit the shareholders of the target firms, as we have seen in the case of Hidrocantábrico. Exceptions are known, however, as Enersis shareholders were to discover in the late 1990s. Consumers in the countries of target firms tend to benefit more from cross-border acquisitions than those in the countries of acquiring firms, since the strategies adopted by the latter often (though by no means always) reflect local restrictions on product market and corporate control market competition. Political issues have also been seen to play a significant role in most transactions. The continuation of this wave of takeovers in forthcoming years should enable researchers to undertake a more complete assessment of the winners and losers in such transactions.

NOTES

1. See Arocena (2001).
2. In addition, I thank Joan Cals for reminding me that, in Spain, in the second half of the twentieth century up to the nineties, banks and savings banks (albeit to a lesser extent) were obliged to comply with a so-called compulsory investment coefficient, by which they had to buy public debt and the securities issued by electricity companies. Thus the latter benefited from the existence in the economy of privileged circuits of financing.
3. See Trillas (2001).
4. In the US, one area that historically had been regulated was the possibility of expansion by electricity firms. The repeal of the Public Utility Holding Company Act in 2005 removed this constraint.

5. Some authors have suggested the coincidence of liberalization and privatization processes in the utilities sectors with the narrowing of profit margins in traditional financial markets as the cause for the large increase in savings banks' non-financial equity stakes in the 1990s. See Cals (2005). In roughly the same period, a reduction occurred in the equity stakes that large banks held in other businesses, which had traditionally been sizeable.
6. Sevillana and FECSA had a diversity of shareholders in 1996, and today are subsidiaries of Endesa. Viesgo is a subsidiary of the Italian firm Enel.
7. Unión Fenosa is another Spanish electricity firm with significant investments outside the energy sectors – for example, in the airports sector in Mexico, and in the engineering sector through its subsidiary, Soluziona. Although diversification outside the energy sectors has been punished by investors, the participation of a firm in electricity and gas markets is broadly accepted as a value-creating development, because of productive efficiency gains obtained through mainly vertical integration in the provision of gas as an input in electricity generation, and to joint offers in the retail supply of gas and electricity.
8. Chile has maintained a completely open stance to the presence of foreign investors and multinationals, but has retained national public ownership of its main natural resource – copper.
9. Arocena (2001) describes the historically favorable bias towards incumbent firms of electricity regulation in Spain. But, interestingly, following strong activity in the market for corporate control, there was a loss of unity and efficiency in the owners' electricity association, UNESA, which became divided after the takeover by Gas Natural of Endesa in September 2005. This was backed by Iberdrola in exchange for an agreement to share some assets in the newly created firm.
10. See López Duarte and García Canal (2005).
11. See Parisi and Yáñez (2000).
12. See for example Arocena (2004).
13. It is difficult to distinguish, for example, between multiple good objectives and collusion between managers and policy-makers.
14. See Helm (2005).
15. See Glachant (2003).
16. On the role of state-owned firms in competitive environments, see Geddes (2004); and on the role of partially privatized firms, see Sidak (2001).
17. In Spain, this argument has finally been accepted, albeit reluctantly, when it involves non-dominant firms. In the telecommunications sector, the Spanish government did not intervene to stop the sale of cell phone operator, Amena, to France Telecom, or the entry of France Telecom to the broadband market through Wanadoo. In the electricity sector, the government (eventually) allowed the control of Hidrocantábrico by EDP and Viesgo by Enel (see section 3 above).
18. Operators that cannot be taken over incur other costs too, such as the impossibility of enlarging their capital base by going to the capital markets, or the declining efficiency incentives recorded by their managers.
19. See Hope (2005).

REFERENCES

Arocena, P. (2001) "The Reform of The Utilities Sector in Spain", Research Discussion Paper 2001/13, World Institute for Development Economics.
Arocena, P. (2004) "Privatisation Policy in Spain: Stuck between Liberalisation and the Protection of National Interests", Working paper CESIfo: 1187.

Cals, J. (2005) *El éxito de las Cajas de Ahorros. Historia reciente, estrategia competitiva y gobierno* (Madrid: Ariel).
Geddes, R. R. (ed.) (2004) *Competing with the Government. Anticompetitive Behavior and Public Enterprises* (Stanford, Calif.: Hoover Press).
Glachant, J. M. (2003) "The Making of Competitive Electricity Markets in Europe: No Single Way and No Single Market", in J. M. Glachant and D. Finon (eds), *Competition in European Electricity Markets* (Cheltenham: Edward Elgar).
Helm, D. (2005) "The Assessment: The New Energy Paradigm", *Oxford Review of Economic Policy*, 21(1): 1–18.
Hope, E. (2005) *Market Dominance and Market Power in Electric Power Markets* (Stockholm: Swedish Antitrust Authority).
López Duarte, C. and García Canal, E. (2005) "Multinacionalización de la gran empresa española: la valoración de la Bolsa de Madrid", *Universia Business Review-Actualidad Económica*, Madrid.
Ontiveros, E., Conthe, P. and Nogueira, J. M. (2004) *Investor Perception of Regulatory and Institutional Risk in Latin America* (Washington, DC: Interamerican Development Bank).
Parisi, F. and Yáñez, G. (2000) "The Deal of the Century in Chile: Endesa España's Takeover of Enersis", *International Review of Financial Analysis*, 9(1): 103–16.
Sidak, G. J. (2001) "Acquisitions by Partially Privatized Firms: The Case of Deutsche Telekom and Voicestream", *Federal Communications Law Journal*, 54(1): 1–30.
Trillas, F. (2001) "The Takeover of Enersis: The Control of Privatized Utilities", *Utilities Policy*, 10: 25–45.

CHAPTER 15

A Deal Too Far: The Case of the Killer Acquisition

Tyrone M. Carlin, Nigel Finch and Guy Ford

15.1 INTRODUCTION

Mergers and acquisitions have long been, and seem likely to remain, objects of fascination within the world of finance. While scholars puzzle over the theoretical motivations and value impacts of such transactions, practitioners devote their efforts to fueling what has become a burgeoning juggernaut.[1] The result of these twin streams of effort has been the creation of an unresolved, though clearly important, paradox.

Many researchers interested in mergers and acquisitions (M&As) have expressed deep skepticism as to the fundamental rationale for undertaking acquisition transactions (Roll's "hubris hypothesis" being perhaps the best-known exemplar of this trend), arguing that there would be far fewer such events if shareholder value creation was their true aim. They have also gathered large quantities of empirical evidence, which at the very least raises serious doubts as to the likelihood that acquisitions generate value for the buying party (Sudarsanam, 2003).

That is not to say that the literature on acquisitions does not throw up examples of acquisitions that have apparently been well-motivated or which, irrespective of motivation, appear none the less to have resulted in the generation of net increments to economic wealth for acquiring parties. Indeed, some recent analysis suggests that there are three key reasons why the results of empirical studies into the performance effects of acquisition transactions have shed such a consistently dim light on them. First, the wrong transactions were being studied – with many small transactions being excluded from the datasets being used by researchers. Second, the wrong measures of performance were being used; and third, the wrong measurement timeframes were being adopted (Harding and Rovit, 2004).

Despite all this, we do not turn in this chapter to an examination of the preconditions for value creation in acquisition transactions. Instead, the focus lies on transactions that lead not just to value dissipation for acquiring parties, but that result in such a profoundly negative outcome that the fact of the consummation of the transaction in fact results in the onset of financial distress and potential liquidation for the newly-enlarged firm. We refer to this as the "killer acquisition problem".

Of course, pre-existing literature has hinted at this problem. Sirower's (1997) elegant analysis of the so-called synergy trap in acquisition transactions certainly points to the issue. He conceptualizes acquisitions as a special case of the capital budgeting problem, in which the question of value creation or destruction resulting from each transaction is explained most forcefully by balancing the present value of any premiums paid to effect change of control against the present value of any synergies resulting from the combination.

Viewed through this lens, were the value of the premium paid to effect an acquisition sufficiently large in the context of the financial resource base of the acquiring firm, and the synergies (if any) to be sufficiently delayed,[2] it is possible to conceive of financial distress as one outcome for the acquiring firm. But beyond reference to excessive premium for control and lack of timely synergy realization, this approach fails to yield a more clinical set of factors upon which to found a reasonable expectation of financial failure of the type examined here.

Similarly, though previous literature has cited a range of factors that appear to be significant in differentiating the characteristics of those acquisition transactions that fail (that is, destroy value) from those that succeed, including relative size of target and acquirer; strategic relatedness; acquirer track record; combined entity market power, whether domestic or international; and form of consideration (to produce a non-exhaustive list), little attempt has been made to study factors that are likely to be associated with catastrophic outcomes for acquirers (Jensen and Ruback, 1983; Franks *et al.*, 1991; Agrawal *et al.*, 1992; Healy *et al.*, 1997).

Therefore, this chapter contributes to the literature by focusing on a specific under-researched phenomenon – the catastrophic or killer acquisition – and the factors associated with such events in particular, as opposed to value dissipating transactions in general. Given the lack of a substantial extant literature, a case methodology is employed as a means of yielding insights with a capacity to contribute to the development of a more theorized approach to the understanding of this phenomenon (Yin, 1989).

The remainder of the chapter is organized as follows. Section 15.2 provides an overview of and background to the focal case organization, Australian wine producer Evans & Tate Limited. Section 15.3 explores a sequence of acquisition transactions undertaken by this company, their strategic context and their impact on Evans & Tate. Section 15.4 focuses in specific detail on one of these acquisitions – the company's 2003 purchase of Cranswick Premium Wines. This section of the chapter outlines suggested explanations for both why the transaction itself was so dangerous and of the particular traits of the acquiring entity that led it to pursue and complete the deal notwithstanding its obvious risks. Section 15.5 contains a synthesis of the research and offers some conclusions in relation to the incidence of the killer acquisition phenomenon.

15.2 OVERVIEW OF THE FOCAL COMPANY

Evans & Tate is an Australia-based wine producer. The business was established by John Evans, Jan Evans, John Tate and Toni Tate[3] in 1971, with a small land holding in the Perth Hills. Within a short period of time the wine-growing potential of the then nascent Margaret River region[4] was recognized by the founders, and by 1974 the company had expanded to include operations at Redbrook, situated within the Margaret River district.[5] In the years that followed, the company successfully established a number of key brands which still remain an important element of the business.[6]

Though "Evans" precedes "Tate" in the company's name, the destiny of the company has for the greater part of its lifespan rested with the Tate family, and the Evans interests left the business in 1983.[7] This dominance was cemented firmly in place in 1987, when Franklin Tate, son of founders John and Toni, joined the company.[8] At that point, the business was a minnow, with annual sales of just US$700,000.[9] By 1992, with the business growing rapidly, Franklin Tate was elevated to the role of managing director. By 1995, annual sales had reached US$5 million, and doubled again, to US$10 million, by 1998.[10]

Though the years to 1998 saw the transformation of the company from being a small firm to becoming a substantial commercial enterprise, the following year represented a watershed in the organization's history. By 1999, the company had swallowed Margaret River rival Selwyn Wines, owned 260 hectares of prime Margaret River vineyards,[11] and two fully-equipped wineries[12] and was achieving annual sales of US$12 million. Most significantly, chief executive and chairman, Franklin Tate, determined that the time was ripe to transform the family business into a listed public company.

This was achieved through the execution of a successful, fully-subscribed initial public offering which closed in late December 1999, during which the Tate family sold 42 percent of their holdings and the company raised a total of US$26 million. At the close of the first day of trading, IPO participants had achieved stagging profits in the order of 20 percent, and the freshly-listed company enjoyed a market capitalization of slightly more than US$50 million.

Though the business had experienced rapid growth during the 1990s, that had come off a very low base. Even at the time that Evans & Tate made the leap from family-run to public company, it could still be best thought of as a parochial niche producer, and more than 90 percent of its sales at that stage were restricted to the State of Western Australia.[13] Yet only five years later, the firm's asset base had ballooned approximately tenfold, from US$26 million to US$272 million[14] and its revenue flows would have increased by a similar factor, from US$12 million to US$104 million.

In that same period, the company was transformed from being an organization filled with brash optimism to one so ridden with financial disease as to be a heartbeat away from death. The broad brushstrokes of Evans & Tate's trajectory in its post-listing era are encapsulated in Tables 15.1 and 15.2. The first sets out details of the company's revenue and earnings history as a listed vehicle, while the second provides insight into the size of the firm's asset portfolio and financing strategy.

Table 15.1 Evans & Tate, post-listing revenue and after-tax earnings history

Year	Revenue (US$)	Year on year growth (%)	After-tax earnings (US$)	Year on year growth (%)
1999	12,335,000	24	701,000	n/a
2000	19,718,000	60	2,376,000	238
2001	29,269,000	49	2,682,000	13
2002	30,200,000	3	2,925,000	9
2003	63,143,000	109	4,431,000	51
2004	101,643,000	61	7,624,000	72
2005	104,123,000	3	(49,800,000)	−750

Source: Evans & Tate.

Table 15.2 Evans & Tate, post-listing asset and liability history

Year	Total assets (US$)	Year on year growth (%)	Total liabilities (US$)	Year on year growth (%)
1999	26,124,000	n/a	16,581,000	n/a
2000	44,545,000	71	18,826,000	14
2001	53,929,000	21	36,144,000	92
2002	80,353,000	49	48,237,000	33
2003	201,796,000	60	148,203,000	207
2004	215,408,000	7	138,881,000	(6)
2005	272,401,000	26	164,363,000	18

Source: Evans & Tate.

A number of trends quickly became evident even after a brief review of this data. First, the firm's revenue grew by a cumulative total of approximately 750 percent between 1999 and 2005. Over the same period, the firm's asset base grew by approximately 940 percent while liabilities expanded by 890 percent. Put simply, between 1999 and 2005, the firm massively increased its gearing in order to fund a substantially enlarged, though obviously underperforming, asset portfolio. The result was a loss in 2005[15] of US$49.8 million, or US$2.50 for every dollar in post tax profits earned by the company in sum between 1999 and 2004 (inclusive).

Clearly, the story of Evans & Tate between 1999 and 2005 was of rapid, and ultimately deeply unhealthy, growth. But the firm's growth was of a particular character. As Figure 15.1 shows, though part of the firm's expansion was organic, the dominant portion of it stemmed from the firm's acquisitiveness.

Specifically, during the period under review, the firm made three acquisitions. First, Selwyn wines, another Margaret River producer; second, Oakridge Estate, a tiny Yarra Valley concern;[16] and finally, Cranswick Premium Wines. Figure 15.1 shows the revenue of each of these acquired firms at the time they were purchased by Evans & Tate, juxtaposed against that firm's total revenue growth between 1999 and 2005.

As will be evident from the data above, the firm's post-IPO story was dominated by its involvement with a string of acquisitions. However, these were not of a consistent character, and one in particular – the 2003 purchase of Cranswick Premium Wines – was of such a magnitude, in both an operational and financial context, that it had the capacity not only to transform Evans & Tate – but also to sow the seeds of that firm's downfall were all not to go to plan. It is to this possibility and the reasons for it that we turn in section 15.3.

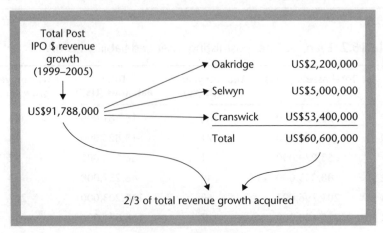

Figure 15.1 Source of growth
Source: Evans & Tate.

15.3 A STRING OF ACQUISITIONS

Prior to the initial public offering and acquisition of the Selwyn wine business, Evans & Tate could best be characterized as a vertically integrated[17] boutique producer of premium, super-premium and ultra-premium branded bottled wine (with the greatest emphasis on super-premium products).[18] However, over the course of the next four years, the company metastized into an organism vastly different in scale and emphasis from that profiled to investors in the 1999 IPO.

This change began with the Selwyn acquisition, which Evans & Tate rationalized as a key plank of its strategy to develop a meaningful non-branded wine operation.[19] This business differed somewhat from the business the company had previously developed, in that its central economic tenet revolved around volume, rather than margin.

The Selwyn acquisition also resulted in a vineyard management business being bolted on to the pre-existing wine-making business, creating a service revenue stream to accompany the company's product-based revenue streams.[20] However, on balance, the acquisition was not of a character or a size that would result in either a fundamental transformation of the Evans & Tate business or a significant threat to it.

The total value of the Selwyn transaction, at approximately US$6 million was small in comparison to the level of resources available to Evans & Tate. Further more, the physical assets acquired (principally vineyards and wineries) were similar in character and geographically close to Evans & Tate's existing operations.[21]

Some further change to the business mix came with the company's subsequent decision to acquire the companies that undertook the distribution of much of Evans & Tate's production in key markets. Thus Evans & Tate acquired US distributor Scott St. Portfolio,[22] European distributor Australian Wineries UK,[23] and Australian distributor WineSource.[24] No data published by the company provides an insight into the contribution of this group of businesses as a stand-alone segment to the overall profit or loss of the Evans & Tate group. However, since these businesses are essentially predicated on assisting the company to sell its own product, it can be assumed that they play a useful, though auxiliary, role in the context of the group overall.

After digesting Selwyn, Evans & Tate engaged in two further acquisitions of wine production businesses. The first involved the acquisition of Oakridge Vineyards Limited in 2001. This deal gave Evans & Tate access to a small winemaking facility[25] and vineyard located within the premium Yarra Valley district of Victoria (and thus a degree of geographical diversification), but was otherwise unremarkable.[26] Oakridge was a tiny operation, and the total consideration paid to effect its acquisition was in the order of US$2 million – a relatively trivial sum in the context of Evans & Tate's operations at that time.

This lay in stark contrast to the company's acquisition of Cranswick Premium Wines, via a scheme of arrangement completed on March 17, 2003.[27] Cranswick was a volume giant compared to Evans & Tate (even after the incorporation of Selwyn and Oakridge). In the year ending June 30, 2002, Cranswick produced over 1.9 million case equivalents and crushed 41,500 tonnes of grapes at its two wineries.[28] Cranswick owned 390 hectares of fully developed vineyards located across sites located mainly in New South Wales (NSW) and Victoria[29] – a transcontinental distance from Evans & Tate's key operations. Evans & Tate, by comparison, crushed approximately 7,500 tonnes of grapes and produced approximately 500,000 cases of wine in the same period, and owned developed vineyards less than a quarter of the total size of Cranswick's holdings.

Scale, though, was not the chief difference between the two businesses. Indeed, aside from the fact that both organizations produced wine, there were very few points of similarity. Whereas the pre-Cranswick Evans & Tate business had defined itself as a dominant player in the very small (though lucrative), highly brand-driven Margaret River niche, Cranswick produced a downmarket product that appealed to consumers more on price than on any other dimension.[30] Evans & Tate had been a domestic sales success, achieving almost 90 percent of its sales in Australia,[31] while Cranswick was highly export-focused and had built up a viable distribution structure in the UK and continental Europe.[32]

The vast distances involved, and differences in scale, production techniques and brand propositions between the Evans & Tate business and Cranswick are all factors that would probably have conspired to reduce the size of potential synergies arising when the business were combined. However, as troubling as these issues might have been in and of themselves, it was the financial dimensions of the Cranswick acquisition that most strongly signalled the potential for dangerous after-effects.

The first announcement that Evans & Tate and Cranswick were in merger negotiations came in early June 2002. By August, Evans & Tate had reported that the purchase due diligence process was proceeding well, and that the putative value that would be placed on Cranswick for the purposes of the acquisition would be approximately US$57 million.

However, by September, Cranswick had been forced to make a range of embarrassing confessions about its financial position – including that it would make a full year loss of US$23 million, having suffered declining revenues, the after-effects of the liquidation of its distribution arm, and a range of impairments to key asset categories, including inventories and intangibles.

Despite this, and extensive press speculation that Evans & Tate would walk away from the proposed deal in the light of these revelations, the facts of Cranswick's damaged position seems only to have hardened the resolve of Evans & Tate to complete the transaction – albeit at a lower price than had originally been contemplated – the value of the proposed deal being reset to approximately US$45 million by late September. Ultimately, this was price that Evans & Tate paid for Cranswick the following March – and it is to the detail and context of this transaction that we turn in the next section.

15.4 EXPLORING A KILLER DEAL

Though Evans & Tate attempted to cast its acquisition of Cranswick in a positive light, the truth of the matter, ultimately revealed two years after the completion of the deal, was that it had in fact acquired a business so flawed, and in a transaction of such a scale that its own financial existence was called into question.[33] Cranswick's business model was to produce and sell high volumes of relatively low-margin product, primarily to export markets. While achieving the first of these objectives, the margins it had generated on this business were so thin as to place the long-term financial viability of the business in jeopardy.

Thus, in purchasing Cranswick, Evans & Tate had extended itself financially to purchase a firm that controlled impaired brands and was generating negative cashflows because of poor management of working capital. Prior to its acquisition of Cranswick, Evans & Tate had reported small though consistently positive net cash inflows from operating activities. After the transaction, however, the firm's cashflow position rapidly deteriorated as margins fell and stock turnover remained unacceptably low. The substantial alteration to Evans & Tate's financial affairs post-Cranswick (2003 and after) compared to the pre-Cranswick (2002 and before) position is captured well in the data set out in Table 15.3, which includes information relating to revenues and margins on a per-case-sold basis, as well as the overall stock turnover position of the firm.

Table 15.3 Evans & Tate, key financial indicators

Year	Revenue per case (US$)	COGS per case (US$)	Interest per case (US$)	Gross margin less finance costs per case (US$)	Inventory days (No.)
2000	144	73	5.82	65.18	486
2001	99	53	3.67	42.33	577
2002	96	51	4.73	40.27	602
2003	70	43	4.04	22.96	687
2004	61	35	5.34	20.66	698
2005	58	40	5.53	12.47	657

Source: Evans & Tate.

The disjuncture between the firm's position pre- and post-Cranswick is stark. Not only did margins fall dramatically, but the average holding interval for stock widened by an appreciable margin – despite Cranswick being in the business of producing wines that did not require extensive maturation or cellaring prior to sale.

Whatever else might be said about the transaction, it certainly cannot be argued that Evans & Tate could only have been in a position to learn of the poor state of Cranswick's finances until the post-completion period. As discussed previously, Cranswick actively signalled its situation soon after Evans & Tate began merger talks, by reporting a very substantial operating loss, negative cashflows from operations, and material inventory and intangible asset impairments.

These were unlikely to have been transient events – on the contrary, they were anchored firmly in a series of industry trends whose momentum and import ought to have been obvious to all who chose to examine them. Data published by the Australian Bureau of Statistics (see Table 15.4) tells an eloquent tale of an industry gripped by increasing competition on the one hand, while being dogged by sustained overproduction on the other. This, combined with a fundamental reshaping of liquor retailing scene in Australia, such that market power was dramatically transferred from producers to two key retail groups that had grown their share of the trade tenfold over the space of less than a decade, spelt a period of substantial turmoil even for financially well-balanced operators.

Thus, all other things being equal, the better view of the transaction must be that Evans & Tate pursued the matter with its eyes wide open. This raises serious questions about the strength of the control and governance systems and processes in place at Evans & Tate in its post-IPO period, and whether these had changed sufficiently substantially to measure up to the challenges associated with the firm's 1999 metamorphosis from family-owned company to public corporation. Arguably, the lack of a strong

Table 15.4 Key industry trends

Year	Wine producers	Cases produced	Domestic case sales	Export case sales	Inventory estimate cases
1999	1,104	94,571,444	38,816,556	24,016,556	121,064,778
2000	1,197	95,462,889	41,030,111	31,659,444	132,421,222
2001	1,318	119,615,333	42,760,778	37,587,667	152,987,111
2002	1,465	135,596,889	42,914,667	46,488,111	174,504,000
2003	1,624	120,665,000	44,719,889	57,626,889	175,760,333
2004	1,798	163,469,778	46,375,333	64,933,000	206,056,222

capacity to rationalize the Cranswick acquisition on either operational or financial grounds suggests that an alternative explanation for the deal lies in the phenomenon of governance failure.

Of course, the quality of a firm's governance is inherently more difficult to judge, especially with only the benefit of publicly available information, than dimensions of an organization's performance such as the financial outcomes it generates. Yet enough circumstantial evidence does exist in relation to the quality of Evans & Tate's governance to facilitate contemplation of the impact of this matter on the decision trajectory exhibited by the firm.

A review of the available evidence suggests several areas for concern. The first is the apparently unchallenged position of Evans & Tate's cornerstone shareholder, chief executive officer (CEO) and board chair, Franklin Tate. Having assumed the role of CEO in 1992, Tate also took on the task of chairing the company's board from 1999 onwards.

The board he assembled was small in size (varying between four and five members in total), and poorly balanced. Tate was the only executive director, and to ensure the continuity of his capacity to control the board, his wife Heather acted as an alternative non-executive director. Further, the skill mix brought to the table by the board's members was constrained – dominated by those with a legal background, but devoid of strong financial, industry and marketing experience.

This weakness at the board level seems also to have been replicated in critical areas of the firm's internal management. For example, between November 2003 and January 2006, the firm had four different chief financial officers (CFOs), an unusual degree of turnover for such a critical role. Further, the lack of strong board financial experience coupled with a lack of continuity in the CFO role may have rendered Evans & Tate less capable of assessing independently the nature of advice tendered to it by key outside stakeholders, such as its primary creditor, ANZ Bank, which was involved directly and indirectly in all of the acquisition transactions undertaken by the firm in its post-IPO guise.

In particular, it seems relevant to note that ANZ had been a creditor to the financially weak Australian Premium Wines when in 1999 it assisted Cranswick to purchase that company, and was a creditor to both financially weakened Cranswick and Evans & Tate when the latter acquired the former in 2003. ANZ's investment banking arm had also played a key role in Evans & Tate's 1999 IPO, the acquisition of Selwyn wines and of the Oakridge estate.

This dominant lending and advisory role serves at very least to raise questions about the possibility that there existed asymmetries between the motivations of ANZ and Evans & Tate in entering into the string of transactions in which both were involved, and, given the apparent weaknesses in the latter's internal financial functions, the capacity of Evans & Tate to conserve its own interests in the face of the advice tendered to it.

Overall, then, the available evidence seems to suggest that the dominant motivation for the transaction undertaken was the pursuit of growth. Evans & Tate chairman and CEO, Franklin Tate, appears to have been intent on rapidly expanding the ambit of the firm's operations on a range of key dimensions (product portfolio, geographic scope, market reach) within a highly constrained time-span. This desire led to the creation of a deep chasm between the company's ambition and the resources available within the organization to fuel the fulfilment of that ambition. It was a void that would, of necessity, be filled by debt-propelled acquisition activity.

Elementary analysis suggests that during the three-year period spanning the Cranswick acquisition (2002–2004), Evans & Tate's sustainable growth rate averaged 3.23 percent per annum, while over the same period, the firm's actual rate of expansion lay close to 50 percent per annum. Debt financing, provided and facilitated almost exclusively by ANZ, provided the means of bridging the resulting financial void – yet, as has been demonstrated above, this significant increase in appetite for financial and operational risk came at a time when the market for Evans & Tate's products was being buffeted by an almost perfect storm.

The dangers associated with driving growth at rates substantially in excess of sustainable limits, rapid increases in leverage, and the distractions associated with the need to manage large one-off transactions such as acquisitions would normally be expected to place internal governance mechanisms on notice and elicit a counterbalancing response.

Yet in the case of Evans & Tate, it appears that this simply was not a meaningful possibility. The firm suffered from poor management systems and controls – particularly in the key area of financial management. Meanwhile, at board level, the range of skills required to effectively critique the quality of outside advice (for example, from principal creditors) and understand its ramifications was severely limited. There was no functioning counterweight to the influence of Franklin Tate – architect of the firm's strategy, cornerstone shareholder, chief executive officer and board chair. The rest, as they say, is history.

15.5 CONCLUSION

It is well known that acquisition transactions can represent a moment of considerable danger for those firms that use them as a method of embarking on a high-growth trajectory. Largely, however, the literature that has contemplated the propensity of acquisition transactions to result in value destruction for acquiring parties has not extended to an examination of value destruction so profound that it has the effect of threatening the ongoing financial viability of the acquiring party.

In contrast to most pre-existing literature, this chapter has focused on this possibility in particular, and on some of the phenomena that might prove to be responsible for its existence, of which three in particular emerge from the case analysis above: first, the financial condition of the target firm at the time the acquisition takes place; second, industry conditions and trends contemporaneous with the acquisition; and third, the quality of the internal governance processes that act as checks and balances on deal proposals brought to the acquiring firm's board by both interested internal and external stakeholders.

Of these phenomena, we propose the third as the most important, since effective governance review would arguably result either in deal avoidance or appropriate price protection in relation to deals proposed where either or both of the first two nominated phenomena presented.

In the case of Evans & Tate however, it appears that there was little opportunity for effective checks and balances being brought to bear on deal proposals. In that firm, a dominant chief executive and board chair bent on growth found an ally in a financial services provider no doubt content to generate growing fee streams while assisting the fulfilment of that desire in conditions where neither other directors or internal finance executives appear to have been in a position to offer an effective counterbalance.

It may well have been the case that neither the Selwyn nor Oakridge acquisitions that pre-dated the Cranswick deal – the subject of this analysis – represented transactions motivated by a cogent investment thesis. Individually, however, this would have been of relatively little importance in terms of the survival prospects for the acquiring firm, since both transactions were very small in scale.

The Cranswick deal was of a markedly different character. As a target, it was large in size compared to Evans & Tate. It had a highly geared balance sheet, poor cashflows and a portfolio of chronically underperforming assets. Its key operations were geographically remote from those of the acquiring business. Its customers were profoundly different in terms of their location, their product and their pricing preferences. Being a primarily export-orientated business, Cranswick was exposed to a plethora of risks (for example, currency risk) which would not have had an impact on the almost wholly domestically-focused Evans & Tate business to any meaningful degree prior to the acquisition. And, of course, the key competitors of the Cranswick business were not only far larger than the key competitors to the more boutique Evans & Tate operation – but also to be found all over the New World.

That so many obvious risk factors existed and would have been evident to a dispassionate observer contemporaneously with the completion of the transaction raises serious questions about how such a deal could have been executed – because there exists an enormous gulf between a dangerous deal proposal and a dangerous deal actually done. Our analysis has led us to the conclusion that the primary explanation for the fact of this deal was Evans & Tate's lack of – for want of a better term – a functioning immune system.

Where swarms of directors armed with pertinent questions about the strategy underpinning the transaction; its risk characteristics; financial simulations showing base case, worst case and best case scenarios for the impact of the transaction and the like should normally have surrounded the chief executive and his coterie of bankers, and prevented their forward motion until satisfactory answers had been provided – and there were none. There was nothing, in other words, to prevent the ingestion of pathogens into the body corporate. Once that state of affairs came into being, it was only a matter of time until opportunistic parasites happened upon and exploited a compromised host.

In this chapter, we have scrutinized just one case in detail. However, this detailed contemplation has led us towards the development of propositions amenable for empirical testing aimed at understanding more comprehensively the killer acquisition phenomenon.

In particular, we posit that firms with higher levels of turnover in key financial management positions – particularly the position of CFO, with unbalanced boards, with high reliance on a single financial services provider, and with high CEO power concentration, are more likely to be susceptible to this form of risk phenomenon than firms that do not share these characteristics. In consequence, it would be to these factors we would suggest future researchers turn their attention as they seek to expand the boundaries of knowledge on the subject.

NOTES

1. According to data produced by Thomson Financial Securities, the global value of completed M&A transactions totalled approximately US$3 trillion, having increased at an annualized growth rate of 33 percent over the decade of the 1990s. The value of acquisition transactions completed fell sharply to US$1.2 trillion in 2002. However, Thomson Financial Securities estimates that the annualized growth rate in global acquisition deal total value since that time has been 46 percent.
2. This assumes that positive synergies result from the deal. However, as some commentators have noted, it is also entirely possible that negative synergies flow from a business combination – for example, loss of a key customer as a result of becoming the owner of a competitor firm (Wasserstein, 2000).
3. Evans & Tate Prospectus (1999) p. 1.
4. The Margaret River region is located approximately 300 kilometres south of Perth, the capital city of Western Australia. Benefiting from a Mediterranean climate and excellent terroir, it is widely recognized as one of the premier wine-growing districts in Australia. Wine produced in the Margaret River region is exported globally and commands premium prices.
5. Presentation by Phillip Osborne, Evans & Tate Chief Operating Officer, to Evans & Tate Annual General Meeting, November 30, 2004.
6. These included: "Redbrook", "Gnangara" and the "Evans & Tate Margaret River" range.
7. Evans & Tate Prospectus (1999) p. 1.

8. His initial appointment was as sales and marketing manager.
9. Evans & Tate Annual Report (2001) p. 4.
10. Presentation by Franklin Tate, Evans & Tate Chairman and Chief Executive Officer, to Evans & Tate Annual General Meeting, November 6, 2003.
11. Approximately 80 hectares of this total was under vine by the end of 1999.
12. These were: The Selwyn Winery – acquired in 1999, and a new purpose-built winery built on the Lionel's vineyard site in 1999. The two facilities were located approximately 1 km from each other.
13. Considering that Perth, the capital of Western Australia, is by far that state's largest population center, but also holds the distinction of being the most isolated capital city on earth, the narrow niche filled by Evans & Tate at the time in question should be graphically evident.
14. The reported value of total assets in the firm's 2005 financial statements was US$215.8 million. However, this figure was derived after allowing for asset write downs to a total value of US$56.6 million in the year ended 30 June 2005. Therefore, to facilitate consistent analysis, this sum has been written back to the balance sheet.
15. The loss was triggered by substantial asset write-downs.
16. The Yarra Valley is one of Australia's premier cool-climate wine-growing regions, with a particular reputation for excellent Pinot Noir. It lies very close to Melbourne, located at the very south of Australia's eastern seaboard. Flying time between Perth – the capital city nearest to Margaret River – and Melbourne – the capital city nearest to the Yarra Valley – is approximately 4.5 hours.
17. That is, the company owned its own vineyards and winery, and had on-site access to bottling and packaging. Further, the company had developed a reasonable distribution and sales capability.
18. These were: the ultra-premium (US$30–50 per bottle) Redbrook range; the super-premium (US$15–30 per bottle) Evans & Tate Margaret River range; and the premium (US$10–15 per bottle) Gnangara range.
19. No cogent rationalization for this "strategy" was ever stated within the prospectus.
20. The viticultural services business represented approximately 3 percent of revenue in 2001, 8.5 percent in 2002, 5 percent in 2003, 5.5 percent in 2004, and approximately 5 percent in 2005 (all dates referring to financial, not calendar, year ends). Overall, this business does not represent a material element of the overall activity portfolio of the Evans & Tate group, nor is the success or failure of the group (as configured) likely to turn on the performance of this element of the enterprise.
21. The distance between them was approximately 1 kilometer.
22. L. Gettler, "Wine Group Buys Taste of U.S. Market", *The Age*, March 14, 2002, p. 3. The consideration paid was approximately AUD 625,000 in a mix of Evans & Tate shares and cash.
23. A 49 percent share of the equity of this company was acquired when Evans & Tate took control of Cranswick Premium Wines in 2003. Subsequently, in 2004, Evans & Tate arranged to acquire the remaining equity in this business for a reported consideration of AUD 2 million. See L. Gettler, "Evans & Tate Tightens Grip on UK Distribution", *The Age*, March 27, 2004, p. 2.
24. This transaction also took place in 2004, costing an initial cash consideration of AUD 11 million with the possibility of additional payments to the vendors totalling no more than AUD 3.34 million contingent on the financial performance of the business in the years ending June 30, 2005 and June 30, 2006. As at the time of writing, a further AUD 1.2 million was payable to the vendors of the business under this variable consideration arrangement – see Evans & Tate Limited, "Running Sheet for AGM", November 30, 2005.
25. Approximately 18 hectares in total of vineyards.

26. The key assets of Oakridge were an 18-hectare vineyard, a modern, purpose-built winery capable of crushing 1,100 tonnes of grapes per annum, and the Oakridge Estate brand name. In the year of the acquisition, Oakridge produced approximately 54,000 cases of wine. By way of contrast, Evans & Tate produced more than 500,000 case equivalents in the same period. At the time of the acquisition, Evans & Tate's market capitalization stood at approximately AUD 50 million, while the total value of consideration payable in respect of the Oakridge acquisition was in the range of AUD 4 million. See the Scheme Booklet for the Scheme of Arrangement between Oakridge Vineyards Limited and Evans & Tate Limited, August 2001.
27. See Evans & Tate media release: *Completion of Schemes of Arrangement*, March 20, 2003.
28. One winery was located in Mildura; the other in Griffith.
29. See the Explanatory Statement for Schemes of Arrangement between Cranswick Premium Wines Limited in relation to the Proposed Merger with Evans & Tate Limited, December 2002, p. 44.
30. Its most successful product, the "Barramundi" range – principally an export brand – was selling more than a million cases per annum by the time of the acquisition. This range was priced in the sub-AUD 10 per bottle segment of the market. See S. Evans, "Cash Lubricates Tate, Cranswick Wine Merger", *Australian Financial Review*, September 27, 2002, p. 54.
31. L. Gettler, "Evans & Tate Merger Fails to Excite", *The Age*, June 15, 2002, p. 3.
32. J. McCulloch, "Evans & Tate Chairman is a Family Man", *Perth Sunday Times*, June 23, 2002, p. 47.
33. Indeed, post-July 2005, Evans & Tate has survived mainly for one reason – the fact that it has been propped up by its chief creditor, ANZ Bank, without whose support the firm would undoubtedly be insolvent.

REFERENCES

Agrawal, A., Jaffe, J. and Mandelker, G. (1992) "The Post Merger Performance of Acquiring Firms: A Re-Examination of an Anomaly", *Journal of Finance*, 47: 1605–21.

Franks, J., Harris, R. and Titman, S. (1991) "The Post Merger Share Price Performance of Acquiring Firms", *Journal of Financial Economics*, 29: 81–96.

Harding, D. and Rovit, S. (2004) *Mastering the Merger – Four Critical Decisions that Make or Break the Deal* (Boston, Mass.: Harvard Business School Press).

Healy, P., Palepu, K. and Ruback, R. (1997) "Which Takeovers Are Profitable: Strategic or Financial?", *Sloan Management Review*, 38: 45–57.

Jensen, M. and Ruback, S. (1983) "The Market for Corporate Control: The Scientific Evidence", *Journal of Financial Economics*, 11: 5–50.

Ross, R. (1986) "The Hubris Hypothesis of Corporate Takeovers", *Journal of Business*, 59: 197–216.

Sirower, M. (1997) *The Synergy Trap – How Companies Lose the Acquisitions Game* (New York: Free Press).

Sudarsanam, S. (2003) *Creating Value From Mergers and Acquisitions: The Challenges* (Harlow: Prentice-Hall/Financial Times), esp. ch. 3.

Wasserstein, B. (2000) *Big Deal – 2000 and Beyond* (New York: Warner Books).

Yin, R. (1989) *Case Study Research: Design and Methods* (Newbury Park, Calif.: Sage).

CHAPTER 16

Trends in Chinese M&A: A Look at Lenovo's Acquisition of IBM PC

Margaret Wang

16.1 INTRODUCTION

May 2, 2006 marks the first anniversary of a Chinese company (Lenovo)'s acquisition of the personal computer (PC) division of the world's third most valuable brand, IBM (behind only Coca-Cola and Microsoft) (Smith and Rushe, 2004). It shocked the world when the proposed deal was first announced in late 2004. Rather than simply being a target of foreign investments, as China had been since the late 1970s, China's potential to be an acquirer of foreign multinational corporations, particularly the PC division of a company that was an American icon (namely, IBM or "Big Blue"), had suddenly been realized – and in a major way too – as this deal represented a "milestone in trans-pacific commerce: the first billion-dollar takeover in the U.S. by a mainland Chinese company" (Hitt, 2005).

Considering that Lenovo had only been established for approximately 20 years at the time of acquiring IBM PC, which has 93 years of history, it is not surprising that the acquisition has even been described as "a snake swallowing an elephant". This chapter explains the key elements of the transaction and its economic rationale. The chapter also considers whether this might be an indicator for future M&A transactions involving Chinese companies as acquirers.

16.2 HISTORY OF LENOVO

Before examining Lenovo's acquisition of IBM's PC division, it may be appropriate to describe briefly the history of a company – that is, Lenovo – that had previously been relatively unknown outside China. Lenovo's precise history is rather difficult to trace, as "the Lianxiang Group [Lenovo's Chinese name; note also that Lenovo's previous English name was "Legend" until 28 April 2003 (Temporal, 2006)] began to think of itself as having a history only after becoming a large company" (Ling, 2006). Having said that, there is one thing that is certain – Lenovo had a humble beginning. From the evidence gathered, it can be established that:

The company started out in a small building of twenty square metres that had two rooms, front and back. It stood in front of the Computer Institute Compound at Number 2 Academy of Sciences South Road. In China, such small one-storey buildings in front of a compound served as guard posts … After much discussion, Lianxiang's current management set the official date of the founding of Lianxiang in this building as November 1, 1984. (Ling, 2006)

The first meeting Lianxiang had was the "meeting to set up the company", which was dated October 17, 1984, and this meeting then became known as "the first Conference in the Guard Post" and was attended by eleven staff – which at that time represented the entire company, all of them members of the Computing and Technology Research Institute (Ling, 2006). The Computing and Technology Research Institute was part of the state-funded Chinese Academy of Sciences, and Lenovo was still partially state-owned when it entered into the agreement with IBM to acquire its PC division in December 2004 (Chao, 2004).

Lianxiang grew exponentially from its small beginnings: from eleven staff in 1984 to approximately 12,000 employees in 2004, and incorporating approximately 10,000 IBM PC employees into the company after its acquisition in 2005 (Ramstad, 2004; Fay, 2005; Ling, 2006).

16.3 LENOVO'S ACQUISITION OF IBM PC

Lenovo's unprecedented acquisition [of IBM PC] provides the possibility for it to set a price for the world's PC market. However, as far as the transaction itself is concerned, this new project of Lenovo would either "fly up to the sky or be beaten into hell…". (Liu Chuanzhi, chairman and founder of Lenovo Group, Annual Report 2005)

When Lenovo's acquisition of IBM's PC division was announced in December 2004, the world was shocked. No longer was China just a destination for foreign direct investments and the site for the world's manufacturing, but the ability of Chinese companies to acquire a division of an icon of the world's largest economy (IBM, in the USA!) had suddenly been realized. Such a shock to the West has been described as follows: "the plot by global western enterprises to gulp up a large share of the Chinese market was, in the eyes of some people, being dealt a powerful blow" (Ling, 2006). Not only did this news shock the world, the Chinese were also shocked – though in a different way – when the deal was announced by Mr Liu in Beijing; even before he concluded his speech, there was a long period of applause (Lou, 2005).

The specific details of Lenovo's acquisition of IBM PC were that IBM would receive US$650 million in cash and approximately US$600 million in Lenovo Group common stock as a consideration for the transaction (thus giving IBM an 18.9 per cent shareholding interest in Lenovo), with the deal totalling US$1.25 billion (NE Asia Online, 2004; *The Wall Street Journal Asia*, 2004; Lou, 2005). In addition, Lenovo would assume approximately US$500 million of net balance sheet liabilities from IBM, which brought the total value of the deal to US$1.75 billion (Keefe, 2004; NE Asia Online, 2004; OECD, 2006).

In exchange for the US$1.75 billion, Lenovo would take over the entire personal computer division of IBM (IBM PC), including its some 10,000 employees (Fay, 2005). Additionally, Lenovo would have the right to continue the use of the "Think" (including "ThinkPad" and "ThinkCentre") (Smith and Rushe, 2004) and "IBM" brands for eighteen months (Musil, 2004; Smith and Rushe, 2004; Lou, 2005). After this time, co-branding such as "Lenovo-IBM" could be used (Dickie *et al.* 2004; Lou, 2005) or, as Yang Yuanqing, Lenovo president and chairman-designate said in an interview, "perhaps, 'IBM, manufactured by Lenovo'" (Dickie *et al.* 2004).

16.3.1 Why did Lenovo acquire IBM PC?

When questions such as "Why did Lenovo, an unknown Chinese company, acquire IBM PC, an American icon?" are raised, it is often appropriate also to look at the other side of the coin – "Why would (and did) IBM wish to sell its PC division to Lenovo?" After all, IBM was a household brand for PCs (Smith and Rushe, 2004). It has been reported that "today, more than one hundred million people have computers carrying the IBM trademark" (Ling, 2006). In fact, IBM PCs were so famous that they were endorsed by IBM's competitors – years after other manufacturers, such as Hewlett-Packard, Compaq and Digital had started producing PCs, their machines were still labelled "IBM-compatible" (Smith and Rushe, 2004). In addition to the surprise of the news of Lenovo's acquisition of IBM PC, an even more surprising item of news was that it was IBM that initiated the deal – IBM had sent a delegation to Lenovo's Beijing office as early as the year 2000 to try to arouse Lenovo's interest in taking over IBM PC (Lou, 2005).

This question may be answered from both sides: on the one hand, why did IBM wish to sell its PC division; and on the other, why did Lenovo wish to purchase IBM PC?

Why did IBM decide to sell its PC division?

There have been various suggestions as to why IBM decided to sell its PC division – the division that helped IBM to make the American "Big Blue" a household name. Regardless of the reasons proffered, there is a consensus – "the problem is that it's just darn tough to make money on PCs today, given how cutthroat compeition has driven down prices ... On some of the cheapest PC models, manufacturers can expect to make only a few dollars' profit" (Keefe, 2004). Further, it has been commented, "loss-making PCs had no future at IBM" (Aylmer, 2004).

On examining the financial position of IBM PC division in recent years, it becomes clear that "losses for the PC division totalled US$965 million for the period from 2001 to June 30, 2004 (US$397 million in 2001 on sales of US$10.1 billion; US$171 million in 2002 on sales of US$9.2 billion; and US$258 million in 2003 on sales of US$9.6 billion). The loss widened in the first half of 2004 in contrast to the same period in 2003, with a figure of US$139 million on sales of US$5.2 billion, compared to a 2003 first-half year loss of US$97 million on sales of US$4.3 billion"(Temporal, 2006).

When Sam Palmisano took on the position of IBM chief executive in 2002, he was reported to have made it clear that, "he was not going to keep businesses that did not fit his strategy, or did not make any money" (Aylmer, 2004). As such, it was obvious that the loss sustained by IBM PC outlined above met neither of his criteria, and Palmisano concentrated his efforts in moving IBM up the economic value chain (including the US$3.5 billion purchase of PricewaterhouseCoopers' management consulting business) (Aylmer, 2004). Therefore, as IBM PC did not fit Palmisano's strategy of moving up the economic value chain, nor was it profitable, it became clear that IBM PC would have to be offloaded.

Why did Lenovo acquire IBM's PC division?

Just as the West was shocked by IBM PC being acquired by a Chinese company, China was shocked by Lenovo's decision to purchase IBM PC. After all, Lenovo had been the leading PC brand in China and across Asia (excluding Japan) since 1997, and its annual revenue in 2004 was US$3 billion (of which 98 percent was from China) (NE Asia Online, 2004; Temporal, 2006). Furthermore, Lenovo PC was already ranked number one in the Asia-Pacific (excluding Japan) market, with a 12.6 percent market share in 2003 (NE Asia Online, 2004).

In terms of worldwide market share, Lenovo had 2.6 percent of the world's PC market by the third quarter of 2004 (Keefe, 2004). As Lenovo, a *Chinese-government-backed company*, was already doing so well, why would it want to purchase IBM PC, a loss-making division of an American icon?

One reporter cynically questioned – "Can a frog turn itself into a prince by buying the prince's cast-off clothing?" (*South China Morning Post*, 2004).

It was reported that Lenovo is a prime example of the dilemma faced by Chinese consumer-goods companies – in the sense that they won market share (Lenovo brand PCs have been best-sellers in China for seven consecutive years, commanding a 27 percent unit share of China's PC market in 2003): (NE Asia Online, 2004) by undercutting their foreign rivals with ever-lower prices, but eventually found themselves trapped among hyper-competitive, low-margin businesses at home (*South China Morning Post*, 2004). Then it reached a point where it was "virtually impossible to generate the profits necessary to invest in the research and development that would enable them to move up the ladder to higher-profit products" (*South China Morning Post*, 2004). On this point, it has been commented, "in these days of rapid technological changes and shorter product cycles, Chinese companies simply do not have the luxury of time to pursue [the] protracted option [of building capabilities through in-house organic growth, like the Japanese and South Korean]" (Wu, 2005). Therefore, "outright acquisitions – like the Lenovo–IBM, become the shortcut route to address the 'twin deficit' [that is, lacking in global branding power and advanced technology]" (Wu, 2005). This line of thinking may be seen from Yang Yuanqing's speech of March 26, 2004, in which he said, "we are not yet an international company, but we are in the process of expanding overseas" (Ling, 2006).

The financial side has also been beneficial to Lenovo. Lenovo's acquisition of IBM PC gave it a market share of 8.6 percent in worldwide PCs, (figures from the third quarter of 2004) (Keefe, 2004). Further, the acquisition enabled Lenovo to obtain a combined PC revenue of approximately US$12 billion and a volume of 11.9 million units (based on 2003 results), a fourfold increase in Lenovo's PC business (before the merger, it was US$3 billion) (NE Asia Online, 2004). In addition to quadrupling its revenue, other reported benefits to Lenovo include doubling its workforce and buying up top talent on a global scale (Fay, 2005). On this point, it was reported: "With the IBM acquisition, Lenovo gained not only a powerful brand name, but some of the most seasoned IT executives in America and a worldwide network of highly skilled computer sales and distribution employees who know tax laws and invoicing practices in 66 countries" (Fay, 2005).

16.4 AFTER THE MERGER

Concerns have been raised over what happens to both Lenovo and IBM PC after the merger. Major topics include: What happens to IBM PC employees? Is Lenovo remotely controlling its IBM PC operation from Beijing? What is going to happen to the IBM brand on Lenovo's PC products? Will there be any cultural shocks from a division of a US-founded company being governed by a Chinese style of corporate governance?

When Palmisano announced the news of the Lenovo–IBM PC merger to IBM PC employees in the winter of 2004, there was reported anxiety among IBM PC employees. Apart from the nervousness associated with potential job losses, other feelings were also evident – "one employee cried, 'I worked for years for IBM, and now I work for a company that I've never heard of!' Another employee wailed on the company's internal website: 'our pension funds are going to be turned into RMB'"(Ling, 2006). In fact, very soon after the deal was announced, Lenovo proved that these matters were not of great concern:

Less than 24 hours after the two companies announced the acquisition on December 8 [2004], the human resources department at IBM's PC division released a 59-point question-and-answer memo to employees informing them that they would become employees of Lenovo, their compensation and benefits would remain identical or fully comparable to their IBM package, and they would not be asked to relocate ... The memo also made it clear that employees could accept employment with Lenovo or leave, with no separation pay. IBM would not consider them for a transfer within IBM or recruit or hire new Lenovo employees for two years. As Lenovo opened a new door for them to join a high-growth company fully committed to personal computers, IBM – determined to complete its transition to business services – quickly closed it behind them. (Fay, 2005)

While the acquisition involved moving all 10,000 IBM PC employees to Le-novo, it was reported that "the workforce transition was a non-event" (Fay, 2005), and that the entire project was "polished off in a matter of months" (Fay, 2005).

As to the concern over the PC division of an American icon being run and controlled by a Chinese-government-backed company located in Beijing, it appears that Lenovo did everything possible to avoid this perception – it moved its headquarters to Purchase, New York in 2004/5 (Merritt, 2004; *Computer World*, 2006) and planned a further move to Raleigh, North Carolina in March 2006 (*Computer World*, 2006). Lenovo's CEO and President, Yang Yuanqing, also moved to New York (Chao, 2004). In fact, Lenovo appears to be so determined to avoid giving the impression that it is a Chinese company that "in the few weeks before Christmas in 2004, Yang made this announcement to his senior staff: 'I want you all to know that we will be adopting English as the official language of New Lianxiang (Lenovo's Chinese name)'" (Ling, 2006).

When it comes to the anticipated cultural shocks that IBM PC employees might experience, perhaps one may look as a pointer at the cultural shocks experienced during Lenovo's earlier attempts at globalizing its company. It was reported that, as early as 2002, Lenovo went to Silicon Valley to recruit middle managers, and a handful of US-educated Chinese were hired (Chao,

2004). However, about a year later, almost all of them had left (Chao, 2004). One former employee described Lenovo's culture as "so different that most employees who had been educated abroad left" (Chao, 2004).

A few reported cultural differences described by former employees of Lenovo's earlier recruiting efforts include:

Twice a day, the sound system broadcasts throughout the company's headquarters in north-western Beijing a song formally known as the Number Six Broadcast Exercises, a set of gentle stretches and knee-bends that any child who has grown up in communist China has learned. Participation is voluntary but highly encouraged. (Chao, 2004)

Employees who are late to meetings, especially internal meetings, sometimes are forced to stand behind their chairs for the first minute to encourage punctuality in the future. (Chao, 2004)

Lenovo also has a company song that is played in the building at 8 a.m. each day and is sung by workers at the start of company-wide meetings. (Chao, 2004)

Employees' time is strictly monitored. Time spent outside the building during work hours must be accounted for, and if no reasonable explanation is given, a deduction may be made from an employee's paycheck. (Chao, 2004)

Apparently, the culture at Lenovo fits with its chairman and co-founder Liu Chuanzi's military background (Chao, 2004). Undoubtedly, "thinking globally is new for all of us in the former Lenovo operation", commented Liu Jun, the chief operating officer (Lohr, 2005).

With respect to concerns over the actual brand/s to be used by Lenovo (it was still permitted to use IBM and Think brands for five years after the deal following the acquisition agreement), in mid-2005, Lenovo announced that it "will start to sell its namesake personal computers outside China in the first quarter of next year [that is, 2006] as part of its long-term plan to build the world's leading PC brand" (Gu, 2005). Lenovo's then CEO, Steve Ward, announced "we want to grow Lenovo into a worldwide brand. In five years, we will have a strong change to be the leading brand in PC" (Gu, 2005).

In fact, in March 2006, Lenovo began introducing itself to the rest of the world with the launch of the first Lenovo-branded personal computers (instead of IBM or Think brands, or Lenovo–IBM brand) to be sold outside China (Bulik, 2006).

16.5 CONCLUSION

The Lenovo–IBM PC merger indeed came as a surprise – not only because it was a young company that was not all that well-known outside China acquiring a US icon, but it was also reported to be the first billion-dollar takeover in the USA by a Chinese company. When this deal was announced, questions over the reasons for the merger were raised from both sides – that is, why did IBM wish to sell its PC division: after all, that is how IBM acquired its reputation among households worldwide; and why did Lenovo wish to purchase a loss-making entity? Among the reasons speculated on were: on the one hand, IBM's desire to move up the economic value chain and concentrate its efforts on its divisions and products that were profitable; and, on the other, Lenovo wishing to acquire IBM PC's "global" brand and expertise as well as its global market share.

One point of interest that might appropriately be raised here – if Lenovo were to acquire IBM PC for its global brand and market share, why did it start launching its own branded personal computers in March 2006, less than a year after the acquisition? After all, this might lead to the impression that the concern raised by Illinois Representative Donald Manzullo (chairman of the House Small Business Committee and an advocate of closer scrutiny of the Lenovo deal) might have some merits. In scrutinizing the deal, Manzullo stated, "Essentially, it is the Chinese government that is the buyer of this company" (Hitt, 2005).

One extension of the above question, if it has any merit, may be – would the Lenovo–IBM PC transaction set the trend for future M&A transactions involving Chinese companies as acquirers?

REFERENCES

Aylmer, S. (2004) "Loss-Making PCs Had No Future at IBM", *Australian Financial Review*, 10 December: 20.
Bulik, B. (2006) "Lenovo Launches Its First Branded PCs Outside China", *Advertising Age*, 6 March: 15.
Chao, J. (2004) "Union of Lenovo, IBM Unit a Cross-Cultural Experiment", *Austin American-Statesman*, 27 December: D1.
Computer World (2006) "Lenovo Cuts 1K Jobs, Moves Headquarters", 20 March: 6.
Dickie, M., J. Lau and S. London (2004) "Lenovo/IBM Deal; IBM Brand Loyalty Holds Key for Lenovo", *Financial Times*, London, 9 December: 26.
Fay, H. (2005) "International Business Machine", *Workforce Management*, 1 July.
Gu, W. accessed (2005) "Lenovo Sees Itself as Top PC Maker in Five Years", http://www.extremetech.com. (29 August).
Hitt, G. (2005) U.S.–China Tensions Seem Poised to Mount Even as Ties Deepen", *The Wall Street Journal* (Europe), 10 February: A1.
Keefe, B. (2004) "IBM Sale Could Be Start of Trend", *Atlanta Journal-Constitution*, 9 December: E1.
Ling, Z. (2006) *The Lenovo Affair: The Growth of China's Computer Giant and Its Takeover of IBM-PC* (Singapore: John Wiley (Asia)).
Lohr, S. (2005) "Lenovo Charts New Course in PC World", *The New York Times*, 1 October: 15.

Lou, Y. (2005) *The Merger between Lianxiang and IBM* (Beijing: Chinese Textile Publishing) (author's translation).

Merritt, R. (2004) "China Tackles Marginalized PC", *Electronic Engineering Times*: 1.

Musil, S. (2004) "Big Blue Tips the Balance of Power by Essentially Bowing Out of the PC Business, Handing the Reins to China's Lenovo", http://www.CNET News.com. (accessed 10 December).

NE Asia Online (2004) "Lenovo Acquires IBM PC Business for US$1.75 billion", 13 December.

OECD (2006) *OECD Investment Policy Reviews China: Open Policies Towards Mergers and Acquisitions* (Paris: OECD).

Ramstad, E. and W. Bulkeley (2004) "Lenovo Stock Falls on Deal Worries", *The Wall Street Journal* (Asia), 10 December: A8.

Smith, D. and Rushe, D. (2004) "Devoured by the Dragon", *The Sunday Times*, Business Section, 12 December: 5.

South China Morning Post (2004) "Don't Expect a Fairytale Ending", 13 December.

Temporal, P. (2006) *Asia's Star Brands* (Singapore: John Wiley (Asia)).

Wu, F. (2005) "China Inc., International: How Chinese Companies have Discretely Internationalised their Operations", *The International Economy*, 22 September.

Index

abnormal returns   163
   buy-and-hold abnormal return (BHAR)   10, 19
   calendar time abnormal return (CTAR)   10, 19–20
   cumulative *see* cumulative abnormal returns
   Turkey   86–7, 88; average abnormal returns   91–3
accuracy (absolute financial analysts' forecast errors)   142, 145–50, 151, 152
ACS   217, 218, 224
Adelphia   132
agency problems   215–16
   see also diversification
agency theories   1
Agrawal, A.   16–17
AHT Corp.   126, 127
airlines   163
Airtours/First Choice deal   132
Alford, A.W.   141
Ali, P.U.   180
Allied Signal   130
Amihud, Y.   33
Andrade, G.   2, 7, 10
Ang, J.   6, 15–16
announcement of merger/acquisition   6–7, 8
   acquirer stock performance in announcement period   12–17; robustness checks   13–17
   combined firms' stock performance   17–18
   stock market reaction   28–31, 67
antitrust legislation   2, 129, 155–67
   empirical studies   163–5
   statute and case law   160–2
   theoretical literature   151–60
ANZ Bank   243, 244
AOL–Time Warner   56
arbitrage, merger *see* merger arbitrage
arbitrage spread   119, 123
   between Honeywell and General Electric   130
arbitrageurs, number of   129
Arellano and Bond estimator   199
Arthur Andersen   139
Asda   132
Asian crisis   139
Asquith, P.   15
Asturias region   221
AT&T Broadband   129
attitude to takeover *see* management attitude
Auna   223
Austral Coal   181–5
Australia   97–99, 104, 113, 114–15
   Austral Coal takeover   181–5
   Evans & Tate   236–44, 245–6
   Federal Court   184–5, 185
   Takeovers Panel   181, 182, 183–4, 185
   wine industry trends   242
Australian Competition and Consumer Commission (ACCC)   35
Australian Premium Wines   243
Australian Wineries UK   239, 247
average abnormal returns   91–3
Aylmer, S.   252

Baker, J.   164
BancFlorida Financial   125, 126, 127
Bank Act   1987 (Canada)   45, 52, 54
Banc One   122

INDEX

banking 2–3
  National Bank of Canada *see* National Bank of Canada
  performance in domestic and cross-border M&A 189–212; literature review 190–2; methodology 198–200; results from empirical analysis 200–6, 207–8; sample definition 192–3; variables 194–198
Banz, R. 13
Basel 2 capital agreement 206
Bass/Interbrew deal 132
BBC Hardware 34, 35, 38
BBVA 189
Bell Atlantic/GTE merger 162
Berger, A.N. 190–1, 200
Berger, P.G. 141
Bhagat, S. 97, 106
bias in FAF errors 143, 145–51, 152
bidding firms 1–2
  CARs for Turkey 88–89
  expanding firms in energy sector 221–28
  impact of share price rise in offer period 28–41
  size and merger premium 13–15
  stock performance: announcement period 12–17; long-run post-merger performance 18–20; pre-merger performance 22–4; robustness checks 13–17
  structural changes in behavior of returns 90–1
Bioshield Technologies Inc. 126, 127
Bishop, S.R. 33
Black, B. 185
board's monitoring 58, 70–3, 78–9
Boesky, I. 118
book-to-market ratio 10–11, 14, 16
Bowditch, J.L. 200
branding 251, 255
Bresnahan, T. 164, 166
broadcasting 2–3
Brooks Brothers 129
Brown, K.C. 98, 99
Buffett, W. 118
Bulik, B. 255
Bunnings 34, 35, 38
Buono, A.F. 200
buy-and-hold abnormal return (BHAR) 10, 19

'Caixa, la' 218, 219
Cajastur–EDP 220–1
calendar risk 128, 129

calendar time abnormal return (CTAR) 10, 19–20
Canada
  Bank Act 1987 45, 52, 54
  impact of cross-border M&A on financial analysts' forecasts 139–54
  National Bank of *see* National Bank of Canada
Canadian National Bank 42, 54
  structure of 43–50
capital budgeting problem 235
carbonated soft drinks 162
Carroll, R. 101
cash-based M&A 3, 6–7, 29–30, 31
  cash bids and price volatility 99, 103–10
  cash bids and trading volume 111–12, 113
  factors influencing form of consideration 32–4
  merger arbitrage 119–22; example 120–2
  stock market misvaluation 7–24
  Wesfarmers' acquisition of Howard Smith 35–6, 39–41
cash flows 61–2
cash-settled equity swaps *see* equity swaps
Cecchini Report 189, 209
Celler–Kefauver Act 1950 (USA) 155, 161
Centennial 181–5
CEO's decision rights 57–8, 60–6
  board's monitoring 58, 70–2, 78–9
  choice of diversified vs focused strategy 64–6
  monetary incentives 58, 67–70, 75–8
champions, national 228–32
Chaney, M. 34
Chang, J.J. 140
Chao, J. 254–5
Chen, Y. 6
Chile 223, 231, 232
China
  dilemma of Chinese consumer-goods companies 252–3
  Lenovo acquisition of IBM PC 249–51
Chow test 89–91
Clayton Act 1914 (USA) 155, 160–1
clinical econometric case studies 164
CNE (Spanish energy regulator) 220, 228
Coca-Cola/Dr. Pepper merger 162
collar offers 125–28
combined firms' abnormal returns 17–18
common informational events 99–101

INDEX

common legal system   202–6, 207–9
community   171–2
Compaq Computer   129, 251
competition policy
  energy sector   228–31
  see also antitrust legislation
computing sector   249–57
Computing and Technology Research Institute (China)   250
conditional volatility equations   102, 108, 109–10
conglomerate mergers   2, 156, 157, 160
consideration *see* payment, form of
contract rights   172–3, 174–5, 175–6
control of shares, equity swaps and   180–1, 182–5, 186
coordination costs   65
corporate scandals   132, 139, 216
corporate social responsibility   173
costs
  reduction and types of merger   157
  vertical mergers and raising rivals' costs   159
Cournot oligopoly   158
Cranswick Premium Wines   238, 240–4, 245–6, 248
credit losses, provision for   51–2
cross-border M&A   2, 3, 84
  banking performance in domestic M&A and   188–212
  energy sector in Europe   220–31
  impact on financial analysts' forecasts   139–54
  Turkey   85, 91–3
CS/Tremont Merger Arbitrage Index   132–6
culture
  barriers and banking M&A   191
  Lenovo–IBM PC merger   254–5
cumulative abnormal returns (CARs)   1–2, 10, 104
  announcement period: bidding firm   12–17; combined firms   17–18
  pre-merger stock performance   20–4; bidder firms   22–4; target firms   20–2
  Turkey   87–89

Davidian, M.   101
Davidson, C.   158–9
Davis, D.   165
debt ratings   225, 226
decision rights *see* CEO's decision rights
delta hedging an option   126–7
Deneckere, R   158–9

Department of Justice (USA)   129, 156, 161–2
deregulation
  banking sector   188–9
  energy sector   216–17, 223, 230
Deutsche Bank   189
Dickerson, A.P.   194, 198, 199
Digital   251
Directive on cross-border mergers, proposed   206–9
Directive on Takeover Bids   209
disclosure requirements   181–2, 183–5
discount, trading at a   66–7
diversification   1, 56–82
  costs and benefits of synergies   64–6
  diversified strategy   63–4
  empirical implications   66–7
  focused strategy *see* focus
  literature review   58–60
  and merger premium   15, 16–17
  model structure   60–2
  robustness   67–73; board's monitoring   70–3; CEO's monetary incentives   67–70
dividend cuts   53
dividend spread   123
domestic M&A
  banking performance in cross-border M&A and   188–212
  Turkey   85–94
Dong, M.   6, 8
Dr. Pepper/Coca-Cola merger   162
Dufwenberg, M.   165
Duke Energy   223

Eckbo, E.   163
economic globalization   3
economic growth   134–5
EDP   220–1, 226
efficiency   1, 84
  domestic and cross-border M&A in banking sector   190–1
  market power/productive efficiency trade-off   156–60
effort, CEO and   60–4, 67–70
Electrabel   220
Electricité de France (EDF)   214, 228, 231
employees   253–4, 254–5
employment rights   174
EnBW   220, 228
Endesa   218, 219, 220, 221, 222, 224, 228, 231
  E.On takeover   214, 218, 225–28
  expansion in Latin America   222–3

ENEL 214, 220, 226
energy sector 213–33
  behaviour of target firms 217–21
  competition policy and national
    champions 228–31
  expanding firms 221–38
  issues at stake 214–17
Enersis 223, 225, 231
Enron 132, 139, 216
environmental pollution 174
E.On 214, 217, 218, 221, 225–28
Epps, M.L. 99
Epps, T.W 99
equity markets 134–6
equity swaps 178–87
  hedging of swap exposure 180
  takeover battles 180–5
Erwin, G.R. 141, 145
ethics 168–77
  ethical approaches 168–73
  literature review 173–5
Europe 3
European Union (EU)
  banking performance and M&A 188–212
  Directive on Takeover Bids 209
  GE/Honeywell merger 131
  M&A in energy sector 213–33
  proposed Directive on cross-border
    mergers 206–9
  Second Directive on Banking
    Coordination 189, 191, 206
Evans & Tate 236–44, 245–6
  acquisition of Cranswick 240–4; analysis
    of a killer acquisition 241–4
  post-listing history 236–8
  string of acquisitions 239–40
event studies 1–2, 84, 224–5
  Turkey 85–94
exchange ratio 30
expanding firms 221–8
expenses ratio 45–6, 53–4
experimental economics 165

failed bids
  failed merger arbitrage 119, 129–32
  and price volatility 98, 103–10, 110–11,
    112
family ownership 92–3
Farrell, J. 157–8
Fay, H. 253, 254
Federal Court of Australia 184–5, 185
Federal Trade Commission (FTC)(USA)
  129, 156, 161–2
Ferroatlántica-EnBW 220
fiduciary duty 170, 171, 174–5

financial analysts' forecasts (FAFs)
    139–54
  conceptual framework 141–2
  data 143–5
  empirical results and analysis 145–51,
    152
  measures of FAF errors 142–3
financial scandals 132, 139, 216
financial services fees 45
Financière Banque Nationale 52, 53, 54
firm size see size
firm-specific factors 91–3
First Choice/Airtours deal 132
First Data Corp. 120–2
First Union 125, 126, 127
Fishman, M. 32
fixed collar offers (fixed exchange collars)
    125–8
floating collar offers 125–8
Focarelli, D. 191, 194, 199
focus
  cross-border M&A and financial analysts'
    forecasts 141–2, 145, 147–8, 151, 152
  strategy 56, 57, 60, 61–2, 61, 64; CEO's
    monetary incentives 68, 69–70; costs
    and benefits of synergies 64–6
foreign partnership 92–3
France 214
French legal system 202–6, 207–8
Friedman, M 174
friendly bids
  and price volatility 99, 103–10
  and trading volumes 112–13, 114
FTC v. Procter & Gamble 162
Fulghieri, P. 59–60
Fuller, K 16, 125, 127

García Canal, E. 224–5
Gas de France 214, 226
Gas Natural 218, 220, 222, 226
  bid for Endesa 214, 217, 225, 227
GDP, natural logarithm of 196–7
General Electric (GE) 56
  failed bid for Honeywell 119, 129–32
German legal system 202–6, 207–8
Ghosh, A. 33
Glencore 181–4
Global Crossing 132
globalization, economic 3
Gneezy, U. 165
golden shares 216, 228
Goldman Sachs 118
governance 243–4, 245–6
Governance Codes 206, 210
Graham, B. 118

Graham, D. 159
greenmail 170
Grossman, S. 159–60
growth, pursuit of 244
GTE/Bell Atlantic merger 162
Gu, W. 255
Gugler, K. 83

Hamermesh, L. 29
Hansen, R. 32
Harding, D. 235
Harford, J. 2, 83
Hart, O. 159–60
Hart–Scott–Rodino Act 1976 (USA) 155, 161, 166
Haw, I. 140, 141
Haynes, M. 202
health care 2–3
Heath, C. 141
hedging
  delta hedging an option 126–7
  of swap exposure 180, 182–3
Helm, D. 229
Herfindahl index 195, 197
Hewlett-Packard 251
Hidrocantábrico 217, 219, 220–1, 222, 224, 228
Hitt, G. 249
Hodrick, L.S. 59–60
Holmstrom, B. 2
Holt, C. 165
Honeywell 119, 129–32
Hope, O.-K. 140
Horizontal Merger Guidelines 162
horizontal mergers 156, 157–9, 160
hostile takeovers 2, 128
  ethics and 170–5
  and price volatility 99, 103–10
  and trading volumes 112–13, 114
Houston, J.F. 194
Howard Smith Ltd 31–2, 34–41
  value of combined entity after Wesfarmers takeover 37, 38–9; before synergies 37, 38–9; with synergies 37, 39
  value of control to Wesfarmers 37, 38
  value prior to takeover announcement 36–8
Hu, H.T.C. 185
hubris hypothesis 6, 7–8, 11–24
Hughes Electronics 129
Hutson, E. 97–8, 104, 108, 113, 114–15

Iberdrola 218, 219, 220, 222, 224, 226
IBM PC–Lenovo merger 249–57
  IBM's motivation for merger 251–2
  merged company 253–5

incentives, monetary 58, 67–70, 75–8
industry 10
  conditions and killer acquisition 242, 245
influence activities 59
information barriers 191
informational events 99–101
initiative effect 65
institutional ownership 2
Interbrew/Bass deal 132
interest paid by arbitrageur's broker on cash proceeds 123
interest rates 50–1
  interest rate spread of Canadian banks 43–4
internal capital markets 59
International Accounting Standards (IAS) 206
international activity 92–3
international competitiveness 228, 229–31
Istanbul Stock Exchange (ISE) 83
IT&T 56

Jensen, M. 59, 174, 192

Kahle, K. 10
Kaplan, S.N. 2
Kearney, C. 97–8, 104, 108, 113, 114–15
Keefe, B. 254, 255
killer acquisition problem 234–48
  exploring a killer deal 241–4
Koch, C. von 191
Kohers, N. 15–16

La Porta, R. 202
Lai, G.C. 119
language 191–2
large-scale econometric studies 163–4
Latin America 221–3
Lee, C.M.C. 97
legal system 202–6, 207–8
Lehman Global Aggregate Bond Index 132, 133
Lenovo 249–57
  acquisition of IBM PC 250–3; Lenovo's motivation for purchase 252–3
  history 249–50
  merged Lenovo–IBM PC 253–5
Levy, H. 97
Lhabitant, F.S. 129
Lindblom, T. 191
Ling, Z. 250, 254
Liu Chuanzhi 250–1, 255
Liu Jun 255

London Electricity 231
long-run performance 3–4, 84
  market-manager rationality framework
    10–11, 18–20
López Duarte, C 224–5
Loughran, T. 32
LTCM 132, 137

Maksimovic, V. 163–4
management attitude 128, 129
  and price volatility 99, 103–10
  and trading volumes 112–13, 114
  see also friendly bids; hostile takeovers
management ownership stake 33
managerial motivation 83–4
Mant, J. 185
Manzullo, D. 256
Maquiera, C. 16
Margaret River region, Australia 236, 246
market effect, and price volatility 101–2, 106–19
market-extension mergers 156
market foreclosure 159
market-manager rationality 5–27
  abnormal return of combined firms
    17–18
  acquirer stock performance:
    announcement period 12–17;
    long-run post-merger performance
    18–20; pre-merger performance
    22–4; robustness checks 13–17
  data and descriptive statistics 8–10
  hypothesis development 7–8
  long-run method 10–11
  short-run method 10
  target stock performance pre-merger
    20–2
market power extension hypothesis 159
market power/productive efficiency trade-off 156–60
market power theories 1
market share 196, 198
market structure 157–8, 164
market timing theory 5–6, 7–8, 11–24
matching 59
Matsusaka, J.G. 59
maximum likelihood estimator (MLE)
  47–8, 49, 50
McGee, R.W. 169, 171, 172, 173
mean equations 101–2, 106–9
mean reverting process 46–50
Meckling, W.H. 59
Megginson, W.L. 16
merger arbitrage 97–99, 118–38

historical performance 132–6
  key sources of merger arbitrage risk
    128–32; calendar risk 128, 129;
    example of a failed arbitrage trade
    129–32; transaction risk 128–9
  as a strategy 119–20; cash transactions
    19–32; stock transactions at a fixed
    rate 123–5; stock transactions at a
    variable rate 125–8
merger premiums 3, 29, 119, 128
  market-manager rationality and 7–8,
    13–17; acquirer size 13–15; book-
    to-market ratio 14, 16;
    diversification 15, 16–17;
    pre-merger stock performance of
    target and acquirer 20–4; relative
    size 14, 15–16; target origin 15, 17
merger-specific factors 91–3
Microsoft 124–5
Miller, M. 32
misadventure 28–41
  acquisition of Howard Smith by
    Wesfarmers 34–6; assessment of the
    transaction 39–41; financial analysis
    36–9
  factors influencing the form of
    consideration 32–4
mismatching problem 10–11
Mitchell, M. 2, 10, 98, 135
mixture of distributions model (MDM) 97,
  99–101, 109
mobile telephony 162
Modigliani, F 32
Moeller, S.B. 13
monetary incentives 58, 67–70, 75–8
Moore, K.M. 119
Morck, R. 16
mortgages 43–4
Mouvement Desjardins 55
Mueller, D. 160
Mulherin, J.H. 4, 10

Nanda, V. 59
National Bank of Canada 42–55
  low P/E ratio for the stock of 53–4
  new merged bank 50–3
  structures of the two merged banks
    43–50
national champions 228–31
natural monopolies 214–15
  see also energy sector
net income ratio 46–50, 51
Norman, G. 159
notification procedure, pre-merger 161, 166

INDEX

Oakridge Estate   238, 239, 243, 245, 248
oligopoly model testing   164
operating costs ratio   44–5, 52–3
Oppenheimer, H.R.   119
ordinary least squares (OLS)   47, 50
Ordover, J.   159
organizational capabilities   59
other income ratio   45–6
   spread between National Bank of Canada and all banks   52–3
outcome of bid
   and price volatility   98, 103–10
   and trading volumes   110–11, 112
   see also failed bids

P/E ratio   53–4
Palmisano, S.   252, 253
Panel on Takeovers and Mergers (UK)   181, 185
Parisi, F.   225
Pautler, P.   163, 164
payment, form of   28–41, 128
   acquisition of Howard Smith by Wesfarmers   34–41
   factors influencing   32–4
   and price volatility   99, 103–10, 115
   and trading volume   111–12, 113
   see also cash-based M&A; share-exchange M&A
Paymentech   120–2
Pepall, L.   159
Pepsi/Seven-Up merger   162
performance extrapolation hypothesis   16
Perry, S.E.   141, 145
personal loans   43–4
Phillips, G.   163–4
physically settled equity swaps   178–79
   see also equity swaps
Pitts, M.   99–101
poison pills   170, 175
politicization of control market   223–4
pollution   174
popular capitalism   215
post-bid period
   price volatility   104–6, 106–7
   and trading volumes   110–14
post-merger stock performance
   long-run   10–11, 18–20
   short-run   17–18
Powergen   225, 226, 227
Pozzolo, A.F.   191, 194, 199
pre-bid period
   price volatility   104–6, 106–7
   and trading volumes   110–14

pre-merger notification procedure   161, 166
pre-merger stock performance   20–4
   acquiring firms   22–4
   target firms   20–2
Price, C.   185
price volatility   96–117
   econometric analysis   101–10; conditional volatility equations   102, 108, 109–10; data and preliminary results   102–6; econometric results   106–10; mean equations   101–2, 106–9; model   101–2
   previous research and theoretical background   97–101
PricewaterhouseCooper   252
private benefits   61–2
private equity   3
privatization   215, 216–17, 230
product differentiation   158–9
product-extension mergers   156
productive efficiency/market power trade-off   156–60
profitability, banking   194, 195, 199–200, 200–2, 203–4
project choice decision of CEO   60–4, 68–9
property rights   172–3, 174–5, 175–6
Provincial Bank   42, 54
   structure of   43–50
   see also National Bank of Canada
Public Choice School   169
public interest   228
public target firms   142, 150–52, 152
Pulvino, T   98, 135

Quebec   51

Rajan, R.   67
Rau, P.R.   16
Ravenscraft, D.   163
Raymond, M.V.   98, 99
real options   54
reciprocity   230–1
Red Eléctrica Española (REE)   217, 222, 224, 226
regulation   115
   barriers to banking M&A   191–2
   cash-settled equity swaps   179–80, 181, 185–6
   energy sector   214–16, 223, 231
   regulatory approval and merger arbitrage   130–31, 132
   time inconsistency problem of   214–15
Reinganum, M.R.   13
relative size   14, 15–16

Repsol 218, 222
research effort, CEO's 60–4, 67–70
resource-based theory of diversification 59
Rhoades, S.A. 200
Rhodes-Kropf, M. 5, 6
rights-based ethics 172–3, 174–5, 175–6
risk 128–32
 calendar risk 128, 129
 transaction risk 128–9
risk arbitrage *see* merger arbitrage
robustness
 checks and stock market misvaluations 13–17
 diversification and synergy 58, 67–73; board's monitoring 70–3, 78–9; CEO's monetary incentives 67–70, 75–8
Roll, R. 6
Rosenthal, L. 98, 99
Rotemberg, J. 59
Rovit, S. 235
Ruback, R.S. 192
Ruhrgas 225, 226, 227
Ruland, W. 33
rule of reason 160, 166
RWE 214, 220, 226

Sacher, S. 164
Safeway 132
Sainsbury's 132
Saloner, G. 59
Salop, S. 159
same-industry M&A 91–3
Samuelson, W. 98, 99
Santander Group 189
scale efficiency 84
Scandinavian legal system 202–6, 207–8
Scheffman, D. 159
Scherer, F. 163
Schmalensee, R. 164–5
Schwert, G.W. 101
Scott St. Portfolio 239, 247
Second Directive on Banking Coordination (EU) 189, 191, 206
Selwyn Wines 236, 238, 239, 243, 245
service sectors 2–3
Seven-Up/Pepsi merger 162
Shapiro, C. 157–68
share-exchange M&A 28–30, 31, 99
 acquisition of Howard Smith by Wesfarmers 35–6, 39–41
 factors influencing form of consideration 32–4

merger arbitrage 123–8; fixed exchange rates 123–5; variable exchange rates 125–8
share price, rising for bidding firm 28–41
shareholder value 70–3
Sherman Act 1890 (USA) 160, 166
Shleifer, A. 5, 6, 60
short-run performance 84
 M&A in Turkey 85–94
 market-manager rationality framework 10, 12–18
signalling hypothesis 32
signed financial analysts' forecast errors 143, 145–51, 152
Silicon Valley 254
Singal, V. 163
Sirower, M 235
size 10–11
 acquirer size and merger premiums 13–15
 M&A in Turkey 92–3
 relative size and merger premiums 14, 15–16
Smith, B.F. 97
Solnik, B.H. 141
sovereign loans 43
Spain 213–14, 217–18, 231
 expanding firms 223–8
 Spanish firms as targets 220–1
Stafford, E. 10
stock market misvaluations 5–27
stock market studies 163
 see also abnormal returns
strategic objectives 228–9
structural changes in behaviour of returns 89–91
structure–conduct–performance studies 164–5
Stulz, R. 33
successful bids
 and price volatility 98, 103–10
 trading volumes 110–11, 112
Sudarsanam, S 234
Suez 214
Sydkraft 225
synergy
 acquisition of Howard Smith by Wesfarmers 37, 38–9
 diversification and 56–82; costs and benefits of synergies 64–6, 74–5
synergy trap 235

Takeovers Panel (Australia) 181, 182, 183–4, 185

INDEX 267

target firms 1
  behaviour in energy sector 217–21
  CARs for Turkey 88, 89
  origin and merger premium 15, 17
  ownership structure 128
  poor financial condition and killer acquisition 240, 241–2, 245
  pre-merger stock performance 20–2
  price volatility *see* price volatility
  structural changes in behaviour of returns 91
  trading volume 96, 99–101, 110–14
target pricing model 98
Tate, F. 236, 243, 244
Tauchen, G.E. 99–101
taxation 1
  and form of consideration 33
technology bubble 139
Teece, D. 160
telecommunications sector 2–3, 162, 223
Telefónica 222, 223, 228
Telemundo Communications Group 129
Temporal, P. 250, 252
Tempus Group 129
Tesco 132
Texas Utilities 220
Think brand 251, 255
Thompson, S. 202
3M 56
time inconsistency problem of regulation 214–15
Toronto Dominion Bank 49, 50, 54
trader-specific informational events 99–101
trading volume
  General Electric and Honeywell 130, 131
  impact of takeover announcement 96, 101–3; findings 110–14
transaction risk 129–30
Travlos, N. 32
Trillas, F. 225
Turkey 83–95
  average abnormal returns 91–3
  CAR for bidder and target firms 87–9
  data and methodology 85–7
  likelihood of observing abnormal returns 92–3
  rise in M&A activity 84–5
  structural changes in behaviour of returns 89–91
Tversky, D. 141

Unión Fenosa 217, 218, 219, 220, 222, 224, 226, 232

United Kingdom (UK) 214, 231
  Panel on Takeovers and Mergers 181, 185
  stock market misvaluation 7, 8–24
United States (USA) 254
  antitrust merger law 2, 129, 155–67
  Celler–Kefauver Act 1950 155, 161
  Clayton Act 1914 155, 160–1
  Department of Justice 129, 156, 161–2
  FAF errors in cross-border M&A involving US target firms 142, 148–50
  FTC 129, 156, 161–2
  Hart–Scott–Rodino Act 1976 155, 161, 166
  price volatility study of tender offers 102–14, 115
  Sherman Act 1890 160, 166
  waves of M&A activity 2–3
United Technologies 130
Unocal Corp. v. *Mesa Petroleum* 174–5
US v. *Brown Shoe* 161
US v. *Northern Securities* 160
utilitarian ethics 168–72

Vander Vennet, R. 191, 202
'vanilla' equity swaps 179
Veba 225
Vermaelen, T 16
Vernon, J. 159
vertical mergers 156, 157, 159–60, 160
Viag 225
Viesgo 220
Vijh, A. 32
Vishny, R. 5, 6, 60
Visio Corp. 124–5
Viswanathan, S 5
Vita, M. 164
Vivendi 216
volatility, price *see* price volatility

Walker, M. 10
Walkling, R. 10
Ward, S. 255
waves of M&A activity 2–3, 83
  energy sector 213–14
Weiss, L. 165
welfare economics 155, 156–60
Werden, G. 164
Wesfarmers Ltd 31–2, 34–41
  offer for Howard Smith Ltd 35–6
  value of acquisition of Howard Smith to 39–41
  value of combined entity after acquisition of Howard Smith 37, 38–9; before synergies 37, 38–9; with synergies 37, 39

value prior to takeover announcement 36–8
Williamson, O.E. 58–9, 157
wine industry 242
   Evans & Tate 236–44, 245–6
WineSource 239, 247
Woodstock Theological Center 173
WorldCom 132

Wu, F. 253

X-efficiency 84

Yáñez, G. 225
Yang Yuanqing 251, 253, 254
Yin, R. 235
Yoder, J.A. 97